Praise for America's foremost criminal defense lawyer Gerry Spence and

THE SMOKING GUN

"Spence has done it again with this mesmerizing account of a 'hopeless' case with another side. Spence educates, advocates and entertains with his experience, his humor and his unique homespun approach to storytelling. This one is quite a tale. You won't put it down until you find out what happened."

—Alan Dershowitz

"This disquieting book shows that the facts don't speak for themselves, innocence is rarely presumed and justice is far from a first priority in America's courtrooms. Spence is a gifted storyteller and his rhetorical skills are mesmerizing . . . [a] thrilling account of injustice barely averted."

—*Publishers Weekly* (starred review)

"THE SMOKING GUN is a vivid, sometimes painfully persuasive look at the nitty-gritty of the American criminal justice system, where often mundane settings become a stage for extreme emotions."

—Larry McMurtry, author of *By Sorrow's River*

"Sometimes self-righteous, sometimes merciless: an unforgettable account of the state's power against individuals who might be innocent."

—*Kirkus Reviews*

"The pages of Spence's latest legal drama are smokin' like the murder weapon he ultimately crammed down the DA's throat. He is the best lawyer storyteller I know. This is by far his best tale—and it's all true."

—Morris Dees, founder of the
Southern Poverty Law Center

"A courtroom drama that keeps the reader riveted as it moves from crime scene to trial. It is more than a book about a poor Oregonian woman and her son, charged in 1985 with a crime they didn't commit. It's more than a book about their lawyer's considerable talent and humanity. In short, it is a sad tale about our criminal justice system that occasionally fails. Sadder still is the number of innocent defendants who do not have Gerry Spence to help them."

—Geraldine Ferraro

"THE SMOKING GUN is many things. Certainly, a gripping murder case told by a master storyteller, one who also happens to be America's premier criminal defense attorney. It is also a fascinating anatomy of bitter courtroom battles and behind the scenes strategizing by the prosecution and defense. Finally, and perhaps most importantly, it is a story that should be frightening to all Americans—that without the best legal representation possible, innocent people can be convicted of murder."

—Vincent Bugliosi

"See a murder trial, THE SMOKING GUN, through the eyes of Gerry Spence. There is no better seat, no better equipped luxury box, no better insider's position than through Spence's unflinching vision."

—Judge Jim Randall, Minnesota Supreme Court

"Trial lawyers who read THE SMOKING GUN will often get that familiar knot in the stomach, as the twists and turns of this actual murder case unfold. Spence's wonderful felicity of expression (with the written word as well as the spoken) will also grip the general reader, especially those who like the white-hot drama of the courtroom. And, it is my fervent wish that the book will inspire able civil trial lawyers to go down into the arena of justice to do battle for poor persons who are facing, alone, the awesome power of the government."

—The Honorable William Wilson,
U.S. District Court Judge

"THE SMOKING GUN should be required reading for anyone contemplating life as a defense lawyer. It is a story that examines the heart and art needed to defend an accused person in a system where the cards are stacked against them. Gerry Spence is the best of the best and Sandy Jones was lucky to have him."

—Linda Deutsch, veteran trial journalist

Praise for Gerry Spence's courtroom thriller

HALF-MOON AND EMPTY STARS

"This richly-textured page-turner kept me on the edge of my seat until the dramatic—and unexpected—conclusion."

—Alan M. Dershowitz

"A splendidly-written novel. . . . No reader will be left unshaken by the devastating ending."

—Vincent Bugliosi

GERRY SPENCE

THE
SMOKING
GUN

POCKET BOOKS
New York   London   Toronto   Sydney

POCKET BOOKS, a division of Simon & Schuster, Inc.
1230 Avenue of the Americas, New York, NY 10020

Copyright © 2003 by G.L. Spence and Lanelle P. Spence Living Trust, dated November 8, 1999

Originally published in hardcover in 2003 by Scribner

All rights reserved, including the right to reproduce this book or portions thereof in any form whatsoever. For information address Scribner, 1230 Avenue of the Americas, New York, NY 10020

ISBN: 0-7434-7052-4

First Pocket Books printing July 2004

10 9 8 7 6 5 4 3 2 1

POCKET and colophon are registered trademarks of Simon & Schuster, Inc.

Cover design by John Vario
Author photo by D.J. Bassett

The photo of Sandy Jones holding the smoking gun is a public document. All other photos are courtesy of Kent Spence.

Manufactured in the United States of America

For information regarding special discounts for bulk purchases, please contact Simon & Schuster Special Sales at 1-800-456-6798 or business@simonandschuster.com.

Every trial lawyer worth a damn needs to have a good murder case.

—GERRY SPENCE

THE
SMOKING
GUN

INTRODUCTION

This story is timeless, and it is true.

Most of us have never faced a serious criminal charge that hauls us before the justice system. If suddenly, during these fearsome times, we were forced to peer into the mythical safe box where our rights are said to be stored, what would we find? Are we still guaranteed a fair trial? Have we ever been? If we're charged by the state with a penitentiary offense, can we adequately defend ourselves? How is it that in these days so many helpless innocents find themselves behind bars, some even awaiting the executioner's needle? When we look into this safe box of sacred rights is it, indeed, filled to the brim, or do we discover little more than an old folder of empty promises?

As a criminal defense attorney I've searched that safe box of rights on behalf of the accused for more than half a century. Faced as we are with the daily erosion of our freedoms, I find this case of several years past more relevant now than ever, for it represents in plain, stark reality what is now and has, for decades, been widespread across this land—a system of justice that is more wishful than real. Today the question is not how many rights must we sacrifice for our security, but, instead, how can we *recover those we have already lost* so that the average citizen, innocent or guilty, may at last obtain a fair trial?

This case, more than any other I've tried in my entire

career, exemplifies the terrible odds we face when the state launches all of its forces against us. Most of us live in a sort of curious denial—that the criminal law is irrelevant to us. Yet, in certain hidden places, we hear a small voice warning that someday, under circumstances we cannot foresee, what happened to Sandy Jones might happen to us—that we might be called upon to face the invidious charges of the state—perhaps even a charge of murder.

This story, based on the actual record of the case, asks the dark and frightening question, How will justice be delivered to *you* when *you* are called before the criminal bar? What if you can't find a skilled trial lawyer to defend you, one who cares about you? What if your lawyer turns out to be one who'll fight for you only if you have the money to buy that which has become another commodity in America—something called justice—and you don't have the price? What if you are left to fend for yourself as were Sandy Jones and her child fighting their battle against the good old boys of Lincoln County, Oregon?

In this book I take you with me in and out of the courtroom in a hopeless murder case. I take you behind the scenes, into the judge's chambers, into our worried, sometimes frightened hearts as lawyers who must garner the skill and the power to ward off the inevitable, the conviction of our client, who was, in this case, captured at the crime scene on film with a smoking gun in her hands. This case, or parts of it, might have been your case, and Sandy Jones might well have been you. Read on.

GERRY SPENCE
Jackson, Wyoming

1

The Lincoln County prosecutor, a friendly man, shoved the photograph under the noses of anybody who wanted to look. The woman in the photograph, tall and blond, was locked on her target, her mouth pulled askew against the stock of her rifle. Smoke puffed out from the end of the barrel as she fired. Sandy Jones was the woman's name. She'd been charged with murder, and the reporters were scrambling for the story.

Something about a murder case fascinates as well as frightens me. If you lose, the state hauls your client off and locks him up in some dank hole for the rest of his life, or an anonymous state-sanctioned murderer pulls the lever and your client is burned to death in the electric chair or gasps and turns purple and foams at the mouth in the gas chamber. And what happens to the lawyer who defended the poor bastard? If he was worth a damn and cared, a part of him dies along with his client. He drowns in his nightmares. He thinks that if he'd been more competent, prepared better, or called one more witness, maybe he could have saved his client.

A small-time real estate developer named Wilfred Gerttula was dead—shot cleanly through the chest. Not only that, the prosecutor had an eyewitness to the murder, the dead man's wife, Monica, who said she'd seen Sandy Jones murder her husband, shoot him point-blank with the gun in the photograph. She ought to know, she said. She took the photograph. Then Monica said this Jones woman drove off with her dying husband in her husband's own pickup. It had been a cold-blooded, premeditated killing.

Sandy Jones was thirty-nine years old at the time she was arrested. She hadn't lounged in a bed of roses. Out of high school she'd gone to work in a cannery sorting berries. After that she managed one of those small motels that brags with its flickering neon sign that it's "modern," which means it has running water, sometimes. Sandy saw to all of the maintenance, painted, fixed the leaking faucets, and filled in the chuckholes in the driveway. Earlier a drunk driver ran into her, injuring her back and ribs. She and Mike Sr. had had a stormy marriage. He drank. They separated. He quit drinking. They got together again. And during his comings and goings their two kids, Little Mike and Shawn, were seeded and born.

Big Mike, as the family called him to distinguish him from their young son, Mike Jr., was a broad, muscled man of average height with wavy red hair, a red beard, an outdoor face, and powerful arms. He'd been a fisherman in Alaska, but that was before he'd been hurt working in the woods. After that, to feed his family he fished for salmon in the Siletz River and worked at whatever odd jobs he could find.

When, in the last days of July 1985, Sandy and Little Mike, by then fifteen, were both charged with murder, Mike Jones was like a lot of folks who face the crushing power of the state. He didn't know what to do; he had to find a lawyer to defend both his wife and son, and he had no money. The Joneses never had much. When their bills weren't paid, the phone company shut their phone off, and sometimes the power company shut off the electricity. They lived on a twenty-nine-acre swamp-bottom farm in a rickety, leaky-roofed house that was little more than a shack with a porch. The boundaries of their small, severely overgrazed pasture were marked by a dilapidated fence, the rotted posts leaning, the wire sagging. Derelict car bodies, rusted and in parts, were strewn here and there along with an assortment of other junk and a couple of outbuildings, one of which served as a barn for the kids' pony and the milk cow, and the other as a well house. The bank's mortgage was attached to the place like a cop's chokehold on a suspect.

The dead man, Wilfred Gerttula—in his fifties, tough, grizzled, and humorless—had insisted that the road that cut through the Jones property was a public road. Little more than a trail, it crowded within six feet of the corner of the Joneses' bedroom and then meandered steeply up a densely forested mountain through fern and heavy undergrowth to some granite outcroppings the Native Americans called Medicine Rock. After that, the trail snaked through the wet Oregon jungle to the top of the mountain and past a wire gate that marked the Joneses' farthest boundary. There a person could look down the steep canyon side to the river a couple hundred feet below. Beyond the Joneses' gate, the trail puttered along to other lands and eventually led to what Gerttula claimed was his subdivision.

"That's a county road," Gerttula proclaimed. "Always has been. And that woman won't let me or my buyers come through. Stops us cold ever' time." The good old boys of Lincoln County had had some experience with the Jones woman before. She was a troublemaker all right.

But Sandy Jones made her own speech. "The county and nobody else has ever had any right to cross our land. He says he has a subdivision up there? I can show you it was illegally established. Besides, a public road on that unstable ground

would give way in the rainy season. It'd be dangerous."
Beyond that, the Indians, with whom she held continual
counsel, claimed that Medicine Rock was a sacred Indian
burial ground. And Sandy Jones was one who was willing to
fight for the rights of her Indian friends. "This is America,"
she declared, "and the good old boys in Lincoln County are
not going to make us give up what rightfully belongs to us."
Sandy herself was one-eighth Sioux.

There'd been lawsuits brought by Gerttula against the
Joneses over the road and countersuits by Sandy Jones.
Not satisfied with suing the Gerttulas, she sued the judges
and the prosecuting attorney himself. Her first half-dozen
attorneys dropped her, mostly because she couldn't pay,
but she blindly forged on representing herself.

After the shooting on that muggy July day in 1985, and
in panic, Sandy Jones had driven the Gerttula pickup
down the mountain to get help for Gerttula, who was
doubled up in the seat next to her. He was dead when she
parked the truck at the neighbor's house below and ran in
to call 911. That had ended the argument between Sandy
Jones and Wilfred Gerttula.

It's true I'd often said that a trial lawyer without a good
murder case isn't a real trial lawyer. Those who represent
large corporations and like to stay sprayed in the perfumed
mist of corporate dollars, who won't get down in the pits and
get bloodied in the wars where human beings are at stake,
are not real trial lawyers. If a trial lawyer won't take on a
murder case because he doesn't want to get his hands dirty
or because there isn't any money in it, the system fails. It not
only fails the accused, it fails the rest of us. Someday when
some fair-haired prosecutor with the governor's chair glow-
ing in his mind's eye decides to charge one of us or one of
our kids with a crime—well, that hated, scorned, and
damned of the legal profession, the trial lawyer, better be

around to see that we get a fair trial, and that if we're innocent, we walk out the courtroom free.

One day in November 1985, I got a letter from a woman named Carol Van Strum. She and her husband were waging their own lonesome battle with the Forest Service. She wrote me that a citizen in Lincoln County, Oregon, had been charged with murder and that the woman's husband, a man named Mike Jones, whom she'd never met, had driven two hours in the cold of night to ask her for help. He had a small girl with him, his daughter, Shawn, about ten. The child was sick with the flu, and the woman put the child to bed while she talked with him. Why Jones had sought her help she didn't know. But from what he told her she thought something was fishy. The cops were holding the man's wife in isolation. The cops had their excuses. Van Strum wrote:

> The only person allowed to visit her other than her attorney was her Native American Church minister. Approximately a month before, the minister himself was arrested for blocking the road on the Jones property, booked and released. The police claimed he was infected with hepatitis A. After that even he was barred from visiting Sandy and she's been kept in isolation for four months on the excuse that she's been exposed to the disease. She's received neither medical attention nor blood tests to establish the presence of the hepatitis antibodies. None of the jail staff or police officers involved in the minister's arrest have been similarly quarantined.

When Mike Jones asked the Van Strum woman for help, the only help she could think of was to write to me.

"That's a bunch of bullshit," I said to Eddie Moriarity,

my partner of many years. I slammed the letter down. "If you put everybody in isolation who's been exposed to hepatitis, the whole world would have to be cooped up."

After a couple of calls, Eddie reported back. "It's true: the Jones woman's been in jail since July. Four months! The chief judge assigned a guy named Gardner to hear the case. Gardner won't let her even touch her kids."

"They're twisting her for a guilty plea," I said. I'd been defending murder cases for more than three decades, and if I'd learned one thing it was that trials do not seek the truth, nor are they always intended to deliver justice. Trials are wars—wars that are won more than 90 percent of the time by the state.

"There's not one murder case here, there's two," Eddie said. "The Joneses' fifteen-year-old boy is charged with murder in the juvenile court. The kid was up there when Gerttula was shot. Shawn, the little girl, is cryin' for her mom. Her mom can't make bail. No collateral. Even their chicken house is mortgaged."

I see it in nearly every case. Innocent or not, hold them long enough in some miserable jail, frighten them enough, make them desperate enough, and the state wouldn't have to prove its case. And you have to remember: some charged with murder are innocent. They're usually poor and usually helpless to do much in defense of themselves. Under our Constitution, every person charged with a crime is presumed innocent until proven guilty beyond a reasonable doubt. In truth, most people charged with a crime are *presumed guilty* even by the jurors who hear their cases.

"How come they charged the kid in juvenile court?" I asked. "Most prosecutors would have charged him as an adult. These must be good guys."

"Oregon law required 'em to file the case in juvenile

court," Eddie said. "But the legislature passed a new juvenile law that became effective on October 10. Ulys Stapleton, the DA, threatened Michele Longo—she's Sandy Jones's court-appointed lawyer—that if the kid didn't turn himself in fast, Stapleton would charge him as an adult. Boy came in on his own a few days after the shooting. But before he came in, Stapleton threatened Longo he was going to send out a tactical team to take the kid out. Jesus! Threatening a tactical team to take out a fifteen-year-old!" He shook his head; the Irish smile vanished. "They have the smokin' gun and the eyewitness," Moriarity said. "Easy case to prove. Take about ten minutes. Why those tactics?"

"Maybe there's something wrong with the state's case, or maybe they're just used to those brownshirt tactics up there."

"Maybe," Eddie said.

"Maybe we'd better go see what's going on in Lincoln County," I said.

2

A lumbering, damp, gray November day. We climbed the steps to a squatty little courthouse, that sanctuary of justice in Lincoln County, Oregon, its redbrick facade, its squinting windows, the place as drab and miserable as the day.

The woman behind the jail bars was dressed in men's prison garb that hung loose on her bones and mocked what had once been her good looks. Her bare feet were stuffed in rubber sandals. No socks. She sat huddled on the steel prison cot embracing herself against spasms of shivering. I could see she was tall and slender with blue eyes. Her dark blond hair, uncombed and stringy, hung to her shoulders.

I told her who we were. Without looking at either of us she said, "Never heard of you." Then speaking to no one, she began her liturgy of complaints: "They won't let me have a doctor except that Vargo." Dr. John Vargo, an osteopath, had attended Wilfred Gerttula's autopsy and was a witness for the state. She wouldn't talk to him. She said he gave her some antibiotics, but that they were trying to poison her. She wouldn't eat the food. She began to shiver again.

"Where's your socks?" I asked.

"They took 'em. Can't feel my feet." She went on as if talking to someone who wasn't there. "I got a rupture." The once regular features of her thin face were stretched against the skull, the eyes in shadows behind sunken sockets, dull and empty. I stood looking at the woman not knowing what to say, feeling as if I'd intruded into an ugly, private place of pain and should get the hell out.

"Maybe we could help you," I said.

"They got Little Mike. He never did anything." She spoke to the concrete walls. "I keep seeing blood. I keep seeing it over and over like in a bad dream." Her voice was hollow. "There was blood all over everything—the grass, the sky—it was in my eyes like looking through bloody sunglasses. I feel numb. At first I thought I was going into shock or something. I should have just let Gerttula take my gun from me, but then I thought, no, he would have shot me. Then I saw that blood on the wall." An insanity plea skipped across my mind.

She struggled to her feet and walked to the wall, her steps small and hesitant like a frail old woman's. "I checked it out up close for the blood. I asked a jailer about it." She sat back down, still not looking at me. "I prayed and asked God what it meant and my heart told me that the blood is on the courthouse walls. It was the county's blood. The walls were the county's hands. 'It wasn't your fault,' I heard the voice. 'It was their fault.' Then I was all right again."

Finally she looked at me, and then past me. "I sat for hours. I was swaying to the drums and the chanting. I could even follow along a bit. It was comforting. When the jailer came in, I asked if my friends were out there in the parking lot beating on their drums. He said he didn't hear any drums. I could still hear them. I thought he was lying to me. Finally he said, maybe he could hear them, and he laughed."

"What's that?" I asked, pointing to a poster pasted above the sink of an angel with a flaming sword.

"I don't like looking at my face anymore. It's old," she said, barely touching her cheek. "I can't even recognize myself. So I don't look. I covered the mirror with the picture."

She stared out the high, small, barred window at the end of the walkway that separated the cells. "I can't breathe in here," she said. "The air's so stale, don't you think?" She stood staring in the direction of the window. "I dream of touching the earth again. This concrete is so cold. And all you can hear in here is the clang of the doors and the people hollering."

"Do you remember when they brought you in here?" I asked.

"They made me undress. Three women watched me. They took all my clothes. They stripped me naked and searched me—made me bend over and spread my cheeks while they watched. Then they put me in these." She put a finger on her prison clothes. "Wouldn't give me underwear. I can't get used to not wearing underwear."

The cell was barren—two steel bunks, one on top of the other, and a toilet stool in reach of the lower bunk, a sink next to the stool, a table, and a two-way speaker. Like living in a water closet.

"The floor was sticky like somebody vomited. Smelled like it," she continued. "Then I started to throw up and I couldn't stop. The second day they took me to the hospital and gave me some antibiotics for my urinary-tract infection. And Mike Berry came with his pipe and asked to be allowed to have a ceremony with me, but the jail staff wouldn't let him in. He could talk to me through the window. He said that the Sundance People were all saying prayers for me. I felt like everything was a dream. Still feel that way." Her eyes were like blank pages. "I think I had a fever. Maybe that caused me to get confused so I couldn't tell what was a dream and what was real."

Suddenly I needed to put my arms around her, a father holding a child. And when I let loose, she held on longer. Then I hollered for the jail-keep. You could hear him coming, multiple doors slamming, steel on steel.

"Ever been sued?" I asked the jailer. He was the pot-bellied kind with a face you couldn't pick out of a lineup.

"What ya talkin' about?" he asked in a reedy voice.

"Take a look at this woman. She look comfortable?"

He shrugged his shoulders.

"Maybe I could borrow your socks?" I said.

He looked at me as if he'd better find a padded cell. "When I come back, she better have socks—the heavy wool kind, and a warm sweater. Otherwise I'll be asking you a lot of questions on the witness stand in front of the judge." I walked up close to the man, gave him a big smile, and offered my hand. He didn't take it.

By the time I'd left the jail a thick, sick feeling had come over me. I was glad to get out of there. It isn't that any old murder case will do for a trial lawyer like me. A lawyer needs to feel for his client, and I felt for this woman, alone, help-less, charged with a murder she probably didn't commit. Once I saw her huddled up and half-crazy from her pain, I had no choice but to take her case. If I hadn't, it would have said something about me that no man would like to hear about himself.

Eddie and I met Michele Longo and Steve Lovejoy for breakfast at the Salishan Lodge. They looked like kids to me—Lovejoy, tall and slender, brownish hair, with a face like a first-year college boy and a nose that finally decided to turn up on the end. Michele, an attractive brunette, had a smart, competent look about her and a quick, easy laugh. Put robes on the two of them and they'd look at home in any choir. But both had been around the courtrooms of Oregon.

When Sandy was arrested, Longo's name had come up on the list of lawyers who would take court appointments, which is how she got into this case. She was the direct, no-nonsense kind. Nobody messed with her. She was the kind who struggled for her clients until she dropped despite that the state paid only $45 an hour and she had to run an office out of that and live on whatever was left. Then, from the same state that was trying to convict her client, she had to beg money to hire expert witnesses and an investigator. The state has access to all its needs—the prosecutors, the police, the sheriff's office, the FBI, and an unlimited budget. But appointed defense attorneys have to fight for every dime. Then they face some judge, usually a former prosecutor, who isn't especially passionate about the rights of the accused, but is deeply committed to keeping his job and getting reelected on a record of having been tough on criminals.

From the prosecution's point of view the thinking goes like this: The poor commit crimes. Then the poor want the state to provide the best lawyer in the history of American jurisprudence to get them off. No. The state would provide the accused just enough of a defense so some smart lawyer couldn't spring the bastard on appeal because the state had failed to provide due process.

In the same way, Steve Lovejoy's name had come up on the list, and he'd been appointed by the juvenile court to represent Little Mike. You don't come across his kind too often—someone who actually believed there was a palpable difference between right and wrong and wanted to do something about it. I asked him about his first contact in the case.

"Well," he said, "after the shooting, the boy ran into the pucker brush and stayed there about a week. His dad found him and they voluntarily went in. My first meeting with Little Mike was at the old juvenile department next to the courthouse, about a week after the shooting. Mike Sr., the boy, and several Indians were there along with the director of juvenile services.

"Then Mike Berry, Sandy's 'spiritual adviser' and the leader of the Indians, walked up close to my face and said that even though I'd been appointed by white men to represent the boy, I had to be screened by the family's support group at Medicine Rock before I could interview the boy. I was terrified going out there and facing that tough-looking bunch. On Saturday I drove out to the Jones place. Mr. Spence, I'm telling you, the place looked like it was under siege: locked gates, people on guard. When I got there, I was escorted to one of the tepees. There were five or six Native Americans there along with Mike Sr. Inside the tepee it was dark and smoky. I was sweating, but not from the heat. It was plain old white-boy fear. Frankly, I've blocked out the questions they peppered me with. But I passed!" He laughed again.

"The plan was to come up with a strategy to get Little Mike out of the lockup where they were holding him. Norma McMillan, a neighbor lady, offered to take custody of the boy if he was released. She and Mike Sr. and I prepared a game plan that weekend. That Monday, after a battle with Josh Marquis—he's a deputy DA—Judge Gardner released Mike to Norma's custody. I was in with the Indians—big hero." He laughed again.

Lovejoy said Little Mike was just a kid, like any kid trying to defend his mom. "And they're trying to put him away for that." I could hear the frustration in his voice.

"They have the kid charged with murder," Michele said, "and they have Sandy charged with the same murder. They won't tell us who they claim did the shooting.

Charge 'em both, let the law sort it out. That way they can't lose. Sandy told me Gerttula shot at her kids, actually *shot* at Shawn and Little Mike when they were riding their ponies one day. Scared the kids half to death. The day before the shooting Sandy tried to get a restraining order against Gerttula—but no luck." Michele took a sip of her coffee and looked directly at me. I liked what I saw in her face, a caring that loosened the edges of her eyes when she spoke about her client.

"So this guy'd been shooting at her kids and she kills him for it, right?" I said, testing.

"No. She was defending herself," Michele said.

Steve Lovejoy nodded agreement. I liked these two young lawyers.

Then Lovejoy said, "The DA claims Sandy maliciously killed Gerttula over the road fight. But if she testifies that Gerttula had been shooting at her kids, the DA'll claim she took the law into her own hands and shot him. First-degree murder either way you look at it."

"And they're trying to play us against each other," Michele said. "They want to give Little Mike a deal to testify against his own mother. His *own mother*! They're trying to separate us. But they aren't going to get the job done."

"What do you mean?" I asked.

She was mad and having trouble getting her words out. "They're trying to use Little Mike to get Sandy to plead guilty. Stapleton told me she'd better plead guilty to attempted murder, assault two, and menacing, or she'd wish she had. That'd put her away till she's gray-headed and on Social Security. They're trying to force Sandy to plead guilty to save her son. That pisses me off beyond belief."

"Has the kid given the cops a statement?" Eddie asked.

"Yeah," Steve said. "But we're trying to get it thrown out."

Longo had asked her best friend, a tough criminal defense lawyer from Portland named Jenny Cooke, to help Steve in the boy's case. Cooke was an expert on criminal procedure and juvenile law. Cooke and Lovejoy filed a motion to suppress Little Mike's statement. At the hearing they'd called Detective Thomas Groat of the Lincoln City Police Department and grilled him about how this cadre of officers, Groat, Stapleton, and one of Stapleton's deputies, had manipulated the boy into giving a statement without reading the kid his rights.

Groat said that when they arrived at the Jones farm, they spotted Little Mike running through the field. They hollered at the boy. "I had to ask him several times to come over to the fence," Groat said. He admitted he was wearing a gun, but claimed it wasn't visible, unless, of course, his unbuttoned coat flew open.

Jenny Cooke had pushed on in her questioning. "So had the boy come over to the fence as you ordered him?"

"Yeah."

"And if the boy hadn't come over the fence, you would probably have gone after him?"

"Yeah."

In that case, Cooke argued, the boy wasn't free to leave and was in "constructive custody"—the same as custody—and they should have read the boy his rights.

As I listened to this story, I turned to Eddie. "How old do you have to be, Eddie, before you have rights?"

Eddie knew I was already arguing the case. "You have to be really old," he said. "You have to be a member of the good old boys' club before you have rights."

Little Mike, alone, surrounded by officers, and without having been advised of his rights, had, of course, talked.

He told Groat he hadn't fired the family .30-30. But it was apparent to Groat that more than one weapon had been fired up there. Little Mike said that after the shooting started he couldn't remember anything, but he did see Gerttula holding his stomach. He couldn't remember how many shots were fired.

The officers weren't through. They took Little Mike up to the scene of the shooting. No parent, no guardian, no lawyer, no friend with him.

"Kid woulda been scared shitless," Eddie said.

Then they hauled him back to the house and Groat demanded that the boy tell him where the .22 was, the one Sandy had been carrying. Groat claimed he told the boy he didn't have to give the officers the gun, that he had a right to refuse the search—he had to say that or the search would have been illegal. Anyway, the boy ended up retrieving the .22 for the officers—"all voluntarily," Groat insisted. Then Stapleton, the DA, and one of his deputies came into court and backed up Groat's testimony.

Josh Marquis, Stapleton's chief deputy, who was opposing Cooke and Lovejoy on their motion to suppress the kid's statement, asked Groat, "What did you do about getting him to talk to you?"

Groat replied, "I told him that he wasn't in trouble, that I needed to talk to him about the incident, that someone had been killed and we needed to know what had happened to assist us in the investigation of the homicide."

That he wasn't in trouble? Before the week was over the boy had been sent to the state detention center to await trial on a charge of murder.

"What we have here," Jenny Cooke argued to Judge Robert Gardner, "are all these grown men, including a police officer and a sworn officer of this court, engaged in a shabby conspiracy to deprive this fifteen-year-old of his constitutional rights."

But Deputy DA Marquis argued that Little Mike didn't have to be advised of his rights unless he was in custody. The officers claimed he wasn't a suspect at the time. What he said and did was totally voluntary.

In response Jenny Cooke argued that Stapleton had deliberately kept the child out of physical custody so he wouldn't have to read the boy his rights under *Miranda*. "He wasn't under their control?" she cried. Cooke's argument had been eloquent. "Where on earth was the child to go with four officers standing along with an armed officer? His mother had been taken into custody. The child saw his mother beaten up, a man shot to death. The child was traumatized. He was upset and reluctant to talk. And did Detective Groat ever tell him he didn't need to talk to him? No. Detective Groat showed him his badge and said, 'I am a police officer and I need to know what was going on here.'"

Judge Gardner took the motion to suppress under advisement. He'd probably overrule the motion. Just needed time to figure out a legal position that wouldn't be overturned by the appellate court. Judges play such games.

"And one other thing," Steve Lovejoy had said to Judge Gardner. "We will file two other motions. The first, to dismiss this case against Mike Jones Jr. because of a complete lack of any evidence tying this boy to the crime, and if that motion is denied, we will ask the court to grant us a jury trial."

Marquis had laughed a high, ridiculing laugh. "You don't get a jury trial in juvenile court!"

"And, Your Honor," Lovejoy pleaded, "my client has had no personal contact with his mother for months. Little Shawn is sitting here waiting also." The children were looking over at their mother, the woman wan and sick, and sick for her children. "And just on behalf of Mike Jr., I'd like to ask the court some indulgence, to let these kids see and touch and feel their mother for a few minutes before the court locks her up."

Judge Gardner said he'd talk with the sheriff about it later.

Michele handed me a couple of sheets of rumpled paper. "These are some notes from Sandy," she said. They were written in a careful hand. I began to read aloud at the breakfast table. "'I am an earth child,'" Sandy had written. "'The coyote is my brother. My father in heaven blessed me by allowing me to be born free like the eagle in a country that was founded under Him—by men who praised their freedoms and rights and were willing to defend them to the death.

"'As I sit in this bare cell which has the cigarette butts and tobacco leafs nine former prisoners have strewn about the floor, and their art work upon its walls, I think about things like democracy and justice.'" I looked up from the paper in my hand. The young lawyers were intent on my reading. I read on. "'The murder, assault and menacing charges that hang over my head are a weight that burdens my heart. My family split into pieces, a life's dream in shambles—because the judges, district attorney, and the courthouse hierarchy have used their powers to teach this earth child her place in their society. A lesson to any other upstarts who make waves by trying to change things that are not right.

"'The greed and hate of a neighbor boiled in his heart when he found the justice system would condone his every illegal activity against the earth child. When the earth child's man was run over, when her children were shot at, animals killed, vehicles vandalized, fences cut, the justice system turned its head away.'"

"What's she talking about here?" I asked Michele.

"It's her inventory of her trouble with Gerttula."

I began to read again. "'When a dead raccoon was put in her drinking system, the justice system was blind. Its eyes were only open for the complaints against the earth child and her family. After he cut the fences and the earth child's animals strayed, the justice system cited her for allowing animals to run at large.'" On another page she'd written and I read aloud, "'The newspapers have been using Little Mike's name, stating that he's accused of committing murder. The DA wasn't supposed to release his name because he's a juvenile.'"

I read on: "'Last night at about nine P.M. the jailer told me that he'd gotten orders to the effect that if anyone made contact with me in the courtroom again, referring to Little Mike hugging me, he was to jerk me out and bring me back to my cell. I asked where those orders came from. He said he heard it was high up.'"

About her health complaints she'd written: "'I said to the nurse that Judge Gardner told me to call him, and that I could have a doctor. The nurse said she wasn't going to call the judge, that she left the legal things to county counsel. I told her that my back and shoulder were hurting, and could I have a back brace. She said I'd have to talk to the doctor about it. I said I have a brace at home. Could I use it? She said only if a doctor says so. I told her about my veins. She said, "You're getting old." Then she left. The jailer came to give me an antibiotic. I told the jailer that DA Stapleton had been trying to intimidate Little Mike by staring at him in court and mouthing, "You murdered him." She shrugged and said, "Well, that's bad, but we could have someone worse."

"'My shoulder was really hurting earlier after breakfast. I asked to take a shower. The female deputy always comes in and stares at me.'"

Done reading, I handed the pages back to Michele. I felt an anger and was glad for it. Without anger a trial lawyer is just a mannequin mouthing meaningless legalisms.

"They got a warrant to search the Jones property," Michele said. "Ever since Sandy's been in jail the cops have been constantly out at the farm. They found one hundred and eighty-seven pounds of salmon and deer meat that Mike Sr. had taken to feed the family and hauled him off to jail."

"Christ," Eddie said. "They let those big corporations dump their crap into the river and kill most of the salmon, and when a crippled man takes a few to feed his kids, they want to hang him."

Just as Carol Van Strum had written, something fishy was going on. This woman was being treated as if she were a member of the Manson family. Nothing added up. The state had a photograph of Sandy firing the .22 rifle. But Gerttula had, in fact, been shot with a large-caliber gun. Despite his denial, Little Mike had fired the family hunting rifle, the .30-30. But, according to Lovejoy, all of the bullets had been accounted for. None could have hit Gerttula.

I saw those decent young lawyers sitting at the breakfast table with us. They looked first at Eddie and then at me, not wanting to appear as if they really needed help. "What do you think, Eddie?"

Eddie Moriarity just gave me that look that said, "Every trial lawyer worth a damn needs to have a good murder case."

3

In the afternoon of November 25, 1985, we sat in that dreary little windowless, blond-wood-from-the-fifties courtroom waiting for His Honor, Judge Robert Gardner, to take the bench. The case, entitled "In the Matter of Michael Jones, Jr., a child," was set to be heard in the juvenile court of Lincoln County, Oregon. The state intended to try Little Mike first and leave his mother moldering in jail. When the judge found the boy guilty, maybe the mother would cave in to save her son. For us to represent both mother and son created a potential conflict. But I thought, One case at a time. We'll cross that bridge when we get there. We entered our appearance for Little Mike.

Waiting for His Honor to take the bench, I suddenly turned to Eddie Moriarity. "Eddie, let's do something defense attorneys never do. We don't know Stapleton and Marquis. Let's give 'em the benefit of the doubt. Let's lay our whole case out for 'em. Why would they want to try a case against us if they don't have one?"

"I don't trust 'em," Eddie said.

"What do you think?" I asked Steve Lovejoy.

He seemed excited. "The facts are the facts. Little Mike couldn't have killed Gerttula. I sent an engineer out there. Reconstructed the scene. None of the bullets Little Mike fired came close to Gerttula. They can't change the facts—not now. What do we have to lose?"

I sauntered over to Stapleton and Marquis. "Gentle-men, let's get the judge in here for a little pretrial confer-ence."

They looked surprised. Then they followed me into the judge's chambers, the door open. "Could we talk to you on an informal basis, Your Honor?" Stapleton shrugged his shoulders, and the judge, expressionless, got up and led us into the jury room. He sat down mechanically and folded his hands, waiting.

"I want Mr. Stapleton and Mr. Marquis to know what our case is—no surprises," I said. The judge's face was stony.

I went to a large paper flip-pad on an easel. "The family hunting rifle in the hands of Michael Jones Jr. was a Win-chester .30-30. It holds seven cartridges in the magazine. All seven cartridges can be accounted for. Three were fired— and there was a dud on the ground. The police recovered two live cartridges out of the gun. That's six. The crimi-nologist discovered the seventh cartridge in the chamber when he examined the gun several weeks ago at the State Crime Lab."

I walked to the board and drew a profile of Gerttula's pickup truck at the scene. "Shot number one went through the right rear tire. Shot number two lodged in an alder tree. The state has a picture of it and the tree in which it was embedded." I drew in the tree behind and above the bed of the pickup. "Shot number three went through the pickup bed." I sketched in the path of that bullet. "The state has pictures of that bullet hole as well." I turned to Judge Gardner and then to Marquis and Stapleton. "Given these facts, why are we here?"

The judge was making notes. I waited for him to finish and look up. When I had his attention, I said, "Your Honor, our expert, Dr. Brady, whom you know and respect, is the single most outstanding forensic pathologist in the State of Oregon. He's spent a lifetime testifying in cases for the state. Dr. Brady says that the slug that killed Wilfred Gerttula did not come from a high-powered rifle. It came from a pistol."

I waited again. "But whose pistol?"

I turned to Stapleton and Marquis. "There's something wrong with this case, gentlemen. A boy shouldn't be put on trial for murder under circumstances such as these. These are undisputed facts. These are the facts gathered by the state itself. I'm going to ask you gentlemen in all good faith to dismiss this case."

Marquis looked at Stapleton and then laughed. Marquis was the youngish, dark assistant to Stapleton. "This is nothing but another contrived fiction by Mr. Spence," Marquis said. Then, as if to underline his confidence in his case, Marquis said that they would put Monica Gerttula on the polygraph, and if they were satisfied she'd lied, they'd dismiss the case.

I glanced at Eddie. He made a quick face that said, "I told you."

We followed the judge into the courtroom and watched him ascend the bench. The prosecutors took their table, and we ours. Once more we were back in the formal mode of the courtroom. Both the judge and the prosecutors seemed more comfortable.

Judge Gardner opened the file on his desk and looked up. "About the deposition of Mrs. Gerttula?" he began. His face was molded in mortar. He wore an obvious black hairpiece. We'd subpoenaed Monica Gerttula, the deceased's wife, for her deposition. I told the judge we wanted a chance to ask her questions under oath, with her answers accurately recorded. She was the state's only eyewitness to the homicide. We thought she knew why the state's case didn't hold up and we wanted to take her testimony before Little Mike's trial began.

Marquis had moved to set aside her subpoena. But even before the judge had ruled on his motion, Marquis had taken it upon himself to instruct Mrs. Gerttula that she needn't appear. Marquis was already arguing: "This is an attempt by the defense, at best, for discovery and, at worst, to intimidate and harass a witness who they know to be emotionally wrought up in these circumstances." He argued that the juvenile court was akin to a criminal process, and a deposition in a criminal case was not permitted.

I stood before the bench. "They've already told Mrs. Gerttula she doesn't have to abide by the subpoena," I said, "as if *they've* made the decision, not Your Honor."

"Your Honor," Stapleton shouted, "could you advise counsel to get back where he is supposed to be? I mean, you know, wandering around the courtroom!" He was referring to a strange rule that required all attorneys to stay seated at their tables during argument.

"I should hope, Your Honor, that we have more important matters before us than my standing here," I said.

"I'll allow some leeway," the judge replied. I got chilly when he spoke. After that the judge set aside our subpoena. The juvenile court, he held, was akin to a criminal proceeding, and depositions were not permitted in criminal law.

Then what about a jury trial for Little Mike? If this were a *criminal* proceeding, then surely the boy was entitled to a jury. But in Oregon, citizens under eighteen don't get a jury trial in juvenile court. The judge hears all the facts and makes the decision both on the facts and the law. And this judge was going to hear *both* the boy's case and his mother's case as well.

"No matter what decision you make as the fact finder in this case," I said to Gardner, "it will affect your judgment as you decide the issues that come before you in Mrs. Jones's case. The basis for asking a judge to step down from a case is when the judge can't retain some kind of objectivity." I let the words settle in. "If you hear the facts in the boy's case, you'll have made a decision as to what you believe he did. And that will affect how you view the facts and the legal rulings that you'll need to make in Mrs. Jones's case. It's a situation that places Your Honor in a very uncomfortable position, or it should."

Again I waited. Finally I said, "I don't know how to say it any more honestly than I have. I think it would benefit justice if Your Honor were insulated from deciding any facts in this case and gave that duty over to a jury."

His Honor seemed unmoved.

I began another tack. "I think because a boy is fifteen years old, that shouldn't deprive him of his rights as a citizen of the United States."

This time Marquis argued that this *wasn't* a criminal proceeding at all. It was a juvenile proceeding. "There's no right to a jury trial for juveniles. Juveniles have a tremendous number of rights, virtually everything, but no right to a jury trial." His Honor agreed.

By eight-twenty in the evening the various pretrial arguments had come to an end, mostly because the lawyers, if not His Honor, were exhausted.

One thing was clear: it was going to be a war. And in a war one should have an accurate view of the enemy. The enemy was neither prosecutors set in concrete nor a judge sunken in dead calm. The enemy was the endemic meanness of the system. Every day the state hauls into court the dregs of society. These miscreants fill the courtrooms with the sounds of their contrived excuses and their tinny pleas for mercy. We despise them for the injuries and pain they impose upon us. The accused are mean. Their crimes are mean. Murder is mean. And meanness is contagious. The system has caught it.

Yet through the system runs a thin, golden streak of humanity, hairlike, barely capable of discernment, which declares no matter how evil, the accused is still presumed innocent, and that the state, despite its need to bring vengeance upon him, must provide a fair trial, and still more: it must prove its case beyond a reasonable doubt. We believed in the system. And we thought Little Mike was being railroaded.

4

Once more we gathered at the breakfast table. "They offered us a plea," Steve said. "Little Mike can plead guilty to manslaughter and go to MacLaren until he's twenty-one. I been tryin' for probation. But his mother had Michele take a message to the kid: that to plead guilty to something he didn't do was wrong. Besides, he doesn't want to plead guilty."

"They offered me manslaughter for Sandy, too," Michele said. "Sandy said for me to give them *her* offer: they can drop all charges against both her and Little Mike and she won't sue the county. She said she shouldn't give 'em that much, the way they treated her."

"She's got a lotta spunk," I said. I liked that kind, something about a person who has the courage to stand up against power. I found myself caring about Sandra Jones. If we didn't defend her and Little Mike, I'd feel as if we'd left behind something important about us.

"I finally got the reports from the criminologist," Michele said. "DA's been sitting on 'em. And I'll tell you why: Monica Gerttula had gunshot residue all over her hands and face. Enough for the guy at the state lab to conclude that she likely shot a gun that day!"

"So that's it!" I said. The fog started to lift. "What we have here is Monica Gerttula claiming she didn't shoot a gun, the scientific evidence saying she likely did, and the prosecution telling us that if they give her a lie detector test and she's deceptive, they'll dismiss the murder case against our boy."

"Right," Eddie said.

"This morning we're going to get the results of that test," I said.

"Want to bet on it?" Eddie said. "I got a dollar says we get zip." He emptied his coffee cup.

"Let's go," I said.

It was the second day of December 1985, in Newport, Oregon, the county seat of Lincoln County, the first day of Little Mike's trial on a charge of murder. The boy was a fifteen-year-old replica of his father without the beard: red-headed, with freckles, the blue eyes, the open face.

"Don't worry, Mike," I said. The boy, dressed in freshly ironed overalls and a clean flannel shirt, was sitting at counsel table next to me. Steve was on his other side trying to comfort him. "It's going to be all right."

Then I heard them at the courtroom door. I turned to see Sandy Jones being escorted in by a couple of deputies. She was in prison garb and cuffs. She took a step toward Little Mike, but the female deputy in charge held her back. Shawn and Big Mike were sitting up front. The child got up to run to her mother. But the deputy ordered the girl back.

"Your Honor," Deputy DA Marquis began, "both the state and the defense may call Mrs. Jones as a witness—and if she were able to sit in the courtroom and hear all of the testimony, and then be able to, perhaps, change her testimony according to that, I think a great injustice could be wrought." But in a juvenile court hearing, the parents have a right to be present. And what of the child's right to have his parents there?

"This is a pretty lonely proceeding and a pretty frightening place for a boy charged with first-degree murder," I said, "and to be sitting here alone in a courtroom having his case tried by a judge without his parents present."

"He's obviously not alone," Marquis said. "He's represented by all these attorneys." He made a sweeping gesture to our table where Eddie, Steve, and I were sitting.

Marquis wanted Big Mike excluded from the courtroom as well. "They're attempting to get as many witnesses as possible into the courtroom to frustrate the purpose of the court excluding the witnesses," he argued, his voice loaded with anger.

But Gardner ruled that the parents could be present. That was as far as his ruling went—they could be present. The deputies kept Sandy separated from her children and Big Mike, away from their touch, the family members not able to say the first word of comfort to each other.

Later that day in chambers I said to the judge, "One thing that distresses me: I said to Sandy a minute ago—'Sandy, have you talked to your son yet this morning? Have you seen your boy?' She looked at me with eyes full of tears and said, 'They won't let me talk to him.' I turned to the female guard from the sheriff's office, and do you want to hear what she said, Judge?"

The judge made no indication he was interested.

"The guard said, 'I don't want her to talk to him.' Now, Judge, I ask the court to let Mrs. Jones talk to her son during the trial in the presence of the sheriff's officers."

Marquis objected. "Sandra Jones is an adult charged with murder. She's in the custody of the sheriff. She's present here because the court has allowed it. I guess Mr. Spence would have these people wander around the courtroom and do anything they like because it's a juvenile proceeding."

"I can't believe what I'm hearing," I said. "This is just plain orneriness on the part of the prosecutor. I'd expect him to say, 'I join you in this, Mr. Spence.' I just can't understand that, Your Honor."

I looked at Marquis and Stapleton. They could have been a couple of guys you'd meet at a Rotary Club luncheon. I could see them leading a troop of Boy Scouts. I wouldn't charge them as cruel men. They were acting in the role of prosecutors. They wanted a conviction. And no big-shot lawyer from Wyoming was going to stop them.

The judge peered down with his earthenware face. He said he'd take my request under advisement, but he wanted to talk to the security commander first.

Despite the phony hepatitis quarantine Sandy was under, Michele continued to meet with her. Sandy's brother was a minister, and she sought him for spiritual guidance. But she was refused even that comfort—the officer's reason: Sandy couldn't have a peace-pipe ceremony with the Indians and still be a Christian. Not once during this time was Mike Sr. permitted to embrace his wife, to hold her in his arms and comfort her, not even for a moment. Not once had Shawn or Little Mike been permitted to touch their mother.

As I saw it, Sandy Jones was *presumed guilty*. She was denied bail and condemned to sit in a freezing cell without adequate clothing. She was sick, and the state had refused to provide her proper medical care. In the meantime, the state was playing mother against child. The game was evil, I thought. A Rockefeller would have had visits with her child, a Kennedy, from his priest, and both would have had plenty of warm clothing and medical attention, and both would probably be out on bail in a case where manslaughter had been offered. But as an ex-prosecutor, Judge Gardner probably saw it from the standpoint of the state: the woman and her kid were killers.

Who were we to judge? We were the rascals of the legal system who were paid to get murderers and rapists out of jail through some legal loophole. That Eddie and I were serving without fee from the state didn't change our status. Yet, something was wrong here.

Little Mike was a wide-eyed, scared little kid, the innocent kind if I'd ever seen one. Never had a run-in with the law. He did his chores, took care of the cow, fed the ponies, gathered firewood, went fishing with his father for salmon, hunted deer in the fall to help feed the family. He was a boy who knew more about the woods and the rivers than about drugs and crime. He'd been home-taught by his mother and isolated from the rampant temptations rife in public schools. He could just as easily have been seen as a hero, a boy who'd tried his best to frighten off a man who was attacking his mother.

But the charges against Little Mike were broad. The state claimed he'd shot Gerttula intentionally, or, if not, that he was guilty of the crime of murder as an accomplice. We asked the court to order the state to elect which of the charges they'd proceed on.

Marquis argued back, "Let's say we were to elect accomplice liability, and then Michael Jones Jr. takes the witness stand and gets up there and says, 'Aha, I am not an accomplice. I shot Gerttula. I did it. Therefore I'm not guilty because the state elected to proceed against Sandra Jones as the one who pulled the trigger.'"

I said, "He's wanting to play games with this child. The game is 'Guess what we're going to prove.'"

My arguments failed to move Gardner. "It's quite clear," he said, "that the state is not required to elect in this case."

I hadn't won a single substantive motion. At the recess

I said to Eddie, "Eddie, no use talking to this judge anymore. What we say in here we say for the benefit of the record for our appeal to the Oregon Court of Appeals."

"I agree," Eddie said. "But we've pulled worse ones than this out of the fire." He gave me a smile and a wink, the eternal optimism of the Irish.

I pressed on after the recess. "Your Honor, we want to make the specific objection for the purpose of an appeal to the United States Supreme Court that this proceeding is in violation of this young citizen's rights under the Sixth Amendment of the United States Constitution. This child, merely because he's a child, cannot be deprived of a trial by a jury in a case in which the charge is murder."

Gardner seemed bored. He'd heard it all before.

I asked the judge for special findings of fact, to state specifically in writing who killed Wilfred Gerttula and with what weapon. Did the boy intend to kill Gerttula or was he merely defending his mother? What about Sandy Jones? If she shot the man, did she do so in self-defense? And what weapon did she use?

The prosecutors, of course, objected that such findings by the judge might adversely affect their case against Sandy Jones. But His Honor said, as if in passing, "I will probably give some brief reasons for the court's ruling."

Into this arena, this hybrid trial that was neither criminal nor civil, a battlefield already brimming with hostility, a child just turned fifteen was dragged before the court on multiple charges of murder, while his mother was charged with identical crimes in the criminal courts and locked up in the Lincoln County jail.

I confronted Judge Gardner head-on about his rulings. "I want to tell you what bothers me: It's my belief, Your Honor, that in a juvenile court proceeding the guiding light has to be 'What's for the benefit of the child?' It certainly isn't for the child's benefit, when he's charged with murder, for the court to take the strict legal position of a technician who says, 'Unless there's a duty on my part to give this right to the child, I will not give it to him,' so that we end up in a proceeding in which the child has fewer, not more, rights than if he'd been charged as a vicious criminal."

I asked the judge: How was I to explain to Little Mike why murderers and rapists in this country go before a jury but a jury couldn't hear Little Mike's case? "What do I reply when the boy says, 'I understand Monica Gerttula has changed her testimony. Why can't we take her deposition?'" I went on. "I'm asking Your Honor to be a fifteen-year-old for a moment. You've just seen a man shot before your eyes. Your mother has been hauled off to jail, and you're surrounded by armed police officers and you're scared. Now the state says that whatever statements they obtained from you cannot be suppressed because they were voluntary?"

Again I waited. The judge gave me a rocky stare. Finally I said, "An understanding court would say, 'No fifteen-year-old boy under those circumstances is going to be stuck with what he did or didn't say to the officers at the time. I'm not going to hear them call this child a liar because he said he didn't shoot a gun, and therefore, because he lied, he's a murderer.' These are the things, Your Honor, that hurt me."

The judge said, "My understanding of the proceeding is that Michael Jones Jr. will receive all the rights that appertain to the criminal trial, with the exception of the right to a jury trial."

"So he has fewer rights than if he were tried in the criminal court," I said. "It's an anomaly for the legislature to pass a Juvenile Court Act hoping that a child should have better treatment and then end up in a proceeding like this where he has fewer rights. That, I think, is the cruel joke here."

Then I brought up the polygraph that Marquis had promised they'd have administered to Monica Gerttula. I reminded the judge that after Marquis said the state would submit her to the polygraph, these same prosecutors had asked for a continuance in order to test Mrs. Gerttula's truthfulness. I asked for the results.

Marquis began to argue that I'd previously called lie detector tests "the test of charlatans."

"Has she taken the polygraph?" I asked Marquis.

"I'm not going to answer Mr. Spence's question."

Gardner said to Marquis, "My recollection of the telephone conversation was that if the state could obtain a continuance, they'd be willing to make one of the conditions of that continuance to place Mrs. Gerttula on a polygraph, and if she proved deceptive, that you would dismiss the case."

"That's a correct statement of what my statement was," Marquis said.

Then the judge asked, "Was she subjected to a polygraph?"

Marquis said, "I don't think that is discoverable. It's not admissible evidence. If counsel will stipulate to the polygraph test, we will stipulate to—"

I interrupted. "The question is *whether she's been given one.*"

The results of the polygraph might not be admissible, the judge said, but there could be statements in the notes and the like that might be discoverable. I wondered what the state was hiding.

Marquis continued to argue. "As Your Honor knows, with polygraph tests, you can't have subjective answers. You have yes or no answers. So there are no statements, *per se*, of the witness." Once more Marquis tried to direct the argument away from the results of the polygraph: "Any conclusions would not be admissible unless they are willing to stipulate to what they may be."

Eddie whispered, "Gerry, if she had a good result, we couldn't keep him from broadcasting it to the whole world."

"Right," I said.

"He's bluffing," Eddie said. "He knows you won't stipulate in the blind to what the results of the test were."

I said, "Your Honor, he's being deceptive. All he has to do is tell us, 'Yes, there was, or no there was not, a polygraph given.' If there was, then Your Honor can look at the results himself and decide whether or not we should have them."

Finally Judge Gardner said, "I'll require that by one-thirty you advise Mr. Spence whether a polygraph was given, and if so whether there's a report or notes of the operator, and provide any copies of reports or notes and the name of the operator."

"We'll never get it," Eddie said to me. "Remember, I got a dollar on it."

5

Eddie, Steve Lovejoy, and I huddled during the recess. Michele Longo sat on the other side of the courtroom watching over Sandy. Sometimes Sandy cried out in loud whispers, her visions of what was happening around her often at hard variance from our own.

Yet she had bravely refused to plead guilty, as Stapleton had demanded. "I'm not guilty of anything," she said, "and I'm not pleading guilty to anything." We told her of the DA's warning—if she didn't plead guilty to manslaughter, the DA was going back for an additional charge—attempted murder.

"Little Mike didn't do anything either," she said. "If he had, he would have told me."

I looked at Eddie. Mothers believe their kids. Mothers will fight for them. Then what she said surprised me. "I told Little Mike he could do what he wanted to do. He's fifteen. If he wants to nail me and do a deal with Stapleton to save himself, I told him to go ahead. It was up to him. But I am not pleading to something I didn't do."

By order of Judge Gardner, Little Mike had been placed in the care of Norma McMillan, an elderly friend of the family's and a retired schoolteacher. He and Shawn, separated from each other, lived under a relentless cloud of fear. You could see it in their tight, small faces. What would become of them, of their mother, who was surrounded by armed deputies? I saw Big Mike sitting in the audience with Shawn. He was holding on to her hand—the heavy longing in the room for the mother.

This small team of lawyers was the last, desperate hope of Sandy Jones. She said Eddie and I, these two from the far-off mountains, had descended like angels. Her view of us offered as much reason for our presence as our own.

Despite my appearance to the contrary, I felt small and weak. Always do. Here I was, a well-known lawyer with many a successful trial under my belt—I'd written books, lectured the bar, and often appeared on television. Yet I never had enough power to ensure that an innocent client would walk free. I had a recurring nightmare—the cops fastening the cuffs and shackles on my client and seeing his frightened eyes as they dragged him away. As he looks back at me for help, he wants to cry out like a child but he's too afraid to cry out, and I stand there helpless to stop it.

With this judge I felt as if I were screaming into the void. My words landed on the judge's ears all right, but I was only part of the legal machinery, the rattling, sometimes exploding, steam and noise. The machinery ground out case after case, day after day. The machine had one purpose—to process the cases, which usually meant to convict those accused.

"Here's the state's situation," I said to my young colleagues. "They give Monica Gerttula a lie detector test. Did she shoot a gun that day? She's probably failed the test. Now they're trying to explain away the gunshot residue on the woman's hands and face. They're in trouble with the facts."

"Why would the facts make any difference?" Eddie asked, his question tinted with cynicism born from many a struggle in the courtroom, where he'd found that facts didn't always decide the case.

Cops all know that when a cartridge is fired, small particles of antimony and barium from the cartridge's primer escape. The particles can land on the shooter's hands, face, or on someone very close to the muzzle of the gun. The crime lab had done a test firing of the .30-30 that Little Mike had fired at the scene. The lab tried to duplicate the residue found on Monica Gerttula with a test on a mannequin. But the results of that test had not been provided us.

When the judge took the bench again, we asked for test results. Marquis claimed the crime lab hadn't completed its tests yet. Further he said, "In many of these cases, Your Honor, there are no such things as test results."

Judge Gardner: "But you *are* going to check that out?"

Marquis: "I am going to check that during the lunch hour."

Moriarity, whispering: "Want to bet another dollar, Gerry?"

Precisely at the hour of one-thirty in the afternoon we reconvened as ordered by the judge. What about the tests on the mannequin? I asked. Nothing existed, Marquis claimed, except, of course, the indecipherable notes we already had.

"Verify which figures are key to the mannequin test before the end of the day," the judge said.

"Another dollar?" Eddie whispered to me. "I don't wanna break ya."

"Anything further at this time?" the judge asked.

"Yes," I said. "I'm still waiting for Mr. Marquis to provide me the information on the lie detector test that you ordered for this time."

Marquis began a high, strained discourse. "A polygraph test was administered on Friday at approximately eleven

A.M. by Stephen Toliver, who is an employee of the District Attorney's Office."

"Was there a report prepared?" the judge asked.

"There was no report prepared. There are the questions that were asked and, I think, some notes about the background of Mrs. Gerttula. Mr. Toliver—I'm talking about everything I found that—you know, that he wrote down."

"Ready to pay up?" Eddie whispered.

"Now, it's my position that this comes awfully late in the game," Marquis continued. "I mean, we talked about this before. All of a sudden counsel is demanding this. It wasn't prepared with the anticipation of offering it. They are the only notes he took when he did the polygraph examination. It is our position that, (a), they are not exculpatory, they contain merely questions; (b), they are work product; (c), they are not admissible in evidence under any possible scheme. And the only reason the defense is doing this is to throw chaff up at this point. If the court directs me to, I will give them—"

"Why don't you disclose those by five o'clock today," the judge said.

"I will do it right now, Your Honor." Marquis handed me a copy of the notes with the questions. But there were no findings by the polygraph operator!

Josh Marquis opened his notebook, cleared his throat, and began his opening statement. This was to be one of the deputy DA's most masterful performances. He'd been a news reporter and knew the value of a sound bite. He was young, talented, and driven.

"Your Honor," he began, "the state will prove Michael Jones Jr. shot and killed Wilfred Gerttula on July twenty-third, 1985, in Lincoln County, Oregon, and that he did so intentionally."

Marquis claimed that the core of the Joneses' resentment against Gerttula was a fight over a county road. Sandy Jones had wrongfully blocked it. When the evidence was in, the court would see a young boy who'd been pulled out of school at an early age and who'd lived an isolated life, and a family who saw the Gerttulas as their sworn enemy. The boy killed Wilfred Gerttula with the family .30-30 hunting rifle.

Marquis told how earlier that same day a couple of woodsmen by the name of Dick and Nye had driven up the disputed road with the Gerttulas to the Gerttula property. They were on their way down when they were confronted by Sandy Jones and Little Mike at the Joneses' upper gate. The boy held his .30-30 at the ready, the mother the .22. Then Sandy Jones told them, "Don't come up here again or I'll shoot you. Who the hell do you think you are, coming here?" Michael Jr. had brandished the rifle. The men, frightened, left. And after that, according to Marquis, Sandy Jones "was in the brush outside" and Michael "was up on the hill just beyond the gate." An ambush!

Now he spoke of "the classic smoking gun," the .22 Sandy Jones had fired at Gerttula through the windshield of his truck. She had tried to kill the man. Before the shooting started, Mrs. Gerttula had gotten out of the truck to take pictures of the Joneses with their guns. The state had this photo of Sandy Jones shooting the .22 moments before the murder. It was one of the photos taken by Mrs. Gerttula herself. And Sandy Jones had shot out at least one tire on the Gerttula pickup. Mrs. Gerttula, no expert on guns, knew that both Sandy and her son had "long guns" at the scene. But, Marquis quickly added, "she won't be able to specify the caliber or anything like that."

Marquis, like a veteran in the courtroom, waited for the judge to complete writing a note. When the judge looked up, Marquis continued, "And for the most part Mrs. Gerttula lost track of Michael Jones Jr. because her attention, as the court will find, was extremely distracted by Mrs. Jones, who was firing at her husband, and it was Sandy Jones who ended up beating Mrs. Gerttula severely with the barrel of her gun."

According to Marquis, Mrs. Gerttula suddenly heard "a big bang," and Wilfred Gerttula crumpled over, crying, "Oh, my God!" and started to bleed and die at the front of the pickup.

"The evidence will be that Mr. Gerttula had *no gun* in his hands," Marquis said with all the power of his voice, "that if, in fact, he had had a gun in his hands, he would have been the most restrained individual on earth, a virtual saint, because at this point he will have already been shot in the face by Sandy Jones. His wife is being beaten by Sandy Jones. He comes out of the pickup. The defense, I assume, will contend that he started beating Sandy Jones with a handgun. But she had no injuries on her."

He mentioned the marks in the dust on the pickup hood where Gerttula rested his arms after he was shot and the blood splatters that extended down to the bumper where he bled. Then the dying Gerttula had climbed back into the pickup and collapsed.

Not only had the Joneses killed Wilfred Gerttula, but after that, Sandy Jones had taunted Mrs. Gerttula. "'What good is your money now? What's it worth?' she hollered." Marquis claimed Sandy Jones knew her picture had been taken by Mrs. Gerttula. "'You are not going anywhere until I get that camera,' she said."

Marquis admitted there was a tape recorder at the scene, one belonging to the Gerttulas. (They hauled it along wherever they went in order to record any untoward statements made by Sandy to them.) How it got thrown down over the side of the road Mrs. Gerttula didn't know. She didn't throw it there. Then his voice quieted. We listened. The judge listened. "Monica Gerttula will testify that she did not have a gun that day, that, in fact, she and Mr. Gerttula had never owned a handgun."

I saw Eddie sitting next to me writing: *Never owned a handgun.*

"They've owned several rifles," Marquis continued. "But she did not have a gun that day and her husband did not have a gun that day."

Eddie wrote some more: *Didn't have a gun that day.*

Then, wise to the counterpoint in the argument, Marquis said, "The people who had guns that day were Michael Jones with this .30-30 and his mother with this .22 and, perhaps, a couple other pistols owned by the Joneses that they turned over to some people called the Clevelands, who will testify early on in the state's case."

Eddie leaned over to me and whispered, "They got Sandy trying to shoot Gerttula in the face. There's the attempted murder they're talking about. Then they got Little Mike finishing the job." He looked worried. We both knew you could take the same bricks and build a stately castle or a morbid death house. But Marquis had some problems in his evidence—that gunshot residue on Monica Gerttula's hands and face to begin with. Now we heard his explanation.

Little Mike "grappled with Mrs. Gerttula for some time," Marquis said. That was how he claimed the gunshot residue was transferred from Little Mike to Monica Gerttula. Besides, Marquis insisted, the gunshot residue was of little importance. "It will be the state's contention, Your Honor, that gunshot residue tests can many times be helpful, just like the weather can be helpful. But sometimes they aren't. And in this case they don't really prove anything. Someone could just as certainly argue that Sandy Jones fired that pistol because Sandy Jones has high levels on her hand, too. And the levels on Monica's hands are on the wrong hand."

And what would be the testimony of the state's crime lab technician concerning the gunshot residue? Marquis soon told us. John Amish, from the state lab, would testify "that the levels on Monica Gerttula's face are much too high to have fired a revolver, that they are entirely consistent with somebody who has had antimony and barium transferred and then grabs their face—does something like that."

At last Marquis in his opening took us to the murder scene. Mrs. Gerttula had been beaten and was hysterical, he said. Sandy Jones had crawled into the driver's seat of the pickup after she and her son had forcibly wrested the truck keys from Mrs. Gerttula. Sandy Jones then ordered Mrs. Gerttula to open the gate, and when she did, Sandy Jones drove off in the pickup with the dying Wilfred and left Monica Gerttula screaming down the road after the truck. Michael Jones Jr. followed Mrs. Gerttula down. Then, according to Marquis, he went into the house, where he left the .22 rifle.

"The boy put the .30-30 in the pickup," Marquis claimed. "He wouldn't want to be found with that because the .30-30 was the murder weapon. The boy was seen carrying the .22."

Marquis claimed Sandy "abandoned" the pickup at the Cleveland residence and that Mr. Cleveland, a former mortician, came out, took one look at Gerttula, and pronounced him dead. Marquis told the judge, "Sandy Jones, in a methodical effort to get everything arranged for what she knew was a certain arrest, went out and collected their guns—the .22-caliber pistol that her son had, a .38-caliber Charter Arms that she apparently carried sometimes, the

.22-caliber rifle that she had, and the .30-30-caliber rifle which was left in the pickup."

Eddie was still making notes. He shoved the pad to me: *Little Mike left the .22 rifle at the house. How did it get down to Clevelands?*

And when did Sandy go back to the house to pick up the .22 pistol that wasn't at the scene?

Marquis pressed on. He told the judge that his expert, Dr. John Vargo, an osteopath, would testify that the wound suffered by Gerttula was "entirely consistent with that of a .30-30." He argued it was one of the least powerful of the rifle cartridges.

At last Marquis was ready to sum up his case. "The evidence, when we get past all of the hoopla and all of the possibles, will show that Sandy Jones and her son, for whatever reason, wanted a confrontation with the Gerttulas. So they went up there that day. They blocked their path of escape by locking the gate, by blocking the road. They brandished their weapons. They threatened people that day—Nye and Dick—and later the Gerttulas, and when Mrs. Gerttula had the effrontery to take a picture of what they were doing, they decided *that was it*. It wasn't any express agreement, but that's clearly what happened.

"Mrs. Jones started firing her gun and her son decided to join in. He shot at least two rounds into the pickup and started moving around. And when Mr. Gerttula came out to help his wife, who was being beaten, Michael Jones shot him through the chest and murdered him."

With a flourish of voice and a slap of his folding notebook, Marquis said, "That will be the state's evidence." He looked up at Judge Gardner, a smallish smile on his face, like a son waiting for his father's approval.

* * *

I walked in front of the judge's bench. He looked down at me without expression. I wanted the judge to know this boy, this not much more than a child he was about to dispose of in one way or another. Little Mike, frightened and timid, could hardly paint a lucid picture of himself. I'd have to do it for him.

"This boy was taught as we like to teach our sons," I said to the judge. "He was taught to respect his parents. He loved his father. He loved his mother. They were not perfect people. They were different than most folks.

"Mr. Jones had worked four and a half years in Alaska to save enough money to make the $5,000 down payment on this small, twenty-acre farm, the balance for thirty years at $195.27 a month. Paid $32,500 for the place. And the family had a different life's goal than we. Where you and I might wish to have power or prestige or money or position or honor or social acceptance, these were values that meant nothing to them."

I looked over at Sandy Jones. "This woman who is within hearing of my voice cared little for fashion. She cared little for acceptance by her peers, or by other women. But she had a great deal of love and caring in her heart. And what she wished was to do something good and decent for the Indian people. This was her life's goal."

The stony face stared down, the judge's eyes not blinking. Only an occasional small twitch at the corner of his mouth.

"If you were to ask Sandy Jones today what her life's goal is, she'd say, 'I wish to help the Indian people in their worship. I wish to preserve their historical monuments.' One of the historical monuments was a place called Medicine Rock, a burial ground.

"These folks didn't want money. They lived on the land. They had a milk cow. She worked her separate job.

He worked. They had simple goals that were related to the land, to this beautiful area where they'd chosen to live and raise their family.

"Now this boy was taught in another way than our sons are taught. He was taught to be brave. It's hard for a boy to be brave. It is hard for any of us to be brave." I looked at the judge for a long time. He stared silently back.

I told how Little Mike had once seen his father's neck cut with a chain saw that had jerked out of his father's control and had nicked a major vein. The boy had packed the wound and the doctors gave the boy credit for having saved his father's life.

"Now Mike was a boy who was frightened like other boys," I said. "He lived a life in constant fear of the Gerttulas. Mr. Marquis would like to interpret that as a passionate hatred. But the evidence will show there wasn't a hateful bone in Mike Jones Jr. Despite the fact that he has been dealt with as a hardened criminal and does not understand why the law treats him as it does, nevertheless, the fact is, Your Honor, that Mike Jones doesn't now, nor has he ever, hated anybody."

I turned to look at the boy sitting next to Steve Lovejoy. "He's a boy whose face reflects a great deal of love. He has only been taught to love. He has been taught to love nature. He has been taught to love his parents. He has been taught to love God. He has been taught to love the animals. He has been taught to love his neighbors.

"And one of the things I'm going to ask Your Honor to do as you judge the conduct of Michael Jones Jr. is to somehow try to go back to the time when you were fifteen." Could any of us remember? What we recall is tainted by the years, by the judgments we've made and by those that have been made against us. We cannot remember innocence.

"This is a fifteen-year-old boy who did the best he could under the circumstances. He was a boy you would be proud of, who conducted himself with honor and bravery as you would expect your son to act. He'd been taught to respect and obey the law. And he had respected the law and obeyed it. But he didn't come to this situation on July twenty-third with an empty mind. His mind had already been programmed by his experiences, experiences that caused him *not to hate, but to fear*.

"His father was often gone off working. Big Mike had been gone that day. During such times Mike Jr. became the man in the house. He had a huge responsibility at fifteen—to protect his mother, and his little sister, and the farm and the animals."

I explained the long history of intimidation and harassment that Wilfred Gerttula had brought against this small family. I told the judge how Little Mike had once seen Gerttula knock his father down with his pickup truck, saw it happen right there on the family property as Gerttula went driving through, his father not walking fast enough to get out of the way, and how his father had been taken to the hospital, at first paralyzed. He'd been in the hospital for a week or more. "And so what I'm trying to say to you is that Mr. Gerttula was a frightening man. The family talked about it every day at the table. Often Little Mike had to stay alone. And he tried to be as brave as he could."

I explained to His Honor our version of how the shooting took place. I quoted the statement that Sandy Jones had given to Michele Longo. Sandy had said, "I heard this blast over my head. I was down wrestling with Mr. Gerttula in this fashion. I was trying to keep hold of my gun. He was hitting me over the back of the head with what I thought was a gun. I saw the black barrel. He was hitting me. And all of a sudden I heard this blast come—

and I thought, 'Oh, my God, I've been shot.' I started to look around to see where the shot had hit me. As I held on to my gun and was looking at my own body, I could see the blood starting to come out of Mr. Gerttula, and I realized that he was shot."

After the shooting Little Mike had been driven to the Clevelands by Ben Kowitz, an elderly man who lived nearby. "He was frightened and was crying," I told the judge, "and his mother said to him, 'Mikey, it will be all right. Mikey, say the Jesus prayer.' It's the prayer these folks say together when they're frightened and in need of help. And Little Mike said the Jesus prayer, Your Honor. And Little Mike has said the Jesus prayer a thousand times since that day.

"Now one final thing," I said to the judge. "Every lawyer has to make a decision in his case about a very important matter—whether to put his client on the stand. I have mixed emotions about that. If I don't put him on the stand, Your Honor will think he's not willing to tell his story, and therefore he must be guilty. On the other hand, if I put him on the stand, it's natural for people not to believe him. Everything he says will be seen as gratuitous statements—lies to help himself. They have already charged him as a liar.

"I'm struggling with this decision. I don't want to put him through the misery of being beaten up by a prosecutor who is hungry for this case. If Your Honor won't believe the physical facts, you probably won't believe him any better.

"This boy is not guilty," I said. "It's my job to defend him and to protect him. It's my job not only to protect him from the charges that are brought against him, but also from further injury as he becomes involved in this court proceeding.

"I think he has gone through quite enough for a boy

now fifteen years old. And the Jesus prayer has stood by him well. We have arrived at the end of the road, a time when perhaps this boy's bravery can finally end."

It turned out to be the longest trial in the history of the juvenile court of Lincoln County, one that mounted a score of witnesses and consumed three weeks. During Little Mike's trial, Ulys Stapleton made good his threat. When Sandy refused to plead guilty as Stapleton had demanded, he went back to the grand jury and obtained an amended indictment charging Sandy with yet another crime, attempted murder, leaving Sandy now to face not only that charge but murder, second-degree assault, and menacing as well. If he couldn't get her on one charge, he'd get her on another. Then Stapleton hauled Sandy back before the same judge, Judge Gardner, to enter her plea.

She stood in her prison garb looking up at the judge. Her arms hung from her shoulders as if both were broken. She was sick, that much anyone could see. She struggled to hold up her head. But when the judge asked her how she pleaded, she said in a voice as loud as she could muster, "Not guilty. That's how I plead. I didn't do anything, and they know it."

She was near exhaustion, this mother who'd watched the prosecutor attack her child day after day, and she, helpless to defend him, to even speak to him or touch him. We, too, were exhausted. I began to feel as Sandy Jones must have felt—like some hapless animal who'd wandered into the hunter's trap. We could cry out. We had. We could argue endlessly for the rights of the boy. We had. We could beseech the judge, beg him, flatter him, even attack him. And we had. Finally, in desperation, I asked the judge to meet with the lawyers in chambers.

"I go to my room at night, Your Honor, and I don't

sleep. And the reason I don't sleep is because I don't know what's going on in this courtroom," I said. "These good young lawyers and I talk about it into the night. I understand the court's ruling, but I don't understand the reasons for the court's rulings. I'm no newcomer in this business."

Marquis interrupted, "I know about the informality of this. But these private, sort of from-the-heart talks—you're an experienced-enough judge that it probably won't make a difference, but I just have to object to them. I don't think it's proper."

"How am I going to defend a boy," I replied, "where everything that even comes close to him is permitted to go to Your Honor as evidence of his guilt?" I complained that Marquis interrupted my cross-examination with countless groundless objections. "Finally it comes to the place where my cross-examination is totally frustrated. I'd be better off not to cross-examine at all."

The judge gazed at me as if he were looking at something miserably monotonous.

"I've come to the conclusion that we can't get a fair trial in this case," I said. "I don't think we are getting a fair trial."

"Is this a motion for a mistrial?" Marquis taunted.

"It is." Why not? I thought. We were going to lose the case. Anyone could see that.

But Gardner was not without a response of his own. "I cannot believe that an attorney of your reputation and standing could appear in this court and question witnesses in the way you have. I think your motion for a mistrial is entirely unjustified and unfounded, and"—he showed his lower teeth—"it is denied."

I pressed on. "I want to renew my motion on Dr. Vargo," I said. Vargo, the osteopath, had not been present at the autopsy when the corpse was first opened up. He wasn't a pathologist or even an MD. And one thing for certain: he wasn't an expert on firearms.

Marquis groaned his impatience. "For the record, I am going to continue to object to these further runs Mr. Spence is taking." True, I'd been overruled by the judge on this same issue before. But why give up? Under cross-examination Detective Longley had admitted that quite a crowd of people had gathered around the cutting table at the mortuary to watch the autopsy. Murders didn't occur too frequently in Lincoln County, and nobody was going to miss the party.

"I think you can see what was taking place at the autopsy," I said. "Everybody was having a good time—the prosecutor, his deputies, his clerk, and his two secretaries. They are all gawking. Vargo finally comes in after the man has been completely opened up and they're ready to close him—and now Vargo comes into court and testifies as an expert." Again Judge Gardner overruled my motion.

6

Marquis called Mary Ross, the victim's rights assistant in the DA's office, to the stand. In July, just before Gerttula was shot, Sandy had gone to Mary Ross for help. Gerttula had shot at Little Mike and Shawn. We knew Ross was prepared to testify that Sandy said if she didn't get some help, she'd probably end up having to kill Gerttula herself. I objected. Ironically, as a victim's rights lawyer, Stapleton, the DA, became *Sandy's lawyer* because Sandy's children had become Gerttula's victims and both Sandy and her children had rights. Mary Ross worked for Stapleton, and whatever Sandy said to the DA or his representative, Mary Ross, was privileged. It was our position that therefore Mary Ross could not testify against Stapleton's client, Sandy Jones, in the matter. If a victim couldn't talk to her lawyer without the lawyer or his representative testifying as to what she had said, then no victim would ever be safe to use the services of that office. Michele Longo joined in the objection, claiming a privilege on behalf of her client Sandy Jones.

But it was Marquis's theory that since Little Mike was present at the Victim's Rights Office and had heard his mother's statement, and since the boy and his mother were in this murder together, what his mother confessed as *her* intentions also bound the child.

"Again, I move for a mistrial," I said.

Judge Gardner: "Well, if it's admissible, that can hardly

be the basis for a mistrial. Do you agree with that?" I didn't answer. "Do you agree with that?" he demanded. Still I didn't answer. Then he turned to Michele and rebuked her: "Mrs. Jones is not involved in this case, Ms. Longo." Michele had been sitting in the courtroom with Sandy. "Mr. Marquis, you may finish," Judge Gardner said.

Ross claimed that Sandy told her Gerttula had shot over the kids' heads, but when I pressed her on cross-examination, she conceded that Sandy may have said Gerttula actually shot *at* the kids. That he shot at all would be hard to prove beyond a reasonable doubt, Ross argued. Ross said she thought it was a civil matter and that Sandy should hire a lawyer. Hire a lawyer? Sandy had no money to hire a lawyer to sue Gerttula for shooting at her children. Moreover, it was clearly the prosecutor's job to prosecute him criminally for his assault on the children. After that, Sandy told Mary Ross it looked like Sandy would have to handle the matter herself. Then came Ross's bullet-to-the-heart testimony: Ross claimed Sandy said that the time she'd spend in jail for killing Gerttula would be better than spending her whole life being harassed by the man.

I asked Ross, "What would you tell a person who told you she'd been to a lawyer, been to the police, been to the sheriff, been to the judge, and she couldn't get any help? What would you tell them then to do?" I waited. "Would it surprise you if she said I may have to shoot the man myself? Would it surprise you that she might say I may have to take the law into my own hands?"

Yet Ross hadn't notified the police about Sandy's supposed threat. I said, "So we can take it from the fact that you didn't tell the sheriff, didn't tell the DA, and didn't tell any other law enforcement officer, that you took her statement to be one that was given out of frustration, isn't that right?"

Marquis cried, "Objection."

Judge Gardner muttered, as expected, "Sustained."

Then I turned to the judge and spoke slowly and deliberately. "That one point is the total issue of my cross-examination."

Judge Gardner: "I think you have made that point, Mr. Spence. I am sustaining the objection."

Then I said to the witness, "Now, none of your testimony is to be taken as indicating Mike Jr. agreed to anything that Sandy said?"

Again Marquis objected.

Again Judge Gardner sustained his objection: "My understanding is that he [the boy] was standing there, looking in their direction, and didn't say or do anything." Was this fifteen-year-old boy supposed to realize that under the law his mother might be placing on him a guilty intent by what she said to Mary Ross, and that he should deny or contradict her or be charged himself with an intent to kill? That is the cruelest legal fiction I'd ever seen dumped on a child by a judge. Ross even admitted Little Mike had been fidgeting around, and she didn't know if the boy had been listening. It made no difference to His Honor.

Then Marquis wanted the judge to know the tone of Sandy's voice. I'd been objecting without success to a series of Marquis's leading questions. Now he asked another one. "Did she say it in the voice I just used?" which was unusually loud and hostile.

I objected to the leading question.

The judge overruled my objection.

"How did Sandy sound?" Marquis asked this time without leading.

"Angry and mean," Ross said.

I, too, would be angry and mean if someone had shot at my kids and no one would listen to me and no one would help—not even the "victim's rights assistant." But Marquis had set the stage, and skillfully. Ross's testimony established Sandy's motive and intent to murder, and by the judge's ruling, Little Mike's as well. According to Marquis, Little Mike was part of the scheme, that he shot Wilford Gerttula and that he was guilty of intentional murder, as was his mother.

Judge Gardner, a thorough man, had decided to visit the scene of the homicide. Of course, he took us lawyers with him. The sheriff's deputies stood back, watching as if we might tamper with the evidence. We walked upward along the trail from the Jones house on the two tracks Wilfred Gerttula claimed had long been established as a county road. The tracks were muddy. The judge was in the lead, Marquis on one side and I on the other.

I tried to make small talk. The gray-barked alders were much like our quaking aspens in Wyoming and like the birches in the East, I said. Same family. The judge nodded but said nothing back.

The road upward from the house was sometimes steep. Judge Gardner, trim, in good shape, walked fast enough to press me. He kept his eyes on the ground, measured his steps to avoid as much mud as possible, a protruding rock as a footstep here, another there. I could hear Marquis's heavy breathing on the judge's other side.

We came to where the trail passed an outcropping of granite.

"This is a sacred place to the Indians," I said. "This is Medicine Rock."

"That's not in the evidence," Marquis snapped.

The massive slab of rock rose steeply up from the river below. The river ran deep there, engineers having sounded the bottom in places at sixty feet. Upstream, what remained of a faint, single trail led to the top of the sacred rock. At its top an old Douglas fir with a double-snagged top known as Medicine Tree took in the folding hills below, forested with fir and alder.

Then where the road turned, an overhanging bow caught the judge's hairpiece and lifted it neatly from his head. I pretended not to see as he plucked it off the branch and stuck it back in place. I glanced at Eddie with a scowl. Eddie knew. The faintest grin could do us in. We walked on, the silence painful, the judge acting as if nothing untoward had happened, nothing at all.

At the top of the climb we came to the third gate, the wire one where the shooting had taken place. His Honor examined the gate carefully. Then he walked over to where, at the time of the shooting, Little Mike had been standing in a small clearing. On the other side of the road he could look steeply down to the river, where I believed Monica Gerttula had thrown the tape recorder and where I believed the culpable pistol might still be found.

I'd said it in my opening, "The evidence in the case, Your Honor, is going to show that the gun that killed Wilfred Gerttula has never been recovered by the state. They know it's missing. They knew as late as this week that they should be looking for it. They planned a further search but they never conducted it."

There at the gate the judge saw the alder tree, its bark marred by the bullet hole, the scene exactly as our engineer had drawn it. He saw where the struggle for the truck keys between Monica Gerttula and Little Mike had taken place so that the gunshot residues were supposedly transferred to the woman's hands and face. But that was impossible. During the trial even Marquis's own experts had been unable to duplicate that far-fetched scenario.

As we walked back, Steve Lovejoy, Eddie, and I held to

the rear of the procession out of earshot. "What do you think, Steve?" I asked.

He didn't answer. He took long steps as if he wore built-in stilts.

Eddie said, "He's out here trompin' around because he wants to prove to the court of appeals that he knows more about the case than they ever could. They weren't here. He was."

"You're a cynic," I said. I laughed.

"You think he's going to turn Little Mike loose?" Eddie asked. "What elected judge ever turned anybody loose? He has to answer to the prosecutors. He has to answer to the voters. He has to answer to the good old boys. Only ones he doesn't have to answer to is us."

I'd told the judge in my opening statement, "You're the jury. You're the twelve men and women we sought in this case. I haven't had much of a chance to select my jury. I inquired about you and what I found was good." That's all I could say.

At the scene we showed the judge where Gerttula had attacked Sandy Jones with his pickup, the woman backed up against the gate. We showed him where the acceleration marks were left from the pickup tires as Gerttula gunned the truck at her, braked it, gunned it again and again, the tires spinning in the dirt leaving not skid marks but "burn out," as an officer later called them during the trial. We showed His Honor where the boy was when he shot at the rear tires, and where his mother had stood trying to shoot out the front tires of the attacking truck. She was trying to stop the truck from running over her, I said.

In my opening statement I told the judge how Gerttula, a large-chested man, got out of the car and wrestled with Sandy for her rifle. And all Little Mike wanted was for the man to leave his mother alone.

"The boy screamed, 'Leave my mom alone! Leave my mom alone!' It was then that the boy began shooting at the pickup. And what about Monica Gerttula? What was she doing during this time?"

We'd tried to find out.

Once more before the trial began I'd addressed the court on the matter. I asked the judge's permission to talk to the officer about the polygraph he'd administered to Monica Gerttula. "I think the court correctly suggested that if there were any kind of answers in the polygraph that would be exculpatory, we should have them, and that the officer's conclusions on the polygraph might themselves be deemed exculpatory and lead to the discovery of additional evidence.

"You asked me to talk with Mr. Marquis about that, or otherwise for Mr. Marquis to tell me whether or not there was anything incriminating in the polygraph. We have had no communication about that except I have asked him and he has said, 'I have nothing to say to you about it.'

"Now I would like to talk to the officer," I said. "The answers that Monica Gerttula gave are not recorded. He gave us only the questions. The answers she gave to those questions are not there. They have for some reason been omitted."

I walked a few steps closer to the judge. "I take it that if her answers had clearly been consistent with telling the truth, they would rush forward to tell us so. I think we are entitled to sit down with the officer and talk with him about it. That's all I want to do. It's their officer. It seems to me that it would be fair for us to have that opportunity in a case like this."

Marquis jumped up. "Mr. Spence can assume anything he wants. The court can properly assume that if there were deceptive answers that the state—if we thought Mrs.

Gerttula was not telling the truth, the state would not be proceeding with this case. And I understood the court's ruling . . ."

His Honor said, "My ruling was, if they were deceptive answers or some statements that she made that were reported or something—tape recordings or things of that nature would have to be—"

Marquis interrupted, "There are no such statements."

But the judge refused to permit me to talk to Steve Tolliver, the officer who'd administered the polygraph, or even to call him for examination in the judge's chambers. I could call him as a witness, the judge said, if I could make his responses relevant to our case, which, of course, I could not since the results of a polygraph test are inadmissible.

"Want to pay me my dollar now?" Eddie whispered. He looked from Marquis in disgust.

I would have objected to any attempt by the state to introduce the results of a polygraph test had my client taken one. But Marquis, on behalf of the state, had offered to submit its principal witness to the polygraph to assure everyone, especially His Honor, that the gunshot residue on Monica Gerttula's face did not get there from her firing a gun that day. If her answers on the polygraph had been deceptive, we believed the prosecutors promised they would dismiss the case. But now we were not to have the answers she'd given or the polygraph operator's opinion as to whether she'd lied!

1

Days ago, at the end of the state's evidence, had the judge followed the law, we could have taken Little Mike home with us. The state had failed to make its case against the boy beyond a reasonable doubt. I'd moved the court to dismiss. It was the judge's duty. But power often knows no duty.

It had been difficult to try this case to a judge. I'd spent a lifetime before juries. In a jury trial, the judge rules on matters of law. The jury finds the facts. But when the judge took on the role of both judge and a twelve-person jury, as in this case, it cramped my style. At the conclusion of the state's case I openly spoke to Judge Gardner about this.

"It's a difficult thing for us to be engaged in a trial where the trier of fact is also the judge. It's hard for us and I know it's hard for Your Honor. It's hard to raise objections, to be a strong advocate for your client, to work out on the edge where a lawyer should work, not back in some nice, safe place. It's hard to fully advocate for your client without placing yourself in a position where you may gather the wrath of the judge who is also your jury. Judges don't like lawyers out on the edge.

"And I have pushed," I confessed. "When I have a jury, I force the issues with the judge as far as I can because the judge is not going to decide the facts of the case. But the judge in this case, with whom I have forced these issues, is also going to be my jury. From the standpoint of fully advocating for my client, I have frankly been at a loss to know how to deal with that."

I have always believed that truth carries the strongest argument. I told the judge the truth. "I understand that it is not easy to be a judge. I think it would be very difficult to be in your hide, Your Honor, to have lawyers suggesting that I wasn't giving them a fair trial when I was trying to do so. I think it would hurt me. And I want the court to know that I understand that, that I appreciate and I respect that."

Judge Gardner said, "I think I have felt through the trial some of the tensions you've indicated. I expect lawyers to be advocates for their clients. I think one has to approach a court trial differently than a jury trial. I appreciate your remarks and share those concerns."

Then I pointed out that the judge had been extremely technical in his rulings, but that that road ran both ways. Now, at the conclusion of the state's evidence, was the time for the court to be as technical *against* the state as it had been *against* the boy. I wanted the judge to dismiss the case.

"There cannot be freedom and there cannot be democracy and there cannot be a Bill of Rights that protects us all unless it also protects the least of us." The judge gazed down on me void of expression. "Unless this young man who sits here has the exact, technical, beautiful kind of protection that you've granted to the State of Oregon, then justice will become a mockery."

I pointed out that the hostile witness, the only eyewitness, Monica Gerttula, never once claimed that the gun that killed her husband was in the hands of the boy. "All we know is that Mrs. Gerttula said, when her statement was first taken, that she thought that Sandy shot her husband. She never once blamed Little Mike."

I argued that having charged Sandy Jones as the principal, the state should have let the boy go. "Instead, they've charged them both. And they've done it in a way I think is quite insidious—to turn mother against son and son against mother—that somehow in the squeeze of mother against son something would happen. This is the game they're playing."

I went through the entire litany of the state's failed evidence. I said, "If the court can't make heads or tails out of this case, remember, it's not the court's duty to do so. It is the obligation of the state to prove its case beyond a reasonable doubt."

I argued that the state had failed to call Trooper Geistwhite, who had first taken the statement of Mrs. Gerttula shortly after the shooting when she claimed Sandy Jones had shot her husband "point-blank with the .22." He was the one who made a second visit to her after which she changed her story. He took the gunshot residue swabs from Mrs. Gerttula. He was an important and material witness. "Why did the state fail to call him?" I asked. "I think you know, Your Honor. The law requires you to conclude that his testimony would have been against the interests of the state's case. That's the law."

Then I turned to a more painful matter. Who shot Wilfred Gerttula? Monica Gerttula had those gunshot residues on her hands that were consistent with her having recently fired a gun. The state, I said, had refused, as promised, to provide us the results of her polygraph. I felt justified in suggesting one other possibility—that there'd been a gun in the pickup, and that Monica Gerttula, thinking she was defending her husband, had accidentally shot her husband in this affray.

I had been unmerciful in my cross-examination of the woman. I said, "I saw this poor woman crumple and fold and weep and defend herself as best she could. It must have been a horrible experience for her after what she saw at the scene to go through that again in the courtroom. I have to be frank with Your Honor. I felt less than proud of myself after I finished. But we have raised the question. And the state must prove beyond a reasonable doubt that Wilfred Gerttula wasn't shot by his wife as a result of an accident."

I argued there'd been no evidence of malice, of hatred, as claimed by Marquis, a necessary element that the state had to prove for murder. Instead, the evidence showed that the Joneses were deathly afraid of Gerttula. "The state has the burden to show evil intent. They must show it by evidence beyond a reasonable doubt. The mere fact that somebody is dead, that somebody has been shot, doesn't mean that a crime has been committed."

And manslaughter was out. "The reason it's out, Your Honor, is because there was no gross act of recklessness that could be charged against this boy under any stretch of the imagination. Further, it's the burden of the state to prove that the shooting was *not* done in the defense of his mother."

Then I'd closed my argument on my motion to dismiss. "I have a fear in this case, and I want to share it with you. My fear is this: I come from a different place and I have a national background. And that's a disadvantage because people say, 'Well, he's a fancy lawyer.' But I think you've seen me. I'm not a fancy lawyer. I think you see that I make mistakes, that sometimes I can't phrase questions like I should. I'd like to be seen as a lawyer who cares about his client, one who cares about his case and who has worked hard to present it correctly to Your Honor. I would like to be seen in that light and no other.

"I hope there isn't some kind of subliminal contest that inserts itself into the case. I couldn't bear that. It would be a great disservice to my client. I want the facts and the law, and nothing more, to be the sole consideration in your dismissing this case and letting Mike go home." But the judge wasn't convinced and overruled our motion to dismiss.

It was time for us to put on our defense and we chose not to call Little Mike to the witness stand. How could we turn a fifteen-year-old over to the likes of Marquis? The boy would have had no chance against him. And we had not called Sandy. She had wanted to defend her son, but I argued against it.

"Sandy," I said, "Little Mike has always been the bait to trap you. Your testimony won't help him. The judge, if he's going to find against Little Mike, won't believe a mother. He knows that mothers say what they must to defend their children." At last she said again that we were the angels from the mountains, and she would do as the angels said.

We called the state's own expert from the crime lab, a young man named John Amish, who said the gunshot residue on Monica Gerttula's hands and face made it more probable than not that Monica Gerttula had fired a gun that day. We called the engineer who proved that all the shots from Little Mike's .30-30 had been accounted for, and none could have touched Gerttula, and we called Dr. William Brady, who said that the slug that killed Wilfred Gerttula, in his opinion, came from a pistol, not a rifle. Then we listened as Marquis tried to dismantle our defense. I thought his final argument to the judge was a splendid work of obfuscation. Words are as powerful as the sculptor's knife in forming the image. Marquis's tools, his words, had argued for a case of murder.

According to Marquis, nothing was redeemable about Sandy Jones. She had intended to kill Gerttula in cold blood. Her first shot with the .22 had been through the windshield at the man's head. In the same way, nothing of worth could be said about the child. According to Marquis the boy cared more for the whereabouts of the family horses after Gerttula was shot than the life of the dying man. He'd been in hiding for eight days after the shooting, hardly the conduct of an innocent boy, Marquis claimed.

Monica Gerttula, on the other hand, was the innocent, traumatized victim. She'd been beaten up by Sandy, seen her husband shot, had fought and lost with Sandy Jones, the larger woman, who'd driven their pickup off with her dying husband aboard. No wonder she couldn't remember what had happened. No wonder she originally thought that her husband had been shot point-blank with the .22 by Sandy Jones and, of late, had not been able to remember exactly the details of the shooting.

"So Monica Gerttula is scared," Marquis argued. "She's on the ground. She's trying to find the camera. She's trying to get her glasses. And she hears a series of shots. She hears the tires being shot at." He claimed that the gunshot residues on Monica Gerttula's face were deposited when her face was near the muzzle of the boy's gun. "What does she complain about at the hospital?" he asked. "She complains of her ears. And it is marked right on the hospital records."

Next Marquis reduced the state's own chemist to a mere unreliable amateur. Amish, the chemist, was "a nice young man," Marquis said. "He has testified in exactly one case before. He testifies that Monica Gerttula couldn't get those levels of barium and antimony from the .30-30." Then with a shrug of his shoulders Marquis said, "There is no evidence in this case that you can get those levels of antimony and barium from firing any other kind of weapon." And, of course, since the results of Monica Gerttula's polygraph on whether she'd fired a gun on the day of her husband's death had been withheld by the state, Marquis made no mention of them whatever.

"Now if Mr. Gerttula had a gun in the pickup—let's assume he is an ordinary man—would he not take it out at that point? Sandy Jones has already shot at his wife, shot at him. Is he so saintly, so restrained, that he doesn't even think about the gun back there? Common sense tells you no."

But the scientific facts pointed to the existence of a weapon that the state hadn't produced. The residue on Monica's face was not consistent with that of either the .30-30 or the .22. The tape recorder had been found thrown over the side of the road. A few feet more and it would have landed in the river. Sandy told us Monica Gerttula had been left behind when Sandy drove off in the pickup. Was it possible she'd cleaned things up before she appeared at the Cleveland residence a half hour later? If she'd thrown the recorder over the side of the road, which she denied, had she also thrown the missing gun there as well? The state had failed to search the river for the gun. Why? We'd raised the issue before trial. Were they afraid they might actually find it?

Then Marquis, always colorful, said, "Instead of a bushy-haired stranger in this case we have a bushy-haired gun. We don't know what caliber it is. We don't know if it was an automatic. We have no evidence that the Gerttulas own it. There is nothing at the scene to indicate it."

Marquis claimed the engineer's drawings we presented were defective. The shell casings were ejected from the rifle so that no one could establish exactly where the boy was standing when the gun was fired. But he couldn't refute the physical evidence: the three shots from the .30-30 were accounted for. None of those three could have hit Gerttula. The only argument left was for

Marquis to claim that a fourth shot had been fired. And, unless the Joneses kept a shell in the barrel of the gun when it was stored in the house—a matter contrary to standard rules of firearm safety—all the bullets in the .30-30 had been accounted for. If there'd been a fourth shot, where was the fourth casing?

After several hours of argument Marquis said, "What we have here is overwhelming circumstantial evidence of Michael Jones Jr.'s guilt. The state urges the court to do justice, because justice needs to be done for Wilfred Gerttula, who is dead. Justice needs to be done for all the people of our society who obey the laws and who don't take the law into their own hands. And justice needs to be done for Michael Jones, for if Michael Jones were to get away with this, it would probably be a worse tragedy for him."

As Marquis closed his final argument to the court, his voice changed and he spoke quietly. "The Joneses needed a miracle. They needed Gerry Spence. They needed an eloquent, spellbinding orator to try to take some fantastic scenario and get a judge to believe there was some credibility to it even though there is no testimony, no physical evidence, to back it up, even though common sense doesn't back it up."

Marquis had ended his argument powerfully: "When I went to college and I became a newspaper reporter, I started covering the criminal justice system. And as I chose a career, I decided I wanted to help the poor and the indigent and the helpless, until I came to realize that the poor and the indigent and the helpless are the victims more often than not, and that the role of the prosecutor and the role of the criminal justice system and the role of the law is to protect everyone.

"It is to protect Monica Gerttula, to protect Will Gerttula, who is dead, who will never celebrate a Christmas again or Thanksgiving or anything"—his voice broke—"because his life was taken from him violently, without his consent, and without any reason at all. And it was taken by this boy and by that woman because of their hate and their paranoia and the fact that they would not accept what the courts had said about a road—a piece of land."

Then quickly recovering from his grief, and as prosecutors often do, he began to portray his opponent as untrustworthy. "Mr. Spence is very eloquent. In fact, in preparation for this case I listened to a tape recording of Mr. Spence addressing the Oregon State Bar. I think it was a year or two ago. And he gave a talk up there. I was driving on Highway 101 listening to it. And he talked about how you have to be a preacher if you're going to be a good trial lawyer. You've got to make them believe that you believe. And like a very eloquent preacher who has his audience spellbound, Mr. Spence can tell us a marvelous tale. That is his job.

"But he forgets, just like the preacher who doesn't know the Bible very well, there are some paramount things we cannot forget. We cannot forget the basic commandment in our law, in our life. And that commandment, the one that these people refused to follow, was 'Thou shalt not kill.'

"Thank you." And he sat down, the small smile still on his face.

Judge Gardner left the bench at nine-thirty in the morning on December 20, 1985, and locked himself in his chambers to deliberate his decision. He didn't bring the experience or common sense of twelve ordinary people into the room. He brought only a disadvantaged self, a man who seemed to me to have an entirely different vision of the case from the one the facts supported.

The day was dark. The faces of the lawyers, the mood of the milling people in the hallway waiting, were dark as well. It was nearing three in the afternoon. The lights in the corridor glared in our eyes. The place smelled of smoke and the bodies of the restless crowd.

We gathered up close, Michele, Steve, Eddie, and I, waiting for the judge's decision. We knew what it would be. Little Mike stood on one foot and then the other, hands in his pants pockets. His father leaned up against the wall, silent as timber, his arm around his son. I tried to find something light to say. Nothing came.

"It'll be all right," I finally said. Big Mike's lips moved slightly without words. We were fighting against a pervasive fear in a doomed case, a boy the victim. Perhaps it paralyzed the father. Perhaps it was only my own fear that I saw in the eyes of the man.

I saw the face of the boy, the young flesh as if frozen. Caught in an eternal nightmare, he'd relived the killing with each witness. Little Mike wasn't one to say much, the son like his father. I saw the boy watching the people, the people glancing in his direction and then looking quickly away.

Judging was an art, I thought. It's in the eyes of the beholder. We should test judges, test them for self-interest, for prejudice, for courage, for their fear, test them for caring. Justice is hard and cannot be defined, steeped as it always is in the needs of whoever defines it, especially the judge. My need for Little Mike was different from the judge's and the prosecutors'. They saw a corpse and a grieving widow. They saw the power structure in the community demanding revenge. I had to face the representative of the power structure, Marquis, and speak to the judge in a voice that could be heard over the background grinding and gnashing of bitter reprisal. I had to speak for

Little Mike, who was innocent, but who could not speak.

What was taking the judge so long?

Earlier the deputies had put the cuffs on Sandy and hauled her back to the jail. But now the deputies were bringing her into the courtroom. Perhaps the judge was ready. More people filed in, people in their work clothes, some hard-looking from their labor, but soft in their eyes and with quick, passing smiles.

Carol Van Strum, the woman who'd written asking me to take the case, had been in attendance every day, her home many miles from the courthouse. A funny, little round hat was perched on the top of her head. Without saying any words she gave me a quick hug. Then she walked away.

Marquis sauntered past us and entered the courtroom, that small, sure smile still on his face. Eddie gave me a nod to say he was with me. He'd always been with me.

I looked once more at Little Mike. How could the judge convict this boy on the evidence we'd heard: the gunshot residue on Monica Gerttula not satisfactorily explained, her changed statements, our engineer having established that all of the bullets fired by Little Mike had been accounted for and that none could have touched Wilfred Gerttula? And finally, our respected pathologist, Dr. Brady, had testified that the bullet came from a pistol, not a rifle, and even Marquis contended that the only pistol on the scene was Sandy's and it hadn't been fired. Surely all of that established reasonable doubt. And even if the judge believed that Little Mike had fired the shot that had killed Gerttula, he also had to conclude that Little Mike fired to defend his mother, and killing in the defense of another demanded an acquittal under the law of Oregon or any other state.

We were still waiting for the judge to take the bench

and announce his decision when we saw five extra deputies filing into the courthouse. They were armed with night-sticks. They took strategic positions in the building and around the courtroom.

"This is why the judge kept us waiting," Lovejoy said. "We've been waiting for the extra deputies to get here."

"Why the extra deputies?" I asked. I already knew the answer.

Michele knew the answer as well. She nodded her head.

It was Eddie who said it. He walked up to me and in a quiet voice that Little Mike and his father couldn't hear said, "He's gotta have extra deputies because he's going to hold against us, Gerry. He's afraid there's gonna be a riot or somethin' from these people."

"Why?" I asked. "These are just ordinary people. Neighbors. Hardworking, good people."

"It's gonna go against us," Eddie said. "His own deci-sion is spooking him. Thinks the people might mob him."

Suddenly the bailiff burst into the hall and motioned us to the courtroom. When His Honor, Judge Robert Gard-ner, hurried up on the bench, the people became suddenly silent like frogs along the pond that cease their chirping when the coyote walks by. He looked up from the file in front of him. But he didn't look at us. Now at three-thirty in the afternoon on December 20, 1985, Judge Robert Gard-ner cleared his throat and began to speak. I took Little Mike's hand and squeezed it hard. I glanced at the boy. He was staring at the judge, his mouth open, his eyes as wide.

Then we heard the judge's vacant voice: "As counsel knows, this court must decide this case on the basis of the evidence that has been presented. And, of course, the court, as I would tell any jury, cannot base its verdict on specula-tion or guesswork."

He spoke in an icy dispassion that put me in mind of

the inquisitors, those judges in the Dark Ages who looked down on some poor woman and decreed the wretch a witch, as kindling wood to be burned alive at the stake. No passion was permitted in such business. Nothing changes, I thought. Still, something in me suspected that beneath the ice lay a caring man whose vision of his role as a judge required him to conceal all evidence of feeling. His Honor continued in his reading.

"This court finds that the juvenile, Michael Jones Jr., is within the jurisdiction of this court under Oregon law because the state has proved beyond a reasonable doubt that Michael Jones Jr. committed acts which, if done by an adult, would constitute the crime of manslaughter in the first degree; that is, unlawfully and recklessly causing the death of Wilfred Gerttula under circumstances manifesting extreme indifference to the value of human life."

I heard Marquis slamming his notebook shut in victory.

I felt sick. I wasn't surprised, but still we'd clung desperately to hope. Yet hope often erases reality.

Steve Lovejoy sat speechless in disbelief.

I looked over at Marquis. He had that same small smile on his face. He was tapping his fingers.

I thought I could have better accepted His Honor's judgment had he spoken in anger. Ought not a man feel anger at a boy who recklessly killed another? I could have better accepted His Honor's judgment had he spoken in sorrow. Ought not a man feel the deepest sorrow for a child who, at such an early age and for the rest of his life, should forever wear the thorny cloth of a reckless killer?

The judge continued, his white hands steady on the paper, "Now, the next issue before the court this afternoon is Mr. Michael Jones Jr.'s release status. I have received a series of reports on Michael Jones Jr. all throughout this proceeding. And all of those reports have indicated consistently that Michael Jones Jr., with the assistance of family and friends, has fully and completely complied with all of the court's requirements for reporting.

"I set a series of very restrictive requirements. And, quite frankly, I did not expect that Michael Jones Jr. would meet all of those requirements because some of them were very restrictive. In fact, they have all been met. So based on his performance, I am going to continue him on the same release conditions." He could have sent the boy to jail, even to the juvenile detention center at MacLaren pending the time when he'd decided what sentence to level against Little Mike. That said something about the man.

"And in view of the fact that Mrs. Jones's trial is set to begin in several weeks, I do not feel that it is appropriate to set a dispositional hearing on Michael until that other case is tried." He wasn't going to sentence Little Mike until *after* Sandy's trial? That meant the judge left Little Mike as the bait in the trap. Without leniency from the judge, the boy faced the next six years of his young life at MacLaren. Rotten place for any kid. He'd enter there as a condemned killer, and they'd treat this innocent, naive kid as such. When he came out, he'd be stained with the depravity of all such hellholes.

His Honor went on reading. "The parties have requested that this court make specific findings of fact. I reviewed this request but I conclude that there is no legal authority or requirement for the court to make specific findings of fact. In fact, I think in this particular case that there probably are some very good reasons why the court should not make specific findings of fact. One in particular is that there is another case yet to be tried.

"But to honor the request made by the defense and,

perhaps, to assist any appellate courts if this matter is appealed, I have made specific findings of fact. And I have them here." He held up an envelope. "The findings of fact will be sealed and not opened until and if the case is appealed," which was Judge Gardner's way of saying we had no immediate right to know the basis of his judgment. The secrecy of a new-age inquisition, I thought. It also meant he anticipated our appeal.

"We're in recess," the judge said. Then he fled from the bench.

At the moment the judge was gone, the deputies hurried Sandy Jones out of the courtroom. She was not permitted to hold her son, to comfort him. The most she could do was holler across the courtroom, "I love you, Mikey." As they dragged her out the door, she handed Michele a note and said, "Read this to the judge." The note read:

If a judge loses his capacity for indignation in the face of injustice, he may not be less of a judge, but he is less of a man. *NY Supreme Court Justice Samuel Hofstadter.*

Marquis sauntered over to counsel table. He had a copy of my first book, *Gunning for Justice,* in his hands. It was worn from reading. "Congratulations," he said. His smile. "You got the kid off."

"What do you mean I got the kid off?" I felt numb.

"The judge only found him guilty of manslaughter in the first degree. We wanted murder. Big difference."

"What difference would it make? If the judge found Little Mike guilty of anything, he'd be at MacLaren until he's twenty-one—murder or manslaughter—makes no difference."

"I wanted a murder conviction," Marquis said, still smiling. He pushed the book I'd written in front of me and handed me a pen. "Could you autograph my book for me?"

I opened the cover and in the front leaf wrote, "To my friend, Josh Marquis, who beat me fair and square, mostly. With respect, Gerry Spence."

I don't like losers without grace and with excuses.

He read what I wrote and smiled. "You won't be able to say you never lost a criminal case, not after today." He laughed as if he were making a small joke. "But one thing I always said about you, as they say in the most beautiful language in the world, which is Italian. *Se non è vero, è ben trovato.*"

He saw the blank look on my face. "'If it's not true, it's at least a good story,'" he translated, and laughed again. Then he gathered up his files, stuffed them in his briefcase, and swaggered out of the courtroom with quick, smallish steps.

After a while we got up and walked into the hallway. I looked down at Little Mike. He looked up at me. "Am I free?"

"For now," I said. "The judge said you did good. Followed every one of the conditions of your release."

"What are they going to do with me?"

"You'll be okay," Steve Lovejoy said, his voice kind and reassuring.

Big Mike stood silently by waiting for us to explain what had happened. "The judge found Mikey guilty of manslaughter," Steve said.

"I never shot anybody," Little Mike said.

"How could he be reckless when Gerttula was tryin' ta run over Sandy?" Big Mike asked.

"There wasn't any way he could have found that," Steve

said. "We're gonna appeal. Don't worry. The appeals court will throw it out."

I said nothing—the power of hope once more twisting reality.

Then through the courthouse window we saw the judge hurrying to his car in the parking lot. He was escorted on either side by a deputy sheriff.

"Look!" Eddie said. "This guy thinks somebody's gonna do him in. He's got deputies guarding him."

We're all afraid, I thought, and of different things. My fear had been I would be inadequate to save an innocent boy from a hurt that would scar him forever. My fear was that I could never right the wrong. But I thought the judge's fear came from another place.

Suddenly the road ahead became clear. Unless we could stop the judge and the prosecutor, Sandy Jones would end up in the penitentiary—probably for life. Judge Gardner couldn't have decided Little Mike's case without having decided hers. The evidence in the two cases was identical. And this judge was determined he'd preside over her trial as well.

Now I knew how trapped Sandy Jones felt in her cell. No one would listen to her. The machine was deaf. Nor would the machine listen to us. And unless we could stop the machine, two innocent people would soon be ground up.

That evening I sat staring at the walls of my small room. I saw Little Mike, bewildered by events he didn't understand, his innocence in plain view. I saw his father, a replica of the child, as bewildered and innocent. I saw Sandy caged, the woman shivering and sick. And nothing I'd done had changed any of that. Never in a long career had I felt such deep feelings of impotence.

8

You can worry about your case until you lose the thin thread of truth you must follow. But if you don't worry, you don't care. And if you don't care, you're already lost.

We'd worried about Sandy Jones. She might die in jail awaiting trial. Michele had demanded yet another bail hearing. With the new evidence from the state crime lab showing it was more likely than not that Monica Gerttula had fired a gun that day, Michele thought she had a chance. Gardner brought in Judge Greg Foote from Lane County to hear it. I said to Judge Gardner, "If you want to whisper in the ear of the judge who's coming in for this bail hearing, you could tell him how she's being treated."

In front of Judge Foote and in one last desperate move to get Sandy out of that hellhole, Michele called a bevy of witnesses, among them Dr. Vargo. He could establish that Gerttula had not been shot with a .22, the rifle that Sandy had carried. Michele got after Monica Gerttula to show she'd changed her story a couple of times. And she called Richard Geistwhite, who'd taken the gunshot-residue swabs from Monica Gerttula that indicated she'd fired a gun that day.

But Ulys Stapleton put Detective Ronald Peck on the stand. He'd led the investigation at the scene. And the DA called Jack Dick, who this time testified that Sandy confronted him at the gate and said, "You ain't gonna cut no

goddamn timber here. Get back in your car or I'll kill you."
Then Stapleton put the Ross woman on the stand again,
who repeated her previous testimony—that Sandy had said
she might have to kill Gerttula.

Stapleton told Judge Foote that he was bound by the
previous rulings of Gardner, which was meant to remind
the judge that he ought not to overrule a fellow judge.
Foote was impatient to rule and get the hell home. He'd
given Michele's plea for bail a perfunctory listen, like one
glances across the obituaries without a sense of the pain
represented on the printed page.

"Counsel, I think I've heard enough," he said, interrupting Michele's argument. "I'll rule. The issue before the
court is whether or not the proof of guilt is evident—
whether there is a strong presumption of guilt. Mrs. Gerttula's perception as to who fired the fatal shot may have been
wrong at the time. Circumstantially, the court could conclude that the shot through the windshield was fired by the
defendant because it was a small caliber and it caused the
face wounds on the deceased.

"The court could also conclude that the son was acting
in her direction based upon her previous threats and the
efforts that she made in directing her son to prevent the
escape of the victims, and also preventing them from
getting the help they were trying to seek after the wound
had been inflicted. I believe that very little has changed
since Judge Gardner made the findings that he made. The
motion for release is denied and she'll remain in custody."

Stapleton, the state incarnate, could have risen up like
a towering warrior for justice and agreed to let Sandy go
home to her kids and await trial there on her little isolated
farm. She'd never before been arrested, much less convicted of anything. She was steadily employed. She was a

mother. Her child needed her. Her small daughter, Shawn, needed her. The woman was not going to pick up her kids and flee the county.

Michele had arranged for Sandy's mother to put up her home in Portland as security. Her mother was poor but her home was free and clear. Michele explained to the old lady what signing these papers meant: If Sandy didn't appear for trial, the judge could take her home—no hearing, nothing. The state just comes in and takes it. But, no, the judge said. No. He was not going to grant bail for this woman.

"Well, I'm not surprised. It's probably all over the courthouse," Michele said. "I'll bet all the judges know. I'll never get her out on bond."

"What do you mean?" I asked.

"One day back in October I met Judge Littlehales in the hall. He said Sandy came to him, before this all happened, to see if he'd sign a restraining order against Gerttula and set a hearing. She handed him forty dollars as a filing fee and demanded her hearing immediately. Littlehales told me Sandy threatened him. She said, 'What do I have to do to get justice—join an organization that advocates the assassination of judges?' Littlehales said he advised his staff that he wouldn't have that woman in his courtroom again without full security. He said that she was suffering from a mental disorder, that he'd testify to that, and that she was an extremely obsessed person."

"Well, I'd be obsessed, too, if the good old boys were trying to force a public road within six feet of my bedroom," Eddie said.

I'd said it many times before to whoever would listen: The presumption of innocence is a glorious fiction. A fair trial is a cruel, colossal myth. Prosecutors aren't interested in a fair trial for the accused. They're interested in a conviction. They need to be seen as winners, and as tough on crime. Judges, too. And prosecutors and judges alike want to be reelected.

Even jurors take care of their own needs first—to be seen as good citizens who aren't about to let a killer escape through some clever lawyer's legal loopholes even though the loopholes prove to be our constitutional rights. And the newspapers? They have needs, too—to sell papers. You don't sell papers by reporting that the defendant is presumed innocent. You sell papers by sensationalizing— the woman with the smoking gun in her hand, the strange kid who didn't go to school, who lived on that isolated farm and ended up murdering a good old boy. That sold papers.

The leavings—what's left after everybody else takes care of his or her needs—that's what Sandy Jones and every other defendant gets. From their desperate motions, their aggressive arguments, and their hostile cross-examination of cops who often lie, defense attorneys scrape up the few bits that remain for a "fair trial." Sure, the accused would get her rights as guaranteed under the U.S. Constitution so long as her rights didn't interfere with the needs of anybody else. Sandy Jones could stay in jail. Rot there. Die there. Those who administered the law owned the law.

In jail, things were getting worse for Sandy. This tall woman seemed to have shrunk, her spirit diminished in the darkness of her cell. "I can't have someone bring in the herbs and medicines I need because they claim it would violate security." Then she said to Michele, "I told the guard, 'It's not against the rules to die.'"

"I'll try to talk to the judge again," Michele said. "It makes me sick, too, Sandy."

"I haven't been allowed to go outside for fresh air and exercise. The sheriff's breaking a court order by denying me this. What can I do when I can't take care of myself and Lincoln County won't take care of me either?"

Michele said she just held Sandy's hand for a long time and then Sandy said, "I need to hug my kids as much as they need me. And the sheriff won't speak to me about how they broke in my home while I've been in jail and stole my legal papers. He said he'll only talk to you."

"He hasn't talked to me," Michele said.

"The newspapers and TV have been using Little Mike's actual name—saying he's accused of committing murder. The DA wasn't supposed to release Mike's name. It's against the juvenile court laws."

"I know," Michele said.

At Michele's urging Sandy had kept a diary of her physical complaints. They read like a nurse's notes in the emergency ward:

Friday: No light. Picked up heavy book. Hurt stomach. Back hurts.

Saturday: 200 watt light on this morning. Headache. Excessive water in stool. Back hurts.

Monday: Headache, severe side pain, vomiting. Jailer threatens me they will take away my privileges if I don't mop and sweep.

Tuesday: Sore muscles, headache, side pain, vomiting. Back pain. Nurse gives Ben-Gay. I am sick. Back hurts.

Wednesday: Side pain, headache, back pain. Got a hot water bottle.

Thursday: Side pain, headache, back pain.

"They think I'm crazy," Sandy said. "They called in a psychiatrist. She wouldn't come into the cell. Probably thought I'd attack her. She talked to me through the cell door. She asks me things like 'What does it mean when they say, "When the cat's away, the mice will play"?' I said it was like what was happening at the farm—some of the people out there were doing things that they wouldn't do if I was there—stealing my stuff. Then she asked me some other questions, and pretty soon she said under her breath that the cops should be the ones taking the test."

"It'd be good if we could test everyone's sanity in this case," Michele said.

"Yeah, and they raid my cell all the time. Take away my rubber bands that I use to put my hair up to keep from vomiting on it. They go through everything."

"Trying to wear you down," Michele said. "As long as you know their game, we can win it, Sandy."

"I know," she finally said. "They put this biker chick in with me."

"Jesus! You didn't tell her anything, did you?" Michele asked. We were constantly alert to the possibility that they'd put a snitch in with Sandy and come up with some trumped-up confession—a woman-to-woman thing—give the snitch a deal if she'd testify in court against Sandy. That's standard for prosecutors across the country.

"The biker chick was crazy," Sandy said. "She didn't know what was going on. She'd supposedly stolen her mom's car. She said her mom loaned her the car. The woman was on heavy medications of some kind. She banged her fists till they were bloody. She was going to choke me. I was on the top bunk praying hard."

Then Sandy finally said, "I was praying and all of a sudden I felt a shield go around me and the biker chick started to cry. She got in a corner. She was naked. She wound her clothes into a noose. I got down and put my arms around her and prayed for her. She said she planned on choking the jailer. She screamed for two days straight. Can you imagine that? Can you imagine being within three feet of someone screaming for forty-eight hours?

"They claimed you could hear her clear out on the highway. The jailers wanted me to sign an affidavit to have her committed. I told 'em I would help her sue 'em for not giving her her rights and her medications. I refused to sign their paper saying she was nuts. I told the woman I didn't care what she did. Just leave my library books alone. She broke the TV, the toilet, and really made a mess for them. The jailer told me that Judge Littlehales had to cancel his court because he couldn't think, she made so much racket."

I'd already talked to Judge Gardner about Sandy's torture in the jail. At one of the recesses in Little Mike's case he was speaking of a proposed trial date for Sandy. I said, "We could be pretty relaxed about a trial date if I didn't have the specter of a woman who's frozen up there in that jail. It's cruel. It's having some serious effects on the woman's psyche. It's hard for us to deal with her and it's hard for her to survive."

"I can recognize that," His Honor muttered into something he was reading.

When he looked up, I said, "It hurts me to see it. She sits here in the courtroom and I can't get the sheriff to let her put on socks. I want to bring her a pair of warm socks. She's sitting there in a pair of rubber sandals with her feet sticking out and she's freezing. She said to me, 'Feel my feet.' I reached down to feel her toes and they were ice-cold. It breaks my heart to see this happen to a human being. And I would like to get her out of this jail."

Stapleton chimed in with scorn in his voice, "This is no concern of ours. I don't want to sound cold. But we want to get this case over with and tried. Whether she does or doesn't get out of jail, from my standpoint, doesn't change the fact that we want it tried in early January if that's at all possible, because this case screws up our whole calendar."

We put on our jogging shoes, Eddie, Michele, Steve, and I—for a run down to the sea and then along the endless sandy beach. I was weary. I wanted to lie down, not run.

I heard Eddie say, "We got to get rid of Gardner. He's got it all figured out. He thinks Little Mike pulled the trigger and that Sandy had him do it."

"Right," Steve said. "We had a damn good case. He just didn't hear it. And he isn't going to hear Sandy's case any better."

"We gotta get rid of that judge." It was Eddie, running alongside Michele.

I said, "Michele, file your affidavit against him. Let's see what he does."

"He'll have a fit," Michele said.

"He's not going to get off of this case," Eddie said. "This is the biggest case going in the state right now."

"What if he won't get off? And he won't," Steve said. He ran with long steps that covered the ground in half the time.

Running in sand was like running in a bog. I slogged along. "I have a sign over my bridge at the ranch. The sign reads, 'Do not cross this bridge until you get here.'"

"What's that supposed to mean?" Michele asked. She took a look at me and laughed. I was fiftyish, florid, and fatigued.

"Ask Eddie," I said, too winded to answer.

During Little Mike's trial, Gardner, sounding as if he were making only a friendly inquiry, asked—and he asked with the court reporter present—if there wasn't something in the rules of ethics that prohibited me from defending *both* mother and son? I thought he was setting me up. In the future, if the DA made a complaint against me to the bar, the bar could point its long, white accusatory finger at the record where I'd been forewarned by Gardner. I knew that and the judge knew I knew that.

"He wants to get you off Sandy's case," Michele said. "He's had enough of you."

"I know," I said. "Feeling's mutual." This judge should have known all about conflicts. If anybody was in conflict, it was the judge himself, who was determined to sit on both the boy's case as well as the mother's.

I saw a dirty little legal game brewing, the prosecutor in the lead, the judge running interference. The law prohibited a lawyer from representing both mother and child if the legal and factual position of one might be to the detriment of the other. Simple example: Sandy could claim that Little Mike shot Gerttula on his own. Little Mike could say the same against his mother. Mother and son had individual rights, and an attorney who represented both mother and son could not protect both if their interests were in opposition.

"This's silly," Michele said. "Sandy isn't going to turn on her own son to save herself. She couldn't anyway. They both see the facts the same. Little Mike didn't shoot anybody. Neither did she."

"Stapleton and Marquis are going to play it to the hilt," I said.

I'd told the judge that the conflicts in this case weren't all mine. He, himself, might want to consider whether he should sit on Sandy's case. I told him our team was thinking about asking him to step down. Then on December 23, 1985, Gardner set up a conference call among Stapleton, Michele, Steve, and me. Eddie and I had gone back to Wyoming for the holidays. The judge wanted to know if we were going to file a formal motion to get him off Sandy's case.

"Are you missing me?" I asked the judge, cheerful-like. Silence from the judge. Silence from the prosecutors. No room except for gloom.

"I want you to make a decision on your position," the judge said. "Are you or aren't you going to file against me?"

Stapleton said, "I sit on the Ethics Committee. And I'm telling you that in Oregon it's improper for you to represent the mother after you've represented the boy. I don't know what you do out there in Wyoming," the sneer in the voice.

"You've put me in a tough place," I said to the judge. "You're holding back on your decision on what you're going to do to Little Mike until after Sandy's trial. I'm very concerned about what will happen to the boy if I ask you to get off Sandy's case."

"I have no particular interest in trying her case. But another judge would have to relearn it. Judicial efficiency."

"You're very efficient, Your Honor," I said. "I'll give you that. But let's be frank: If someone asks you to get off a case, if someone is worried about getting justice, why wouldn't you just get off? Plenty of other judges in Oregon."

Stapleton was shouting, but I went on, "It's not fair to require us to go to court to prove prejudice against you— against the very judge who'll be deciding Sandy's case if we lose our motion against you, the very judge who'll decide whether her son goes to MacLaren or not. That's a rather serious conflict in itself, wouldn't you say?" We told the judge we'd advise him as soon as possible concerning our decision.

Later, on the phone again, Michele said, "He'll be pissed if we file an affidavit against him. If we file and he doesn't step down, we're screwed."

I said, "Look, what do we have to lose? We can't win

Sandy's case with a jury with the judge ruling against us every chance he gets like he did in Little Mike's case. He can't hurt us any worse than he already has. It's a no-lose situation." I embrace no-lose situations. "If he won't step down, we have another shot at him in the Supreme Court."

"Okay, here we go!" she said.

On the same day as Gardner's call, Michele filed her affidavit against him in which she pointed out that Gardner had made findings, but his findings were kept secret. How could a judge find a boy guilty of reckless homicide and hold secret the facts upon which he based his decision? Then she said that by Gardner's having found Little Mike guilty beyond a reasonable doubt, the judge had also necessarily made findings of fact beyond a reasonable doubt that pertained to the guilt of Sandra Jones. She concluded her affidavit saying, "My client is entitled to a clean slate upon which her case can be heard and considered. I do not believe Sandra Kaye Jones can receive a fair and impartial hearing before this court." She signed the affidavit before a notary and filed it.

But Gardner was not about to give up the throne. On December 26, 1985, he filed his letter decision. He said that Sandy had already excused three judges in Lincoln County. (These were the judges who'd been involved in the litigation over the road fight, one or more of whom she had individually sued.) Gardner then wrote, "The upcoming case will be a complex case and it would, in this Court's opinion, be very difficult for a judge who has no involvement with this case to prepare for trial and to be able to adequately rule on legal issues raised at trial, many of which have already been litigated."

"What that means," Eddie said, "is that nobody is as smart as Gardner."

"No, what this means is we're fucked," Michele said.

The judge's decision went on. "The case is somewhat unique because, although this Court has heard the juvenile case, this Court has never yet had an opportunity to form any opinions regarding either the credibility of Sandra Jones or Michael Jones. Neither has testified either at the juvenile trial or at any of the motions."

"I think we may have him," I said. "He's made a decision beyond a reasonable doubt against Little Mike and he's complaining he didn't get to hear Little Mike or his mother to determine their credibility. What if he'd heard Little Mike and believed him? Doesn't sound like he made a decision beyond a reasonable doubt to me."

"He's got a worse problem," Michele said. "He's commenting on their right to remain silent. Did he forget that?"

He then ended his decision insisting he had no personal reason not to try Sandy's case. He had to travel from his district, and this case interfered with his duties at home. Yet he was willing to make this sacrifice "in the interest of judicial efficiency."

I kept saying it: "I think we may have him! 'Judicial efficiency' is not a legal ground to refuse to get off of a case where you're in conflict like this guy is." I began to laugh. There was nothing else to do.

Eddie joined in with his high Irish laugh. We all needed to laugh. "Yeah," Eddie said. "We didn't nail him. He nailed himself in his own decision." But in the end, nothing was funny. We just needed to laugh.

9

I thought Gardner had a passive-aggressive style. He struck back in subtle ways that when read from the cold pages of the record didn't reveal what I was experiencing in the courtroom. In truth, he likely thought he was a good, fair, patient judge—especially patient. I couldn't say I altogether blamed him for the defenses he constructed around himself. We were from two different molds. If I'd been the judge, you could have heard me from the halls of hell if I thought something was wrong. But I don't have what lawyers call the *judicial* temperament. Just the temper.

After Gardner had adjudged Little Mike the killer, Eddie and I spent one last day in Newport with Michele and Steve before we left for Jackson Hole. We'd been gone from our families and home for over a month.

Michele said, "Gerry, before you leave, we all need to talk." We were gathered around a table in the back of the Galley-Ho, a one-story, reddish orange brick restaurant on Highway 101 at the north end of Newport. Elbows on the table, Michele rested her chin on her hands. She was trying to hold back. "Stapleton called me. They're after you, Gerry, and me, too. I talked to him yesterday. He said when you file your appearance as Sandy's lawyer, he's filing against you with the state bar. Said he didn't have any choice. Said if he was lucky enough to get a conviction against Sandy, she'd raise all sorts of hell on appeal claiming there was a conflict of interest and that she was entitled to a new trial. So he wants you off the case."

"Even if there were a conflict," Steve said, "what kid could bear to grow up knowing he'd turned on his mother to save himself? Little Mike would never do that, even if he could."

"This is a family defense," Michele said. "And this family's going to *hang together*."

"Yeah," Eddie said. "That's what they got in mind for 'em."

"If they could get us split up and fighting, they could win it all, easy," Steve said.

"The law creates the problem. It can solve it," I said. I didn't know what else to say. Then we packed our bags and left for home.

Before Sandy's trial was scheduled to begin, Stapleton called Michele again. He wanted to know when my appearance was going to be filed in Sandy's case. Michele called me in Wyoming.

"Hey, Gerry. . . . Yeah, it's still raining. Listen, Ulys said that when I file your appearance they're going to object to your coming into the case. Said Marquis was writing a memo about the conflict. Stapleton says you're not going to get out of this unscathed." She didn't say anything for a minute. I waited. Then she said, "I want you to know what he said before you get into this mess. He's threatening you through me. They're after you."

"We're a team," I said.

"And Ulys is threatening me. He said, 'You know, Michele, I have no control over what the Bar Association will do to you if you file Spence's appearance in Sandy's case.'"

I waited. Then it came: "And get this," Michele said. "He told the press that you had an ethical problem if you represented both Sandy and Little Mike. Actually said that! It's all over the radio stations, too." There was silence on the other end for a moment. "What if the judge kicks you off?"

"Don't forget the sign over my bridge," I said.

"You talk about conflict," she finally said. "I'm the one who's in conflict. I shouldn't have got you into this mess."

I started to answer her. She interrupted, "No. Let me get it off my chest. The minute I file your appearance for Sandy, that's the minute they start after you. Then you'll not only have to defend Little Mike and Sandy, but you'll have to defend yourself."

"So, what am I supposed to do? Cut and run? It's the law that's in conflict. If lawyers always follow the law like a blind man, sometimes the people the law's trying to protect get hurt worse. Eddie and I are big boys. We knew what we might be getting into when we took this case."

Michele said, "I didn't want to tell you then because you were concentrating on Little Mike's case, but Ulys was sending me notices of all the witnesses he's going to call against Sandy."

"So?"

"First letter was on December third. He's going to call Sandy's mother and her brother and sister-in-law as witnesses against her."

"What would they testify to?" I asked.

"Nothing. Just trying to harass me, I guess. Then on December fifth, while Little Mike was still in trial, he sends a letter saying he's going to call Little Mike against Sandy."

"Still trying to mess with your head," I said.

"Yeah, right. He's trying to scare Sandy into a plea. Then on December ninth, he sends a letter listing a Sandra Valdez, who was in Sandy's cell with her."

"The usual jailhouse snitch, I suppose."

"Don't know. Sandy says she didn't say anything to the woman. Then I get a letter that says he's going to subpoena Little Shawn to testify against her mother, and Mike Sr. to testify against his wife. All in all he's going to call fifty-six witnesses."

"It's all part of the scare tactics," I said. "Takes a lot of witnesses where there was only *one* eyewitness and that witness flunked the poly and had gunshot residue all over her."

On New Year's Eve, Michele drove to Salem and filed our papers in the Supreme Court of Oregon. They were entitled "Petition for a Writ of Mandamus," better known among our little team as "the papers to kick Gardner off the case." Mandamus is a four-bit legal word meaning "do what you are legally required to do."

We also asked the court to order Gardner to release his findings of fact to us. We wrote in our brief "that the child, Michael Jones, existed in a Kafkian nightmare in which he was never informed as to the exact charge brought against him, and never learned what verdict has been rendered against him. Nor is he permitted to know what the punishment will be, which is, of course, the mental torture and the cruel deprivation of due process which has been condemned throughout history."

We argued that Michele's affidavit was sufficient in law to require the judge to remove himself from the case, that Judge Gardner had found Little Mike guilty of manslaughter and made specific findings of fact regarding what both Little Mike and his mother had done at the scene of the crime. To arrive at his findings the judge had to believe or disbelieve certain evidence. He would continue to hold those beliefs in Sandy's case, and he would not be able to set them aside. And we added, "A trial court judge cannot refuse to follow the law on the basis of 'judicial efficiency.'"

We waited.

But on the same day we were busy filing the writ to take Gardner off the case, he ordered Sandy's trial postponed until January 14, giving us little more than an additional week to prepare for what Ulys Stapleton's fifty-six witnesses were going to say against Sandy.

During that week Gardner wrote another letter. In it he continued to assert that there were no legal grounds for taking him off Sandra Jones's case. However, he thought another judge should hear the issue against him. The judge turned out to be someone he knew personally, Judge Frank Knight.

Shortly after Judge Knight made his appearance in the Lincoln County courthouse, Michele went in to talk to him. Stapleton was there, of course. She told us that suddenly, out of the blue, Knight volunteered that he'd had some discussion with Judge Gardner about Sandy's case.

"It seemed like he intentionally brought up the subject," Michele said. "It was as if, for whatever reason, he wanted me to know that he'd talked with Gardner. I told him in that case I'd file a motion to get him off as well. We were supposed to get a fresh judge with a clean slate. I told Knight that I was going to subpoena him to establish under oath and on the record what had been said between Gardner and him about Sandy's case." Took a lot of guts to talk to a judge that way. Michele, as usual, was laying it all down for her client.

Then Michele said, "After talking to Judge Knight, Ulys Stapleton and I were waiting around to see what Knight was going to do, and the judge's assistant came up and said that the judge had ordered that we both remain there on the third floor of the courthouse until three-fifteen. She said the judge didn't want to talk to us. After his assistant was gone,

I wandered on down the hall just in time to see the judge hurrying down the steps in his hat and overcoat."

He never came back.

The seventh of January, 1986, was a big day for this little tribe of besieged lawyers. I'd been slumped in front of the judicial slot machine for months, pulling the handle with desperate legal motion after legal motion, objection after objection, argument after argument. The machine had gone on, and on, spinning up its eternal lemons. But the house has to let you win occasionally. If you can't win once in a while, no one will play. On that day the Supreme Court of Oregon issued its "Alternative Writ of Mandamus." It was the first order from any Oregon court that had come down in our favor. *Jackpot!* It kicked Gardner right off the case unless he wanted to appear before the judges up there and fight it. And Gardner didn't want to fight us in the Supreme Court. He filed his certificate of compliance on January 8, my fifty-seventh birthday, and did as the Supreme Court ordered. He packed his bags and went back where he had come from.

But Gardner still had jurisdiction over Little Mike. And he was still considering what to do with the boy. Like God, with a vengeful nod of the judicial head, he could send him to MacLaren, where he could rot as a condemned killer until he was twenty-one years old.

10

January and still raining, the incessant, endless rain on the Oregon coast. People worked in the rain, their faces wet, the rain matting their hair, the sweat under their yellow raincoats soaking them from within. I saw the men working at the gutters clearing away the debris. I saw fishermen on the back decks of boats parked at the fish plants unloading their catch in the rain.

Judge Gardner had also worked in the rain under the public roof. I could see him sitting at his desk, his face as impassive as when he had stared down at us from the bench. But he probably wasn't a happy man. Not only had the Supreme Court told him to get off Sandy's case (or show the court why he shouldn't), but he was also ordered to release his secret findings of fact in Little Mike's case.

On the thirteenth of January, 1986, Steve telephoned us. We were in our motel room getting ready for trial. Steve said that Gardner's findings of fact in Little Mike's case had arrived in the mail. Did we want to read them?

We walked out into the rain, no umbrellas, our clothes wet in minutes, the sky dark as dusk. I sat in Steve's office looking out the window to rain-drenched firs, drops of rain hanging on the needles. Steve shoved Judge Gardner's secret findings over to me without saying anything.

*　　*　　*

This court finds beyond a reasonable doubt the following:

1. On July 23, 1985, in Lincoln County, Oregon, Michael Jones Jr. did unlawfully and recklessly cause the death of Wilfred Gerttula under circumstances manifesting extreme indifference to the value of human life by shooting Wilfred Gerttula in the chest with a bullet from a .30-30 rifle.

2. Michael Jones Jr. fired the fatal shot.

3. That neither Mr. Gerttula nor Mrs. Gerttula had in their possession or fired a pistol or rifle.

4. That the state has disproved beyond a reasonable doubt the defenses of self-defense, defense of another, and the defense of property by Michael Jones or Sandy Jones.

"He had it all boxed up real pretty," Eddie said. "Ribbon on it and everything. What's left to try in Sandy's case?"

Steve said, "We'll appeal the damned thing. There isn't a whit of evidence in that record to support those findings. He musta been dreaming."

I stared out the window. The eaves were dripping. Then in the southern sky I thought I saw the sun shining through a weak place in the cloud cover. I looked at the place for a long time. Pretty soon the sky began to clear.

"We got rid of the judge," I said. "Maybe we ought to get rid of the prosecutors, too. I've about had enough of those two—all those intimidation tactics they've been handing you lately, Michele. It's another one of those no-lose propositions. I think we got a shot at it."

Suddenly it stopped raining.

* * *

I was sitting in the Lincoln County courtroom wondering what had happened to me. Why was I there? Judge Gardner wanted me to go home. The prosecutors wanted me the hell out of Dodge, and I wanted to go home. The client couldn't pay our expenses, much less a fee. Besides that, Sandy Jones was a hard one to represent. All she could think and talk about was the damned road. She talked incessantly about how the judges had screwed her out of her rights and how the attorney against her had represented both the county and Gerttula and how Gerttula had been trying to break her with a series of bullshit lawsuits she had to defend herself because she was broke. I began to understand what Michele had been going through trying to work with the woman those last six months. It was easier to rail against the good old boys and her road than to face her own fear of what was likely in store for her—and for her family—in the criminal court.

She'd taken that one step that had changed her life. That first step had been when she'd decided to walk up to the top of the mountain carrying her .22 rifle. The next thing, a man was dead. The first simple step, I thought. And that first step was also one she took for me. What lawyer with any experience and any judgment would voluntarily have gotten into a case like this? A wild-eyed, penniless client, this woman who had an Indian for her minister, who fought the town fathers and who kept her kids out of the public schools? Why would a lawyer who had cases that were crying for his attention, a man with a wife at home he was in love with, kids at home and grandkids—why would any lawyer voluntarily put himself on such a case for no better reason than that questionable postulate that every lawyer worth a damn needs a good murder case?

That wasn't all. I was afraid. You don't tell people you're afraid. Sometimes you have to act as if you can take on the whole world single-handedly. But I was afraid. And of what? I could go home. I hadn't made my appearance in Sandy's case yet. I had a good excuse—Gardner had given it to me on the record—his backhanded way of suggesting I was facing an ethical problem. Stapleton, too, had given me the same out. I didn't need to lay it all down for this woman. Why, as Michele asked, should I put myself in a position where I had to defend not only Sandy, but myself as well? Hadn't I done enough already? Stapleton said he was going to turn me in to the bar. No lawyer needs that.

But I cared about these great young lawyers, and truth known, I cared about Sandy and Little Mike. Yet why should I? Maybe I cared about her because I thought she was brave, braver than I. A man couldn't walk away leaving a woman like her in a trap. When fear comes welling up, you decide how it will move you—to run away or to charge. I always found it easier to charge.

In the meantime Michele and I had gone to the jail and met with Sandy in what Lincoln County called "the attorney room." The room reflected what the folks there thought of lawyers—a small, L-shaped space with a sink and an open toilet, metal table and chairs, a veritable paradise. We brought along a court reporter, who took down every word.

Michele, as Sandy's lawyer, apprised her of every conceivable conflict she could think of. She explained to Sandy that based on the facts Sandy had told her and those that Little Mike's attorney, Steve, had told her, she saw no conflict of interest in their defenses because neither Sandy nor Little Mike had shot Gerttula and neither contended that the other had. With the reporter taking it all down in the record, Sandy waived all possible conflicts and asked that I enter my appearance on her behalf. Then Sandy looked over at me. "You wouldn't leave now, would you, Spence?" She looked frightened. She always called me Spence. The reporter transcribed the record; we sealed it and filed it in the court file.

Steve Lovejoy brought Mike Sr. and Little Mike into the tiny law library of the courthouse. No one else around. We shut the door. The father was, of course, the boy's natural guardian. Again we had the court reporter present, who took down everything that was said. Steve told Mike Sr. that if I represented Sandy, the boy could never raise a conflict of interest as a defense both on a motion for a new trial or on his appeal.

"Well, me and Mom, we didn't shoot anybody," Little Mike said again.

Big Mike said, "We're in this together. We don't want our family split apart by attorneys fighting each other." What if a deal were offered by the state to Little Mike to testify against his mother in exchange for leniency? Little Mike couldn't agree to a deal if he continued to insist that neither he nor his mom shot Gerttula.

"I wouldn't testify against my mom," Little Mike said. Then again on the record, both Little Mike and his father as his guardian waived any conflict of interest that might arise by my representing Sandy, remembering that I continued to represent Little Mike as well in his case. It was a *family defense,* not two members of a family defending themselves at the expense of the other family member. That's how they saw it. The question was, of course, whether anybody else—the judge, the prosecutors, or the bar—would see it that way.

On January 28, 1986, Sandy Jones entered the courtroom, still surrounded by burly, scowling deputies. But she looked better than I'd ever seen her. Michele said Sandy wanted to look her best in front of this new judge. She'd given Michele explicit instructions. Told her to go to her house and retrieve some things: Big Mike couldn't find women's stuff. Men are like that. She wanted a pantsuit. Earth child or not, she was going to wear a bra, and panty hose, and she wanted her makeup and mascara, her eyebrow pencil, her frosted lipstick, the pink spongy curlers.

Then Judge Harl Haas came marching up to the bench. He walked with his feet out. He was about my age, a little younger maybe, balding, brown hair the color of a beaver hide. He had one of those ducktail noses, the kind that gave him an impish, boyish look. He was plump with a round face and had an elfish smile—as if he were going to play a joke on you any minute.

By reputation Harl Haas was the kind of judge who'd give you every benefit of the doubt until a jury convicted you. Then God help you. He'd served in the Oregon legislature and had been elected district attorney in Multnomah County, Portland being the county seat. After that he'd been in private practice representing injured people and had been appointed and then elected to the bench. By all reports he was a good judge and a decent man. Lawyers liked to appear before him. He'd let you try your case.

Now this new stranger (and in court, strangers are always put in charge of your life) was to be in control of Sandy Jones's life. Chief Justice Peterson of the Oregon Supreme Court had decided to go to Portland for a judge. He simply asked the judges there if anyone wanted the case. Haas said he'd give it a shot. Now why?

Why would a judge want to take on this miserable case down in this pinched-up, little backwater town that was all but washed away in the great tides and the incessant rains on the Oregon coast? He didn't need this case any more than I did. Maybe he needed to prove something. I was wary.

No sooner had Haas taken the bench than Marquis

and Stapleton started after me. They wanted me off the case. Marquis jumped up, huffy and squinty-eyed. "Mr. Spence has filed a request for association of counsel in Mrs. Jones's case. We have a problem with that. A proper waiver has not been executed. We believe that this has the potential of creating very grave problems."

I told the judge about how we'd fully advised both the boy and his mother of the potential conflict of interest, that each had been separately represented by their attorneys, and that both had waived any potential conflict. I explained to His Honor how the court reporter had taken it all down, that it had been transcribed and that I had filed it under seal in the court file. That stopped Marquis and Stapleton cold, but just for a minute. They then started demanding that the judge should see if it was sufficient, and that it should be sworn to.

Finally Judge Haas said, "I'll accept Mr. Spence's recitations." If there were confidential attorney-client matters contained in the papers, as I had asserted, he said the papers should remain sealed until the appellate court needed to get into them.

It was my turn. I said, "May we proceed now on the question of the debarment of the prosecutors from this case?" That was the beginning of the war to come.

11

I stood to address His Honor, Judge Harl Haas, on my motion to have Marquis and Stapleton thrown off the case. The judge took a quick look at me. Then I saw him glance at Sandy—half a second, no more. The trained eye.

"Now, Your Honor," I said, "Mrs. Jones sits in jail. She's been in jail for six months without bond. She's entitled to bond. Her applications for bond have been resisted on every occasion by these prosecutors. We'll show that during this prosecution their conduct has been vindictive and hateful.

"I have been asked by Mrs. Jones to defend her. I have over thirty-five years experience in trying cases, many of which have been murder cases. This woman has no money and no way to defray our expenses. I was here for over a month defending her son. And I brought my first partner, Mr. Moriarity, who's a skilled trial lawyer, to help me and who provides my brains more often than I wish to admit. So we have deprived a small office in Wyoming of its two principal lawyers to defend Michael Jones Jr. and we are about to go into a four-week trial here.

"Now I am not here to laud myself or to seek praises or to condemn myself for being that fool. But such altruism has its limits. We intend to prove it's the plan of the district attorney to launch a continuous and systematic campaign of threats, intimidation, and defamation against me and Ms.

Longo, to the end that the price of our representation of Mrs. Jones will be so high that we cannot continue."

I turned to Stapleton. "He's made statements to the press that have been defamatory in nature, saying that it's unethical for me to represent the defendant because of an alleged conflict of interest. When he tells the people of this county that Ms. Longo is unethical, he has already deprived Mrs. Jones of a fair trial. The whole community now looks at Ms. Longo and me as unethical lawyers. Certainly the law authorizes no prosecuting attorney to make defamatory statements for the sole purpose of intimidating counsel and to thereby manipulate who the defendant can get to represent her.

"By that process I think he attempts to increase his chances to get a conviction against her in a case that he knows is weak, that he knows, in fact, is nonexistent." I was letting it go, letting the words come up from the deep places where passion is stored and sorted and then emerges in civilized language.

"To face the bar's Grievance Committee, where lawyers are deprived of their due process rights, is one of the most devastating experiences a lawyer can have. Such a threat to a young woman who's just beginning her career is an extremely serious matter."

The judge was listening, making notes, scowling appropriately, a fleeting look of astonishment appearing when called for. Sometimes he took a quick glance at the prosecutors to catch their reaction to my foray. Their heads bobbed up and down with the exclamations they stabbed with their pens on their notepads.

"It's one thing for a lawyer and his client to be attacked in a courtroom by proper evidence, proper procedures, and proper motions under the supervision of a learned and careful judge. It's another for attorneys to be personally attacked *outside* the courtroom, to be called unethical in the newspapers that every juror has an opportunity to read, and to state that the lawyer will be subject to discipline by the Oregon bar, especially when that comes from the mouth of a member of the Ethics Committee who, himself, violates the canons of ethics when he makes those statements."

I heard the judge clear his throat. But he said nothing.

I wanted the judge to see this family. I painted the picture. "The Joneses live a different kind of life than we do. They milk their cow, have a few chickens, and fish the river. They live a simple, meditative, open, and religious life. They believe in a good God, and that they are required to do certain good and honorable acts in this world, one of which is to preserve for the Indians their burial ground. Mr. Gerttula, the deceased, had threatened the lives of Mrs. Jones's children and had run over her husband. The evidence will show a continued aggressive, hostile conduct on the part of Mr. Gerttula against this family.

"Now what does that have to do with the conflict of interest I claim against these prosecutors? She called upon law enforcement officers for protection. Most often she was cut off and spurned and ignored entirely. She was a person without power. She had no money. She was one of that large mass of poor and helpless people. When she called the sheriff, she got a response commensurate with her power—she got nothing."

I told the judge how she had gone to the district attorney's victim's rights representative, and after telling her story about how her children had been shot at and then being given no assistance at all, she had said that maybe she'd have to shoot Mr. Gerttula herself if she couldn't get help.

I told the judge we believed that Mr. Stapleton was

aware of the investigating officer's report about Gerttula's shooting at Sandy's children. I said, "It's a case manyfold better than the case he brings against Sandy Jones."

I turned and spoke to Stapleton, my back to the judge. "He gave her no help." Stapleton glared back. "And Mr. Stapleton was charged with the knowledge that if she didn't get the kind of help that she needed, the possibility of her engaging in self-help was clear. He knew that. Anybody knows that. Everybody within the sound of my voice knows that."

I argued that Gerttula's death was totally preventable had the DA acted in a lawful and diligent fashion on the information that was available to him. "Now that puts the prosecutor in this kind of a position, Your Honor."

The judge leaned forward from the bench.

"If we were to crawl into the prosecutor's hide—when Mr. Gerttula was shot, Mr. Stapleton had to justify his failure to take any action in this case. And the methods that he has undertaken to justify that failure have been unbelievable.

"This woman has been in jail without bail. There's been no reason why she shouldn't be with her little eleven-year-old daughter. She's been cold and in jail without adequate clothing. I had to go to the judge to even get socks for her."

I held the judge's eyes for a long time before I said, "There's a conflict of interest that's been created to the prejudice of Mrs. Jones, *because Mr. Stapleton is the attorney for Mrs. Jones.*" I waited for that idea to sink in—the DA was Sandy Jones's attorney? "His office, the Victim's Rights Office, *represented her.* The minute Mr. Stapleton opens his mouth in this case, he has a conflict of interest and this court must prevent that!"

The judge put his pencil down and leaned even farther

over the bench. "Mr. Spence," he said, "one might argue that the prosecutor may very well have acted much like a private attorney in that he didn't accept the case, therefore, no attorney-client relationship." He sat back waiting for my answer.

"Let's assume that Your Honor is a private attorney," I said. "I come to you and I say, 'Mr. Haas'—may I call you Mr. for the purpose of my example?"

"Sure. I've been called much worse."

A rattle of laughter in the courtroom.

"I say, 'Mr. Haas, I'd like you to represent me in a case. I want to sue one of my partners.' And you say, 'Tell me something about the case.' And I do and after I've told you, you say, 'I don't like the case.'"

Judge Haas nodded, adding, "And then I go and represent one of the partners. I see your point."

"Although you didn't take my case, you are disqualified to take my partner's case." Stapleton couldn't have it both ways: He set up a Victim's Rights Office as a politically smart move, and then when people came in for help, he used what they said against them. I argued that the same rules that govern other attorneys applied equally to the DA.

I saw the judge pick up his pencil again and attack his notebook with quick, decisive jabs. I waited for him to look up. When he did, I said, "The third ground for the disqualification of the DA is that he's a witness.

"The universal rule is that a lawyer can't be a witness to a material fact and act as an attorney in the same case. That's why we use investigators." I explained how Stapleton had been at the scene, and when we attempted to suppress the boy's statement, how Stapleton had been called as a witness. "And why did he advise the officer that the boy shouldn't be given his Miranda rights? He admitted candidly, unbelievably, that the reason was because the boy wasn't under arrest and therefore they could take the boy's statement without giving him his Miranda rights. That hardly sounds like fair play," I said to the judge. "Mr. Stapleton is a witness."

The judge was writing again. I looked down at Eddie, sitting at my side. He gave me that look with the slight raise of an eyebrow. It meant I was doing all right.

"We intend to show that the purpose of the prosecution in this case is to vindicate Mr. Stapleton. We will show the unfair tactics that have been outlined in his pervasive, relentless efforts to unlawfully obtain Mrs. Jones's conviction to justify his own nonfeasance, which resulted in the death of Wilfred Gerttula." I sat down.

Stapleton reserved his argument, which meant he would give it at the conclusion of the hearing. For me, I want to speak to the judge or the jury at the first opportunity—*first impressions*. I never want it to appear that I'm holding something back or playing some clever waiting game.

I called Michele as our first witness. The judge looked up over his half-glasses and watched her walk to the witness stand. Then he looked down at his notes and sat back, ready to listen. She folded her hands across her lap and got that expression on her face that said she was ready for the war.

I plunged right in. She said Sandy Jones wanted me to represent her, that she, Michele, had tried only one murder case, that she was afraid that if she had told me of Stapleton's threats, I might withdraw from the case. And she was afraid that an ethics complaint against me would also end up being a complaint against her since she had sponsored my admission into the case.

She testified, "Steve called me and said, 'Seen the paper yet?' 'No, why?' I asked. 'Well, you're on the front page and it's bad,' he said. 'Why?' I asked. He read the story to me over the phone—how Stapleton said I'd be disbarred and all. I was speechless. I put my head down on my desk and just sobbed. It felt like everything I'd tried to do for Sandy was just pulled out from under me."

She'd gone to see Stapleton. Stapleton told her he was going to file an ethics complaint if Spence entered the case. He asked her what she was going to do, and Michele, the tempered resignation in her voice, finally asked him if he'd ever seen the movie *Risky Business?* "He just looked at me, blank. I held out my arms, palms up, and said, 'Hey, Ulys, sometimes ya just gotta say, "What the ———?"' He stared at me. I don't think Ulys saw movies like that."

Then she looked up at Judge Haas. "I thought these threats both to Mr. Spence and to me were done to intimidate Mr. Spence and to cause our withdrawal from the representation of Sandra Kaye Jones."

I introduced the stories from the *Oregonian*, the state's only newspaper of general circulation, and the *News Guard*, a paper in Lincoln City that was religiously scrutinized by the local folk. The stories quoted Stapleton: if the Joneses were represented by me, there'd be an ethics problem—a conflict of interest "because an attorney can only represent one client accused of the same crime." He was quoted as saying Michele could be disbarred if such a conflict of interest were found.

"Frankly," Michele told the judge, "I was sick to my stomach about it. For an ethics complaint to be filed against me would dirty my reputation as a lawyer in this community." She said she literally lost sleep over it. "Mr. Stapleton's repeated statements were beginning to cloak Mr. Spence and me with an aura of unethical lawyers. It worried me about how jurors would sit and look at Mr. Spence and me after having read these articles."

I read to the judge from one of the Disciplinary Rules that governed lawyers' statements to the media. A lawyer, including a prosecutor in a criminal matter, "shall not make or participate in making an extrajudicial statement [a statement made out of court] for public communication in relation to the trial, parties, or issues in the trial or other matters *that are reasonably likely to interfere with the fair trial,* except that he may quote from or refer without comment to public records of the court in the case [emphasis added]."

With a leading question I summed it up: "Now, what's happened is that a woman charged with murder is represented by unethical attorneys, is that correct?"

"That's correct," Michele said. "Sandy Jones is being deprived of a fair trial."

On cross-examination, Stapleton, skilled at the art, took after Michele. He was all over her. I wanted to go up and grab him by the neck and pull him off.

"Miss Longo"—his voice was hard—"in your representation of Sandra Jones have you done anything or failed to do anything because of these articles *other than worry?*" She had not.

Had she failed to assert any motions? She had not.

Had she failed to do any investigation, to interview any witnesses? She had not.

Had she failed to assert any defenses or any possible defenses because of the newspaper articles? She had not.

Had she failed in any manner to zealously represent her client because of the articles? She had not.

"Do you feel that Mr. Spence is intimidated by this?"

I objected, "I don't think she is qualified to say."

The judge overruled.

"Yes."

Stapleton went through the same litany of any failure on my part to fully represent my client on account of his statements to the press. Michele admitted my worry had not affected my work.

Then he quoted from Disciplinary Rule 1103, subsection A, which he claimed required any lawyer aware of a violation of the Disciplinary Rules to report the violation to the Bar Association. Lawyers had a legal duty to rat on one another. He asked, didn't he have a duty to report Mr. Spence if he believed Mr. Spence had violated a disciplinary rule? Michele said she couldn't say.

Then Stapleton turned his attack against me. He wanted to know if she was familiar with my early statements to the press when I said I didn't feel that I could represent the boy and his mother at the same time.

She said she was aware of that statement.

And didn't she also know that Mr. Spence had said to the press, "If we find she and her son are innocent of the crime, we'll ask the Oregon court if we can defend her along with her present attorney"?

She was familiar with that quotation as well, she said.

"Did you feel it was a comment on the evidence or the merits of the case where, in the same article, Mr. Spence said, 'It's obviously a case of a powerless woman caught in a system in which the power structure is of men. This woman and her son wanted protection from the system and she never got it.' Did you feel that was a comment on the merits of the case?" The questions were hard and his voice a blunted weapon.

"No."

He quoted the Disciplinary Rule that made it unethical for a lawyer to represent multiple clients who have an *actual* as opposed to a *potential* conflict. She argued there was no conflict between the defenses of Sandy and Little Mike.

"Wasn't the conflict of interest issue initially raised by Judge Gardner while Mr. Spence was still participating in the juvenile case?"

I said, "Ask whether she was present. There has to be a foundation," which meant that Stapleton had to show that Michele was present when Gardner made the statement.

Michele said, "Judge, I don't believe I was present."

On my redirect-examination of Michele I asked if I was representing Sandy Jones when I made the statement to the press concerning a poor woman facing the power structure. No, she said. I was representing only Little Mike.

Finally, Michele stepped down from the witness stand. She looked tired and drained, her face white. As she walked past me and headed for the courtroom door, I thought the man had beaten her up pretty well, but he didn't get her, and she knew he didn't get her and the judge knew it, too. Then the judge called a break.

Later she walked up to me where I was shuffling through papers getting ready for my next witness. She said, "I had a talk with Ulys in the hall."

"What was that about?" I was surprised.

"He had tears in his eyes when we talked. He said, 'Michele, I never intended to hurt you.' I said, 'Ulys, I know. I can't talk to you.'"

"You believe him?"

"Yeah." She had tears in her own eyes. "I think he was being real. I know the man. He's like me. He's got a big mouth. Gets him in trouble. At least he tells you what's on his mind."

We didn't talk about it the rest of the day. Maybe she

was right. Maybe the man never intended to point his gun at her. He was after me. But he'd hit her.

I called Steve Lovejoy to the stand. He took those Lincoln-like steps to the witness chair and raised his hand to take the oath—the long fingers, the serious, boyish face, his legs, always in the way, sprawled out in front of him. Yes, he knew Michele Longo, she had worked as a law clerk in the District Attorney's Office and later passed the bar. She was a good lawyer. "She's the type of lady that gives her client one hundred and fifty percent of herself."

He'd read the story about Michele's potential disbarment and said he thought somebody ought to break the news to her gently, like a death of a friend or something. When he read the article to her, she kept saying, "This is terrible, this is just terrible." Steve said he tried to talk to her, but all she could say was " 'This is terrible.' She was in a state of shock."

After that, Steve said three or four people came up to him and asked if Michele would be disbarred because she was representing Sandy, and from such a number in such a small town he thought the rumor mills had carried the message around pretty well. He said, "I felt that Michele was coming apart because of this."

I asked, "Did you try to comfort her?"

"Yes."

Marquis objected. "This is not a personal injury case. If we can get to the issue—please!"

The judge turned to Marquis, the smile gone, but the smile creases lingering behind. "Sustained," he ruled.

And after Marquis's cross seemed to go nowhere, I announced my next witness: "Call Mr. Stapleton to the stand."

12

Ulys Stapleton sauntered in confident steps to the witness stand. He wore his blond hair in a Dutch-boy cut over a broad Aryan face with strong orbital bones. He held his head high like a man treading water. He wore large, dark-rimmed glasses. His clothes were not stylish. Instead he presented a rumpled agrarian look. I thought I might have met him at a county fair somewhere. I saw the judge quickly look the man over, the way an old trial lawyer takes in a witness and instantly knows much about him.

I couldn't read this judge. He seemed friendly enough. He listened and had a sense of humor, which is always the first overt sign of intelligence. Machines do not laugh. But who he was, I couldn't tell. When judges make decisions, they reveal more about who they are than what the law is. Knowing the judge in a long case is like a marriage. You don't know your spouse until the honeymoon is over.

I walked to the podium and gave Stapleton a long look. He glowered back as a fighter in the ring looks at his opponent just before they touch gloves. He was admittedly aggressive, "a volatile sort of guy," by his own account, although he'd lately told the press he was "mellowing out." Although he was a devout Mormon, he'd confessed, "In this job you can really hate defendants without trying very hard." He once admitted he had pushed a defense lawyer out of his office and once he might have made an obscene gesture to an accused during trial. Among some lawyers his reputation was that of a prosecutor who would use any legal means to make life difficult for defendants before or after trial. He told a reporter that his first priority was not pleasing the voters. His highest allegiance was to God. That seemed oddly incongruous. I thought if God stood for anything, He would surely stand for tolerance and forgiveness.

I had to harness my anger, had to let it out a little at a time in solid, simple questions, as when my mother was canning peaches and the steam from her pressure cooker was released in small spurts so the thing didn't blow up and kill everybody in the room. I was canning peaches.

"Do you recall having a telephone conversation with me in which you questioned my entry into this case," I asked, "the conversation when you told me it would be unethical for me to represent Mrs. Jones?"

"Yes, I do."

"You raised the subject, Mr. Stapleton, not me." Let just a little steam out.

"I'm sure I probably did," he said indifferently, raising a ready eyebrow. He denied he wanted me out of the case to increase his chances to convict Sandy. "It might make it easier to convict her," he finally admitted, "but that's not the reason I would be turning you in to the Bar Association, sir." And he admitted he'd told a number of other people he wanted me out of the case.

Stapleton had warned me he was a member of the Ethics Committee—he admitted that, and he further admitted that he had told Carmel Finley, a reporter for the *Oregonian*, that if I entered my appearance as Sandy's lawyer, it would create an unethical conflict. I thought the man was shooting in the dark with both eyes closed. He didn't know for sure what our defense was going to be. He didn't know if either Sandy or Little Mike would testify. He didn't know if our clients had filed waivers. Yet despite his monumental lack of knowledge, Stapleton had told the world, including all prospective jurors who read the paper, that it would be unethical for me to represent Sandy, and that Michele might be disbarred for sponsoring my admission into the case. Ethical people don't need rules to be ethical.

Sometimes in the heat of battle I lose composure and my anger shows. Anger sometimes frightens jurors and alienates judges. I walked back to counsel table to see if my seething was showing. "How'm I doing?" I asked Eddie. He knew what I meant.

"You're right on," Eddie whispered back.

I saw this member of the Ethics Committee sitting there, plentifully pious and sanguine in his judgments.

"Do you think your statement 'Longo could be disbarred if such a conflict of interest was found' was a statement you should have properly made under the Disciplinary Rules that govern *your* conduct?" I asked.

He raised his chin slightly. "I do not believe that was a violation of the Disciplinary Rules."

"Did you talk to Michele Longo about the possibility that she could be disbarred?"

"Yes."

"Do you think that frightened her?"

"She says it did. I have no reason to doubt that it did. It wasn't my purpose to frighten her. I wanted her to know that if you were coming into the case, she might end up holding the bag."

"To your left, Mr. Stapleton, sits Judge Haas. Do you recognize him as a proper authority to whom problems of this type might be addressed?"

"In some circumstances, yes." No animation in the voice, the slow blinking of his eyes.

"Do I take it you made your statement to the press solely for the purpose of doing a favor for Miss Longo?"

Finally, after he had talked around the question, I said, "Let's be frank with the court, Mr. Stapleton. You made a concerted effort to make reference to this supposed unethical conduct to intimidate Ms. Longo, isn't that true?"

"It depends on what you call a 'concerted effort.'" His arguing about the meaning of simple words said to me he wanted time to think through his answer.

"Don't you think Michele Longo is capable of taking care of her own ethical problems without help from you?"

Marquis could see his witness starting to fray and objected angrily that my question was argumentative. The judge sustained the objection.

Then I quietly said, "I'm asking you, please, whether or not you gave any consideration to the effect such a charge against us would have on a jury?"

"No."

"Don't you recognize that a juror might sit there and say, 'Well, this is a woman charged with murder and she's represented by an unethical attorney. So she must be guilty'?"

"No."

"What you tried to do throughout this case, Mr. Stapleton, has been to put this mother and son at odds—to get the mother to accuse the son and the son to accuse the mother, isn't that true?" my voice rising.

"No. I believe they *are* at odds, but that's not what I was trying to do," his voice rising back.

I asked him about his Victim's Rights Office. "You were aware of the fact that Mrs. Jones had made a complaint that Mr. Gerttula was shooting at her children, isn't that true?" I handed him the police report.

"That's what this report indicates, yes."

"You knew that prior to the time that Mr. Gerttula was killed, isn't that true?"

Finally he said, "I'm sure, because of the dates, that I knew about it before."

Was Stapleton a witness in the case? He admitted he'd been to the scene, heard Officer Groat talk to the boy, might have said something to the boy himself, saw the dead body of Gerttula, saw the .30-30, saw the pickup, the bullet holes, the blood on the hood, the tires—saw it all.

"Your witness," I said to Marquis. Maybe he could put him together again.

I couldn't understand where Marquis was going in the cross-examination of his boss, Stapleton. Marquis was resourceful all right. He created a word maze that often lost me. Probably the judge was experiencing it as well. Finally the judge interrupted Marquis. "Let me ask you a question," the judge said to Stapleton. "I can see why you'd have concern over a conflict. Ms. Longo would and Mr. Spence would. But why the *public* discussion of unethical conduct and disbarment to the press?"

"I guess it's because when Carmel Finley [the reporter] came into my office, we sit down and discuss things pretty freely," Stapleton said.

"You don't discuss unindicted cases, do you?" the judge asked. "You don't discuss investigations?"

"No, I don't."

"Do you generally sit down and discuss the ethical conduct of other members of the bar with the press?"

"No. In this particular case she was asking about the issues."

"I can understand you talking about a conflict, but you're on the Ethics Committee—and you told her [the reporter] that Ms. Longo could be disbarred."

"I believed that was true, Your Honor," Stapleton said.

Marquis interrupted to stop the mayhem, insisting he had more questions, and after he asked several that didn't seem on point, the judge interrupted again. Like my old bird dog, Sam, the judge had picked up the scent and wasn't going to be distracted.

"What's the difference between making the statements about unethical conduct and disbarment to the press and standing up in front of the jury and saying the same thing? You're communicating to the same people, aren't you?"

Eddie whispered, "Maybe we've got a judge here!"

"I didn't mean we would be bringing that to the attention of the jury," Stapleton said.

The judge said, "Well, the jury reads the newspaper."

"Like I said to Mr. Spence, I didn't think that far in advance," the DA said, his petulance thinly concealed. The judge turned away.

On my redirect-examination, Stapleton admitted that his own office had prosecuted Sandy before. The charge: livestock running at large. She'd been found not guilty. Later he'd prosecuted her for an alleged violation of the building code, and again she was acquitted. Both complaints had been brought by Gerttula. Stapleton had prosecuted the Joneses for these petty misdemeanors but had refused to prosecute Gerttula for shooting at the Jones children?

Then I called the reporter, Carmel Finley, to the stand, and she refused to testify until the lawyer from the *Oregonian* came. Marquis tried to block her testimony. "The *Oregonian* takes an extreme view of the shield privilege. They'll probably say that their reporters cannot be examined as to any published or unpublished material. That's just a guess."

"I'd love to see the statute on that," Judge Haas said.

"Witnesses are witnesses." He ordered the woman to testify.

Finley said that after Michael Jones Jr. had been convicted she'd been in Stapleton's office. Michele Longo and Josh Marquis were both there. "I asked Mr. Stapleton, 'Well, is this going to be an ethical problem with Mr. Spence representing Mrs. Jones?' And he said, 'Yeah, yeah, there could be—there could be a complaint to the Oregon bar,' or words to that effect."

When it came time for the DA's arguments on our motion to disqualify him and the members of his office, the judge gave a preview of what was on his mind: "My concerns are the statements made about ethics and disbarment, and the second issue being Mr. Stapleton's potential status as a witness."

Marquis tried to convince the judge that Lincoln County was a small community, and that certainly in a homicide case some member of the district attorney's staff would likely be at the scene. As for what Stapleton had said to the press, Marquis said, "I think Mr. Stapleton would agree if he had it to do over again, he probably wouldn't make that statement. You can't kick a district attorney off a case because you say, well, he did something wrong and we're going to punish him."

Judge Haas asked, "What if a DA in his opening statement to the jury got up and said these two defense lawyers are unethical and are going to be disbarred?"

"You might be able to mistry the case," Marquis responded.

"*Might?*" The judge seemed astonished, his eyes round with surprise.

"Probably would," Marquis said in a high, pettish voice. "But the attorney would know he was doing it with the sole purpose of prejudicing the jury. We have a vastly different situation here."

"Let's say he did it because he believed it," the judge said. "Give him good faith."

"Well, I'll give him good faith, but I assume—"

Judge Haas was unrolling his impatience. "What we're worried about is not so much bad faith. What we're worried about is whether or not we have an unbiased jury."

Marquis begged to differ with the judge. He said that absent a showing of bad faith, the judge had no authority to remove any prosecutor from a case.

"Well, well," Eddie whispered to me, looking straight ahead. "Tell a judge what he can't do and you'll soon find out."

Stapleton himself had admitted he didn't sit around talking about the ethics of other lawyers, the judge said. Why did Stapleton pick these two lawyers? "A fair issue is whether or not Mr. Spence can be allowed to defend this case. But the issue of the disbarment of Miss Longo is unrelated to anything germane to the case, is it not?" The judge stopped a moment and shortly began again. He was thinking out loud. "Carmel Finley said there was more than one occasion when she discussed the matter of ethics with Mr. Stapleton." When Marquis tried to defuse the judge's train of thought, the judge, annoyed, interrupted him again. "And why should I disbelieve the reporter's statement that that's what she got from him, too? He said he said it."

"I'm not asking you to disbelieve it, I'm indicating that—"

Haas was exasperated. He slammed his pencil down. "Well, he said it and she said he said it to her!"

"Then there's not much point in me arguing about it," Marquis said. "I'm trying, I guess, to point out some things that we believe to be significant." He went on to complain that while what Stapleton had said might have been improper, "we are talking about barring the entire Lincoln County District Attorney's Office from trying this case on the basis that Mr. Stapleton made this comment with Ms. Longo sitting there."

"What are you going to do when the defense calls Mr. Stapleton to testify, and after that Mr. Stapleton gets up to make a closing argument?"

Marquis said, "I'm going to resist them calling Mr. Stapleton as a witness."

Stapleton jumped in. "If I was called by my side of the case, I couldn't make an argument. If I was called by theirs, I could. There's a specific rule on that."

"The other side of that," the judge said, "is that a smart prosecutor could always go to the scene and wind up testifying and giving closing argument in the case. I think there is some jeopardy in going to the scene that you may become a witness."

Stapleton was quick to see the opening. "I think your point is well taken, Your Honor. The difference is in this case we haven't been notified I was a witness. That's the difference."

I rose and said, "Please, Mr. Stapleton, *accept your notice.*"

Marquis jumped in again. Was there any legal authority for the entire office to be removed because of an alleged impropriety? He urged there was obviously none. "First, you've got to address, is it improper, and then you've got to go beyond that to determine if it's intentional. This is a very extreme remedy." Then Marquis shut his notebook. "Enough said."

We waited.

The judge was arranging his notes on the bench. Finally the judge looked up. "Let me tell you the way I look at it. We have a case that's well-known in the area. We have a woman accused who has been in jail approximately seven months awaiting trial. The primary function of a judge is to ensure that every consideration be given so that the state and the accused receive a fair trial.

"I think the publication of the statements concerning ethics and disbarment was a substantial error of judgment. I am fearful that the question concerning this lady's innocence or guilt is going to get lost in the smoke of the cross fire between the prosecution and the defense. It seems to me that the danger that this talk of disbarment and unethical conduct represents is that the woman cannot receive a fair trial. If I were she, I would consider it serious.

"I think you have to look at it from her perspective to a certain extent. I think the most important thing is to remove the conflicts that have arisen so that we may focus on the trial. I don't know how we're going to try this case without all of this being retried again. So I'm going to appoint a special prosecutor."

Stapleton and Marquis were speechless and peeled-potato white. Then Judge Haas offered to confer with Stapleton as to whom the judge might appoint. Stapleton, shocked, must not have heard himself saying he thought that the judge's ruling was appropriate in light of the fact that he was going to be subpoenaed as a witness.

The judge said, "It's just going to be a mess the way it is now."

"I understand," Stapleton said. I didn't think he understood.

"I sincerely think it's better for the prosecutor's office and I think it's better for the defendant." The judge mentioned several names that were unfamiliar to me, people he considered skilled, professional prosecutors.

But Marquis quickly recovered. He wanted the judge

to lend *him* to the special prosecutor. I thought he didn't want to give up the limelight, and I thought that if he stayed, he'd try to run the show. His Honor asked me what my position was on letting Marquis remain.

"The reason I say 'no way,' Your Honor, is because one of the underlying problems we face in this matter would not be cured, which is the enmity of this man."

"Now wait a minute," Marquis shouted, jumping to his feet.

"Mr. Marquis is not a witness in the case, Judge," Stapleton said, beginning to awaken.

I said, "It would be a shame for the court to take good and strong and brave action for good and proper reasons and then lose the effect of it. We ought not poison what you've done."

Judge Haas thought a minute. Finally he said, "What troubles me is that the chief law enforcement official of the county, Mr. Stapleton, is going to be a witness in the case, and his deputy is going to get up and argue it?"

Now Stapleton began to talk about some forty witnesses the prosecution was going to call, his argument being that Marquis was necessary to help the special prosecutor understand such a complicated case.

Finally the judge said, "I'm going to give you a ruling on that tomorrow morning."

Stapleton also jumped to his feet, trying to salvage his last hope of maintaining some control in this case, the most notorious in his career. To be thrown off, not to mention his whole office along with him, would be something the voters might not applaud. He began to plead.

"I'm not trying for a situation where Mr. Marquis's going to be an attorney, where he's even going to be addressing the jury or the court. I think it's important that he be allowed to sit at counsel table so that he can assist the special prosecutor. I think that is extremely important."

Marquis joined in with one last desperate thrust. "Just so I understand, Your Honor. You said you were going to reserve the ruling on the issue of my participation?" I could see he was trying to set something up.

"Yes," the judge said. "I want to think about it. But I'll give you a ruling tomorrow morning."

"Before we proceed with the other matters?" Marquis asked, referring to the several motions pending before the judge.

"Yes."

"Our position is going to be—whether we would go along and agree with the court's ruling and not contest it in any way—depends to some degree on whether I'm going to be excluded from participation in the case. This all can happen prior to . . ."

I saw Judge Haas stiffen. He sat straight up.

"Is that a threat, Counsel?" I asked Marquis. One ought not threaten a judge.

Judge Haas peered down at Marquis, his already ruddy face turning red. "You know," he said, his anger welling, "why tell me that? You know, I don't have any problem if you want to appeal it. Appeal it! I don't have any problem."

Marquis said, "No, that's not the issue, Your Honor."

But it had been his threat. And Judge Haas had taken umbrage. With that, he rose and walked quickly from the bench.

"Marquis is going to go hobbling around for a long time," Eddie said as the judge closed the door behind him.

"What do you mean?" I asked.

"He just shot himself in the foot."

13

Michele phoned me, wildly exuberant. "Hey, Gerry, guess what!" She was hollering. "Haas kicked Marquis's ass off, too." I was back in Jackson Hole. On January 30, 1986, Judge Harl Haas entered his order disqualifying all Lincoln County prosecutors from taking part in the Sandra Jones case.

"I'm going to miss the boy," I said.

The judge went one step further: he ordered that all attorneys make "no extrajudicial statements concerning the above entitled case"—a "gag order" on the lawyers as it's called.

"Who did Haas appoint as a special prosecutor?" I asked.

"Guy by the name of James M. Brown."

"Who the hell is he?"

"He was the attorney general for the State of Oregon. He's in private practice now. I've been asking around," Michele said. "He's one of the establishment. Some say he's a nice fella, bright. Tough. He thinks Salem is big time. He was Benton County DA for three or four years. He's quiet, unassuming. Not too tall. Kinda skinny. Real gentleman. Scholarly, low-key, polite, and politically connected. He was a legal adviser to Governor Bob Straub. He won't appear overbearing to a jury, that's for sure."

"Great!" I said. "So Haas gives me the smiling brother,

the loving father of every juror in the State of Oregon. Small. Quiet. The underdog. I'm big and noisy. I can see it all now."

"Like they say, 'Be careful what you ask for. You may get it.'" Michele laughed.

That afternoon I called the guy. Wanted to start out on the right foot with him. Welcomed him into the case. "How come you'd get involved in a case like this, Jim?" I asked as if I'd known him since third grade.

"I was asked by Judge Haas to take the case." He had one of those calm, nothing-can-upset-me kind of voices.

"But why would a man of your stature take a case like this against a poor swamp-bottom farm woman in this remote part of the state? Surely you have better things to do in Salem." I let him have an easy laugh.

"Why did you get involved in the case?" he said. "You're surely more busy than I."

Suddenly changing the subject, I said, "You should dismiss this case." I wanted to see how he'd respond to a small, direct assault. "You got Monica Gerttula with gunshot residue on her hands and face. The crime lab's been trying to duplicate how she got the stuff all over her, and can't. She probably flunked her lie detector test as to whether she fired a gun on the day of the killing. For Christ's sake, you ought to dismiss this one, Jim."

A long silence. Then Brown said, "I'd appreciate it, Mr. Spence, if, when you are talking to me, you wouldn't take the Lord's name in vain. It offends me."

"Well, I'll be damned," I said. "No offense intended."

"I accept your apology," he said. "I'll see you in court."

In February, Judge Haas set the trial for March 17, 1986. Pretrial motions were to start a week earlier. The trial was sure to last for more than a month. Genius in the courtroom is the product of endless hours of work in the lawyer's lonely office with the doors locked and the phone off the hook. I spend as much as ten hours in preparation for every hour I'm in the courtroom. I took the best ideas of Michele and Eddie and Steve and wove them into my own. One of the talents of a successful trial lawyer—yes, a successful person—is to recognize the insights, the gifts, of others.

Problems were already brewing like an impending storm on the horizon. The *Oregonian* wanted to know what was in Judge Gardner's sealed envelope. The newspaper filed a motion to intervene in Sandy's case to compel the release of Gardner's findings to the public. Haas denied the *Oregonian*'s motion and told its lawyer, E. Walter Van Valkenburg, that if the paper wanted to know what Judge Gardner did, go ask Judge Gardner. It was Gardner's call.

Judge Gardner did Haas one better. He wrote to Van Valkenburg, "It was the Court's intention that the findings not be released to the public or the news media until further order of the trial judge who would be hearing the case of *State v. Sandy Jones,*" namely Judge Haas. But Haas threw the judicial hot potato back to Gardner. Haas wrote Van Valkenburg, "With all due respect to Judge Gardner, he made the decision to render findings and to seal them for the reasons stated in his letter. I have no jurisdiction outside the case of *State v. Sandy Jones* and do not intend to jump into the thicket. Simply put, the matter is not before me."

The first interest of the *Oregonian* was obviously not justice. Justice was for the courts. Justice was for juries. The *Oregonian* would not step back, not even until Sandy's case had been tried. They wanted the story *now*, even if its publication might cause an innocent person to be convicted of murder.

"Here's the way it can come down in the jury room," I

said to Michele. "The jury is deliberating Sandy's case. The jury is split. Then somebody pipes up and says, 'Well, what about that judge who heard the boy's case? That judge thought the mother was guilty as hell. Who are we to disagree with a judge?' That could pull the others over for guilty."

On February 18, 1986, the *Oregonian* filed its "Petition for a Writ of Mandamus" in the Supreme Court of Oregon, a suit to require Gardner to release his findings of fact and to lift the gag order on the attorneys in Sandy's case. The *Oregonian's* lawyer reminded the Oregon Supreme Court that the state constitution proclaimed, "No court shall be secret," and that the United States Constitution under the First Amendment guaranteed a free press. Judge Haas saw the handwriting on the wall and beat the Supreme Court to the punch. On February 19, 1986, he signed an order revoking his gag order on the attorneys. A few days later Gardner wrote another letter to Van Valkenburg of the *Oregonian*. This time he said he would release the findings of fact to Judge Haas, who could then decide if the findings should be released to the public. The hot potato. The judicial games.

"He's obsessed!" Michele shouted.

I said, "He's trying to avoid getting kicked in the butt again by the Oregon Supreme Court. He's trying to make it so Haas gets the butt-kicking."

Then we got into the fray on behalf of Sandy. On February 26 we filed our "Motion to Intervene" in the *Oregonian's* case in the Supreme Court. Our position was simple and consistent. The release of the findings of fact and their publication would result in irreparable damage to Sandy Jones's right to a fair trial anywhere in the State of Oregon since the *Oregonian* was read in every nook and cranny, village and backwater, in the state. We also asked the Oregon court to dismiss the *Oregonian's* case because it hadn't been filed within the thirty-day time limit. Nevertheless, the *Oregonian* replied that the true test was not the hard-and-fast rule of time, but the better rule of what was equitable. When you violate the rules, cry about justice.

"Judges are afraid of nothing and no one except the press," I said to Michele. "Occasionally a brave judge will rule against big money and big power, and they can even tell politicians to go to hell. However, judges have to be reelected. They're at the media's mercy. They can't answer back. They can't hold the media in contempt. They can't appeal. The media finally becomes the highest court in the land."

"So we are going to lose?" Michele asked.

"Yeah, we're going to lose."

On March 21, the Oregon Supreme Court issued its writ requiring Judge Gardner to forthwith release his findings of fact. We quickly filed a motion requesting an *in camera* review of the findings by the Supreme Court, a lawyer's way of asking the Supreme Court to take a look at what was actually contained in Gardner's findings of fact before the court poured that poison on the public. Last-ditch hope. Maybe if they read the findings they could understand how detrimental they'd be to Sandy's case. I could see the *Oregonian*'s headline already: "Judge Finds Woman Guilty in Secret Court Ruling." On April 10, 1986, the Supreme Court entered its final order against us, and the following day Judge Gardner turned his sealed document over to the public.

Why couldn't the *Oregonian* wait until after Sandy's trial to report what Gardner had said about her? The people were not being deprived of a free press. The people were asked only to wait until a jury had first heard and decided her case before they were contaminated by Gardner's findings of guilt against Sandy. Judge Haas had kicked Stapleton and

Marquis off the case, in part, because of prejudicial statements Stapleton had made to the press that might affect the jury pool. But no judge in Oregon could silence the *Oregonian*, the mighty press that was free to prejudice Sandy as the sale of their papers dictated.

In a free land, justice is the product of a fair trial. But in Oregon, its one statewide newspaper had the power to deprive Sandy Jones of her chance at justice. The *Oregonian*, not the Supreme Court, was the court of last resort, and that court had just joined the prosecutor's team.

14

On February 20, 1986, Judge Haas held the third bail hearing for Sandy. James Brown, the special prosecutor, was there along with his assistant, Doug Dawson, a man who looked like a nineteenth-century wrestler, with the droopy mustache, the barrel chest that extended past his waist, the grizzly voice. Brown had borrowed Dawson from the Oregon attorney general's staff in Salem.

I said to Judge Haas, "If Sandy Jones were an upstanding businessman, a member of the Rotary Club, the Masons, or the Chamber of Commerce, a judge would say, 'This man has strong ties to the community and has been a law-abiding citizen and is entitled to be released on bail.'"

Judge Haas was listening.

"I don't think it's possible to tell Your Honor what it is to be a woman who has spent her life as a law-abiding person and who has been up in that jail all of these months away from her children and held in that vindictive and spiteful manner.

"She's been cold. As she sits here today she's in need of medical care. She tells me she's been in pain all night. Her blood pressure this morning is very low, which, combined with her hypoglycemia, leaves her unable to think." I could see my words touch the man, the eyes giving hints of it before the quick looking-away.

"This woman has become so traumatized from being

separated from her family and treated like an animal and from suffering up there with her medical problems, including infections that are rampaging in her body, that at times I cannot talk sense with her about her case.

"It is impossible to form her defense. That jail is equipped with big listening devices up on the ceiling in the room where we must talk. I went to the sheriff and asked him about it and he admitted they were there, but he said he wouldn't turn them on. I should believe that?

"So what we have here is discrimination against somebody such as Sandy Jones, who is poor. She is a scared, beaten rabbit tied to a stake, and it's time, Your Honor, to untie the rabbit and let her go back to her family, and let her prepare herself for the defense of her life in this courtroom." I sat down.

The judge turned to Brown.

"We are dealing with a death case," Brown said. "Obviously, I don't think it needs to be said, but throughout our collective history there is no more sober event than death. This is a case in which the state alleges there was a violent death. One person is not here—the victim, Wilfred Gerttula. He was violently shot and killed, and the state alleges that the defendant is responsible for that crime, which is murder."

"The killing was tragic," I replied. "But this woman is presumed innocent. It's been suggested that she's guilty and that we must punish her and keep her in that place, that we must deprive her of the human requirements she's entitled to as one who is presumed guilty." I asked the judge to send her home.

But Brown hadn't given up. He argued that this Jones woman had been denied bond by two judges before Haas came on the scene, and on the same testimony as Haas was considering. Nothing had changed. The law was the same, the facts the same. Therefore, the judge's ruling should be the same. That all seemed logical. However, justice is not always logical. Somewhere in the body of justice a heart is alleged to exist.

I called Sandy's mother, Mrs. Alferetta Emburg, to the stand. She was an old, frail woman with a halting gait made as stable as possible with her flat-heeled, black shoes. She wore a plain cotton dress with a flower design and a necklace of tiny pearls. She owned her home in Portland and understood that if her daughter violated her bail, she could lose her home. "I have a lot of faith in my daughter," she said in a low, quivering voice. No mortgages were outstanding against the property, which, according to Mrs. Emburg, was worth about $65,000.

"I've heard enough," Judge Haas said, throwing down his pencil. "I'm going to let this woman out of jail. She's been there long enough. This woman isn't going anywhere. If she does, the state'll take her own mother's house away from her. Mrs. Jones won't let that happen. Besides, let's be real. This woman belongs at home with her children."

Sandy couldn't say anything. She just looked at me and then back at the judge as if she'd been stricken.

"You're going home, Sandy," I said. Then she began to weep, and her thin body began to shake and her shoulders seemed almost to touch each other, and when she came out of the sobbing, she looked up to see if we were still there. Then I held her until finally she was able to speak. "I'm hungry" was all she could say.

I took the whole crew to lunch to celebrate. Strange, I thought, that freeing one powerless woman of her misery had generated the power to transform this group from a tense, sometimes melancholy band of warriors into a celebrating tribe. The power was in the caring. Caring is contagious. It caught hold of the judge. That power penetrated the lifeless law and gave the law life. And it had given us life.

Caring! How strange that feeling is to the law! In that barren landscape called the classroom, professors stuff their students with empty legal didactics as if to suffocate them, as if to render them as dead as they. They who have never faced a jury, who have never given themselves the inimitable gift of caring for some voiceless wretch, they preach to their students, "As a lawyer you must avoid becoming emotionally involved in your cases." I say nothing, nothing at all, is more void of feeling than the abstract law. But caring is the taproot of justice.

Sandy's first food wish out of jail was for a hamburger and fries. She ate silently, hungrily. I sipped my soup watching her take ravenous bites out of the hamburger. Occasionally she looked up, too busy eating to speak. After that we drove to the Joneses' little farm at the end of Immonen Road, the place that had become the epicenter of this war, but also a refuge where she could begin to reconstruct the remnants of her family. As we drove toward the dilapidated old house, I began to feel a dreary sense of foreboding. The fog lay heavy on the river and had crept up over the banks toward the house. Through the mist, the outline of the buildings and the junk took on strange, amorphous forms. I wondered if Shawn would be home to greet her mother.

Shawn had stayed with a neighbor from time to time while Mike Sr. was off working, trying to provide for his family. One day, without prior announcement, the Children's Services Division pulled Shawn out of her classroom and questioned her. A secret complaint had been filed claiming the child was in danger. I suspected without knowing that the DA had initiated the questioning to put further pressure on the family—Mom in jail, Mike Jr. on trial for murder, Dad in and out of jail on game violations. Now they'd grabbed Shawn. Michele raised hell. Who was making these groundless complaints? But no. The agency wasn't required under the law to reveal the source of the complaint.

When the agency worker took Shawn out of the classroom, the child was terrified. Maybe her mom had died. Michele wrote a letter to the Children's Services Division demanding that they have no further contact with Shawn without the prior consent of her parents or Michele. The Children's Services Division answered saying that under Oregon law the agency was not required to provide notice to the parents if their investigation took place on public school grounds. They had the family in the proverbial double bind. If the child was not in school, that also provided grounds for their investigation.

Although the caseworker admitted that her interview with Shawn showed "no current protective service concerns," she warned that if there were further complaints, they would have to reopen the investigation. This meant, of course, that the DA could, at will, secretly invade this family through the Children's Services Division.

When we arrived at the house, Shawn came bursting out to greet her mother. The little girl held on to Sandy, and the two of them wept; these two children, I thought. I stood back watching mother and daughter clinging to each other on the rickety porch, the natural wood weathered from the seasons, and brown rubber boots, fishnets, and a stack of old tires up against the wall, parts of a car engine on blocks, and a flowerpot near the steps, the flower dead.

Even after Sandy's release, Little Mike had been isolated from his mother by order of Judge Gardner. He was staying in Portland with his grandmother, Mike Sr.'s mother, Pearl Johnston. I thought of the boy away from his parents. Away from the farm. He had little experience in a public school. He had few social skills. The child's total life had been the farm, the family, and the animals.

He'd begged to come home. Sandy couldn't visit Little Mike in Portland because, by the terms of her release, she was not permitted to leave Lincoln County.

We were fearful that, despite the court's order, Little Mike might run away and come home to the farm. Then Gardner would send him off to MacLaren. Yet by all accounts, including those of the hawkeyed Juvenile Department, he was an easy child to supervise. He had a resourcefulness we hadn't counted on. The department admitted he was cooperative, courteous, and respectful. They reported he had a strong work ethic and made all of his contacts as he was required. Perhaps he had taken to heart my advice.

"Mikey," I had said, "you want to beat these people who are after you and your mom?"

He looked at me without response, his eyes wide and waiting.

"You beat them by never giving 'em a chance to criticize you. You beat 'em by doing everything they ask, and more. Be on time. Do what they say. Be polite. Be nice. That's how you beat 'em." But I was afraid for the boy.

Once at home, the harassment never stopped for either Sandy or Michele. Sandy was calling Michele constantly. The cops were knocking on her door claiming they were looking for someone they were supposed to subpoena. The cops were hanging out at her driveway. The county sheriff and the Oregon state police got into it. Sandy said the state cops were surveilling them at night from across the river and were interviewing all of their neighbors at nearby Calkins Acres, and she told Michele that a sheriff and a highway department officer had taken their gateposts down again.

In the meantime, Josh Marquis couldn't purge himself of his epic zeal for the case despite its having been taken from the Lincoln County DA. Marquis was calling Michele wanting to know what was going on, wanting to know when we were going to file our motion to change the venue of the case—wanting to know, wanting to know. On February 26 he called again to see if we'd filed our motion—which we had. But Brown, always deliberate, wanted to consider our motion further. He said he was concerned about the cost to Lincoln County for moving the case elsewhere. A few thousand bucks is more important than a fair trial? The local paper had made much clamor over the high cost of Sandy's defense, a record in the state, the editor claimed, even though Eddie and I were pro bono to the state and paid our own expenses. Judges, tight as sticking drawers, had reviewed and approved every hour of Michele's charges, but that didn't stop the press. What it came down to was that the defendant was entitled to justice all right, but cheap justice.

There were stories about how all of the local judges had been disqualified, and, of course, Stapleton had made his statements about our supposed unethical conduct, which we believed had poisoned the jury pool. A move to Portland would give us a larger pool to choose from outside the influence of the Lincoln County good old boys. Besides, we wanted to keep Judge Haas at home and happy. It would be a long trial, and a happy judge is always a better judge for the accused.

On March 7, 1986, Judge Haas announced his decision

on our motion for a change of venue. In his jocular judicial language he said to us, "Well, boys and girls, I'm going home. See you all in Portland."

Meanwhile, this case took on further baffling ramifications. Brown sent us a terse letter advising that the sheriff's deputy, Detective Ronald Peck, had been suspended from duty. On February 24, 1986, Brown wrote, "I am informed that Mr. Peck may be subject to indictment arising out of allegations concerning his handling of evidence for the Sheriff's office." The sheriff's lead investigator in the case against Sandy was about to be indicted? This was the officer who'd been in charge at the shooting scene. What could this possibly mean for our case? Before we had time to fully consider the implications, Judge Haas set the trial for May 19, 1986, in Portland, Oregon.

15

On a rainy May 19, 1986, the "Jones tribe," as we'd begun to call ourselves, walked into the Multnomah County court-house in Portland. Eddie was carrying a couple of big bankers' boxes filled with files. Michele and I lugged a couple more, Sandy behind looking lost. She was dressed in a baby-blue polyester suit. One thing for sure: she'd arouse no jealousy among the women jurors, and none of the men on the jury would see her except as their poor, down-on-her-luck sister. A lawyer should be acutely aware of any lurking sexual issues in the shadows of the jurors' psyches. If women on the jury become subliminally jealous of your client, even a little, you'll have trouble, and if men are turned on to your client, even a little, you may also have trouble. I want my clients and their lawyers looking clean, wholesome—simply dressed plain Janes and ordinary Joes.

As for me, I wore the same brown coat and tan trousers and a button-down, blue shirt and one of those paisley ties that went with anything. Sometimes I changed into a navy blue coat, but with the same intent. Dress should never become an issue. Too many other issues to deal with in a murder trial—in any trial.

Another thing: there was always a potential danger with this woman Sandy Jones. She had a temper. "Sandy"—I looked her in eyes—"I know you're innocent, but the jury doesn't know. People will say hard things about you in this courtroom, things that aren't true. You're going to hear people lie and that will make you angry. But if you show it, Sandy, do you know what the jurors will see?"

"They better not lie about me," she said almost to herself.

"They'll see you up there mad at Gerttula and encouraging Little Mike to kill him. That's what they'll see. I want you to be like the Virgin Mary. Love 'em. Forgive 'em and don't get mad. Think that way."

Her eyes took a vacation, a far-off look. Then she didn't say any more and walked on into the courthouse ahead of me. "Listen, Michele, this thing is going to be like a barroom brawl," I said. "You gotta protect my back. You gotta keep Sandy cool."

"You got it," Michele said.

The state had thrown the kitchen sink at Sandy with all the dirty dishes. The DA had her charged with murder, attempted murder, assault in the second degree, and menacing. And although he'd come to realize that Sandy Jones had not fired the shot that killed Gerttula, he held to a more pernicious position. He argued that although the boy had been found guilty of only manslaughter, the mother could be prosecuted for and convicted of aiding and abetting murder. Even Gardner could stretch the facts only far enough to find that Little Mike's crime was a reckless act, one that didn't include an *intentional* killing as is required in a murder charge. If Little Mike hadn't intended to kill Gerttula, how could Sandy be guilty of aiding the boy in an intentional killing?

This pretty legal conundrum confused us. It confused the judge. He said, "This is a fascinating question. I've discussed it with some of my colleagues and gleaned no assistance from them."

I argued it would be like the driver of the getaway car being charged with aiding and abetting robbery when the bank robber himself was found not guilty. Haas reserved judgment on the question until the state's case was presented at the trial. But I convinced His Honor to sever the charge of aiding and abetting murder (which carried the same penalty as murder) from the charge of attempted murder. We'd try the charge of attempted murder at a later time with a different jury. The "assault two" charge rose out of Sandy's supposed striking of Monica Gerttula in the melee up at the gate, and the menacing charge was for her alleged threat against Dick earlier that day.

Michele slapped her forehead and slumped down in her chair. "Big favor you and Haas just did us. Even if we win the murder case, Brown still gets a second shot at us down the line on attempted murder. I'm going to be an old lady before this case is over."

"You know that sign on my bridge, Michele," I said. "It says, 'Don't cross this bridge until you get here.' You win these cases charge at a time."

We were in His Honor's chambers, one of the larger rooms provided for senior judges. The walls supported a variety of commendation plaques that reflected some of the judge's public history, certificates evidencing his elections, his memberships in the various bars and admissions to the courts of the land, parchment papers with ancient script and gold seals that said he was a leading and accepted member of his profession. His much marred walnut desk was large, rectangular, and stout enough to support layer upon layer of papers, transcripts, and books constituting the slag heap of a busy judge. He sat behind his desk peering at us over a pile of papers.

Now Brown began singing that same old chorus—

our supposed conflict of interest in representing both Sandy and Little Mike. I thought the matter had been settled long ago. I'd listed Little Mike as one of our possible witnesses. The boy hadn't been sentenced yet. Brown argued as if he were the boy's lawyer. He claimed Little Mike's testimony might influence Gardner's pending decision on what punishment to level against the child. Brown wanted independent counsel to represent the boy.

I held back my anger. A little. "I would much appreciate it if Mr. Brown would be straight with the court instead of suggesting his benevolent concern for Mike Jones Jr." Everyone in the judge's chambers, including the judge, knew what Brown's game was. He was hoping that some appointed lawyer might scare the hell out of the kid. Maybe, frightened, Little Mike would take the Fifth. That way Brown could keep his testimony from the jury. I told the judge that Steve Lovejoy would be present to take care of Little Mike. We didn't need the assistance of Mr. Brown.

Then it was my turn: I brought up Monica Gerttula's polygraph. I told the judge how Marquis promised us that if the poly revealed that the woman had lied, the state would dismiss against Sandy Jones. "But they won't give us the test results," I said. "We have the right to take these results to an expert not under the hire and thumb of the state. We have a right to enforce our agreement. Moreover, the entire file may lead to exculpatory evidence."

Brown seemed shocked. His already colorless face waned. He assured us he'd never heard of the polygraph notes. "Without stipulating to admissibility, which I don't think they are, if there are such things, sure, we'll show them to the defense." Haas said he'd take a look at the notes and then rule whether we could see them or not.

"We're paddling upstream, but we're paddling," Eddie whispered.

More cases are won or lost in these preliminary skirmishes behind the closed doors of the judge's chambers than in the courtroom in front of the jury. The setting is more informal. Lawyers can let their hair down—a little. But I always make sure I have a reporter present. And I talk straight to the judge. Judges long for lawyers to tell them the truth. A lawyer should become a reliable guide. Trials are like wandering through strange woods, and the judge needs to rely on someone he can trust to show him the way.

And what about Brown? How was he playing the game? Here it was mid-May, the trial upon us, and we were just discovering that four months earlier Stapleton had ordered Terry Bekkedahl, the state's criminologist, to perform still more experiments as part of the state's ongoing attempt to explain the gunshot residue on Mrs. Gerttula's hands. We had never been provided these latest Bekkedahl notes, and since the judge had previously ordered that these test results be provided us in a timely fashion, I argued that the judge should be fair: he should order Bekkedahl's testimony excluded.

Haas ruled that Bekkedahl's testimony would be held back until our expert reviewed Bekkedahl's findings, our expert's fees to be paid by the state. Whether Bekkedahl's testimony and the results of his experiments would be heard by the jury was a matter he'd decide when the state offered its testimony later in the trial.

"I can hardly stand this," Eddie whispered. "This judge is actually ruling in our favor once in a while."

While we struggled in the judge's chambers getting ready for the battle to come, the *Oregonian* wasn't finished with its invasion into Sandy's case. Two days following the shooting of Wilfred Gerttula, Ms. Judy Pinckney, a reporter for the *Oregonian*, had just finished interviewing Mrs. Gerttula at her home and was walking out of her house when Trooper Geistwhite came marching up the steps to do the same. Geistwhite had twice before interviewed Monica Gerttula. But by this time the cops knew something was seriously wrong with the woman's story.

Monica Gerttula hadn't known of the just finished autopsy findings when she gave her statement to Ms. Pinckney. The autopsy proved Wilfred Gerttula had not been shot with a .22, and contrary to Monica Gerttula's prior statement, the blood on the front of the pickup proved he'd been forward of the driver's door when he was shot. What Mrs. Gerttula told Ms. Pinckney, compared with what Mrs. Gerttula told Trooper Geistwhite in her recorded statement a few minutes later, might irrefutably establish that Geistwhite had manipulated Mrs. Gerttula into renouncing her first statements to him—that her husband had been shot point-blank by Sandy with the .22.

However, after she talked to Officer Geistwhite, Monica Gerttula suddenly lost her memory. Pinckney's testimony was therefore crucial. We subpoenaed the reporter. But the *Oregonian* wasn't going to let their reporter testify. E. Walter Van Valkenburg, their lawyer, claimed that the "shield law" of Oregon protected the media from disclosing unpublished material. I called Eddie Moriarity to the stand to establish the necessary showing to the judge—that the Pinckney testimony was essential to our defense and that the information was not available from any other source.

After Eddie summarized the case and told the judge of Mrs. Gerttula's conflicting statements, Eddie said that Geistwhite had stopped the tape for twelve minutes—*a twelve-minute gap in the tape!* What Geistwhite told Mrs. Gerttula during those twelve minutes, we didn't know. But one thing we did know: *after* Geistwhite's visit, Mrs. Gert-tula's memory suddenly faded.

The judge wrinkled his brow and made a face as if he'd just tasted something sour. "I get a new major constitutional issue about every fifteen minutes here. I don't want to shoot from the hip. I'd like an evening to review the cases and to give some consideration to this."

Then back in chambers I threw another one at the judge. I'd personally talked with Dr. Vincent DiMaio, an expert on gunshot wounds and a possible witness for us. After he'd examined the X rays of the corpse and the other materials I'd sent him, he concluded that Gerttula's wounds were consistent with a bullet from a rifle. We'd decided to go with Dr. Brady, a pathologist respected by judges and lawyers across the state, who had concluded otherwise. Brady, the former medical examiner for the state, was honest and presented himself as a powerful witness. Now Brown listed DiMaio as the state's witness. I objected.

Dawson, Brown's assistant, tried to make it all proper. He claimed he'd advised Dr. DiMaio not to reveal any confidence that I'd shared with the doctor, an admirable display of dexterity in the art of sophistry, I thought. I was pacing the floor.

"Your Honor, there are thousands of experts in this country who are available. I communicated confidential matters to Dr. DiMaio. Now they tell us they're going to use him against Sandy Jones." I stopped in front of Dawson and pointed my finger at the man. He jumped up from his chair, ready for a physical assault. I said in a voice red-brown in anger, "I think Mr. Brown and Mr. Dawson have acted improperly and contrary to their responsibility to fair play."

Judge Haas motioned us both to sit down. I said, "I notice that Ulys Stapleton wrote the letter retaining Dr.

DiMaio as a state's witness *after* Stapleton had been removed from the case."

Eddie whispered, "You want me to get out a motion for contempt against Stapleton? I'll bet the judge'll sign it right now."

Haas turned to Dawson. "The fact is, Mr. Dawson, you did consult with Dr. DiMaio on exactly the same issue that the defense had consulted him on, and, presumably, you'd then acquired whatever information the defense acquired. Isn't that essentially the case?"

Dawson skirted the issue. It was merely science, he said, and science was science. But no one was fooling His Honor. He knew the reason the state wanted DiMaio and he knew the reason I was trying to keep his testimony out. The judge was tired. So were we. It had been a wrestling match all day. The judge said he'd take up these more troublesome issues the following morning. But before he recessed for the day he denied our motion to strike Mary Ross as a witness, ruling that an attorney-client relationship did not exist between Sandy Jones and the DA through the DA's victim's rights representative.

Then another issue came roiling up concerning a witness named Rocky Marrs. Marrs claimed that prior to the shooting he was working for Gerttula, and one day Sandy Jones came riding up on a motorcycle, pulled her pistol out of her holster, and pointed it at Marrs's head. Brown claimed Marrs would testify that Sandy hollered, "The next time Gerttula comes up here, I'm going to blow him away."

"This guy's been a snitch for the cops before," Michele whispered to me. "He's a convicted felon." But when a witness gets on the stand and says your client threatened him with a gun, snitch or not, it would be like defending your client against another charge, and if the jury liked

Marrs, even if he was a convicted felon and a professional snitch, his testimony could tip the scales for conviction. I argued that the incident, which had occurred several years previously, if, indeed, it had happened at all, was too remote in time to be admissible. Again His Honor ruled against us.

I was exhausted from a long day of arguing in the judge's chambers and didn't look forward to the melee scheduled to begin at 8 A.M. sharp the following morning. After that we'd begin choosing a jury that would determine the fate of Sandra Kaye Jones.

16

On the morning of May 20, 1986, Eddie Moriarity came stomping into Judge Haas's chambers. He was angry. So was I. The judge saw the look on our faces and with a quiet warning in his voice said, "Gentlemen, it's going to be a long trial."

Eddie stayed on his feet. He told the judge that an investigator from the Attorney General's Office, a guy named Stafford, had been trying to talk to Mike Jones Sr., our client. Stafford knew and everybody knew that was against the rules. When Big Mike told the man he'd been told not to talk to him, Stafford demanded to know who told him that. Eddie had overheard the encounter, asked Stafford what was going on, and when Stafford bristled, Eddie told Stafford he'd better come in and talk to the judge. Stafford had first refused.

Dawson jumped in. He admitted they'd subpoenaed Mike Sr. as a witness to testify against his wife, and that Dawson had actually told the state's investigator, Stafford, to talk to Big Mike.

I told the judge we represented the family. But Brown and Dawson wanted to argue about that as well. What family? The grandmothers? Who else? Were the Joneses married? Dawson said he'd heard they were divorced. If they were, the husband-wife privilege that protects each spouse from the other's testimony might not protect Sandy. The judge wanted us to bring Big Mike into chambers and have him establish in the record that we represented him so there'd be no further question. When I went out to find Mike, a woman in the hallway said he'd taken off. He was frightened. Just shaking all over, she said.

It took no shining insight to conclude that the state was continuing its pattern of harassment. Brown had listed Mike Sr., Little Mike, and other members of the family as witnesses for the state. By listing them, whether Brown called them or not, these members of Sandy's family would not be allowed in the courtroom to give her support during the ordeal she was about to face. The *Malleus Maleficarum,* that evil fifteenth-century tome that instructed judges on how to try witches, advised, "Give no witch the comfort of her kin, for in their absence she is more likely to confess."

I said, "Let's get this thing worked out." I motioned to Brown and Dawson. "These are grown attorneys, grown men, and also purportedly human beings—"

Brown interrupted, "Your Honor, I don't think that is necessary. If we could talk about this like lawyers . . .' Judge Haas agreed.

I pressed on, "This woman is charged with murder. Her husband is here to support her, and this is what happens. Ordinary human beings understand that a family is a family, and to start to interrogate an individual member of the family seems to me to be improper." I was containing the steam, still canning peaches. "It's something I wouldn't do."

I took a breath. Then I said, "The day before yesterday Mike was headed towards Portland in his old car to attend his aunt's funeral. This was the woman who'd raised him as a child. She was eighty-two and her funeral was the next morning. One of the officers in this case, Trooper Geistwhite, stopped Mike and asked for his registration. Mike showed him his registration. Then he followed Mike for eighteen miles until he was outside the county. There, three patrol cars stopped him. The officers jerked him out of the car, threw him to the ground, put shotguns to his head, put handcuffs on him, and took him to jail for failure to have the car properly registered. Put him under a thousand-dollar bond."

The judge turned to Brown. "Is that right, Jim?"

Brown denied knowing anything about it.

Stafford, now sitting in the back of the judge's chambers, said, "I think the charge was driving while suspended."

The judge's head whipped around. "Since when do they take people to jail for driving while suspended?"

"I don't know," Stafford said. "I don't work in Lincoln County." Smart-ass, I thought.

I told the judge of the continued display of force by the state. When Judge Gardner rendered his decision against Little Mike, there'd been eighteen armed officers in the courtroom. That frightened everybody. Now this obscene display of force. I'd been shouting, pointing, pacing, snarling. The judge dropped his pencil on his yellow pad with a deliberate holding back and looked up at the ceiling.

A solitary cell in the county jail was as available to lawyers as it was to the accused. When the judge finally turned to me, I smiled, took my chair, and looked silently down. Then in a near whisper His Honor mentioned another case in which both the defense and the prosecution had been held in contempt. "I don't mean this as a threat, certainly. You know, Mr. Spence, your reputation precedes you. I know you're an outstanding attorney."

He turned to Dawson, who had also been stomping and hollering. "I know Doug has done an awful lot of incredible work for the AG's Office." Even Brown had raised his voice a pitch or two. The judge said, "I picked Jim as a special prosecutor because of his experience and background. I don't want to get in a position where I have to call a lawyer down in front of the jury. I think we all know what I'm saying." To stem the mounting tempers the judge called a recess.

Our team went upstairs for coffee, and there, walking single file toward us, came Brown and Dawson with Stafford bringing up the rear. Stafford was as tall as I, over six feet, about thirty-five, with dark, thick hair and a mustache to match and that intentionally casual, on-the-border-of-unkempt look that some women find attractive. He had a bulge under his left arm, the standard holstered pistol. Stafford was carrying a cup of coffee in his hand. As we passed, I bumped into the man, causing him to spill his coffee. The guy flashed. "You do that again, Jack," he growled, "and I'll lay you out."

Brown rushed immediately down to chambers charging that I'd given Stafford the elbow. But before the judge could get to the bottom of that matter, Michele joined in the fray.

It seemed that Mike Sr. had gathered up his courage and had returned to the courthouse. Michele told the judge she'd been standing outside the courtroom and saw Mike Sr. coming down the hallway from one direction and Stafford from the other. Once more Stafford had taken after Mike Sr. She said, "I put down my coffee cup and was going over to Mr. Stafford. He came up within about six inches of my face and said, 'Michele, let's go talk. Let's go talk.' And I said, 'Mr. Stafford, go away.' He wouldn't leave me."

"What's an investigator doing talking to the lawyers?" the judge asked Brown. Brown said he didn't know. "I'm going to ask you to instruct Stafford to have no contact with the defense," the judge said, after which Brown again renewed his complaint that I'd elbowed Stafford.

The judge just looked at the two of us and shook his head. It was war, but not the kind lawyers should be engaged in. I knew that. Then Haas had Mike Sr. come into chambers, and Mike, still frightened and barely able to speak, told the judge we represented the family and he didn't want to talk to Stafford.

In the meantime, the *Oregonian*'s lawyer, Van Valkenburg, had been waiting in the wings. Once more in chambers he demanded that our subpoena of Ms. Pinckney, the reporter, be quashed, saying that the *Oregonian* was protected by the shield law.

When Haas had heard enough, he began his ruling. "The defendant stands charged with murder, and upon conviction could be facing a term of thirty years imprisonment, perhaps a term that she would not even live to fulfill. I think the shield law is certainly a privilege. But there are very few privileges that are absolute. If the notes contain the type of information that I presuppose, I believe that the constitutional right to a fair trial would have to take precedent over the shield law."

Could I be hearing correctly? A judge who was not terrified of the press?

Haas ruled that when Ms. Pinckney appeared to testify, he would review her notes himself, and if they were relevant to the defense, he would allow her testimony and her notes into evidence. However, he left the *Oregonian* an opportunity to appeal his ruling to the Supreme Court of Oregon.

I was afraid the notes would disappear before we'd need them at trial, which could be several weeks or more down the line. I wanted the *Oregonian* to seal the notes and leave them with His Honor.

Judge Haas turned to Van Valkenburg. "Well, can I have the assurance that—"

Van Valkenburg interrupted. He exuded a well-bred charm. "Your Honor, I represent that I will maintain the notes, and that they will not leave my possession."

The judge said, "All right." Then to me he said, "I will accept that, Mr. Spence." There must be some honor remaining in the profession.

Finally, the last of the motions having been deferred until trial, and His Honor eager to get on with the case, he asked, "Gentlemen, are we approaching that golden moment?"

"We are, Your Honor," I said. I gathered up my files. As I walked toward the courtroom, I thought, Thank God for jurors. Give me twelve good, ordinary people. Give me, at last, people who speak my language, people I can trust. I trusted juries, and so long as I remained trustworthy, they had most often trusted me.

I looked at Sandy in her blue polyester suit. She'd been listening, sitting mutely by as the lawyers engaged in two days of endless, what must often have seemed meaningless, haranguing. Perhaps she'd gotten used to the noise, the lawyers pointing their fingers, their pacing, the droning on and on. The lawyers spoke a foreign language, one that had little to do with what was on her mind—her freedom and her family. Perhaps, at last, the lawyers would say something she could understand.

"I hope we're going to be all right," Eddie said as we approached the courtroom door. He looked worried. I wondered what he knew that I didn't know.

"What's the matter?" I asked. But before he could answer we entered the courtroom.

17

A courtroom is a place of both wonder and horror. It is one of the few arenas in which a human being can speak on behalf of another human being about issues critical to life and death. It is also a place where the voices of the poor and terrorized are muted by the grinding machine of justice and by the snarl and hiss of hate and vengeance.

We took our seats at counsel table. I looked around Judge Haas's courtroom. I thought it a menagerie of the man's eclectic choices, impervious to any idea of the standard formality of a courtroom. Paintings were hung here and there on the walls, paintings of ancient judges with wigs and of courtly scenes of colonial barristers stiffly holding forth.

It was one of the largest courtrooms in the building, the walls of both red and black marble. The windows on the north extended to the ceiling but were too high off the floor for anyone but an NBA center to see out. The carpeting was an anemic aqua, and the chairs were a variety of styles and colors, from pure black to blond wood, the court reporter's chair of blue leather, the judge's maroon.

His Honor looked down on us from his bench, which was of blond oak that matched the spectators' pews. The desktop bore the judge's array of papers, books—probably the court rules, maybe a dictionary, and other miscellaneous pamphlets—and in the left-hand front corner of the bench was a small, curious wooden carving of a child on a pedestal.

The clerk's desk, immediately below the judge's bench, was also of blond wood, suggesting that the original decorator harbored a plan long ago tossed to the winds by His Honor. The lawyers' tables faced the judge and were of the same oak. The table to the judge's left was closest to the jury box, which occupied the wall opposite the windows. The jurors' low-backed swivel chairs were also of blond wood, with those little slats in the back to allow the escape of the jurors' sweat from their long hours of painful sitting. We claimed the table closest to the jury, leaving Brown and Dawson in the far-off corner of the room as if they were an afterthought. But the witness chair, again of blond oak, was closest to the state's table and was directly under the judge's right so that the judge could, if he chose, glare down at the top of the witness's head, and if the witness dared speak to the judge, the poor devil had to look skyward as if addressing some descending deity. High up on the wall above the jury box hung the dreadful courtroom clock, a plain, round thing that we saw as our friend when a longed-for recess had arrived, and as our mortal enemy if we were a minute late for court.

I took my seat at counsel table and opened my old, worn leather briefcase. This was a time of fear for me. After more than thirty years I still felt the grip of it as I walked into this place where the futures of human beings were decided. The eyes of the prospective jurors were fastened on me. They were making their first judgments, a look of suspicion on their faces, wondering who this shyster was, what his game would be, what venal crimes he was attempting to cover. I could feel it as I walked in, the silence, those peering, piercing eyes, the bodies shifting uneasily in uncomfortable chairs. I uttered up a small prayer, to what or whom I didn't know.

I spoke to Sandy. Smiled at her so she'd smile back. A glance told me the jurors were also fixed on her, this woman charged with murder. Couldn't they see she seemed harmless enough, that she could smile like other human beings, not a haughty smile but one of enduring, patient sadness? I patted her lightly on the back to reassure her. Everything was going to be all right, I said. I told her to think of this room as if it were full of her best friends, people she would actually trust with her life.

She whispered she didn't have that many friends. I said, "Well, Sandy, at last you have a roomful of them. Be comfortable with them. They like you." She said they didn't know her. If they knew her, maybe they wouldn't like her. She laughed a little laugh at her own nervousness. Michele sat down on the other side of her, like a loyal, solacing sister.

When the judge marched in, the clerk pounded the courtroom to attention with his gavel and we all rose out of respect to the court, a medieval reminder that the judge, then the king, was still the king. Haas looked judgelike all right, the black robe, the man well-fed, the thin, sandy hair cut close as if to announce to the world that he was conservative, predictable, and voted Republican. He was a Democrat. He smiled at the jury, said good morning, told them this was an important case, a murder case, and asked a few questions— whether they'd read or heard about the case somewhere, knew any of the parties, or if any had friends or relatives who were connected with law enforcement.

A woman whose brother was a cop admitted she leaned to the police, and the judge excused her. Another said he had a vacation planned for weeks, and the judge excused him. A man dressed in shabby clothes was excused because he was unemployed. Said he had no means of support and was looking for work. At the bench I said to the judge that I understood why, out of human compassion, he had to dismiss this man, but the danger was we'd end up with an elitist jury composed of only those who had the luxury of spare time and finances to sit for long months listening to the evidence.

Finally it was my turn to question the jury on *voir dire*. Those words were of Anglo-Norman derivation, meaning "to speak the truth." Lawyers have enough trouble speaking plain English and often fail to speak the whole truth. The announced objective of jury selection is to pick those who will be fair to both sides, but neither side wants to be fair. Both want to win, and both want jurors who will favor their case, fairness be damned.

As I walked to the podium, Brown was already objecting, Dawson glowering in support. I was required to sit at the table, Brown complained, something about the local court rules. What lawyer worth his salt ever addressed the court or a jury sitting on his rear? When the judge overruled Brown, he next complained that he couldn't see the jurors. The podium was in his way. I moved it over slightly. Perhaps, I told the judge, we'd eventually get over our pretrial jitters that made us so nervous and testy. I smiled at the juror on the end. He smiled back.

Then I turned to the jury and told the jurors the truth: I *was* nervous. I had the life of another human being in my hands. Maybe some of them were nervous, too, because in the end my client would be in theirs. Together we had a large responsibility here—to do justice. We were in this together. Did any of the jurors share my feelings? The jurors were silent—too early in the process for any to speak up yet. I let the silence fill the courtroom. Finally one woman raised her hand tentatively and admitted she sort of understood what

I meant. I said that made me feel better. I didn't feel so alone. That began to break the ice.

When I ask jurors to reveal to me parts of their personal lives, I must first do the same. It's only fair. They want the lawyer to reveal his own feelings first, which gives them permission to reveal theirs. In the end it's the way we learn to trust each other, to become friends.

Brown was objecting again, but at the bench. This time he claimed I was making an opening statement when I spoke of my anxiety over fulfilling my responsibility to Sandy Jones, that this was not asking proper *voir dire* questions. He kept traipsing to the bench to keep his objections secret from the jurors. But I thought the jurors knew.

Brown's voice approached a high whine. It was unfair, he said, that he was required to continuously react to my "novel" methods.

The judge said, "I don't think any comments that he's made at this point are objectionable for their content. I mean, 'Are you nervous as you sit here today?'" The judge tossed a mirthless laugh to Brown. "So what's wrong with that? We're all nervous."

My voice rose above the standard whisper at the bench. I said Brown was trying to obstruct a fair trial by interrupting my *voir dire*. The judge stopped it: "Okay. Everybody has had their swing. Let's get on with it." Brown walked back to his table with a look and a shake of the head that said, "This guy's getting away with murder."

I talked to the jurors about jurors' rights. I don't take a case if it's one I can't fairly try. They had the same rights. I reminded them this was a murder case. Were any of them hesitant to sit on such a case? Were any of them reluctant to pass judgment on another human being? (Those who are eager to pass judgment on others often have a disposition more akin to that of the executioner.) A juror's hand popped up: "It doesn't bother me to pass judgment." Every answer a juror gives, even an adverse one, is a gift, something that will help me decide if the juror will be open to my case. Another juror claimed she wanted to sit on the case because if she were being tried, she'd want someone as fair as she as a juror. Those burdened with such a perfect view of themselves would be the first to convict Sandy Jones. I noted it on my chart, smiled, thanked her, and moved on.

But the next man was my kind of juror. He said, "As far as judging and sitting on this case, I've got butterflies. I'm apprehensive, but I think it is something I can do." He was aware of his feelings. Many people are not. Another said he would not pass judgment unless he was *absolutely* sure. The juror didn't need to be absolutely sure to convict, only beyond a reasonable doubt. I waited for Brown's objection, but it didn't come. Perhaps I'd finally shut the man down.

I told the jurors that I'd felt helpless many times in my life. I wondered if any had felt that way themselves. Some raised their hands. The juror in seat 11 said he'd never been in a situation he couldn't handle. How, I wondered, could he understand the fear of a woman, alone, trying to protect her children? I made a note to strike him when the time came.

I talked to the prospective jurors about Sandy's being different. Was being different all right with them? That she cared more about the environment and her children than she cared about money—would that seem strange to them? I told the jurors I was trying to get to know them. I didn't want to put Sandy's life in the hands of strangers.

When it was Brown's turn, he wore his robe of piety as if it were affixed to his skin. His face was solemn, white, drawn, and without expression except for a quick beginning smile that seemed more like an uncontrollable muscle tic, his eyes without fire and placid. He spoke in a bloodless voice and told the prospective jurors that the judge would give them the law. Would they follow it? he asked. His countenance was of one who possessed an ineffable, perhaps holy, knowledge that he was not prepared to reveal at the moment. He spoke to the glassy air. He wanted to know if anyone would suffer a hardship sitting on the jury—questions the judge had already asked. Then he began a long question that seemed to confuse what the state's burden of proof was and I rose to object. I said, the burden of the state was proof beyond a reasonable doubt. "That is clean and pure and simple," I said, "and to cloud that issue in any way is objectionable." Brown restated his question and, to my surprise, suddenly ended his questioning and sat down.

I could never let go so quickly. I jumped up to resume my own questioning. The *voir dire* is a time to establish a rapport with the jury. I told the prospective jurors that everyone, including Mr. Brown, agreed that Sandy had killed no one—that she never pulled the trigger that killed Gerttula. But she had a .22 rifle up there and a pistol. She never fired the pistol. But what about her owning and carrying a gun? Some were for gun control. Some against. Some had guns, some didn't. But all the jurors agreed that if "push came to shove," they'd use a gun to save themselves or a member of their family. And by the time I finished my questioning, they understood that the burden of proof was always on the state—I pointed to Brown—to prove beyond a reasonable doubt that the death of Wilfred Gerttula was *not* a result of self-defense or *not* the result of the defense of another.

I asked them about the multiple charges that the state had filed against Mrs. Jones. Did they think she must be guilty because the state had brought so many charges against one woman? Didn't we all understand that the state could file as many charges as it wanted? I called it a "buckshot" charge, and she'd be as dead if one buckshot hit her as if all of them hit her. Maybe they needed to shoot at her with multiple charges with the hope of hitting her with at least one. Perhaps their case wasn't strong. The jurors seemed to understand.

I'd been talking about how the police and the good old boys had harassed Sandy. Finally Sandy beckoned me to the table. She was worried. She wanted me to tell the jury that although she'd had a lot of experience with the cops, she'd never been convicted of a crime. I'd forgotten. A lawyer needs to listen to his client. I told the jury. It had been a long, hard day. The judge was tired and getting testy. We were tired. It was four o'clock in the afternoon, and we decided to continue the jury selection in the morning.

As we started to leave the courtroom, Brown tossed me six hundred pages of information dealing with the indictment of Officer Ron Peck, the man who'd led the investigative team in Sandy's case. Under *Brady v. Maryland,* Brown had no choice but to give us the report since those six hundred pages might contain or lead to exculpatory evidence, evidence the jury could consider in exonerating our client. According to Peck's attorney, Peck had been charged in four separate indictments containing forty-six counts, charges that involved the mishandling of drugs and other evidence. Guns perhaps?

We were staying at the RiverPlace Hotel along the Willamette River. We took our evening run along the riverfront, cleared out the mental mud and the trash that had accumulated during the day. These runs were always painful for me. But after the run and the sweat, the mind begins to clear again. And after supper, sleep would come easier. Then in the early morning shortly after five, we— Eddie, Michele, and I—would meet, have breakfast, and set our strategy for the day.

As I ran along the river sweating, puffing, trying to let loose of the day's struggles, a strategy began to form in my mind. Like a good chef, I thought it my duty to present a different legal fare to the judge each morning, something to keep him invested in the case. But it was more important to present the special of the day to the prosecution. It kept them on the defensive, off-balance, and as Brown complained, it provided something "novel" to which the prosecutors had to react. I wanted them reacting. That left us in control of the case.

As I ran and the strategy took shape, little did I know what a violent turn in the road it would create—starting the next morning.

18

When the judge took the bench, the potential jury panel waiting, I told him that to go forward with this case would make a mockery of the judicial process. I asked His Honor to dismiss the state's case.

From the beginning we'd contended there was a missing gun, and that we thought Monica Gerttula had fired it. Now we'd discovered the state was contending that its own investigator, Peck, had been stealing evidence during the exact time he was investigating Sandy's case. The six hundred pages of police reports alleged that Peck had looted the sheriff's evidence locker of cocaine and a variety of pills—Valium, uppers, downers, and who knew what else? Guns and gun parts were missing, clips, and even a shotgun. Was our missing gun one of them?

Peck would probably take the Fifth if we called him as a witness. Everyone, even Brown, agreed to that.

"So what?" Brown argued. Nearly all of the evidence—the blood on the Gerttula pickup, the bullet holes through the bed of the pickup, the shot tires—could be provided to the jury through other witnesses. Don't forget, Brown argued, the state had its eyewitness, Monica Gerttula. "We believe," Brown said, "that this case is makable without Peck."

Then with a party smile, Brown said, "Your Honor, I take it we're becoming accustomed to encountering novel and intriguing legal issues in this case." He looked at me with an implacable stare. But suddenly he seemed desperate and began arguing that Peck's testimony in Little Mike's case could be read to the jury. I argued that deprived us of our constitutional right to confront the witness, to face him and to cross-examine him.

Judge Haas seemed perplexed, his usual smile wrinkles having vanished. I wanted Peck on the stand. Did he destroy the gun, hide it, throw it in the river? Brown shot back in a storm of words: "The state's position is there never was a gun. That's a total fiction. I want to make it real clear. There isn't a missing gun!"

The judge wanted our formal motion before him. What he really wanted was time to think this through. I said, "I'll go back to my room and start typing." After that, it being Wednesday, May 21, the judge dismissed the jury panel until Friday.

We gathered the next morning in the courtroom, we with our formal motion to dismiss the case all black-and-white and eager in our hands. With Eddie and Michele feeding me details from the files and the case law, I'd typed late into the night. I set out an "A to Z" list of activities undertaken by Peck in the investigation. He was the first at the scene and took the first photographs. He seized the .30-30, which the state alleged was the murder weapon. He searched the scene for what we claimed was the missing gun—on and on to Z, Z being that Peck was the principal consultant to the DA in the preparation of this case.

But there were also things Peck had failed to do, such as take and record triangulation measurements at the scene, which would allow the scene to be reconstructed, something a rookie traffic cop would remember in investigating a fender bender. He had failed to take pictures of the cartridge cases where they were first found and to locate the acceleration marks left by the truck. He had failed to dredge the river for the missing gun and left a cartridge in the .30-30, sending it to the crime lab *loaded.* And he had failed to bag the hands of the deceased to save any gunshot residue that might be present.

We alleged these failures resulted in a loss of evidence that might have acquitted Sandy Jones. In my motion I wrote, "This case has been so stained, tainted, and contaminated by the conduct of the state through its agent, Peck, that a reliable and credible body of evidence cannot be presented to the jury and the case must be dismissed." Moreover, we alleged, "Peck's failures are so gross and the deviations and defects so serious and numerous that it is reasonable to infer that Peck was ingesting the drugs he stole and was under their influence at the time of his investigation and 'processing' of the case."

We quoted Lincoln County judge Charles Littlehales in a recent case, *State v. Braeme,* in which Peck was the investigator. The judge dismissed that case, writing, "The court further finds that Officer Peck's claim in the search warrant affidavit to have identified psilocybin mushrooms through defendant's window was not offered in good faith, was not accurate, and was not truthful."

Under the excuse that he couldn't investigate one of the county's own deputies, Ulys Stapleton had farmed out the Peck investigation to Steve Skelton, a Lane County DA. We'd demanded that Skelton appear before Judge Haas. When Skelton joined us in chambers, he refused to tell us when the grand jury indictment against Peck was to be issued. Nor would he tell us what the indictment contained, claiming it was his duty under the law to keep the work of the grand jury secret. Yet he'd already told Peck's lawyer, Ken Morrow, the indictment was in the last stages of drafting and included some forty-six felony and misdemeanor charges.

By agreement, Peck came to court so we could establish on the record whether or not he'd take the Fifth. I thought we had the state in checkmate. If Peck didn't take the Fifth, I could crucify him in front of the jury on cross-examination. If he did take the Fifth, the case should be dismissed for the reasons set out in our motion. I called Peck to the stand. He was in all ways a medium sort of man—medium of height with medium brown hair and eyes, and his dress was neither formal nor casual, a nondescript sports jacket and tie. He'd gained a few pounds after his months of inactivity following his discharge from the sheriff's office. He was the quiet type, Michele told me, not the typical boisterous cop around the courthouse.

Peck walked with medium steps to the stand. I approached him and stopped a few feet shy of the witness stand. "Would you state your name to the court, please?"

"Ronald Dean Peck," he replied, a lusterless look in his eyes. His shoulders had a certain tight, police squareness.

"Mr. Peck, what do you do?"

Judge Haas stopped Peck's answer to advise him of his rights. If Peck testified about anything, even that he'd investigated the Sandy Jones case, the judge might find that he'd waived his Fifth Amendment privilege and require him to testify across the board, even about the drugs he'd allegedly stolen.

Peck listened carefully. Then he said, "On advice of counsel, I decline to answer on the ground that it may tend to incriminate me."

"Let me ask one other question," I said. "Did you investigate the Sandy Jones case involving the death of one Wilfred Gerttula?"

The sweat on Peck's forehead. "Again, on the advice of counsel, I decline to answer your question on the ground that it may incriminate me." With that, the judge ordered Peck to step down, and Peck left the courtroom with his attorney.

But before Judge Haas ruled on our motion to dismiss the state's case, he wanted proof in the record that we couldn't receive a fair trial without Peck's testimony. Our motion was an enormous request to make of any judge—akin to asking the umpire in the World Series to declare our team the winner because the pitcher, at the crucial moment, the series tied in the last game, the bases loaded, intentionally beans our team's star hitter, disabling him for the rest of the game.

I thought we could shorten the process with stipulations to certain irrefutable facts in the case, but Brown wasn't about to agree to anything. The judge wanted to know how long we thought this hearing would take. I told him it would take as long as the prosecution wanted it to take. We could conclude it this afternoon, or we could conclude it weeks down the road.

"This Brown is driving me nuts," I whispered.

Eddie gave me a grin and a pat on the hand like a father to a child. "Take it easy. We got him up against the ropes. Don't blow it."

Brown, seemingly on the edge of panic, was still talking. "I'm concerned about the burden of proof. If, for example, they claim the sun was purple or something, then does it mean the state has to rebut that or what?"

Finally the judge lost his patience. He looked first at me and then at Brown. "Gentlemen, as someone has said, 'It's not the judge's role to give you the correct decision, but *the* decision.'" He ordered us to be prepared to make whatever record we intended to make beginning at nine in the morning. I told the judge our first witnesses would be Ulys Stapleton and Josh Marquis. The judge ordered Brown to have them in the courtroom ready to testify.

19

The next morning in chambers, the attorneys on both sides pulled up their chairs in front of His Honor's desk and waited. The judge turned to me with a "What now?" expression on his face. Three lawyers who'd been watching my *voir dire* examination of the jury told me they'd overhead a juror say, "We could save a lot of time if we just took 'em out and hung 'em."

I asked the judge to call the juror into chambers. The man looked like a charter member of the National Rifle Association, and of course he denied having said any such thing. Did this juror represent an ambushing undercurrent in the City of Roses? Hang 'em? But before I could worry much, the judge dismissed the whole jury panel. He realized we'd launched into a lengthy hearing that could go on for days. He couldn't keep this jury waiting any longer.

Immediately I took the initiative. "We're concerned here with fundamental, constitutional rights. We have a right to present to a jury this whole litany of Peck's misconduct, his oversights, his omissions, the manufacturing of evidence, and his failure to preserve proper evidence." I was steaming, canning peaches. "We have the right to show, if we can, that Peck was under the influence of drugs when he investigated the case, that he intentionally lost or destroyed evidence, that the evidence in his custody was contaminated or changed, and that he, as the chief officer of that investigation, stands for the state. Fundamental fairness will not permit the state to profit from its own wrongdoing." The way I saw it, Ronald Peck was the state.

"And the state takes the Fifth!" I heard myself shout. I walked to the easel with the big sheets of paper, took a black marker, and wrote the words in large letters:

THE STATE TAKES THE FIFTH!

Brown gave Dawson a disgusted glance, like someone watching a door-to-door salesman's transparent exaggerations. Suddenly, I demanded that Peck be given immunity to testify in our case, a powerful signal to the judge as to how important we felt Peck's testimony was to a fair trial. And asking for Peck's immunity would put unexpected pressure on the three prosecutors, Brown, Stapleton, and Peck's special prosecutor, Skelton, each of whom stood as the state and all of whom collectively had become the state. Skelton probably wanted to prosecute Peck. Big-headline case for him. Stapleton might not want Peck prosecuted at all. He could create political problems. Brown probably wanted Peck to somehow vanish. And I hadn't forgotten that if the state refused to give Peck immunity, and if Sandy was convicted, we had another issue to take to the Supreme Court. As predicted, Brown saw it as another of Spence's novel ideas.

"Day after day, in this courtroom, and at this very moment, prosecutors in every courthouse in the country are granting immunity to whomever they please in order to convict some poor devil," I said. That was all I was asking for Sandy Jones—to immunize Peck so he couldn't hide behind the Fifth Amendment and deprive us of his testimony. The judge just shook his head. He wanted to review the law on the subject. In the meantime we had to go forward with the testimony.

I called Josh Marquis to the stand. He approached in quick, efficient steps, the self-satisfied smile on his face. He crossed his legs and looked over at me as if daring me to ask the first question.

"Mr. Marquis, are you a lawyer?" I asked with a raffish air.

"Yes, I am."

"Really?"

"Really."

"We've had a lot of time together in court?"

"Yes."

"Do you know why you were called to testify here today?"

In a blaze of barely concealed indignation he said he thought he did—something to do with our motion to dismiss the case. Yes, he admitted, Peck had at one point coordinated the police work at the scene. Reluctantly, and only after much urging, did he finally agree that it was Peck who had seized the pickup, the camera, the .30-30 rifle the state claimed was the murder weapon. Yes, Peck took possession of the empty .30-30 shell casings, the gunshot residue taken from Sandy, the tires from the Gerttula pickup that had been shot, and it was Peck who had gathered the bullet fragments from the .22 that Sandy had fired through the windshield.

It had also been Peck who had taken Sandy to the scene right after the shooting, and it was to him that she had first told her story, a story that had never changed: Peck's notes revealed that Sandy had said, "I thought he had a gun. I guess he didn't. I prayed it wouldn't happen." And Marquis admitted it was Peck to whom Sandy had explained that she was trying to drive Gerttula to the hospital when she left Monica Gerttula behind.

"Do you find that to be a possible exculpatory statement?" I asked.

"Yes, in the context we've previously discussed, it's possible. If you're trying to get me to tell you that I believe it is probably exculpatory or likely exculpatory, I can't say that because the way the facts came out, it was not. It is possible."

"If a defendant charged with a crime is trying to take the so-called victim to the hospital, as distinguished from trying to stomp on his head, or hit him with a weapon, wouldn't you consider that a possible exculpatory statement?"

"Since you are asking me as an attorney and not just as a witness, yes, it is possible, but not in the context that this happened."

Tediously, laboriously, question on question, Marquis finally admitted that according to Peck, Nye, one of the men Sandy had confronted at the gate, appeared to be drunk at the time Peck attempted to interview him. This was the witness, along with the witness Dick, upon whom the state relied for its charge against Sandy for "menacing."

After the morning break, Brown suddenly changed his mind. He thought immunity for Peck might be a good idea after all. That told me Brown had learned Skelton would refuse to grant Peck immunity. By agreeing to immunity, Brown could shift the blame to Skelton.

Stapleton and Marquis had been required to dismiss or renegotiate more than twenty felony drug cases Peck had investigated. But Brown would never dismiss Sandy's case. She had fewer rights than all of the drug dealers Stapleton was prosecuting. And no matter what obstacles arose to Brown's prosecution, even when the state itself took the Fifth, Sandy Jones steadfastly remained the target. Such a compulsion to convict was frightening. If convicting Sandy Jones had become a prosecutorial disease, Brown and Dawson had surely caught it.

Still on the stand, Marquis admitted that he'd learned that Peck may have substituted sugar or starch in certain bags of cocaine stored in the evidence locker, and that when these bags were sent to the crime lab, Peck may have substituted drugs from evidence taken in other cases. Marquis wouldn't agree that this was "manufacturing" evidence. He would admit it might be "tampering" with evidence—the word games. A wide variety of drugs were missing, all from the same lockers in which Peck had kept the evidence in Sandy Jones's case. Through all the testimony and arguments that followed, one thing became obvious: Brown, but neither the judge nor any of us, had known about this whole Peck mess for months. But he'd not given us the investigative reports until the day of trial. Trial lawyers call that "trial by ambush." Again we were nearing the end of the day. Marquis stepped down from the stand seemingly as fresh as ever after his hours in the witness chair.

Then I called Stephen Toliver to the stand. He was the polygraph operator in Stapleton's office who'd given Monica Gerttula her lie detector test. I wanted the results of the test that Marquis had steadfastly refused to provide us. Toliver was a short man, thin, with dark brown hair and a mustache—about forty, I'd say. The wrinkles were cut deep in his face. I saw him take his seat, but not with the confidence one might expect from a man shielded with the power of the DA's office. He seemed troubled, his face tight. He reached for a glass of water and took several swallows before I asked my first question.

Toliver spoke with a soft, phlegmatic voice. He said he'd given Mrs. Gerttula a lie detector test and had recorded the results. But the moment I began to probe I was met with objections from Dawson. This was not a time for discovery, he hollered. He stomped up to the bench. He agreed we might interview Toliver out of court, but it was improper in a criminal case to examine Toliver on the stand and under oath on matters that were not material to our motion to dismiss. The judge, ready to go home, sustained the objection and Toliver stood down. "You can interview him over the weekend," the judge said. "Have a good one," and he left the bench in tired steps, his head sagging in heavy thought.

Immediately we motioned for Toliver to take a seat at the clerk of court's desk. Then we gathered around the desk, Dawson and Brown as well. Soon I had Toliver holding up his charts explaining what they meant. All the while I saw Marquis dancing around the edges, bouncing up and down on his toes, trying to listen in. I couldn't believe my ears as Toliver explained his charts. As a veteran trial lawyer I thought I'd seen it all, but we held back our reactions like old cardsharps holding a straight flush.

When we stepped out of the courthouse door onto the busy Portland street, I looked at Eddie. "Jesus H. Christ, Eddie!" I felt light in the head, giddy.

Michele began to laugh. "It's just too unbelievable!"

"I don't see what you think's so funny," Sandy said. She was obviously shocked. It wasn't funny. It was astounding.

"I told ya!" Eddie said. "I told ya!" He was shaking his finger at me and stamping on the pavement like a man keeping time to rock and roll. "Man! Ain't this some profession?" And he laughed again.

20

Monica Gerttula was deceptive, according to Toliver's polygraph charts. If one believed the charts, they said she had lied in answer to the crux question, "Did you shoot a handgun at the scene?" But a lie detector test is only a machine recording of a human being speaking to the machine's operator. Humans can choose to believe or disbelieve what the machine records. The machine doesn't lie. It doesn't tell the truth. It just records.

Sometimes the people who talk to the machine lie, and sometimes the people who read the machine don't read it right. The contraption is mostly a tool to scare a confession out of some frightened accused. "You flunked your lie detector test, you lying sack of crap, so you better tell us the truth before we really get mad." And the guy's sitting there alone, panicked, a bunch of big, armed deputies gathered around like lions over the kill, and he confesses. Sometimes he confesses when he didn't do it. Sometimes he's so frightened and confused that he believes the polygraph before he believes himself.

But what happens when the state's star witness not only flunks the poly but has gunshot residue all over her, and in quantities that force the criminologist from the state lab to admit that Monica Gerttula probably shot a firearm that day? Then what do the prosecutors say? They say they don't believe the polygraph.

"You have to consider who these people are," I said to Eddie. We were sitting on a pile of rocks eating fresh oysters.

"Are these prosecutors evil men, or what?" I said mostly to myself, my mouth full of raw oyster.

"They're caught," Eddie said. "When you get caught, you do stuff."

"I think they think they're doing right. Maybe they think Sandy Jones is a witch or something and it's their job to put her away," I said.

My wife, Imaging, had come up for the Memorial Day weekend. Imaging, "the wondrous one," I called her, looked at me with those great eyes, blue like blue eyes should be on a woman—the black hair, the lips that had put me into a headlong, breathless swoon the first time I saw her and from which I'd never fully recovered. And she had insights about people and about me. I listened to her.

"You always tell young lawyers that they have to believe in their case. These guys believe in their case," she said. "They believe Monica. That's all."

"Right," I said.

"What we have here are two sides who each believe their woman," she said. "You believe Sandy. They believe Monica Gerttula. And if you were on their side of it, you wouldn't let some traveling gunslinger from Wyoming come in and take it away from you."

I stuffed another oyster in my mouth.

"When you were a prosecutor, you never lost a case," Imaging said. "Not one. Do you think you were *that* right every time?"

"Well, I hope so. When I thought I was wrong, I tried to do something about it. I turned a few loose. Got chewed for it sometimes."

"You did what you believed in."

We did what we had to do. This trial business was the historical remnant of men killing each other in the pits. Now we slaughtered each other with words in the courtroom. I saw the prosecutors as bad men. But that's how you see your opponent, your eyes looking up from the depths of your gut, where your feelings are. I had to see them that way. They were committed men, that's all, maybe zealous men. Perhaps they'd lost their objectivity, perhaps they were playing on the edge, but they were not bad men.

We were playing a game, and the stakes were high. Nobody wanted to call it a game. But it was. There were rules to play by, moves that had to be made and boundaries. But no one is made righteous by following rules, and following rules does not guarantee justice. There was a referee, a judge who was supposed to keep things straight and fair. There were winners and losers. Presumably the truth was found by the jury. That depended on some things you couldn't predict and couldn't define. But one fact I knew to be true: if it was a game and we lost it, an innocent person would die. Prison is a form of slow dying.

"Marquis and Stapleton put themselves in a kind of trap," Eddie said. "When Marquis said what he said about dismissing the case if Mrs. Gerttula was lying, he said it because he believed her. He was also trying to mess with you, Gerry. He didn't think for a minute she'd flunk the test. And after she flunked it, what was he supposed to do? Come running into court and say, 'Our witness flunked the test, so dismiss this case and dismiss it this minute, right now'?" Eddie laughed.

"He should have given her another test if she was so upset she couldn't pass it the first time," I said.

"Yeah, but what if she flunked it a second time?" Eddie asked. "And a third?"

"Hey, look," Michele said, "Marquis has never wanted

to face up to the possibility that Monica fired a gun that day. And everybody knows that if she admits it, their case is down the drain, even if she didn't shoot her husband."

Eddie said, "She could have been out target practicing with Gerttula that morning. Remember, Little Mike heard shots being fired that no one's been able to explain. So did Dick and Nye."

"Even so, the prosecutors can still think she's telling the truth and that Sandy Jones is a murderer," Imaging said.

"I don't know," I said.

"Well, what if you're a woman and come up on the scene and there's Sandy with a gun pointed at you. You're scared, right?" Imaging asked.

I waited to see where she was going.

"Say you're Monica Gerttula, and Sandy starts hollering at your husband, and your husband sees Sandy standing there with the gun and the gate closed, and so he figures he's not going to get out of the pickup. He's going to force Sandy out of the way. He starts gunning the pickup at her, and she starts shooting the .22. Shoots a tire out. Shoots through the windshield. What are you going to do if you're Monica Gerttula and there's a gun in the glove compartment?" Imaging waited for me to answer.

"I'd sure as hell take it out," I said.

"Right," Imaging said. "And then what would you do? You see your husband out there trying to take the rifle away from Sandy and you get panicked. The kid is shooting at the pickup from behind you, and the bullets are whining all over the place, smacking through the truck bed, and the tires are being shot out. You hear the tires blow—two of them. Sandy and your husband are all tangled up fighting over the gun. You're scared and you're shaking and you bear down on Sandy and pull the trigger.

And it's your own husband you hit. Then what do you do?"

"You throw the gun into the river," I said. "You get rid of the evidence."

"That's not what I mean," Imaging said. "You can never make yourself believe that you shot your own husband. You're in deep denial. You will *not* believe it. Sandy was the one who shot him."

"Yeah?"

"And later, if you find out that you made a mistake, it doesn't make any difference. If she and her outlaw kid hadn't been there with their guns, everybody would be alive today. It was Sandy Jones who caused the death of your husband. And that's the way you're going to tell the story."

"So, yeah, but Monica's shooting, which was an accident, isn't criminal," I said. "And Sandy and Little Mike didn't shoot anyone. So no crime was committed."

"Let's get back to the prosecutors," Michele said. "Suppose they saw it the way Imaging just laid it out? Shouldn't they dismiss?" She didn't wait for the answer. "You're damn right they should dismiss!"

"They're prosecutors," Imaging said. "They had to prosecute somebody for Gerttula's death. They took a position. Doesn't mean they're lying. Means they took a position, believed it, have to believe it, and right or wrong they're going to stick to it." Then she said, "Monica Gerttula must feel pretty bad when people claim she might have killed her own husband."

"Yeah," I said. "But if I'm wrong, and Little Mike shot Gerttula, he did it in the defense of his mother. Those acceleration marks in the dirt prove it. Gerttula was gunning his truck at Sandy. A truck is a deadly weapon. There's a complete defense in the law for Little Mike, Sandy, *and*

Monica Gerttula. Each of them was either shooting to defend themselves or somebody else."

"Okay then," Imaging said, "so everybody *could* be in the right in this case."

"Yeah, but somebody knows the truth. And we have to find out who, and we have to find out what it is."

Then I ate the last oyster in the carton.

21

I was pacing the floor in the judge's chambers, the primal urges to attack the enemy erupting, exploding to the surface. The judge saw the rising tension in my face and heard the anger at the margins of my words and beckoned me to a chair with a patient smile.

I glanced over at Brown and Dawson. Brown's face was the color of schoolroom paste. Dawson sat silently, his upper lip fluttering slowly, his thick mustache jumping up and down as if some small, half-devoured furry animal were inside his mouth trying to escape.

Toliver claimed he'd given Monica Gerttula a standard test—spent two hours with her and ran two charts on the woman. He explained how the "subject," as he called the person being tested, had to score a plus-six total for the examiner to conclude that the subject was telling the truth. On the other hand, a minus-six total on any relevant question was necessary for the examiner to conclude she was lying.

I got up from my chair and looked down at His Honor, his face open and waiting. "In this case, on the single imperative question, namely, 'Did you fire a handgun at the scene?' she didn't score a minus-six." I stopped. The judge waited. I whispered. "She scored *a minus-fourteen!* It went off the scale." Then I said, "Toliver admitted that his conclusion on her score established 'very strong'—is how he put it—evidence that she was lying on that subject."

I sat down. Finally I interrupted the silence. "But Toliver claimed the test wasn't valid. She was upset when she came in. I told Toliver, 'I suppose everyone is upset when they're given a lie detector test, and if you're going to lie, you'd really be upset.'" Emotional stress was the theoretical basis of the polygraph. "'Did you know she was upset prior to the time you administered the test?' I asked Toliver. 'Yes,' he said. Then I said, 'If her emotional condition was such that the test results would be invalid, why did you give her the test in the first place?'"

He didn't have a satisfactory explanation for that. I knew one thing: if Sandy Jones was upset and had been given the polygraph and failed, it would only have deepened the prosecutors' resolve to put her away.

I told His Honor that I asked Toliver if he was in the habit of giving the polygraph under circumstances that gave him the option in advance of declaring the results invalid. He said no. Yet the entire graph of her responses to simple questions like "What's your name?" or "Where do you live?" was all consistent with truth-telling. The only time she had a problem was when she was asked that question—the one about firing the gun. Then the needle went off the scale. Toliver admitted he never suggested that she be retested. I stopped talking. The judge seemed dumbfounded.

Toliver had, of course, written no report of his findings and interpretations. I told the judge I assumed he'd been advised by Stapleton and Marquis not to make any written findings so we'd be unable to discover them. I said, "This information was kept from us and the failure of the state to make a truthful revelation of those facts is such bad faith that the defendant is entitled to a dismissal of this charge. The state is guilty of prosecutorial misconduct of the kind that I've never seen in my thirty-five years—where there were objective tests made that showed that the chief eyewitness lied on the principal issue of the case—"

Brown interrupted, "May I speak?" His voice was wooden.

Why should he speak? He had failed to speak when he was obligated under the law to speak. Now he wanted to speak when I was speaking. I snapped, "I'm not finished yet." I turned and pointed a finger at the man. "If they hadn't known about this, we wouldn't have seen Mr. Dawson trying to keep this matter from the record. That was a very interesting move that he made."

Dawson jumped up hollering. "Excuse me, Judge, I thought we had an agreement we weren't going to throw the ethical skews around. If there's some evidence of my misconduct, that should be declared. I have a right to make objections."

I jumped to my feet as well. "I recognize that the special prosecutor is a man with a nice reputation in this community." The sound of my words was not nice. "And Mr. Dawson is from the Attorney General's Office. But I'm going to call them as I see them. I think there was an ethical obligation for these prosecutors to come forward with the information openly and not make me dig it out. There is an ethical obligation for them to dismiss this case. There is an ethical obligation for them not to futz up the evidence with those phony Bekkedahl tests that we've heard about." I was referring to the state's latest failed effort to explain the high levels of gunshot residue on Monica Gerttula's hands.

"We have Mr. Peck here, who is the principal investigator in this case and who has now taken the Fifth Amendment. So when you put this all together, it seems to me these prosecutors should stop this game-playing." I was shouting, the judge but a few feet from me. "If Mr. Brown finds these facts as I've stated them, he should dismiss this case! Your Honor, we're at a stage now where we simply can't proceed. At every turn in the road we're faced with another unbelievable, overwhelming disclosure that shows the misconduct of the state in its prosecution of Sandy Jones, and it sucks us dry to the core."

Dawson cleared his throat. "I don't think we have to respond to that. I think it's important to realize that this woman was not just upset. She was crying. She was visibly upset. She had been recently accused of killing—"

Judge Haas interrupted, a frown on his face. "Who chose the time for the polygraph?"

"I don't know, Your Honor."

"The prosecutors?" the judge asked. "How can you argue this was not effective when the District Attorney's Office chose to have the test performed on her at that time and place?"

"I don't know why the polygraph was conducted." Dawson was beginning to whine.

"And apparently, if accurately represented, they indicated enough reliance on the test that they'd dismiss the case if she failed," the judge said.

The judge's thinking had taken a dangerous turn for Dawson. Where before he hadn't wanted Toliver on the stand, now he said, "That's an issue that we should take up in court with witnesses. I want to hear from Toliver, and I want to hear from the deputy DA."

Brown jumped in, "We will present evidence to the court that by the time the police officer interviewed Monica Gerttula, she had involuntarily urinated, she had vomited, she had been struck on the head and bitten by a dog as she ran after this vehicle in which her husband lay." But that was in July and she was given the polygraph the beginning of December. Then Brown added, "Our understanding is that she testified at great length in the juvenile hearing and was subjected, I'm confident, to the most acidulous cross-examination of which counsel is most capable of mounting. In an independent search for the truth, the polygraph is a side issue."

Sandy slipped a note to Michele: *Asidu-what? What's he mean by that?*

I saw Michele write: *He's trying to use bigger words than Gerry. Means "nasty."*

Suddenly the judge made his decision. He ordered Josh Marquis to resume the stand. As I stepped up to the podium to question him, I could feel the sword of ancient times in my hands and I wanted to swing it—hard.

22

My questioning of Marquis turned into hours of painful, muscled verbal wrestling. He spoke in fast, clipped, often abstract language. He admitted that it was his decision to subject Monica Gerttula to the polygraph, that he had agreed that if exculpatory matters were contained in the test he'd advise us, and that if they believed Monica Gerttula was lying, they'd dismiss the case.

"Do you recall that I leaned around Mr. Moriarity and asked, 'What are the lie detector results on Monica Gerttula, Josh?' Do you recall that question?"

"Not specifically, but I know you asked me about that."

"And you answered, 'I'm not going to tell you.' Do you recall saying that?"

"Probably."

"Then I said, 'Well, did she pass it? Were there any exculpatory matters explained in the test results?' To which you answered, quote, 'I'm not going to answer you. Our going forward with the case is your answer.' Do you remember that?"

"That sounds like what I said," Marquis said with a smirk.

"You did give that answer to us and expected us to accept it in good faith, did you not?"

"Yes."

But despite the test results, they believed Mrs. Gerttula, not the test. Because they didn't believe the test, they were not required to deliver any information to us—that was their logic. He claimed he'd never asked Toliver about her scores on the crux question. And after she'd failed the test, he never suggested that she be retested.

Leaning over the bench, Judge Haas interrupted and in a quiet voice asked why, if they thought the test was invalid, hadn't they done another test?

"I had some question why we did it in the first place, Your Honor." Marquis was quick. I thought that if our positions were reversed, I wouldn't have been able to parry a judge's questions so easily. "I had no problems believing Mrs. Gerttula, and I felt very reluctant to subject her again to another test after what she'd been through and what had been out in the paper—Mr. Spence accusing her of killing her husband." He gave me a hard look.

During Little Mike's trial I'd asked, Had she fired at Sandy to save her husband and accidentally shot the man? She'd denied it, denied it vehemently, denied it with a quick little shaking of her head, denied it in high volume you could hear across the courtroom. I had only asked the question.

"The course you chose was the polygraph," the judge reminded Marquis.

"For internal preparation of our office, yes."

"You must place some credence in it."

Marquis quickly shifted around the question. "Different people in our office have different opinions."

At the recess Michele came charging up to me. "Gerry, Stapleton's deputies use the poly all the time! I've been in court with Marquis where he's asked that a poly test be imposed as a condition of probation. Those guys think polygraphs are the neatest thing since sliced bread. Don't let Marquis say the DAs don't rely on them."

When Brown took over on cross-examination, he had Marquis describe Monica Gerttula on the day the test was given. "She was tearful, she trembled, she held herself to a sort of, you know—"

"You're indicating a huddling kind of posture," Brown offered.

"Yes. I've seen a lot of people who get upset in criminal trials. She was extremely upset."

"Was that before or after the polygraph?"

"Before and after. She was worse afterwards."

But why, the judge still wanted to know, hadn't she been retested? Again when Marquis claimed that she wasn't in "a very good mental state," the judge said, "She was good enough to testify in front of a grand jury the same afternoon."

"To test her again," Marquis insisted, "would further tell her we didn't believe her." Besides, he said, "I had no particular reason to think things would greatly improve any time in the future."

Under subpoena, Ulys Stapleton walked to the stand. I thought him a different person from the one I'd previously interrogated. His face was starched, his aura shrunken. He took the stand with his head hung forward as if in penitence.

To begin, I had him admit the obvious—that it would be misconduct for a prosecutor to mislead a judge. He spoke as if he were reluctant to hear the sound of his own voice. But as I got into the issue of Peck's use of drugs and its possible effect on the accuracy and completeness of the evidence in Sandy's case, he became more alert. Stapleton admitted that Peck had a drug problem.

I asked, "Don't you recognize that if someone would alter evidence in a drug case that the same kind of moral deprivation might cause the evidence to be altered in a nondrug case?"

"It might," Stapleton admitted. Yet he insisted that although Peck was to be charged with some forty-six counts, nevertheless he wouldn't hesitate to present Peck as a truthful witness.

Suddenly I changed my tack. "Mr. Stapleton, one of the reasons you put a witness on the polygraph is to satisfy yourself that the witness is telling the truth before you present the witness to the court?"

"Yes."

"And the reason you want to satisfy yourself is you understand you have an obligation not to present witnesses whom you believe may be lying?"

"That's part of it."

"And you don't want to present witnesses to a court or a jury whom you believe would wrongfully convict an innocent person, isn't that true?"

"Correct."

"And isn't it true that that was one of the reasons that you put Monica Gerttula on the so-called box, or polygraph in this case?"

"That was one of the reasons."

I changed tack again. I'd raised the question of a missing gun. Stapleton admitted dredging the river was discussed but never ordered even though Deputy Don Schmidt found the Gerttula tape recorder where it had been thrown over the side of the road, falling just short of the waters.

It was time for a break. But before the recess I told the judge I had a short matter to bring to His Honor. I called a law student, a bright-eyed young woman attending

Lewis and Clark College, who'd shown up to watch jury selection and had returned to hear my examination of the witnesses. Her name was Kathleen Kurtz.

"I take it you have high expectations for the profession?" I asked the young woman.

"Yes." She had a child's timbre in her voice.

"Did you hear something the other day that concerned you?"

"Yes."

"And who was the author of the statement? Could you describe him?"

"Yes, I can. He was a man, I would say about in his forties, perhaps early fifties. He was a heavyset gentleman. He was wearing two plaid shirts, and he was sweating quite a bit. He would wipe his brow with a red-and-white-striped terry-cloth towel. He had a receding hairline and he had a beard, and his beard was salt-and-pepper in color, gray and white."

"Would you call him rotund?"

"I would call him obese."

Judge Haas said, "I won't ask her to comment on me." Muffled laughter.

"What did you hear the juror say?" I wanted to prove that my prior representation to the judge concerning what this prospective juror had said was accurate. Even though the jury had earlier been discharged, I valued every opportunity to establish my credibility with the court. A lawyer's credibility is all he has to offer to judge or jury.

"It was a time when the judge and the two lawyers were going into chambers," the young woman said, "and the gentleman became exasperated, and he slapped his knee and he said, 'Wouldn't a hanging just be quicker?'"

Dawson wanted to make light of it: "Do you know if he

was referring to the lawyers or the defendant when he spoke of hanging?" More laughter.

"I don't know."

"What about the judge?" Haas asked.

A spoilsport, I interrupted, "I don't want to make light of the matter. It took courage for this young woman to make this known. It was an important matter for the record." I turned to her. "Thank you."

"Yes," Judge Haas said, "thank you." And after that I resumed my cross-examination of Ulys Stapleton.

As I called each witness to the stand, question by question, and grudging answer by answer, it must finally have become clear to Brown that a synaptic link existed between Peck and all of the state's machinations in Sandy's case. Nearing the evening recess, Brown tried to recharge his position with Judge Haas. He offered to stipulate that the judge, at trial, could instruct the jury that Deputy Peck, if called, "would decline to answer any questions in this matter on the grounds that it might tend to incriminate him." This would permit us to at least point out to the jury that the state's principal witness had taken the Fifth. Absent Brown's offered stipulation, we'd be unable to make any reference to his absence other than that he was absent. Brown's move was to give a little, so as to save his entire case. I wanted it all.

"The defense ought to think about that," Judge Haas said. "We'll discuss it in the morning."

The next morning Sandy had gotten sick and Michele left the judge's chambers with her and found a bed for her to lie down on in the Victim's Assistant's Office in the Multnomah County District Attorney's Office. It was springtime. In Wyoming the alpine buttercups had begun to follow the receding snow and were hugging the ground with their tiny yellow blossoms, and the geese were exploding in high joy across the great early-morning horizon that held the majestic reaches of the Tetons. I wanted to go home. I thought Sandy's sickness a manifestation of her voicelessness. All these months she'd been gagged. To silently endure the agony of lawyers playing these judicially sanctioned games with her life must have been an insidious torture. I was sick of it. But it was war, and one does not surrender in the trenches because one longs for springtime and buttercups and flying geese.

As my cross-examination of Stapleton, now more energized, dragged on, he finally admitted he'd personally like to see Sandy Jones convicted. Said he thought she was guilty. As the prosecutor it was *his* belief that prevailed, I thought. One only hoped that in a just society a jury's decision would prevail. But that required a fair trial, and securing a fair trial was the reason for this hearing.

Dig long enough in one of these proceedings and you'll not discover gold. You'll uncover dung. I unearthed another pile of it: reluctantly Stapleton admitted there was a strong possibility that Peck had actually planted evidence against a defendant named Muscutt. Under my prodding Stapleton gave a sketchy account.

"There was a vehicle that was not covered by a search warrant Peck had. One of the officers glanced inside the vehicle and didn't see anything. Officer Peck at some time later was supposed to have glanced in and made comments about some drugs being visible inside the vehicle. He then began to point those out to the other officer that was present and then searched the inside of the vehicle."

"He may have planted drugs?"

"Yes."

"You told Mr. Brown that?"

"Yes."

Brown claimed he'd fairly advised us of this previously in open court. But the record and my memory were silent on it.

Next we learned that a number of pistols had actually come into Wilfred Gerttula's possession. His brother, Raymond Gerttula, a convicted felon, had been hauled before the court on a parole violation for possessing firearms—a .38 Special, a .357 Magnum, and a .380 semiautomatic pistol. Peck had taken possession of these weapons and had delivered them to Wilfred Gerttula while Gerttula was married to Monica. Michele, incidentally, had represented Raymond Gerttula on the parole violation.

I suddenly shifted my questioning back to the polygraph. Why had the prosecutors decided to test Monica Gerttula on the poly? Stapleton said it was because of my lay-it-all-on-the-line presentation at the start of Little Mike's case.

"Do you put some credence in the lie detector?"

"Yes."

"Is that based on your experience?"

"And training, yes."

"And one of the reasons you test a witness with the lie detector is to satisfy yourself whether or not the witness is telling the truth, isn't that right?"

"Yes, sir."

"And the reason that you told the judge that you were going to put her on the lie detector was because you wanted the judge to know that you were going to test her and that if the test showed she was lying, you wouldn't go forward with the case, isn't that true?"

"Yes."

Stapleton further admitted that when the test came back showing she was "highly deceptive," he, as had Marquis, simply declared the test to be invalid, that they told the judge nothing, told us nothing, and never retested her.

"When you have a deceptive chart, don't you think you have some obligation to advise the judge of that?"

"No."

"You never even told Judge Gardner at any time that the test was inconclusive, did you?"

"No."

"Don't you think your silence in the case would permit the judge to conclude that the results showed your witness was telling the truth?"

"No."

"If she were so upset, why would you take her to the grand jury? You wouldn't want to take an upset witness to testify before the grand jury if she were so upset it would invalidate a polygraph test?"

"That's not true," he said.

"Wait a minute," Judge Haas interrupted, speaking to me. "Lower your voice a little bit. Let's try again."

"I just want to make sure he can hear me, Judge," I said, trying to smile.

I turned back to Stapleton. "Well, if you thought she was telling the truth, then you didn't need to give her the test in the first place, did you?"

"No."

I wanted to know about Stapleton's apparent intimidation of John Amish, the young chemist from the State Crime Lab who'd found the excessive gunshot residue on Monica Gerttula's hands. Amish had met with me one morning at breakfast during Little Mike's case and candidly told me of his findings—that it was probable that Monica Gerttula had fired a gun that day. But when Stapleton learned of our meeting, he lodged a complaint against Amish with the young man's boss. His boss made Amish file a written report explaining his conduct, as if his speaking openly to the defense were some sort of misconduct. Stapleton denied he was attempting to intimidate the witness.

Then Stapleton admitted that one of the reasons that Toliver, the polygraph operator, was not required to put his report in writing was because if we demanded the report, there'd be no report to produce.

"Do you think that you've dealt in this entire matter in a candid, fair, and professional fashion?"

"Yes."

"Do you think that you've fully met all of the ethical requirements of a prosecutor?"

"Yes."

"Do you think you've met all the requirements of fair play under *Brady*?"

"Yes."

After that, Stapleton stepped down. I felt covered with the thick mud of obfuscation. I complained to Imaging at dinner that night.

"This isn't the way the trial of a case is supposed to go," I said. "Lawyers are supposed to be open. People's lives are at stake. Those prosecutors have all that power, and they can destroy innocent people with it. They're supposed to protect the innocent."

"It isn't like I haven't heard all this from you before in your other cases," she said.

"It's not just my cases. It's the way the system works. Ethics are just rules to get around. *Justice* is an empty word. The prosecutors want to win. They want scalps. They want to be reelected."

"You're preaching to the choir," she said. "But look at poor Stapleton. He's facing a recall petition some people started against him because of Little Mike's case. He's getting all kinds of heat. You got him kicked off Sandy's case. This looks bad to the voters. Do you expect him to lie down with his feet up in the air and cringe like a whipped dog?"

I didn't answer.

"You always want juries to see things from inside the boots of your client. From inside this Stapleton fellow's boots, you're a giant who came pounding into Lincoln County killing everything and everybody in sight. He and Marquis want to beat you. But they don't have the power now. You took it from them."

I listened.

"And Brown, well, he has his own agenda. If he could kill the giant, in Oregon he'd be sitting on top of the heap."

"What about Sandy's right to a fair trial? If I'm the issue, maybe I ought to get the hell out of this case."

"If you weren't in the case, they'd already have Sandy convicted. You're just tired. In the morning you'll be ready to slug it out again. I've seen it too many times. Now," she said with that gentle look on her face, "you come with me."

23

"I brought Your Honor some new goodies this morning."
I gave the judge my best smile and handed him our latest
motion to dismiss the state's case against Sandy.

He smiled back. He was a smiling judge. "You ought to
buy me a great big stocking and set it up by the chimney."

When all was quiet and I had the judge's attention, I
told him I wanted to put the special prosecutor, James M.
Brown, on the stand. I could hear the gasping in the
courtroom. My argument was simple: Marquis claimed
he'd given Brown the polygraph information as early as
February, while Brown asserted with limp words that he
wasn't too clear at all about when he'd received it. I looked
over at Brown, who was frozen in a wince, his brows making small, freshly plowed furrows.

I reminded His Honor of Stapleton's testimony that
Brown had learned of Peck's supposed evidence-planting
in the Muscutt case two weeks before this trial had begun.
Had I not ferreted out that information in long, laborious
searches, we'd likely not have discovered any of this. And
what about Stapleton's effort to put the fear of God in
poor John Amish of the State Lab? I said, "Stapleton's
attempt to intimidate that officer has a chilling effect on
Amish's free and honest testimony, and we think that conduct prejudices the defendant's right to a fair trial."

And one more thing: we'd discovered that after

Wilfred Gerttula was shot, at least two of his brother Raymond's pistols had been picked up by the cops from Gerttula's sister where they had been left. An alleged parole violation. But a third weapon was still missing. We wanted Brown to produce that third weapon, a .380 semi-automatic pistol. Brown, gaunt, sullen, and hunched down, his voice only slightly higher than a whisper, said, "I must confess, I do not understand what specific weapon he is talking about here."

Judge Haas tried to help him. "Let me spell it out for you. What he's referring to is a third handgun. The sheriff's office has furnished nothing to tell us what disposition, if any, was made of that third weapon."

Brown's voice was wavering. "I'm struggling with the defense tactic that anything and everything becomes one more pretrial motion that keeps this matter from coming to issue."

"Well, Mr. Brown, though, with all due respect, I think it should be." The judge's face was solemn, his words heavy in apology. "They got the six-hundred-page report *after* the trial commenced. The revelation of a polygraph and its results, the failure to have a report made so as to make it easier to keep those results from the defendant's attorney—I'm sure all this creates a curiosity when there's an unaccounted-for handgun and when the defense will contend that the weapon that killed the deceased was a handgun." The judge smiled kindly at Brown, granted our motion to produce the third gun, and having given us something, but not everything, said, "Let's plow on with our evidence."

I called Stephen Toliver, the DA's polygraph operator, to the stand, and within minutes, through Toliver's testimony, we were presented a short course in the art of the polygraph. The test is generally thought to be no more reliable than the operator who gives and interprets it. Yet, many lawyers, both for the state and the defense, rely heavily on the machine. I am not among them. Not once have I ever permitted one of my clients to take a lie detector test.

Toliver had been at it since 1977. He said he'd taken a six-week course on the polygraph and that he, himself, had administered more than 450 of the tests. He was the confessed minion of the DA's office, one who could, he admitted, be fired at the displeasure of Stapleton.

Sometimes people aren't fit to test, Toliver said, but he admitted he always had the option not to test them, as when the "subject" says that he just got back from his mother's funeral, or a "subject" might be mentally retarded or on drugs or drunk. Fear is what the poly is based on—plain, old-fashioned fear. The examiner asks his questions and the subject's fear triggers the subject's lie, and in turn, the lie makes the subject's heart begin to race, his blood pressure elevate, his galvanic responses shoot up. Everyone lies, Toliver said. He, I, the judge. I didn't ask about the prosecutors. As a matter of fact, that's how he set the people up for the test to begin with—got them to lie about something unrelated to the test.

He'd asked questions of Monica Gerttula like "In the thirty-nine years of your life, have you ever lied to cover up a crime?" She said no. Everybody commits a crime, even if it's only running a red light. And he asked, "Have you ever deliberately caused anyone to be hurt?" Sometime in our lives we all do such things, Toliver insisted, minor as they might be. And down where our instincts reside, we all know it. He said the machine recorded deceptive on the setup questions he gave to Monica Gerttula.

Toliver said it all started when Josh Marquis came down from court during Little Mike's case: "There had apparently been some mention that you thought Mrs. Gerttula may have been the one who shot Mr. Gerttula, and they wanted her to take a polygraph. She was willing to take it."

I said, "You knew it would be devastating to the state's case, did you not, if it were shown that she'd fired a gun there?"

"Certainly."

A classroom of students entered the court, the judge nodding and smiling his approval at this civic-minded group of youngsters who were supposed to be learning firsthand how the justice system worked.

"Something that's still pretty nice about America, Judge," I said.

"Yes," the judge said. "We all enjoy it."

Then we got back to Toliver, who said that Monica Gerttula had been waiting in the DA's office. It was early afternoon. "Do you remember anything special about her outward appearance?" I asked. "Was she weepy?"

"I don't know if she was at that specific moment. Later on she was."

"You're aware that tears are often a defense mechanism?" I went on to explain, "When we want to defend ourselves, some of us argue. Some of us get angry. Some of us get evasive. Some of us act smart. Some of us cry."

Yes, he understood that.

"It isn't unusual for people to be defensive when they take the poly, is it?"

"No, not at all. But she said she wanted to take the test."

Then I pulled up a chair in front of Toliver at the witness stand and sat down directly in front of him. If he were the polygraph operator and I were being tested, what would he say to me?

"The first thing I'd ask you: 'What is your definition of a lie?'"

Sitting in front of him like one of his subjects, I said, "I would say that a lie is when I intentionally tell you something that isn't true."

"What is the truth, then?"

"Truth is something I believe."

"You're one up on most people," Toliver said. "Most people say the truth is what actually happened. Truth is what we *believe* it to be. So I explain to people that we're dealing with beliefs and nonbelief. A lie is when you tell something you *don't* believe."

He explained how we all grow up lying to defend ourselves: We lied about what we did in our pants during potty training. We lied to avoid a spanking. As a teenager we lied to avoid being grounded. It was about the animal instinct of self-preservation. "We are all animals," he said. "Civilization is something that we wear as a very thin shell, and we are governed in a large part by our animal instincts."

I thought the man was right. What if we put everybody involved in this case on the machine, especially all the attorneys? The damn thing would probably begin to smoke.

"We've all experienced fear." Toliver pointed out that the body goes through physical changes when it prepares itself to fight or flee, and those changes are recorded on the polygraph. "You breathe differently. Faster. The oxygen is carried through your blood to your muscles where it will be used. Your heart beats faster. Your blood pressure goes up. Your body chemistry changes—additional adrenaline, for instance."

He said he told all of this to Monica Gerttula, who said she understood it. He wants his "subjects" to know how the poly works in order to create credibility for the test in the subjects' minds—so that they know that if they lie, they'll be caught, and if they are truthful, that will also show. Some people are able to lie and get away with it, he agreed. But, he said, maybe they believe their lies. Maybe they are in denial.

Monica Gerttula had begun to cry fairly early in the pretest, Toliver said, although he had no notes to substantiate his claim. He'd tried to reassure her, but he said she felt threatened. She was being accused of shooting her husband.

The pretest took about an hour. When it was completed, he put the questions to her: "Did you shoot a handgun during that incident?" "Did you shoot any kind of firearm during that day?" and "Were there any guns in the pickup on that day?"

"From the chart can you affirmatively tell His Honor that she was telling the truth in her answers to any one of these questions?" I asked.

He let out a prodigious sigh. "No."

"How did she answer each of these questions?"

"'No.'"

"You added up the scores on these questions?"

"Yes."

"Now you have a criteria for determining whether somebody is *conclusively* telling the truth or *conclusively* telling a lie by way of a number, isn't that true?"

"Yes."

He then explained: to say conclusively that a person is telling the truth they must score a plus-six, and to say a person is lying the person must score a minus-six. All in between was inconclusive.

"Now do you have the totals for the first chart on the question, 'Did you shoot any handguns during that incident?'"

"Yes, I do."

"What is the total?"

"Minus-fourteen."

"That is about two and a half times what's necessary for you to conclude that the person is lying, isn't that true?"

"Yes, sir."

"What was the total on the second question?"

"Minus-three."

"What was the total on the third question?"

"Zero."

"And on the question 'Did you shoot a handgun during that incident?' when she answered no, that was a strong indication of her deception, isn't that true?"

"Strong indication of threat."

"On the chart itself, based upon the chart itself?"

"Okay. I . . . you know, there were deceptive responses. I'm not saying that was a strong indication of deception."

"Didn't you tell me and Mr. Moriarity at this very table when you were standing at this very spot yesterday—didn't the words 'strongly deceptive' come from your lips?"

"Those are strong indications of deception. That does not mean necessarily deception."

"If somebody brought a chart in to you like this and you never saw the subject, would you report that the subject's response to the question, 'Did you shoot a handgun during that incident?' to which the subject answered 'No,' as scoring strongly deceptive?"

"Yeah. It would score strongly deceptive."

After the test had been completed, she wasn't crying, and she hadn't cried during the test, Toliver said. She'd expressed surprise at her scores.

Then I asked, "When was it in the course of the test

that you came to the conclusion that you would tell somebody it was an invalid test?"

"I felt it was an invalid test during the pretest interview because of her emotional state." He said it with a little quick tilting of the head. She had been upset. Very upset.

"But you gave it anyway?" my voice rising.

"I gave it anyway, yes, sir."

I left him with a lingering stare of disbelief. "Did you make any note that you thought it was an invalid test?"

"I didn't write it down."

He admitted he'd previously refused to give tests when he thought emotional reasons rendered the subject unfit to be tested. "Isn't what you *did* better evidence of what your state of mind was than what you now *say* it was?"

He said no. Then I confronted him about keeping honest records. His voice got low.

"I do keep honest records."

"Well, the fact that you found the test to be invalid isn't recorded anywhere, is it?"

"In my mind, yes."

"Is that a *record*?"

"It is for me, yes, sir."

"Well, since it's in your mind, you can do anything you want with it, can't you?"

"I probably could, yes."

Judge Haas intervened into the sweaty, rhetorical wrestling. "The thing that concerns everybody, I think, is the failure of the records to contain your opinion that the test was not proper."

"Yes, sir."

"If for some reason you had become incapacitated or dead, Mrs. Gerttula would stand in the eyes of the prosecutor as having taken a lie detector test and failed, would she not?"

"That is a possibility, yes."

"And that would be incorrect, would it not?"

"That would be incorrect, yes."

I said to the judge, "You did it much better than I did." He tried not to smile.

Toliver admitted that he knew that, despite her results on the polygraph, the state was continuing to use her testimony. Yet he didn't think it was his duty to resolve the matter before Monica Gerttula's testimony was presented to unsuspecting jurors or a judge.

"You contend now that you shouldn't have given the test and that you knew that you shouldn't have given it to her before you did?" I asked.

"That is also true."

"You didn't leave room in your mind for the proposition that the state's principal eyewitness was triggering a response at minus-fourteen simply because, as your own charts showed you, she was lying?"

"That is a definite possibility, Mr. Spence, yes."

"Well, if that is a definite possibility and you knew it was a definite possibility, why didn't you take some steps to get that matter resolved?"

He was struggling. "Because it is not my responsibility to get those matters resolved."

He freely admitted that he'd told both Marquis and Stapleton that the charts showed deception, but he also claimed that he told them that the test was invalid because of her emotional state. He said he knew the woman had gunshot residue on her hands.

Dawson charged to the podium to cross-examine. He asked Toliver for his observations of the woman that caused him to conclude that the test was invalid.

"She was going to be used as a witness in court, which is an alien atmosphere to her. That was upsetting to her.

She felt threatened by Mr. Spence, that, you know, he is this world-renowned attorney. She had just been accused of probably murdering her husband. She was having a lot of problems at home in trying to keep her ranch in operation, and I felt that, you know, it was not a proper time for her to be taking a polygraph, and, in fact, I encouraged her several times to postpone it and that we would do it later."

Why had he given the test to her?

"I just gave in to the pressure. We were in the middle of a young boy's juvenile hearing. There was going to be an obvious impact on the outcome, you know, and if there was any substance to the allegations, then, you know, it was important that those be found out and found out immediately."

"But you couldn't find it out is your testimony," Dawson said.

"That's true."

"And you knew it?"

"Yes, sir, and, you know, it's something that shouldn't have been done."

Toliver was taking the fall for the prosecutors, perhaps his job on the line. Even if he thought Monica Gerttula was lying, what could he say if Marquis and Stapleton came into his office and started hollering at him?

"Why didn't you stop and tell Mr. Stapleton that she wasn't a fit subject for the test? There had to be a reason," the judge asked. He thought a moment. "There had to be a reason. You're a professional and you know this is a major case for this prosecutor's office."

"Yes, sir." But other than the pressure he felt, he could offer no reason for having given the test. "I knew it was a mistake at the time I did it."

"I'm just troubled," the judge said, "because you have

given a lot of polygraphs, and you can see the sequence of events are disturbing."

"Yes, sir."

"It comes down to the fact that the answer is a dangerous answer for the prosecution."

"Yes," Toliver said, looking up at the judge.

"And Mr. Stapleton's testimony that he didn't want anything written from you in order to prevent the defense from getting it raises suspicions."

"I agree."

Dawson tried to change the subject: "What was the reaction of Ulys Stapleton to the encroachment of a big-name attorney into the local case?"

Toliver didn't rightly know, he said.

"Well, is he the kind of person who is fairly easily agitated?"

"Yeah. He can be."

"Did he display any agitation as a result of the increase in power in the defense camp?"

"I think it probably bothered him."

"How about Marquis?" Dawson asked.

"Yeah, it probably bothered Marquis also."

"Was any of that in evidence at the time they requested you to do a polygraph?"

"Oh, yeah."

"Did that have anything to do with your willingness to give the test in the face of your contrary, professional judgment?"

"Oh, I'm sure it probably did. I wasn't thinking necessarily along those terms. I'm sure there is a lot of things that . . . sympathy for Mrs. Gerttula as much as anything."

"Can you describe the emotional state of Marquis and Stapleton at the time they requested you to run this polygraph, yes or no?"

"My impression of it was that . . . especially Mr. Marquis, was upset, speaking loudly, rapidly. Mr. Marquis was, you know, far more agitated than Mr. Stapleton was."

"And was he expressing what was agitating him?"

"Yes, that Mr. Spence had come up with this third-gun theory out of the clear blue."

When again it came my turn to examine, I said to Toliver, "Let me ask you a question you shouldn't have any difficulty answering." In a slightly menacing voice I asked, "Would *you* be willing to take a polygraph administered by an independent operator, the question: 'Did you think the test was invalid *at the time* you gave it to Mrs. Gerttula?'"

Dawson disintegrated into a massive explosion. "Your Honor! This is not a proper question!"

The judge remained calm. "I think to an average witness, I would sustain it, but this gentleman is a person who's an expert in the field. So I think I'll let him answer the question."

Dawson hadn't given up. He was swimming in a swivet and making jumbled arguments, but the judge wouldn't let loose of the issue. He said, "The problem I'm having here with the state's position is that the polygraph was the vehicle that the state chose, and it represented to the court that such a test was going to be performed. This was the operator selected to perform that test, and he now states that he did so even though he knew it would be invalid."

Dawson was still hollering, but his bulb was growing dimmer. "I know the court has—"

"Do you think what they did was right?" the judge asked.

"I don't think I would do it, okay?" Dawson said.

"Would you have made that information available to the defense?" the judge asked.

"Yes, I would have."

"That's the problem I'm having with it."

But Dawson was off and running again. "I understand where your nose is, Your Honor. But I guess our position is that, number one . . ." He liked to number his points, which gave him time to think what they were going to be.

The judge saved him with an interruption: "But I have before me the general proposition of prosecutorial misconduct, and it seems to me that anything in that area is relevant."

Finally Dawson got to it. "I'm not denying the relevancy. My objection is challenging a witness to take a polygraph."

Finally we all agreed we knew what Toliver's answer would be. Yes, he would be willing to take the polygraph. But all of us also knew that the court had no authority to order him to take it. To save us any further misery I said, "I withdraw the question."

I came back once more to Toliver's claim that Mrs. Gerttula was upset because this big-shot lawyer was going to question her. "Now you say that she was upset with me as a defense attorney. Isn't that consistent with her also being afraid that this so-called big-name attorney might discover and prove facts that would show that she had shot her husband?"

"That is a possibility, yes," Toliver said.

"You can't sort that out, can you?"

"No, I can't."

"And isn't it true that her being upset may have been the result of her having actually shot her husband, and you were going to question her about that?"

"That is also a possibility."

"This was the way you and Mr. Stapleton and Mr.

Marquis set this whole thing up: You knew that if she failed the test, you could always claim it was invalid, right?"

"No."

"Well, you could always claim it was invalid if you wanted to, couldn't you?"

"If I wanted to."

"If she passed it, you had the option of telling everybody she passed it. If she failed it, you would tell everybody it was invalid; at least that's the way it was set up in your hands, isn't that true?"

"No, that is not true."

I gave Toliver a moment to gather himself. Then I said, "You don't know whether it was an invalid test or not, isn't that true?"

Dawson was hollering again. "Your Honor, I move to strike. That is now interpreting his answer." His objection meant I was hitting pay dirt.

The judge said that was the kind of question he was coming down to himself. Then Toliver said, "I can't say one way or the other—even in good probability one way or the other—which is why the test, I believe, is invalid."

Resuming, I asked, "It is possible that Mrs. Gerttula was not upset about any of the things she told you and really was upset that you were going to ask her the question 'Did you shoot a handgun during this incident?'"

"Yes, sir, that is a possibility."

Then referring to Marquis and Stapleton, I asked, "Do these people generally attempt to secrete the results of their tests?"

"No, sir."

"Pardon?" I wanted the judge to be sure to get the answer. The judge looked up from the note he was writing.

"Have you known any other circumstances in which these prosecutors told you not to make a report?"

"I'm not aware of any."

Then I asked, "You have noticed the emotional involvement of Mr. Marquis as sort of excitable, is that right?"

"Yes, sir."

"Would you say that Mr. Stapleton is, too?"

"Not nearly so much as Mr. Marquis."

"Do you think Mr. Marquis was distressed about my involvement in the case?"

"Oh, I'm sure it probably created some distress for him."

"Did he express any to you?"

"Not specifically. It was my impression—and again, I can't pin it down to specific things—but it was my impression that, yeah, there was probably some concern about your being involved in the case, certainly."

"Have you observed the emotional involvement of Mr. Dawson and Mr. Brown?"

"Yes, I have."

"Do you find any distress about my being involved in this case from Mr. Dawson?"

"I'm sure Mr. Dawson could probably think of an attorney he'd rather be trying the case against."

"Do you recognize that Mr. Brown doesn't generally show any kind of emotion about anything?"

"I don't know Mr. Brown that well at all."

"Well, there are people like that, aren't there?"

"Certainly."

"And there are people who are like that who, when they want to, can show emotional concern, isn't that true?"

"I suppose so, yes."

"That's why we have a polygraph, isn't it, to sort that all

out and find who is covering it up and who isn't. Isn't that what a polygraph ultimately is all about?"

"Yes, sir."

After that, the DA's polygraph operator, hearing the blessed words "I have no further questions," bundled himself up and escaped for good from that torturous chair called the witness stand, which, over the centuries, has proven to be the best lie detector of all.

24
___

Every morning began with Sandy. Where was she? Would she make it to court on time? She was staying with her mother in the house her mother had put up for Sandy's bail. If one day she decided not to show up for court, we could lose it all. She bore an altogether antagonistic view of the system and saw the law as a hodgepodge of contradictions and hypocrisies. Couldn't blame her. She thought the law should be just and suffered from the impertinent idea that the people working in it should be honest. Yes, I thought, we strap murderers in the gas chamber for their crimes, but when the state fails to deliver justice and the innocent suffer or die, we shrug our shoulders and say that the system isn't perfect.

Michele was having a time with Sandy. On occasion Sandy wanted to stand up and holler that this was all so much bullshit, as well as the law and the lawyers, and that she wasn't going to wallow in it anymore. I knew how she felt. Yet, so far, Michele had been successful in keeping her fairly reasonable. But how long would it last?

Often she'd arrive in court within the barest of margins, as if she'd decided not to show up and at the last minute had changed her mind. It drove me bananas.

"Gerry," Michele would remind me, "it's amazing she even gets here. She's broke. Nobody in the family can work while this is going on. The two grandmas are supporting the family. She's worried sick about her two kids. If their car starts in the morning, for God's sake, they're having a good day."

Michele was right. But we lawyers were held to a different standard. We gave ourselves half an hour's leeway. One thing a lawyer can never be, and that's late to court. We couldn't start without Sandy—her constitutional right to be present—and she gave us no slack. Up until this moment, Judge Haas had looked upon Sandy with a certain goodwill that might be lost with the first hint of disrespect on her part—tardiness.

Still, every morning she was there. Every time she walked into the courtroom, I thought it was a miracle. I'd told her the day before she was causing me undue stress. Wouldn't she please let me breathe a little easier and get to court a trifle earlier? And she did. Three minutes before court took up, rather than the usual one. I was grateful.

I walked into the judge's chambers with Sandy, Eddie, and Michele. I wasn't going to let His Honor forget his decision yet unmade: Did Brown, as I had demanded, have to take the witness stand? Brown, of course, was the lawyer the judge had brought into the affray, one whose ethics and skills were expected to be beyond reproach. But had Brown got early notice from Stapleton about the Peck investigation? Had he also known the results of Monica Gerttula's polygraph and kept them from us with the same apparent insolence as the DA's office?

In chambers, Brown was his usual distant, abstract self. He wasn't certain about anything. He claimed his records didn't help much. He thought that he'd learned of the Peck investigation on the fifteenth or sixteenth, the trial beginning on the nineteenth.

The judge was like a patient priest listening to the confessions of an amnesiac. Still Brown couldn't remember having ever been told about a polygraph, or at least, if he was told, he said, "It didn't ring a bell."

The judge pressed him, but Brown was still uncertain. He gave the judge a painful grin, and then the judge turned to Dawson. "If I'm not wrong, I remember that Mr. Dawson said he never heard of Mrs. Gerttula's polygraph."

"That's what I said," Dawson said. "I never heard of it."

Finally Brown said with all due caution, "My best recollection or impression is that there was nothing of significance relating to polygraphs that was conveyed to me in my conference with the district attorneys."

The judge said it in plain English: "Like Mrs. Gerttula failed it?"

"Yes—absolutely not. If she'd failed the polygraph, I would have been all over that."

Then Judge Haas said, "Given their history of secreting information, I accept those representations made by Mr. Brown. I think it would be consistent with the way the DA handled this case. It seems pretty clear to me that there was a conscious effort both by Stapleton and by Marquis to keep that information from the defense. I feel the record is clear that they were evasive, and in a very affirmative way." But I didn't want the judge's blessing bestowed on Brown and Dawson, leaving Stapleton and Marquis the fall guys.

I said, "Mr. Special Prosecutor, here, now occupies the same position that Mr. Stapleton and Mr. Marquis occupied." What was Brown going to do to resolve those polygraph charts that revealed his principal witness was not only "deceptive," but "very deceptive"? Was Brown going to pull a Toliver, rise up, and also boldly declare that the test was invalid?

But the judge was still seething over Stapleton and Marquis. Haas had been a prosecutor himself. "I mean, they deliberately, intentionally, and have affirmed under oath that they did not want to reveal it and did not reveal it.... Whether or not the defense has to ask for it—it's just supposed to be given. I think you all ought to know where I'm coming from on that."

"Mr. Brown has got a problem," I said again. "Every time he reaches out to deal with that problem, he gets his hands dirty. Every time Mr. Brown reaches out to embrace this thing, it raises serious questions as to what his own involvement in it is."

I tried to see it from Brown's point of view. Maybe he felt trapped. Still, I said, "He makes those wishy-washy representations on the record. He says, 'I kind of hear this,' or 'I have a vague recollection of this or that.' I think we can get to the bottom of this from his telephone records."

The judge didn't want to go there. He had no intention of smearing Brown with the DA's dirt. "I'm satisfied that the conduct of the prosecution as it relates to nondisclosure was wrong," Haas said, as if that should settle it.

But why stop when you have the judge that near the edge? I kept pushing. I told him Brown's nondisclosures left us with no starting point of truth. "I can't rely on him"—I nodded toward Brown—"because he has to defend a stinkpot, and when he does, I can't separate him from the stinkpot. I can't rely on the officers to provide a truthful starting point in the case, I can't rely on their principal eyewitness," who, of course, was Monica Gerttula. I told the judge I didn't like to say what I was saying about Brown, "but Mr. Brown is going to get sullied in this. I'm telling you that right now."

I thought the judge was near the brink. He was wearied of the endless arguments. Every time an issue popped up, it was immediately tied to this "stinkpot" that Brown had inherited, but around which he had also chosen to enfold his prosecutorial arms. I thought that if the judge was finally convinced I was going after Brown, the man he had dragged into this mess, he might dismiss this miserable case if for no better reason than to save any further damage to Brown, who, himself, seemed helpless to rise to the occasion. Moreover, we were also proving that Peck was an indispensable witness, and because he'd taken the Fifth, we'd been deprived of important constitutional rights.

I said, "Mr. Brown can't save himself. He can't throw in the towel. He can't walk up to you and say, 'Your Honor, this is such a deplorable, unspeakable mess that nobody can move in it. I want out of this case.' He can't do that and fulfill his obligation to the court or fulfill his obligation to his own pride of self." Brown was looking at his hands.

There's a point in every trial that defines the case. It's true of every relationship, of every partnership, every marriage, every battle in the battlefield. The point is often reached through struggle and pain. And at that certain point the case takes on a life of its own. And nothing after that will change it.

We'd reached that point. I opened the door for Brown like a bowing butler: "I'll *bet you money* that if Mr. Brown could frankly and candidly lay out his heart and soul to us, he'd say something like this: 'My God, what kind of a mess have I gotten into that I didn't know about? I might not have accepted this case had I known about all of this garbage in the background.'"

Brown turned to me and offered one of his pale smiles. "I didn't hear counsel mention *how much money* he was going to bet, Your Honor."

I saw the judge's face darken. The smile left. He looked down at his notebook to gather up his composure. Then he said, "Let's get on with the evidence. Let's do it." From that moment on I knew that unless His Honor intervened, we would have to fight Brown to the grueling, bloody, take-no-prisoners end.

I felt saddened and discouraged. How easily Brown could have expunged himself of all responsibility for Monica Gerttula's polygraph and for Peck's having taken the Fifth. With reluctant kindness I'd escorted him to the place where everyone could have been exonerated, where, if he retained any compassion for this kindly judge, he could have saved him from the hard decisions he must surely make and where, from even a small store of compassion, he could have saved Sandy Jones and her family. And he could have saved himself. We make our choices. But sometimes they are made for us.

I called Steve Lovejoy to the stand. We had to make a record showing how Peck's refusal to testify destroyed our defense, and that took an expert in criminal law. It's the record that speaks to the appellate court, the dead, flat, black-and-white record. Our expert was that tall, boy-faced guy, this ace lawyer from Lincoln County, Oregon, Steve Lovejoy.

Steve told the judge what the judge already knew—that Peck's absence was a constitutional catastrophe for Sandy Jones. Peck knew everything. After Peck's hand was allegedly found in the cocaine cookie jar, we should be able to cross-examine him, days of it, weeks if necessary, to show that the whole case was contaminated. Reasonable doubt was the issue, Steve said. Was Peck under the influence of drugs when he did the investigation? Did he steal the missing gun?

Then in meticulous, painful detail Steve outlined how the engineer he'd hired in Little Mike's case, a fellow named Ginther, was able to show that Little Mike would have had to have been standing on a twenty-foot ladder, or higher, for any bullet from his rifle to go through Gerttula's chest at the angle established by the autopsy. If, to accommodate the path of the bullet, Gerttula had been bent over when he took the fatal shot, he would have been *below* the hood of the pickup—a physical impossibility because the hood would have blocked the shot. Besides that, we'd heard it many times—all the shots were accounted for. And Peck's testimony was the foundation for Ginther's calculations.

Then remembering Toliver's claim that the polygraph ought not to be administered to a subject when he's emotionally frayed, Steve told how once Stapleton, himself, had demanded that one of Steve's clients take the poly when the client was so emotionally torn he had to be on lithium, had been hospitalized, and was, in short, a pitiful emotional mess suffering from "hysterical amnesia." Nevertheless, after he'd taken the test, Steve's client was declared a liar by Stapleton because the charts showed the man was deceptive!

Brown didn't offer much of a cross-examination. I thought he must have something up his sleeve. I was soon to find out. Before the evening recess he called a witness who claimed he owned the third pistol, the .380, that had been in the possession of Raymond Gerttula. The pistol had been stolen from the witness and returned to him by the Portland police. I asked him to bring the pistol into court, and he said he would. As the witness stepped down from the stand, Brown gave me an I-told-you-so look. He knew and we knew we were running out of missing guns. Then we recessed.

But all kinds of hell broke loose on Monday morning.

25

We'd spent the weekend locked in the law library searching for the law that would prompt Judge Haas to rise up and shout, "Aha! There *is* precedent!" Oh, how judges love precedent! If only some decision lurked in the catacombs of the law that would nourish Judge Haas's resolve to dismiss this case.

Hadn't the state misled both the judge and us? Hadn't the state taken the Fifth? In the name of Christ, wasn't that enough? If citizens lie, they get prosecuted for perjury. If some poor wretch charged with murder lies, they'll hang him by his scrawny neck. There are more men languishing on death row not for the murders they may have committed, but for having lied about them. Jurors detest liars. But when the state steps over the edge, well, it is only "in search of the truth" as it strolls with all rectitude down the imperious road to justice—as in some prosecutors' perennial argument "What's a little 'loose usage of the language' compared to murder?"

I liked libraries, even law libraries, although I've often observed that you could read every one of the hundred thousand volumes in the law library and learn approximately nothing. You learn how judges think, which often isn't very illuminating. You learn how they talk, which is often as dreary. You learn how they rationalize and avoid the clear intent of the law, the result of which is often disgusting. You learn how they write, which often is in dull, lifeless idioms of the law.

Yet I liked to search the books. Like fishing. You never knew what book might harbor some big lunker of a decision that's been lying under a big judicial rock, one that could save your case. I fished all weekend in the library with Michele and Eddie without hooking a case worth mentioning. But in a legal system umbilically attached to precedent, to the stale and musty past, someone had to be first to dismiss a case on the grounds we had produced. I wanted Judge Haas to be that judge.

The owner of the .380 semiautomatic pistol bearing serial 902098, as he'd promised the week before, came hauling that itinerant firearm into court for all to see, and satisfied it was the third gun, so that none of Raymond Gerttula's weapons remained unaccounted for, we adjourned to the judge's chambers for what the judge euphemistically called "another little get-together."

Even though Haas found that Stapleton and Marquis had misconducted themselves concerning the results of Monica Gerttula's polygraph, he said he was going to deny our motion to dismiss on that ground. He kept mumbling that the results of the polygraph were inadmissible. But he said that didn't save the state's case. The Peck issue was still bothering him. "They're all kinda rolled into one," he said. "It's the law in the gut. What I'm asked to do in this case is to deny the state a trial. It's the enormity of that versus the conduct of the prosecutors."

Then he turned to me. What new goodies were we going to file this morning that would plague him the rest of the day? He laughed. But before I could answer, he began thinking out loud again. Serious constitutional questions were raised, he said—the right to confront the witness and compulsory process. We couldn't subpoena Peck to testify because he'd take the Fifth. That denied us a fair trial. He continued to grouse over the polygraph. It bothered him like a boil on the judicial backside. "They deliberately and intentionally withheld it. It changes the color of the case," he kept saying. "What is a trial? Boy, it's a piece of humanity out there. Give me some law!" But we had no law.

Then suddenly it came like one hears the rattles in the grass and knows it's a snake. Dawson, as if presenting an introduction to a confession, his head jutted forward, began by saying Stapleton had suggested that Judge Gardner knew Monica Gerttula's polygraph had been inconclusive. What? That Gardner *knew* her poly was *inconclusive?*

I jumped up. "That isn't true." I'd heard Stapleton's testimony like everyone else.

Then Dawson came out with it: "I think you ought to know that I'm having Judge Gardner interviewed today."

I couldn't believe what I was hearing. The arrogance! How could these prosecutors, out of our presence—*ex parte* as the law calls it—talk to Judge Gardner? Lawyers do not talk to judges about cases, especially pending cases, without the other side being present. And Little Mike's case was still pending. He hadn't been sentenced yet. Lawyers can get their gonads in the ethical grinder if they do that. So can a judge.

I was suddenly yelling. "If you're messing around with my judge down there, we're going to have more trouble, and I mean lots of trouble! I'll have him before this court, and I'll cross-examine that man in every conceivable way on every issue in this case!"

"Gentlemen!" Judge Haas was trying to fan the smoke out of the room.

"I'm sorry," I said, trying to tone it down. "I can't stand here in these chambers and hear Dawson tell me he's having Judge Gardner interviewed when that judge hasn't sentenced Little Mike and hasn't yet heard the evidence grown out of this trial that we're going to present to get Little Mike a new trial." Based on what we'd learned from Toliver and Marquis, we intended to file that motion as soon as we were done with Sandy's case.

I was pacing the floor. "I've stayed as far away from that judge as possible. It's not proper for me to even talk to him on the telephone or to communicate with him in any fashion. For the state to now talk to him is inconceivable. I can't believe it!"

I turned to Dawson. "I'm asking you to stop that. I'm asking you to pull your investigators off of him. I demand it!"

Haas was speechless.

Now Steve joined in. He didn't want anything done that would in the slightest way aggravate the situation with Judge Gardner. And if I had to cross-examine Gardner—which under ordinary circumstances I would have loved to do—where would that leave us with Gardner when it came to sentencing Little Mike?

I asked Dawson if Gardner had been contacted yet.

"I don't know." I looked at Dawson. Something made me not believe the man.

"Sometimes I wish we didn't have these meetings," the judge lamented.

Then I asked His Honor to find out whether Gardner had been contacted. I established the time in the record. *It was 10:19 A.M.*

I asked the judge to tell Gardner that if he made *any* statement I'd consider it judicial misconduct. Then I thought better of it: "If I begin to make accusations against Judge Gardner, I'm hurting that boy." I was trapped. I threw up my arms. I was seeing white. "I'd be in jail right now if I walked up to Judge Gardner and began to talk *ex parte* to him about the facts in that case. That's what the state is doing."

Brown was curiously silent about this peculiar effort.

Then Dawson gratuitously pushed my conflict-of-interest button again. With the same smirk frozen on his face he said, "I guess that is one of the problems, Your Honor, when you undertake to represent two defendants."

I whirled to face him. "No, Mr. Dawson, it's one of the problems when the state doesn't recognize its responsibility!"

"Don't you lecture me, Spence." Dawson was safe where he sat. I wanted him to get up. Eddie was on his feet.

The judge: "Gentlemen! Gentlemen! Both of you! No more of that!"

Sandy's and Michele's heads were swiveling from me to Dawson as if they were watching a tennis match. When things quieted down, Haas suggested that Steve Lovejoy contact Gardner.

"No," I said. "Steve has no more right to talk to that judge than anybody else."

"There's no ethical reason Judge Gardner can't testify to that conversation," Dawson said.

Finally it began to dawn on me what Dawson might be up to. Perhaps he was looking for someone to contradict Marquis when Marquis, himself, had admitted he'd agreed to dismiss the case if Monica Gerttula was lying. Judge Gardner had been a party to that conversation.

I asked His Honor to contact the chief judge, the one who reigns supreme over all of the trial judges in the state. Have him call Gardner. "This is putting a noose around my boy's neck. The court has to order the state to call off its investigators and Judge Gardner has to be advised as to our position. The chief judge is the one to do it."

"I agree with that and understand that," the judge said benignly.

"My boy's very life is at stake." Send that kid off to MacLaren until he was twenty-one and we'd have killed the innocent kid and replaced him with the hardened criminal. "Would you *please* tell the chief judge what's happened?"

The judge turned to Dawson. "Do you have an objection to that?"

"You can tell anybody you choose what's happened, Your Honor. You're a free agent and not under our control. If you want to talk to the chief judge, that's your business." Sandy and Michele looked at each other in shock.

I tried to contain myself. I said to Dawson. "Let's take it one step at a time. Would you agree to call off your investigators until this matter is resolved?"

"No."

Now suddenly I knew. *His investigator had already talked to Gardner!* "Will you agree to determine whether or not your investigators have talked to Judge Gardner?"

"I'm not going to agree with you on that."

Now I knew for sure. The damage had already been done. The interview had already occurred.

I said, "Then there's nothing else that can be done." I sat down.

A vicious silence set in. Finally I turned again to Dawson. I said quietly, "Mr. Dawson, I put you on notice as a member of the bar, bound by your office, that you have the obligation to see that Judge Gardner is called immediately by proper, independent authority. Someone like the chief judge. I hold you responsible for that, and if you don't, you're going to answer for it."

Dawson said with a nasty, condescending tone, "Let me see. Let me inquire. You're alleging that I am deliberately interfering in the disposition of the Michael Jones Jr. case?"

I was on my feet again. "I absolutely put you on notice of that. You have knowledge of it, and you're an officer of this court." I looked over at the judge, who saw how this was playing out.

"I choose not to become a witness in the Michael Jones case by calling Judge Gardner," the judge said. By then it was eleven in the morning and the judge adjourned the proceeding, hoping things might simmer down during a long noon recess.

We stomped into the judge's chambers after lunch. The first thing I noticed were a couple of reporters sitting there with their wide-lined, white notebooks clutched in eager hands. I ignored them and jumped into the fray again.

"I'd like to know from Mr. Dawson what information he has to report relative to the contact that was made with Judge Gardner."

"I don't have anything to *report*, Your Honor." Then Dawson said, "If counsel is inquiring as to the results of any investigation we're conducting, we would be happy to report what we found out so far."

"I want to know what happened," I said.

"He contacted Judge Gardner," Dawson said.

"*Who* contacted Judge Gardner?"

Dawson ignored the question. "Judge Gardner remembers general conversations involving the polygraph, but no specific recall." Of course, the memory disease that had plagued this case from the beginning.

"I want to know *who* contacted Judge Gardner. I'm entitled to know, Your Honor."

Dawson finessed my statement by referring to "my attitude and manner of expression," his way of calling the court's attention to the fact that I was outraged to the core. Then he said, "Our investigator, Gary Stafford, contacted Judge Gardner, and the interview was conducted by telephone." This guy Stafford was the one I'd accidentally bumped into. Spilled his coffee. Burned him, he said. What goes around comes around. Now he was burning me.

"I'd like to know when the contact was made by Officer Stafford."

"This morning," Dawson said. "I can't tell you the time, but it was between the time we broke this morning and noon sometime." I doubted that. To my way of thinking Stafford had already questioned Gardner by the time Dawson first brought it up. And I thought Dawson knew it.

"And was the conversation between Stafford and the judge recorded?" I asked.

"Yes." *Yes?*

"Did Judge Gardner know that?" I asked, astounded.

"No."

"What!" A long silence in the room.

"It was a telephone conversation," Dawson said.

"It was recorded without the judge's knowledge?" I asked again.

I looked at Michele. Her mouth opened to say something but no words obliged.

"That's correct," Dawson said as if secretly recording a judge were an everyday occurrence.

Another thick silence in the chambers. They had the consummate gall to record a judge without his knowledge? What were their limits?

Finally I said, "I'd like Your Honor to order a copy of the recording."

Bereft of belief the judge said, "Why didn't you tell him he was recorded?"

"I don't know," Dawson said. Then, with a shrug of his shoulders as if there were no earthly reason to amplify his answer, he said, "That isn't in violation of the law."

"I know that," the judge said, shaking his head in disbelief.

"I tell you if I did that, they'd throw me in jail," I said.

The judge, still shaking his head, a deep frown on his forehead, asked, "Don't your investigators routinely tell witnesses when they call them that they're being recorded?"

"Many times when they do a report, they do this to be accurate."

"What am I to judge from that?" Haas asked. "Do you think if you told Judge Gardner he was being recorded, he wouldn't be accurate?"

There was that ominous, heavy silence again. You could hear the breathing. Then the judge said, "No, Doug," still shaking his head and referring to Dawson as if he were his misbehaving son, "I'm just surprised that the judge wasn't advised he was being recorded, and I'm a little concerned about the reason you give for your investigators not advising people when they're being recorded. I don't like this. But I'm being candid." He wasn't smiling.

"Our investigators comply with the Oregon statutes," Dawson said.

"Every time I pick up a phone and talk to an assistant attorney general, should I presume I'm being taped?" the judge asked.

"I don't think so" was all Dawson said, as if he wasn't required to say more.

I felt powerless. No matter how much we learned of the state's misconduct, no matter how much we spread it on the record, the special prosecutors sat there as surly and untouchable as executioners. The state's long-nosed insolence was frightening. The judge, looking bleak and crestfallen, seemed paralyzed. Eddie just shook his head in silence. Michele was staring in disbelief at Dawson.

Suddenly Dawson was on the attack again, this time against the judge. "First of all, I think you should have stated that you invited the press in chambers."

The judge bristled, "I never invited the press in chambers." He hadn't disinvited them either. They'd been sitting there all the time, their eyes as wide as surprised children's.

Then Dawson started at us again. "I object, Your Honor, to the defense's attempt to interfere with our ability to procure witnesses and evidence in this case. I strongly object."

Sandy whispered to Michele, "Now what's he saying?" Sandy knew what threats sounded like.

"It's another threat," Michele said. "If a lawyer tries to keep witnesses from the state, it's called obstruction of justice. They put you in the pen for that."

"Why do you object?" the judge asked, baffled at Dawson's latest volley.

"They've attempted to get Your Honor to order us not to interview witnesses."

"Doug," the judge said, about to collapse, "I can't stop motions."

"I just want to make a record."

I made my own record: "I'm being intimidated by Mr. Dawson. Mr. Dawson's clear indication is that I'm violating the law in some fashion, suggesting a criminal law, and I want the record to understand that we charge Mr. Dawson with unethical conduct, and my motion will reveal that in the morning."

Brown was on the edge of a whimper. "We feel like a defendant sometimes, Your Honor."

A deputy motioned Michele to the door and handed her a paper. She opened it. "Jesus Christ," she muttered. Remembering where she was, she looked up. "Your Honor, I've just been served with a subpoena by Mr. Stapleton to testify in one of my cases in Lincoln County—not the Jones case. It's about one of my clients' failure to appear."

Stapleton knew she didn't have to testify. She'd refused to do so in the past, and Judge McMullen in Lincoln County had ruled in her favor. It was another of Stapleton's harassing moves, she said. Judge Haas shook his head again. Continuing to shake his head, he finally said that if a conflict arose between the subpoena and our trial date, he'd quash the subpoena. He wasn't going to get into anybody else's case but his own.

26

In the heavy, gray hours of dawn we'd prepared another motion to dismiss. By now the sides had been reversed—we'd become the prosecutors, the accusers charging the state with a litany of misdeeds. I thought we were winning. Our motion ended with the claim that the secret taping of Judge Gardner was the last straw. It left us exhausted and our resources depleted. How many low blows should the referee call before he declared the bout forfeited? The court had to stop this. The only way was by a dismissal.

One thing I was pretty sure of: something was wrong with the Gardner tape. We'd listened to our copy. It sounded like foreign matter had been dubbed-in over a part of Gardner's interview. In court that morning I called it the "Rose Mary Woods syndrome," calling to mind Nixon's secretary and their infamous doctored recording. I asked the judge for his order requiring Dawson to produce the original, and with a sad smile of forbearance the judge ordered the same placed in evidence.

Once again His Honor invited us to visit the furtive recesses of the judicial mind. He said he thought that the prosecution hadn't intentionally delayed indicting Peck to frustrate our case. But there was "the Gardner situation," as he called it, where law enforcement had dared to secretly tape-record a judge. Still, over and over he returned to the issue of the polygraph. He couldn't put it to rest. He looked first at Dawson and then at Brown, the sadness in his eyes. I thought he was deeply conflicted, that he suspected something was terribly amiss but recoiled at the idea of dismissing the charges against Sandy. Still, he had a duty. But how far should he go in protecting one small woman's rights to a fair trial to the injury of these honorable men of the bar, and perhaps a frustration of justice?

He began to talk aloud again. He said he thought that prosecutors should perform their job with vigor and that they should try their cases steadfastly, but the question was whether their zeal had overridden their responsibility to see that the accused received a fair trial. How much misconduct was enough to warrant dismissal? He didn't know. "It's when you reach a certain level," he said. He couldn't define it better.

He openly fretted about what the cops had done to Mike Jones Sr. when they threw him to the ground, drew their guns, roughed him up, and dumped him in jail for a mere suspended license. But before the judge could talk about the state having invaded the confidences we'd entrusted to our expert, Dr. DiMaio, Dawson jumped in, announcing they'd decided not to call DiMaio. That made that issue moot. They'd probably found another expert as good.

The judge continued to think aloud, looking for explanations, hoping for resolution. Why had Stapleton called John Amish's superior if it wasn't to intimidate this gunshot-residue expert? Dawson argued we had to show that the alleged intimidation, in fact, caused Amish to change his testimony to our detriment. Weren't we operating under two sets of rules? When I fumed about Dawson having Gardner interviewed, he suggested I was obstructing justice. But when the DA attempted to put the twist on Amish, well, that was perfectly all right?

Now Brown, his sarcasm seeping to the surface, referred to our latest motion, in which I'd stated we were nearly exhausted. "I would inquire whether or not they need a break in order for the defendant to have effective assistance of counsel."

That did it. I jumped up again, the fuse frayed and short. "What we're saying, Your Honor, is that finally, emotionally, you get to the bottom! Every day it gets worse. Every day the infection spreads. No matter what we do we can't stop it. We've been at this for three solid weeks dealing with the misconduct of the prosecution. It never stops.

"There's such a background of arrogance in this case!" I said. "There isn't an attorney within the sound of my voice"—a number of lawyers were seated in the courtroom to hear our arguments—"who feels secure and safe against that kind of ill treatment. It *is* exhausting. If I have to awaken in the middle of the night wondering whether Mr. Dawson is proceeding with some kind of criminal action against me, then I have to tell you that my client *has* been deprived of the effective assistance of counsel." I was on a roll again. "It seems there's nothing Your Honor can do. Nothing *we* can do. And if we can't be protected by Your Honor, if we can't be protected by an honorable prosecutor, if we can't have the protection of the attorney general's office to uphold the laws of this state, then where are we? And yes, I am entitled to say to Mr. Brown, 'We *are* exhausted.'" Everyone was exhausted, especially the judge. I sat down and waited.

The judge tapped his pencil against his notepad.

Brown changed the subject. He wanted to discuss the witnesses he was going to call in opposition to our motion: Fox, the polygraph examiner who'd tested Steve Lovejoy's client; Amish, the gunshot-residue expert; Geistwhite about how Mike Jones Sr. was stopped; Monica Gerttula; Detectives Groat and Longley—all to show that we hadn't been prejudiced. I said the state was intentionally prolonging the hearing. I offered to stipulate to what some of the witnesses would testify, including that the detectives, when they'd been with Peck, didn't believe he was under the influence of either drugs or alcohol. But Brown insisted on going forward with his witnesses. It would take another three weeks. I thought he was trying to wear us down, all right. And how must Sandy feel? Each day I saw Michele react with amazement at the depths to which the state would stoop to get a conviction. But not Sandy. It was the sort of treatment she'd experienced her whole life.

The judge just shook his head some more and told Brown to call his witnesses. True to his promise, Brown put Dennis Fox from the Oregon State Police on the stand to contradict Steve Lovejoy's testimony that Stapleton had previously wrung out subjects with the polygraph, witnesses who were mentally and emotionally distressed. According to Fox, Steve's client, an undertaker named Omsberg, was "very personal, very pleasant and calm." Fox admitted he knew that Omsberg was on a number of drugs, including Thorazine, but even so he thought the man was a candidate for the polygraph. He showed no evidence of tiring and "remained very good throughout."

But on cross-examination I asked Fox, "Before Mr. Omsberg started the test, you knew that he had a very serious mental condition, didn't you?" Fox bristled. I pressed him. Fox's chart showed that Omsberg had breathing problems and high blood pressure. Fox admitted that in sufficient quantities some of the drugs could make a subject unfit for the polygraph. He also admitted that he'd made no inquiry as to how these drugs were affecting Omsberg. Nevertheless, he subjected him to four full tests.

Fox further admitted on my cross-examination that he wrote a report. It was good practice. He said, "If a person is not suitable for a test and that's determined during examination, then a report is written explaining why the procedure was terminated—by standard procedure."

Then the crux question: "If you discover that a subject wasn't fit for a test, would you proceed to give the test anyway?"

"No, I wouldn't." I let the answer hang. I should have called the man as our witness.

After Fox left the stand, I walked up to the bench. The judge gave me a benign smile, but it faded immediately when he heard me say, "Your Honor, I have in hand a subpoena for the Honorable Robert S. Gardner for his appearance tomorrow as a witness in this case." I wanted someone to advise Gardner of the subpoena so that he wouldn't have it dumped on him cold by some process server. We would accept his assurance that he'd appear. Judge Haas didn't want to call Gardner. He thought he'd ask the chief judge to do it, which was all right with me.

In the meantime we'd contacted an expert to determine whether the Gardner tape had been tampered with. The expert said he needed Stafford's recording equipment used in making the recording. I asked Brown to produce it. Brown, growing more sullen, said he was willing to produce the recorder, but he argued that our next move would be our claim that the tape-recording expert wouldn't be able to come up with a conclusion for a couple of weeks, and that the trial would be delayed. Just a few hours before it had been Brown who wanted to delay the trial to give us time to rest after we spoke of our exhaustion.

Judge Haas remained his usual calm self. He gestured

vaguely in the direction of Brown and Dawson. "Bring the machine tomorrow," he said, "and we'll go right on down the road. I may or may not find the results important to my decision."

But something was profoundly troubling to Brown and Dawson about producing the tape recorder. Dawson insisted that I file an affidavit swearing to any allegations against them. After that he threatened to withdraw from the case because he might have to be a witness. A witness to what? I wondered. If he withdrew, the state would require a continuance, he said, because he and Brown had split up the work. All of this over a tape recorder?

The judge, laboring to bring reason to the forefront, said he thought these concerns were premature. "All we're talking about is supplying a machine so the testing can be done." There was no question, the judge said, that the tape revealed Judge Gardner's voice was picked up on the recording *after* he was already into the interview. Already I could smell the blood.

Brown could, too. He said, "I don't like to say this, but the conduct of our opposition has been very aggressive." He gave the judge a solicitous smile. It had been obvious for days that the man saw me as some kind of wild man out of the old West. It was likewise obvious that he felt vulnerable. Did Brown also suspect something was wrong with the tape? He went on with his complaint against me. "There's been a willingness to say things that aren't usually said in the spirit of lawyers in this state. I realize counsel is from another jurisdiction. We have been asked to turn over something that counsel says may be evidence of a crime. I think, given the gravity of the allegation, that we ought to ask the court to consider some mechanism for observation that would protect and guarantee fairness."

"We would prefer that," I said.

Brown wanted the State Crime Laboratory to do the testing. Judge Haas said, "Let's produce the machine. Let's think about this overnight."

Now Brown threw out still another argument: Dawson was from the Attorney General's Office, an office independent of Brown. It was the AG's equipment. Maybe, Brown offered, the attorney general might have some legal concerns about delivering this equipment into court, to which the judge, still avuncular and still speaking softly, said, "Bring the machine." Then the judge asked that in the morning they also have Detective Stafford in court.

Brown, growing petulant, said, "I've got to confess, Your Honor"—he was clutching both hands as if they were about to fly from their wrists—"we get awful tired of having our people moved around for Mr. Spence." But the judge wanted to hear Stafford's explanation for the tape gap in the Gardner interview. To use the judge's words, "there was a lapse in it," and he looked at Dawson in a friendly way so as not to sound accusing.

Suddenly Dawson lurched forward in an instinctive bid for survival and, pushing the judge, said he'd not made up his mind yet whether he'd withdraw. Haas looked at the man for a moment before he spoke. Then he said quietly, "I don't know if I'm right, but my present position is that it would be *my* decision whether or not you'd be allowed to withdraw." With that the judge recessed the court for the day and hurried from the bench like a man escaping from a gallery of screams.

27

Our energy reservoir, like a water well drained dry in a hostile desert, seemed to replenish itself during the night. One day at a time. If only we had the staying power, I thought, we'd find a way to win. On our motions to dismiss, the judge was our jury. As with a jury, we had to be careful not to push him so steadily to the brink that he'd suddenly throw up his hands, overrule all our motions, kick us out of chambers, and set the case for immediate trial. I watched him as I wrestled with the special prosecutors and the witnesses. He was exhausted, his patience fraying. I could hear it in his tired voice, its breaking sometimes, the hesitant comments interrupted with short stretches of silence. We were at a crucial point.

The judge had given us all the room we needed to make our case, which was unusual for judges in a criminal case, but we had to get this damnable hearing over with. I thought if the judge could decide our motions right then, he'd rule in our favor. He had the courage. He'd shown that when he threw Stapleton and Marquis off the case. Still he wanted to protect Brown and Dawson. Especially Brown, I thought. But Dawson was making it hard for the judge with his often belligerent confrontations, his threats and obscure arguments. Dawson played the role of the bad guy and Brown the good. I doubted it was an intentional strategy. The underlying personalities of the lawyers were beginning to show as they always do in long trials. The judge had revealed his patient core as well. Whom did this judge trust? Which side stood for justice? This dynamic in the courtroom would, more than anything else, dictate the judge's decision. But Haas was an old warrior himself, and if we pushed him too hard, the well-contained combatant within could rise up and devour us for supper. Overnight, Brown must have realized that as well.

In the morning Brown was apologetic. He smiled a certain mirthless smile and, in reference to the prior evening's fracas, said that he had a couple of kids at home, and that the time between five and six in the evening was referred to as "the arsenic hour." For me, Brown's metaphors were like the cartoons in *The New Yorker*. I often didn't get them. Then he finally came to his point. "If any of my remarks last night were perceived as harsh, I apologize to the court and counsel." Dawson scowled in silence.

I said, "I think people who are committed should feel free to express themselves as we have. It's healthy." And the judge, hoping to capitalize on this peace initiative, smiled his small, sad smile and said, "This is a tough case, and it's hard on everybody."

Then gently I handed the judge our latest: we'd located the expert who'd examined the "Rose Mary Woods–Nixon tape," a Dr. Michael Hecker. He'd come to Oregon that very week and he'd examine the Gardner tape. But that was the only week he was free to do the work. He had to know by noon if we wanted him, and the best I could calculate, his fee would probably come to about $3,000.

I could hear the wheels whirling deep in the recesses of the judicial cranium. What if the tape had been tampered with? What dreadful reflections might be cast upon the prosecution? Haas said, "I kinda hate to spend the money if we're not going to get there."

But before we trekked out into the courtroom, Brown wanted to make sure the record was clear about something else he claimed he'd forgotten to tell us: since January he'd been the chairperson of the State Indigent Defense Board, which supervised the moneys paid by the State of Oregon for the defense of its indigents. Brown held the purse strings for Michele's attorney's fees and expenses in our case! But he was quick to add that if any matter involving these cases came up, he wouldn't participate. We could be assured of that. Then, with no further adieu, and no comment from me, Brown called Detective Gary Stafford to the stand.

Stafford testified that every word on the tape was in the order it had been originally recorded. Nothing—no, nothing—had been taped over. Stafford testified that the partial recording of Judge Gardner was not the result of a tape-over. He'd simply failed to turn the recorder on at the precise moment when the judge began to talk.

But on cross I wanted to discover if Dawson had misled us when, the day before, he claimed he didn't know if the interview had been completed or not at the time I was trying to stop it. Stafford seemed pulled back and on his haunches. He denied on three separate occasions that he'd altered the tape in any fashion. I wanted to test the truth of his assertion.

I began by asking whether he'd ever taped judges before. He tried to avoid the question. "This is the first time exclusively of doing telephonic." What was that supposed to mean?

"My question to you is a simple one," I insisted. "How many times have you taped judges in the past?"

"I'd say three or four."

But he couldn't remember the name of a single judge he'd previously recorded—the ubiquitous amnesia disease. And, of course, he'd always told these judges, whoever they were, that he was recording them—he could remember that much—but he offered no explanation for the exception in Judge Gardner's case.

And why had he recorded the judge? Well, people talked so fast he couldn't get it all down, he said.

"And you think that Judge Gardner talked very fast?"

"Not especially, no."

"You knew you'd have plenty of time to make notes of his statements, isn't that true?"

"Can you simplify that for me?" Waffling.

"Yes, you knew he was speaking slowly, didn't you?"

"No."

"He did speak slowly, didn't he?"

"Well, it's all relative." I looked up at the judge like the matador does to the gallery. The judge was scowling.

I remembered Dawson told us that Judge Gardner had only said he couldn't remember anything specific about the polygraph. Now Stafford admitted Gardner had said a good deal more. "Judge Gardner told you that, in effect, if there were exculpatory matters in the polygraph, he had instructed Stapleton and Marquis to give that to the defense. He told you that, didn't he?"

"Words to that effect," Stafford admitted. He had to. That much of the conversation still remained on the tape.

"Did you tell that to Mr. Dawson?"

"I don't recall." Stafford's memory was shot in two days?

When I'd been demanding that Dawson call off Stafford from his interview of Gardner, I thought Dawson might have known that Stafford had *already* taped the judge. I'd made a record of the time and the reporter had dutifully written it down: 10:19 A.M. Now I pressed Stafford for times.

He said the original Gardner tape had a yellow sticker on it which set out the exact time when the recording was made. But no one seemed to know where the yellow sticker was. He said he had "two short conversations" with Dawson that morning, and that they were *just a couple of minutes apart.* In the first conversation Stafford claimed Dawson told him not to talk to Judge Gardner about how the polygraph issue might have influenced the judge's decision, and none of that was on the tape.

What time did these two conversations take place? Stafford couldn't remember when he'd arrived at his office on Monday morning. At first he guessed between eight and ten. Then, with some urging, he admitted that he'd gotten to his office between eight and nine. Still, after more wrestling, he admitted it was before the court took up because that was the best time for him to get ahold of Dawson.

According to Stafford, Dawson was actually holding on the line waiting to talk to Stafford while Stafford was still talking to Judge Gardner. If that had been before 10:19, Dawson was in a lot of trouble, because he'd told the court he didn't know if Stafford had made his call or not. But once again Stafford's memory ran out.

"Well, you talked to Dawson a second time, is that correct?"

"Yes. Mr. Dawson wanted to confer with Mr. Brown regarding this matter."

"And did Mr. Dawson get back to you later?"

"Yes, he did."

"And when?"

"That was the call that he was on hold for during the time I was talking to Judge Gardner." I saw Dawson wince and fix a long stare on Stafford like a parent gives a child who is blabbing family secrets to the dinner guests. I saw Dawson lean over and whisper something to Brown.

"All right, so what you're telling me is that in a few minutes Mr. Dawson called back and held on the phone for three or four minutes. You must have been talking to Judge Gardner somewhere *around nine, nine-thirty,* is that correct?"

"It's reflected on my report."

"No, please. Based on your sworn testimony here . . ." At the precise moment I had Stafford all but pinned, Brown interrupted to ask a question, supposedly "in aid of an objection." I knew he was stopping me *in aid of his witness.* He asked Stafford a question or two on matters I'd already covered. Then, acting as if he were satisfied, and with no objection to offer, Brown said to the witness, "Go ahead." But before Stafford could open his mouth, Brown turned to the judge and did what I believe no trial lawyer is permitted to do—to supply the witness's answer to a question, particularly the decisive question. "Your Honor," Brown said, "my recollection of the witness's testimony is that the conversations are occurring between *eleven and twelve.*"

No such testimony existed in the record. Nor, of course, was Brown a witness. I thought Brown's conduct reflected the depth of his desperation. My cross-examination having been frustrated by this crude infringement of the rules, I raged, "I think that was an improper intrusion. It's improper for counsel to give that information to that witness. He knows better than that." I pointed an angry finger at Brown.

But Haas said quietly, "The more we talk the more trouble we get into. So, let's proceed with your examination." Again he called a recess to cool things down. But before Stafford left the stand, I asked Judge Haas to instruct Stafford not to discuss the matter with counsel during the recess. In response the judge said directly to Stafford, "Until cross-examination is complete, you shouldn't have *any* discussion with *any* other witnesses *or* counsel."

When fifteen minutes later the court reconvened, all hell broke loose. This time Brown took the offensive. He complained that Michele had followed Stafford and him up to the District Attorney's Office in the courthouse. "She followed us into the office, followed us past the receptionist desk, and stopped ultimately when I entered the men's room. I don't think it's professional, and I assume it's at the instruction of senior counsel," meaning me. He gave me a menacing look.

I responded, "Rarely have I been in a courtroom with an experienced lawyer, and when his witness gets in trouble on a very serious matter involving a very serious charge with serious ramifications, that the lawyer would get up, and under a pretense of an objection, instruct the witness as to what the testimony of the witness should be. If we're going to talk about professionalism, *that's* a problem."

Then Michele told her side of it. She said she was out in the hallway and saw Brown and Stafford facing each other talking. Because His Honor had just moments before instructed Stafford to have no communications whatsoever with counsel, she was astounded at what she saw. When Brown and Stafford saw her watching, they turned and left, which caused her to follow them. She followed them up the steps, and when they reached an area past the receptionist area, Stafford said she wasn't "authorized personnel" and couldn't follow them in. Nevertheless she did follow them on down the hallway. She said they came to a room with a number of people in it. Then she said Brown began whispering to Stafford, and they both proceeded down the hall until Brown disappeared into the men's room. "I didn't see him gesture, but I saw his head move and I believe he wanted Stafford to come into the men's room with him. Instead there was some conversation, and Mr. Stafford went down to the end of the hall and I believe turned left and went down to a room there."

Brown claimed all he said to Stafford was that the man was doing fine on the witness stand. If he were doing so fine, why, I thought, had Brown deemed it necessary to supply Stafford with the answer he needed?

Brown was grousing again about Michele's inimitable pluck that had caught Brown and Stafford red-handed. He said he was offended. Annoyed. Distressed. He ran out of adjectives.

The judge said back, "Well, Mr. Stafford is, you know, a trained police officer. And I presume he knew what I meant when I ordered him to have no discussion or contact with counsel or any other witness during the recess." I thought the judge was edging ever closer to the end of his long-suffering patience. He looked up at the ceiling for what seemed an endless time. Then he gathered himself together and ordered both sides not to put "trailing agents" on each other. He turned to Brown. "I've tried to be very patient. I've tried to mediate the difficulties between the parties. I don't have the words of Solomon. There's a lot of things I can't determine. But I *can* say that each of you should advise your witnesses when they get that instruction, that if they violate it, I'm going to find them in contempt of court."

Miraculously, of course, after the recess, Stafford had a revived memory. "Did the second conversation with Dawson take place a few minutes after the first conversation or not?" I asked.

"No. It wouldn't have been a few minutes. Now that I think back on it—because Mr. Dawson said he was going to get back to me after he conferred with Mr. Brown—but in the interim Judge Gardner called me, and that was the interruption. So it wasn't a few minutes. It was during the time span with the conversation with Judge Gardner."

"But you very freely and openly admitted before the recess that there were two conversations with Dawson. You said one was about nine o'clock and the second one occurred a few minutes after that. Do you recall saying that?"

"Yes. I'm saying now that's not correct."

He denied talking to Brown during the recess, except that Brown simply told him to go into the DA's office, which he did. I looked up at the judge. The judge gave me one of those looks that said, "What else can I do?"

I marked Dawson's tape recorder and offered it into evidence. Brown objected. It was an expensive and useful item, he said. Looked like one bought at RadioShack to me. Brown asked the court to defer his ruling on admitting the tape recorder into evidence until the examination of the witness was complete.

Back to Stafford. I asked if he usually recorded Dawson, whose voice we heard just preceding Gardner's. He claimed he hadn't intended to record Dawson. He was just testing the tape recorder. Just testing? He said he shut it off as soon as he *discovered* it was on.

I played the recording for him in open court. You could plainly hear Dawson and Stafford come to the end of their conversation and hang up. He obviously had not *discovered* he was recording Dawson in the middle of the conversation. Now Stafford, with no escape, admitted that his prior testimony in that regard was also in error.

"I want to know if it isn't true that at the time you tape-recorded your conversation with Mr. Dawson that you had already finished your taping of the judge?" Stafford denied it.

Next he claimed that he was into the Gardner interview for only about twenty to thirty seconds when he had turned on the tape. He could remember that much. He said he also had conversations with Brown about the Gardner taping, the first having been the day before. But for some reason he couldn't remember whether it was morning or afternoon that he'd talked to Brown about it.

"Is something wrong with your memory, Mr. Stafford?"

Brown objected. But the judge allowed it, not because the question was proper but because, I thought, the judge believed the witness deserved the reprimand inherent in my question.

Now Stafford had suddenly become clear when the conversation with Judge Gardner had taken place—a time well past 10:19. He guessed the time was "between ten-thirty and eleven-thirty." I didn't have time to subpoena the telephone records of either the AG or Judge Gardner. I walked closer to the witness. "Mr. Stafford, could you explain, please, why you earlier testified this morning under oath that the second call was immediately *after* nine o'clock?"

His answer was again the simple answer: "I was mistaken." And, of course, he now said it was the second conversation with Dawson that he had recorded, not the first, and if earlier he had said the contrary, he was once more simply mistaken.

On redirect Brown asked Stafford, "Does the tape fully and faithfully produce the conversation?"

"Yes. It recorded everything I heard over the phone."

"And is the sequence in which those conversations are produced on the tape the sequence in which those conversations, in fact, occurred?"

"Yes, sir."

In the meantime the judge had come alive. "Well," he said to Brown, "he recorded *everything* that he heard?"

"Your Honor, if *everything* was a part of that question—it wasn't."

"That's what came across," the judge said. "Let's make sure we get that clear." He looked down at Stafford and asked, "Did that tape record every word between each and every one of the people whose voices appear on the tape?"

"Yes." Then Stafford added hastily, "With the exception of the approximate first thirty seconds of my conversation with Judge Gardner, yes."

Then Brown helped Stafford again: "With respect to your conversation with Mr. Dawson?"

"No. The entire conversation was not on there."

"Okay," Brown said, and after that he got Stafford off the stand with all due haste.

In a further effort to refute our charges of prosecutorial misconduct, John Amish took the stand at Brown's call. He was the much discussed criminalist for the Oregon State Police assigned to the Medford Crime Lab. He was tall and slender with the sort of resigned look one sees on a good, honest workhorse. No, he said to Brown, he'd never really been intimidated by Stapleton after his testimony in the Mike Jones Jr. case.

On cross-examination I asked Amish to tell the judge how, during Little Mike's case, we'd talked one evening. Before we'd met, Amish had *already* given his findings on Monica Gerttula to Stapleton, and even before Stapleton, to the state's criminalist, Bekkedahl. He'd told me it was more probable than not that Monica Gerttula had shot a gun on the day of the homicide. In view of that incriminating evidence against their star witness, Marquis had chosen not to call Amish during Little Mike's trial although he was the only person in the world who could testify to the amounts of gunshot residue on the woman's hands and face. We'd called Amish as our witness in Little Mike's case, and he said Stapleton had been upset at his testimony and he'd been required by his supervisor at the State Lab to make a written report concerning his contacts with us.

"Did you feel that you were sort of on the carpet for having given your testimony openly and frankly in this case?"

"Well, I did feel some stress, that's correct." Amish looked down when he said it, as if his words said more.

Then Brown called Trooper Geistwhite to ease up the judge's impression of the Mike Jones Sr. arrest. Now Geistwhite asserted that he'd been driving along at night, saw this car with its headlights on bright, blinked his own, and when the driver didn't respond, he'd turned around and followed. Then he stopped the vehicle. It just happened to be Mike Jones Sr. *Just happened?*

He said he asked for Mike's driver's license, got it, and gave him a warning. Then, as Geistwhite was driving away, he called in on the radio for a record check of Mike's driver's license and found out that Mike was driving with a suspended license. He turned his car around and followed Mike some thirteen miles before he finally stopped him. By this time Geistwhite was out of his territory, and during those thirteen miles Geistwhite had called for a backup car because, he said, "of Jones's background." Something about the Joneses' propensity to use firearms.

Mike got out of his car and Geistwhite patted Mike down, handcuffed him, told him his license was suspended for not appearing for a hearing, and placed him in his patrol car. He denied that Mike was slammed up against his car and made to spread-eagle. Mike had tried to explain. He'd gotten a ticket because he couldn't afford to pay the registration on his car. But he said he didn't know his license had been suspended on account of it. Geistwhite admitted that the trooper who was backing him up had a shotgun out and that he heard the trooper slam a shell into the receiver. Then, after Mike was in his car, three more patrol cars drove up. It was all as simple as that.

I took Geistwhite through a series of questions about how many cars, on average, he stopped each night for not having dimmed their lights. He didn't know. Under extended prodding he couldn't even estimate. Finally he admitted he might go months without stopping one. And how many times in a month had he come upon automobiles that didn't dim their lights? He couldn't guess. I thought the judge could guess.

"Isn't it common knowledge among officers that one of the methods by which you can stop a car is to claim that the car didn't dim its lights?"

"Absolutely not." But he admitted that Jones's lights "didn't necessarily bother me."

He also admitted to a long history with Mike Jones and having been to the Jones property a number of times. Although as an officer he was trained to observe, he claimed he'd never seen Mike's old blue jalopy before. He denied over and over that he knew whose car he'd stopped before Mike Jones crawled out of the car. He was utterly implacable on that—just happened to be Jones, the same Jones whose wife was involved in the murder charge pending before this court, the same Jones whose son Geistwhite believed had shot Wilfred Gerttula.

When you stopped him the first time, was Mr. Jones courteous?

"Very."

"And sober in every way?"

"Yes."

"Kind-eyed, quiet-spoken?"

"More or less."

Yet he'd thrown the man in jail and he was held under a bond of $1,000. I asked, "What do you think the bond would be on Mr. Brown for driving while suspended?"

"I can't tell you."

"Did Mr. Jones tell you he needed to get out of jail because he was headed to his old aunt's funeral, the old aunt who'd raised him from the time he was a little child, and that's what he was doing on the road that night?"

"That's what he said, yes."

"You didn't put that in your report, did you?"

"No."

"Did that make any difference to you?"

"No."

"You didn't care whether he was headed toward the funeral of somebody as close to him as his mother?"

"I didn't know who his aunt was, but, no, that didn't make any difference."

I questioned him about the three additional patrol cars that drove up. Finally, he admitted five officers were there, five handguns, and probably that many shotguns.

"Did you know that these poor people had once sued Ulys Stapleton, the prosecuting attorney?"

No, he didn't know that.

"When was the last time, Officer, that you had five cars, five officers, five handguns, and at least two shotguns, maybe more, at the scene to arrest a smiling, kind-eyed man charged with a suspension of his driver's license?"

He couldn't recall a time. But he insisted that wasn't what happened that night, and with that I ended my questions to the witness.

Then, with a hesitant nod toward the courtroom door, Brown said, "Call Monica Gerttula."

28

Monica Gerttula walked to the stand in short, matronly steps. She wore dark-rimmed glasses that turned up at the ends as if the rims were frozen in a frolicsome smile. Her nondescript dark sweater covered a flowered cotton dress that ended below her knees. She had dark hose and shoes she could have gardened in. When she took the stand and was finally settled in her seat, she looked up from her hands, and then around the room, like a small animal trapped in an inescapable cage.

Brown asked his questions seated at counsel table. When she heard his first question, she turned to him, her voice answering like a distant child's. I felt sorry for her. I didn't understand why Brown thought he must put her through the terror of once more testifying under oath in this, a hostile courtroom, about events that must have become a living nightmare for her.

As matter-of-factly as if he were a bank teller speaking absently to a customer through the drive-up teller's window, Brown shoved his first question through to the woman:

"At some point you were given a polygraph examination?"

"Yes. I wanted to take the polygraph. I was telling the truth."

"Were you feeling nervous?"

"I didn't think I was." *She didn't think she was?* "I wanted to take that test and I didn't think I was."

The woman said that after the test she asked Toliver how she'd done. "He told me that I was quite upset and that some of the answers weren't quite conclusive." *He, Toliver, told her she was quite upset.* "I went away not really satisfied with the answers, but he said, 'It's finished.' And I asked, 'If it wasn't well done, would you let me do it again?' And he said, 'No, that wasn't necessary.'"

He said, *No, that it wasn't necessary?*

I was astounded. What about Toliver's credibility now? Not only wasn't she nervous, but it was *Toliver* who told *her* that she was upset. Not the other way around. And it was she who wanted to be retested, and it was *they* who wouldn't give her the poly again!

Brown wanted to know if some of the test questions had to do with guns. She replied, "There was a few. One, if there had been a gun in the pickup. There was not. Had I fired a gun that day? I did not. That's all I can remember."

"Mrs. Gerttula," Brown asked, "what if any feelings do you have in connection with guns, descriptions of guns, depictions such as television portrayal of guns and gunfire?"

"I can't watch. I find myself nauseous when the subject of guns comes up. I can't watch TV. It's upsetting."

Satisfied he'd laid the winning question before His Honor, Brown delivered the woman to me for cross-examination. He closed his notebook with a quiet finality and sat back to listen.

"Mrs. Gerttula," I began, "you own some guns, don't you?"

"Yes." She moved forward in her seat as if to brace herself against the force of my questions. But I spoke to her in a quiet voice.

"You owned a hunting rifle, a .30-30 or a .30-06?"

"My husband did."

"You owned one of your own, didn't you?"

"Yes."

"You own one now, don't you?"

"It's sitting in the corner."

"You own a shotgun, don't you?"

"Yes."

"You have in your possession a pistol, don't you?"

"No."

"Didn't you have a pistol that one of the neighbors loaned you and that you had in your possession after the incident?"

"He loaned it to me, yes."

"You have that pistol now?"

"No, he took it last Sunday."

"I see. Up until last Sunday you had a pistol in your possession, is that right?"

"Yes."

"Loaded?"

"Yes."

Then I went into a series of questions about her having shot wild animals—moose with her rifle, and birds, pheasants, ducks, and crows with her shotgun.

"Do you get sick when you shoot them?"

"No." Then she added, "Not prior to my husband's death."

She remembered that at some point during the polygraph she'd cried, but she couldn't remember when. She said she did get relaxed, and she didn't remember that Toliver ever said she'd been deceptive or that the test was invalid. "He didn't say anything definite about the test," but she was willing, she insisted, to take it again.

When she stepped down, Judge Haas thanked her kindly. I watched her walk away from the stand. I wondered what Brown thought he'd accomplished by bringing the woman into that place of recurring pain. As Brown watched her vanish out the courtroom door, he must have seen that something was tragically wrong. Either both Toliver's polygraph and Amish's gunshot-residue tests had been wrong, or Mrs. Gerttula was in deep denial. Once more I thought of what Imaging had said: If she'd mistakenly shot her husband, how could she ever admit it to herself? On the other hand it was becoming apparent to me that Brown made no room for the possibility that she had. He'd adopted the whole of the state's case as if it were the irrefutable gospel. As I had said to Toliver, truth is only what we believe. And we believe that which serves us best.

I couldn't imagine the courage it would have taken for Brown to stand up in open court and confess, "We were wrong. We made a mistake. Sandy Jones is innocent. We want to dismiss the charges." I'd heard of prosecutors with such mettle, but I'd never had the exhilarating experience of meeting one, not in all of my years in the courtroom. Instead, sadly, when it came down to it, too many prosecutors I'd encountered would rather do wrong than admit they were wrong.

The next morning I got up even earlier than usual to gather my thoughts for my final argument on our motions to dismiss the case. Despite my longing to excoriate Brown and Dawson for what I thought was their complicity in this whole lamentable display, I knew that Judge Haas, no matter his powerful commitment to fairness, would throw up psychic defenses around Brown. If I wanted the judge to join my side of the argument I had to focus on the conduct of Stapleton and Marquis, and, of course, on Peck's having taken the Fifth.

As I stood before His Honor to begin my final argument,

I felt a dull heaviness in the air, a nagging anticipation. The courtroom was filled with many lawyers who'd come to listen. A lawyer does better with an audience. We'd been at these motions now for three weary weeks, the longest motion hearing in my years of practice before the courts of this land. Sandy's case was in the hands of His Honor. If he granted our motion and dismissed the case, she'd walk out of the courtroom a free woman—and if he denied it, she'd stand trial for murder before yet another jury.

The minds of the warriors on both sides had solidified as if there were no right on the other side and no wrong on their own, a sort of patriotism for the case that blinded us all. Sometimes fervor for their case causes lawyers to place winning above ethics, above the law, above justice. Prosecutors lose their sight in these wars so they cannot see the enemy as human, even the innocent enemy. They live in a sort of cultural fascism. Defense lawyers are blinded as well so they see the prosecutors as inhumane, as brownshirted storm troopers. The enemy is the enemy, and whatever crime is committed against the enemy is no crime. There is no penitence. The consciences of good people dissolve in the heat and the sweat of battle.

Yet I could better endure these courtroom wars were they more honest—were we spared that high, elevated language, that uppity, self-righteous stance one so often encounters in the state's lawyers. Lawyers should lay it out plainly, be who they are, be honest about themselves and their cases, tell of their pain, their anger, their surprise—tell it straight instead of standing stiff as boards with their anal sphincters spasmed tight while they utter those starched words as white and high-collared as their shirts that are meant to demonstrate that, although they may not be candid, they are gentlemen, and scholars.

Sometimes I've mused that judges should order lawyers

to take off all their clothes—all but the pretty silk stockings and the garters that hold them up—make them stand naked before the court. Those pin-striped suits and silk ties hanging down over their antiseptic shirts like diseased tongues provide a guileful armor behind which lawyers lie, and lie about the lies with superimposed manners, which is worse than plain lying.

To me, the hearing on our motions to dismiss had revealed a chilling underlying stratum of loathing for Sandy Jones. I thought the prosecutors seemed not only unbending and relentless in their determination to subdue us, they seemed dripping in the sweat of executioners.

I looked up at the judge not knowing where to begin my argument. He looked down at me, his jaw set, as if to steel himself against my latest onslaught. His impish face was tired. The elfish grin marks were still deep in his cheeks, but his mouth was no longer locked in a smile. Worry was in his eyes—I could see it. He was watching. I sensed the wisdom of the man.

Before I began, I needed the judge to be open to my final argument. I needed to crack the door of the soul so that the feeling of my argument could creep in. I'd been raising hell for weeks, pounding with both fists at the door of justice. Now I began quietly.

"I want to thank you on behalf of another human being. Her name is Sandy Jones, who had never before met a human judge." I reminded the judge of the hellhole in which the woman had lived for seven months. But this was a family who had finally been brought together again because His Honor had granted bail and she had been freed from that cold concrete human latrine. "This was a family of ordinary people, poor people, small people, insignificant people . . . and we thank you for that."

With that, I began the argument. "The name of this

case is 'The State Takes the Fifth.' It isn't just some witness who takes the Fifth. It's the *state* that takes the Fifth. The state sent Deputy Ronald Peck out to collect the evidence and preserve it. Sandy Jones could not preserve the evidence. She had no rights there. She was at the mercy of the state.

"The state takes the Fifth because its hub witness takes the Fifth. Having been on the scene and interviewed the witnesses and understood the facts, Ronald Peck won't tell us what he found. He takes the Fifth.

"Mr. Brown had the power to make Mr. Peck testify. All he had to do when Peck took the Fifth was to give him immunity. But Mr. Brown has taken the Fifth. He says to the witness, 'Do not testify because I will not give you immunity.' Instead he wants us to make do with a make-do case. I guarantee, Your Honor, that every young lawyer in this courtroom can win every case if he controls the evidence."

Still in a conversational tone, I said to His Honor, "The state knows that a competent cross-examination of Ronald Peck would be devastating, and so you understand why the state takes the Fifth. But if the *state* needed Peck to make *its* case against Sandy Jones, they'd give him immunity so fast it would make the judicial head spin." I heard a trickle of laughter from the audience.

I told His Honor that young lawyers had come to me and apologized for the Lincoln County prosecutors. "'We're ashamed of that,' they said. 'We want you to know they don't represent our view of what Oregon law is or ought to be.'" The judge was making notes. I waited until he looked down at me again.

"I saw a woman sitting in this courtroom crying the other day, and after the session I went up to her and said, 'Young woman, why are you crying?' and she said, 'Mr.

Spence, it saddens me that these things happen in our beautiful state.' She said, 'It's been a shock to me.'"

Then I got to the treasure trove of deception that we'd unearthed in the case. "The business of Monica Gerttula's lie detector test is one of the worst examples of misconduct that I've ever heard of." I thought of my unforgiving criticism of Judge Gardner. Should I have blamed him so? Hadn't he heard Josh Marquis saying, "If I felt that Monica Gerttula was not telling the truth, I'll dismiss this case"? Hadn't he been entitled to rely on the representation of the attorneys and conclude by their silence that she'd passed the polygraph?

I remembered how Judge Gardner, in one of his finest moments, and speaking directly to Josh Marquis, said that although he didn't want to know the results of the polygraph, "if you ran somebody on a test and you got a deceptive result on the key questions, I would probably consider that exculpatory evidence. It's not admissible, clearly, but I would consider it probably to be exculpatory evidence to the point that it would have to be disclosed to Mr. Spence." He told Marquis if the test was inconclusive, "then I would think in your situation you should probably just disclose it."

I remembered how Marquis had asked, "Do I understand that the court is ordering me to give them the results?"

"No," Gardner had said. "I'm not ordering you to. I would consider that if there was a deceptive result on key questions, that would be—"

Marquis had interrupted the judge and supplied the word for him: "Exculpatory."

Judge Gardner filled in the word himself: "—would be exculpatory."

Marquis had said, "I understand."

We understood. Judge Gardner had left the matter to Marquis under *Brady v. Maryland* in which the Supreme Court of the United States held that exculpatory evidence must be disclosed to the defense. But Judge Gardner had gone one step further. He defined for Marquis what the judge meant by exculpatory—"a deceptive result on key questions."

Now I argued the point that had so disturbed Judge Haas—that Stapleton had admitted he'd ordered Toliver not to make a record of his findings on Monica Gerttula's polygraph because he wanted to keep the findings hidden from us. I looked up at His Honor for a good long time. "If that isn't a cold, overt action on the part of the prosecutor to keep that information from the defense—which is utterly exculpatory—if that isn't the worst kind of misconduct, the worst kind of representation, the worst kind of lying, in effect, by their silence to the judge . . ." I stopped, out of breath. "Don't you think Judge Gardner would have given us the results of the polygraph if he'd known what they were?

"Now the state's refusal to give those results began to infect the case. It was like trying to operate on something that is clean where everything that is handed to you is handed to you with dirty hands."

Quietly I said, "I feel sorry for Mr. Brown. He's had the duty of defending the likes of Marquis and Stapleton and Peck, and the likes of Toliver, and now the likes of their own investigator, Stafford, who has done the most singular thing that I believe Your Honor has ever heard of—to tape a circuit judge without his knowledge. I couldn't believe it." I said if I'd done the same, I'd have been disbarred.

Then I turned again to the Peck matter. "What would you do, Your Honor, if this case were presented to a jury without the testimony of Mr. Peck, and Sandy Jones were convicted on such a make-do case? Would you say she had a fair trial? Aren't we wasting the time of the state to keep breath in this ugly, sodden, empty hulk of a case, a case that the state itself has ruined?

"This case represents the State of Oregon. How can the people retain their respect and their faith in the system that permits a case like this to be tried? Shouldn't Mr. Brown come forward and say, 'Your Honor, we didn't know what we were getting into. We were victims like everyone else. We wish to do justice. That's our job. We wish this case to be dismissed'?"

I told the judge that Brown, having inherited the case from Stapleton, had to clear up Monica Gerttula's truth-telling before he could require Sandy Jones, a woman charged with murder, to come forward and defend herself. "If Mr. Brown won't do that, then under the law Your Honor must.

"Your Honor, they put Monica Gerttula on the stand yesterday. There she sat. They put her under oath. They called her knowing that she'd failed the lie detector test, and without having resolved her truth-telling problem. They had no business putting that woman on the stand until that matter was resolved. The state has a problem. And only Your Honor can save them from themselves.

"Somebody has to stop this." My voice was rising. "It appears that good lawyers cannot extricate themselves from this. It appears that good lawyers, zealous for their case, have gotten zealous beyond reason and propriety. It seems to me that good lawyers who have embraced the rot and the filth in this case have finally themselves been unable to distinguish what is right from what is wrong." Surely the judge could see that Brown had been trapped. The judge got him into it. Now it was the judge's duty to extricate Brown, who, by this time, had become so stuck in the scatological mire he could no longer save himself.

"The court must dismiss this case. Otherwise I think the court puts its seal of approval on this ugly thing.

"This case does not belong to Ulys Stapleton, who seeks to use it as his own property for the selfish glory of nailing big hides to the wall. Nor does it belong to his scheming, clever assistant, who joins in with lip, tongue, and shallow values.

"This case does not belong to Mr. Stafford, who tapes judges with impunity and contempt and would presumably do whatever is necessary to win this case.

"This case does not belong to Mr. Brown, who has marched in the mud and the muck and the mire of this vile mess already too long.

"Nor does it belong to Mr. Dawson, who would jeopardize a child's pending case for small gain.

"This case does not belong to Sandy Jones. Not to me, not to Eddie, not to Michele, nor to any attorney who claims he only seeks justice.

"This case does not even belong to Your Honor. This case belongs to justice."

Suddenly through the open window and from the street below came drifting up, as if on cue, the patriotic strains of John Philip Sousa's "Stars and Stripes Forever." As the band music swelled into the courtroom and the drums joined in, I felt an immense euphoric lift.

"Your Honor," I said to the beat of the drums and the roll of the music, "if justice cannot be heard here"—I was shouting above the music—"if justice cannot spread her protective wings over the likes of Sandy Jones, over the poor and the humble and the forgotten and the damned, if this case does not belong to justice, then there is nothing left, nothing but the mocking black hole of despair and degradation.

"Even hope is gone if this case does not belong to justice."

The music grew louder as the band on the street marched toward us. I stepped closer to His Honor so as my voice began to soften it could be heard over the trombones and the tubas. "Justice is a quiet mate. She is as meek and as gentle as any small, weak person whom she is called upon to protect. She does not cry out. One must listen carefully with caring ears to hear her voice. She is often shouted down and smothered by greed and shame, and the endless struggle of men for power and for glory.

"This is not our case, Your Honor. This is hers. It belongs to justice.

"Thank you, Your Honor." I looked at the judge for one last long moment, then turned and walked slowly back to my chair at counsel table.

"Thank you, Mr. Spence," the judge said, looking toward the window and shaking his head as if to say he couldn't believe that this man from Wyoming who seemingly left no stone unturned had even brought in a marching band to accompany his final argument.

As Brown approached the podium, I whispered to Eddie, "Godamighty, where did this band come from? Did you have something to do with it?"

"No. Must be the angels are looking down on us." Eddie laughed.

I turned to Michele. "Where did that band come from?"*

"Damned if I know," she said. I turned to Sandy. She

*The band was the Casper, Wyoming, Marching Band, which had come to Portland to take part in a national marching-band contest. Serendipitously, it was playing on the street below as I was concluding my final argument.

looked as if this mystery band were her just due from heaven.

Brown stood to address the court, his face ashen, his voice the same. "Your Honor, the nature of this case has been such that I'm not at all surprised that I must compete with music."

The judge laughed. "I thought they were just drumming you in."

Brown smiled a weary smile. "Counsel's argument is a splendid jury argument. It may well be a moving jury argument. It may well be a persuasive jury argument, but the point is that that's what it is, that's where it belongs, and that's where it ought to be made."

But Brown, I thought, had failed to consider that judges are human beings, too. Although their decisions are couched in legalistic terms, their decisions are first made at the level of their emotions. Justice, to be sure, is only an emotion. We do not know what it is. We only feel it when we experience it and deeply feel its loss when we are shorn of it.

Now Brown wanted to examine some of my "wild swings," as he called them, the first being my allegations about the missing gun. He was right. We'd failed to identify a missing gun. As I saw it, the missing gun must have been in Gerttula's pickup all along.

And Brown was right on another count: we'd not been able to show that Peck had actually been under the influence of drugs or alcohol at any time he'd been at work on our case.

What other "wild swings"? He was all over our claim that Mike Jones Sr. had been harassed and abused by Geistwhite. "It's an enjoyable kind of argument for lawyers to keep things all pumped up. The officer, properly and professionally, and late at night, made a stop and took the man into custody, and that was that. I think it's frivolous to make those allegations, and the inability to back them up ought to have a bearing on the other rhetorical claims made by the defense in this case."

He reminded the judge that the state had waived any hearsay objections to the use of Peck's prior testimony in Little Mike's case, and therefore his testimony, if relevant, could be read to the jury in Sandy's case. That, he thought, put an end to the Peck matter. And the polygraph, of course, was not admissible. So what was this very big deal all about, anyway?

"Your Honor, a trial is not a legal beauty contest. We're not getting points for style." And the furtive tape-recording of Judge Gardner was not to concern this judge. It was legal. Perfectly legal under Oregon law.

Then he reverted to an old argument that defense attorneys hear prosecutors make to juries in nearly every case. "I think, without sounding like I'm in a civics class, that I can tell the court I am not the State of Oregon, and Mr. Dawson is not the State of Oregon. And Ulys Stapleton is not the State of Oregon, and Ron Peck is not the State of Oregon. This case is brought in the name of the *people* of the State of Oregon."

The people! All the people! All the people were against this one small woman who was no longer a person herself, no longer a mother and a wife and a citizen with rights. She was merely "the defendant." She had magically been converted from a person to a *defendant* by a piece of paper called an indictment. And according to Brown, Sandy Jones, the defendant, was, in the eyes of *the people*, a murderer.

Then Brown grabbed another weary saw to apologize for some of the witnesses the state had to deal with, and, I thought, to soften the effects of my cross-examinations that had revealed some of his witnesses to be less than candid. "We do not choose our witnesses," he said gloomily. "We can't say, 'Only bring us the ones where six nuns are witnesses, and while you're at it, if there's a meeting of the Junior League in Portland, we'll take any crimes that occurred when those ladies are watching.'

"I've heard again this morning that Ron Peck is a crucial witness," Brown continued. "I felt admiration for Mr. Spence's rhetorical skills, but we come back to where we were before. They haven't met their burden of proof. There's no demonstrative showing that evidence material to the defense has been lost to the defendant through Peck's absence."

Brown gave the judge his usual smile and folded his notebook. At the same moment I jumped to my feet to deliver my rebuttal.

"Your Honor, we don't have to prove a thing, *not a single thing*. We only have to prove that our allegations are plausible. There's an Oregon case on it." I handed him the case.

Then I turned my back to the judge, and addressing the judge, I stood looking squarely at James M. Brown. "I don't think Mr. Brown would have taken this case if he knew what it was about. I don't think he's a bad man. I'm not suggesting to the record that Mr. Brown is a bad man." I turned back to the judge.

"I'm suggesting that he's badly embraced bad people, and bad acts, and bad witnesses, and bad investigators, and he's failed badly to give us our rights. Mr. Brown could give Peck immunity and say, 'If we have a dope head and a thief who is the hub of the case, let's put him on the stand and test him.' The fate of their case isn't in the court's hands, it is in Mr. Brown's own hands. He can make his choice and he made it."

Then I, too, reverted to an old story, a favorite I'd told to countless juries. I thought the judge was ready for a dramatic ending, and I was ready to deliver it.

"Before we leave I want to share with you a story that I tell in nearly every case to transfer the life of my client from me to the person in power. It's a story of a wise old man and a smart-aleck boy who wanted to show up the wise old man as a fool.

"One day the boy caught a small bird in the forest. The boy had a plan. He brought the bird, cupped between his hands, to the old man. His plan was to say, 'Old man, what do I have in my hands?' to which the old man would answer, 'You have a bird, my son.' Then the boy would say, 'Old man, is the bird alive or is it dead?' If the old man said the bird was dead, the boy would open his hands and the bird would fly freely back to the forest. But if the old man said the bird was alive, then the boy would crush the little bird, and *crush it* and *crush it* until it was *dead*.

"So the smart-aleck boy sauntered up to the old man and said, 'Old man, what do I have in my hands?' And the old man said, 'You have a bird, my son.' Then the boy said with a malevolent grin, 'Old man, is the bird *alive* or is it *dead*?' And the old man, with sad eyes, said, 'The bird is in your hands, my son.'

"So I say to Your Honor, justice is in your hands."

"Thank you, Mr. Spence," Judge Haas said. "I will review the authorities that have been supplied me and I'll be prepared to give my ruling on the motions to dismiss tomorrow morning at nine o'clock."

Sandy Jones: the smoking gun at the scene of the homicide

Sandy and Big Mike

Gerry Spence
and his wife, Imaging

Ed Moriarity,
Spence's partner

Steve Lovejoy, Little Mike's lawyer

Spence, preparing for the trial

Kent Spence, Gerry Spence, Sandy Jones, Michele Longo

Doug Dawson *(left)*, assistant to Special Prosecutor
James Brown *(right)*

Judge Harl Haas

Spence, with the judge's
clerk, demonstrating
the angle
of the bullet's path

Getting ready for the final argument *(left to right):*
Gerry Spence, Ed Moriarity, Michele Longo, Sandy Jones

Spence and Sandy
Jones at the time of the
verdict

A hug was the fee

Imaging Spence
and Sandy Jones
after the verdict

After the verdict *(left to right):*
Gerry Spence, Sandy Jones, Mike Jones, Kent Spence

Spence speaking to the press about the verdict

29

Now the time had come for this kindly, troubled man to take on the role of the judge, the godly role, to look down upon us and to pass his judgments. Fear boiled in our bellies. What must Sandy feel? Michele was holding her hand, more for Michele's need than Sandy's, I thought.

We watched His Honor take the bench, giving no hint of his decision—didn't look at us or at Brown. We stopped breathing.

"Don't worry, Spence," Sandy whispered. "No matter how it turns out, ya did good." I tried to smile.

"Good morning," His Honor said without conviction, and began to read from his notebook. He said the first thing he had to decide was whether Peck was an essential witness for the accused. He took care to recite all of the spokes in the case that connected Peck to the hub, his detailed involvement in the investigation and how Peck, as a witness, would be a "mammoth asset" to the defense. He said Peck, an agent of the state, had worked to make a case against Sandy Jones. It was the state that had made the decision to indict Peck, which led to his having taken the Fifth. His status as a witness was within the control of the state. Had the state wanted his testimony, it could have granted Peck immunity. I was feeling the excitement. Could it be possible he was going to rule in our favor?

He read with an even, reportorial cadence, looking up

from time to time with sad eyes. "The decision here leaves us with neither alternative desirable—the state's loss of a trial or the accused being severely impaired in her defense. The constitution of this country and this state afford every accused fundamental fairness. An important part of such fairness is the granting to each accused the right to confront and subpoena witnesses who will testify in their favor, and under the peculiar and regrettable facts of this case, I find a trial of this case would result in a denial of these fundamental rights to this defendant."

He recognized, he said, that there would be many citizens of Lincoln County who would be frustrated by his decision, and he lamented that the circumstances of the shooting of Wilfred Gerttula might never be known. "However, the subsequent events have conspired to fatally flaw this unfortunate case."

The judge's eyes shifted to Sandy Jones. She was sitting as stiff as a corpse ten hours dead. "Therefore, the court orders that the indictment be dismissed with prejudice, and I bar further prosecution against the accused for the same crimes for the reason that I have noted."

We sat silent. Shocked. None of us knew what to say, our long-cherished dreams suddenly exploding into reality. As if he had anticipated the judge's decision, Brown gave us no opportunity for hooting or hollering or hugging. Already he was asking that the judge's order be expedited. The acerbic sound of his voice spoiled the moment. "There are great fundamental and very serious legal issues present, and it is our intention to appeal."

Three weeks of hearings on our motion to dismiss must have given Brown an intimate view of what was wrong with his case. It *was* a fatally flawed case. I'd repeatedly given him the opportunity to stand up and disavow this thing he'd inherited from Stapleton and Marquis. So had the judge.

But he'd refused to walk out. Now the judge had forced him out and had slammed the door behind him, I thought to save Brown as well. By a dismissal of the case, the testing of the tape recording to determine if it had been altered would probably never occur. The charges of improper conduct that might otherwise have gone to the Oregon bar would likely vanish. Sandy could go home and take care of her kids and work with the Indians at Medicine Rock. It could all be forgotten. But no. Brown was going to appeal! Michele got up and walked hurriedly out of the courtroom.

There'd be no end to this case. Never. What if on appeal the Oregon Court of Appeals decided to reverse His Honor's ruling? There were former prosecutors sitting up there as judges. I could hear them arguing in their robing chambers, "You don't throw a murder case out. Prosecutorial misconduct is one thing. Murder is another." Haas had decided to leave the polygraph issue out of his decision since that matter had been cured when Haas removed the Lincoln County DA's office and had granted a change of venue. Was Peck's unavailability as a witness going to be enough to sustain the judge's dismissal? That raised the fearsome specter of a reversal by the Court of Appeals.

I thought we needed still more grounds in the record to support the judge's decision. Before we left the courtroom, I wanted the judge to order the testing of the Gardner tape. Had it been tampered with? Assuming it had, I told His Honor we wanted him to consider whether altering the tape constituted grounds for dismissal as well. I wanted to make his decision as bulletproof as possible.

For me Brown's threat of an appeal laid a pall over our victory. I tried to explain it to Sandy. She seemed bewildered. It wasn't over yet? Finally she said with a far-off sound in her voice, "I thought there was something called double jeopardy in the constitution."

"There is," I said. "But, as the law sees it, you were never in jeopardy, Sandy. The jury in this case was never finally selected. The first witness against you had never been sworn. No. If the Court of Appeals reverses Haas, you'll have to go to trial."

"Nothing changes," she said. "I've always been in jeopardy." Then she said, "I don't know if Little Mike can handle it. Something has to give. He wants to come home." The woman looked suddenly sick again, as I'd seen her the first time in that cold, ugly cell.

"Let's look at the bright side of it, Sandy. As you sit here today, there isn't a charge against you. The judge has ruled in your favor. You're not in jail. We're still in this case." I gave her a big hug, and when I let loose of her, she gave me a weak smile and said, "Thanks, Spence." Then we walked out of the courthouse door together, this little tribe. We'd clung together, and we'd won. But for how long we couldn't guess.

Within days Brown filed a motion asking Haas to reconsider his dismissal of Sandy's case. On June 20, Eddie and I traveled from Jackson back to Judge Haas's courtroom for the argument. Brown's main thrust was that Peck's criminal trial might soon be over. Then Peck would be available as a witness.

Michele argued the point. "I think that is just plain specious. Peck's constitutional right to remain silent will stay with him during his trial, and if he's convicted, his right to remain silent will continue during his appeal." The whole miserable mess could take as long as five years before he could be forced to testify.

Haas agreed. "I think it would be unfair, among other things, for the defendant to have to sit and wait. Mrs. Jones stands before the court at this point presumed innocent of any crime or wrongdoing. She's spent approximately seven months in jail. We're practically a year after the killing of Mr. Gerttula, and to ask her to wait for the wheels of justice to turn on Mr. Peck until some unforeseen date down the road doesn't seem to me to be the thing to do. I'll deny the motion to reconsider."

Still I was worried. I wanted the judge's order to take the form of a *judgment of acquittal*—not a dismissal. It might be stronger on appeal. We could argue that the state had no right to appeal such a judgment. I pled long and hard but His Honor just shook his head: "Finality is a beautiful thing, but I think it would be injudicious of me to deny the state the opportunity to appeal."

Judge Haas had ordered Stapleton personally to appear on that same day. He'd been sitting in the front pew of the courtroom with his attorney. Clearly, Haas had not forgotten Stapleton's conduct in the case. Still it was becoming more and more apparent that the judge himself was not too secure in his decision. In chambers he had fretted. What if the Court of Appeals sent the case back for trial and Stapleton's office was directed to take over the case? Would Stapleton again attempt to influence public opinion with his statements to the media? He'd continued to make out-of-court statements to the press. Stapleton's latest comments to the papers: "When told of Haas's ruling Friday, Stapleton said he felt there was no legal basis for a dismissal of the Jones case, but added, 'I am not surprised Harl Haas did it.' He said he believed the defense had won the case 'by intimidation' and 'by talking loud and long.'"

I thought the judge wanted to bolster the record in face of Brown's threatened appeal and, in the record, to establish his view of the prosecutor's misconduct. And I thought he also wanted to give Stapleton an opportunity to explain himself before the judge took whatever action he had in mind for him. Speaking of intimidation, Haas said he was concerned how Amish had been treated. "His [Amish's] meeting with the defense is certainly proper. He is owned by nobody. He is supposed to be impartial. I note that Mr. Stapleton was upset over the fact that he [Amish] met with the defense and upset with his testimony and contacted his superior." The judge quoted the ABA Standards while Stapleton sat listening stoic as a stump: "'A prosecutor should not obstruct communication between prospective witnesses and defense counsel. It is unprofessional conduct to advise any person not to give information to the defense.'"

Haas went further: "The National District Attorneys Association Standards says: 'No attempt to improperly influence the action or testimony of a witness should be undertaken by the prosecutor.'"

Then Haas jumped on the polygraph issue. "Remember, Judge Gardner was sitting as judge and jury. He was to judge the credibility of the witnesses just like a jury would, and the prosecutor in this case intentionally and deliberately advised that judge, acting as the trier of fact, that he was going to place Mrs. Gerttula on the polygraph. You can't read this record and come away with any other feeling that if she didn't come through, the case was going to be dismissed.

"If it was an invalid polygraph, why go to those remarkable lengths to hide it, to cover it up? Why have Toliver not make a report? Admittedly so the defense wouldn't get it, and so the judge wouldn't know. I can draw only one conclusion—they didn't want either the defense or Judge Gardner to know."

Haas flipped the pages in his notebook and read on. "The Canons of Ethics are pretty clear. 'Intentionally deceiving opposing counsel is grounds for disciplinary action.'" Again he cited from the ABA Standards of Prosecution. "In the commentary to those standards it states that prosecutors have to be squeaky-clean. The reason for that is the awesome power of that office." He read from the commentary: " 'It is fundamental that in his relations with the Court, the prosecutor must be scrupulously candid and truthful with the Court.'"

Stapleton, silent, waited for the storm to subside.

"Mrs. Gerttula's request to do another polygraph, the adamant refusal and decision by the prosecutor not to, to me is pretty remarkable," the judge said. "I note that the ABA Standard 3–11 (c) states, 'It is unprofessional conduct for a prosecutor intentionally to avoid the pursuit of evidence because he believes it will damage the prosecutor's case or aid the accused.'

"The commentary says, 'He may not properly refrain from investigation in order to avoid coming into possession of evidence which may weaken his case, independent of whether he may be obligated to disclose it to the defense.'"

Haas said he hadn't come to this job "virginally," as he put it. "As a prosecutor I had responsibility for around twenty-four thousand felony prosecutions, but as one statement attributed to Justice Story goes, '*Prosecutors are paid to prosecute cases, not talk about them.*' I don't care if they talk about them. I care when I think it is an intentional attempt to influence public opinion." Haas looked down at Ulys Stapleton for a long time, then said, "Quite frankly, Mr. Stapleton, that is the only conclusion I can draw from it, and I think it was wrong."

Then the judge turned to John Ray, Stapleton's lawyer, and invited him to make any comments he wished on behalf of Stapleton. Haas had actually considered appointing Ray as the special prosecutor, but chose Brown instead. Ray rose to speak. He argued that the established policy at the Crime Lab was that their experts, such as Amish, would not talk to defense attorneys without prior permission from the prosecutor involved in the case. "Whether it's a correct policy on the part of the Crime Lab or not, it nevertheless exists." He said Stapleton was upset over Amish's testimony after the young man had had dinner with me.

But Haas would have none of that: "The fact is that Mr. Amish's testimony was very damaging to the state's case. He stated that, in his opinion, it was more likely than not that Mrs. Gerttula fired a handgun at the scene. One might conclude *that* is what upset Mr. Stapleton." But Ray argued quietly that there was no hint of a suggestion that Stapleton was attempting to get Amish to change his testimony.

Ray and Haas carried on a dialogue back and forth, Ray now asserting that it might have been unwise not to prepare a report, but he sang the same song we'd heard so often: the polygraph was inadmissible evidence and therefore need not be disclosed by the state.

Haas jumped on that: "Would you say it would be *material* if you were the judge in this case and you were told by the prosecutor that they were going to give her a lie detector test, that your office gives them frequently and relies upon them, that if you weren't satisfied she was telling the truth, you'd dismiss the case, and that you did, in fact, give her the test"—Haas stopped to catch his breath—"would you think under those circumstances the result might be disclosed?"

"If they were indicative that they were deceptive, yes," Ray admitted.

"And let's say that the chart shows that deception is a minus-six, and on the question 'Did you fire a handgun at the scene?' the witness throws a minus-fourteen?"

Ray skirted the issue. "Not being a polygraph expert, I'm unable to respond specifically to the court's question."

Then Ray went on to assert that in any event an inconclusive result need not be disclosed.

Judge Haas bristled. "You wouldn't tell the court it was *inconclusive*? Instead you'd get up and tell the court, 'We're going forward'?"

Ray demurred again. "Not having been in those circumstances, Your Honor, I can't tell you what I'd do." But he thought that the prosecutor had to rely heavily on the opinion of the examiner.

Judge Haas replied, "My problem is that it was the prosecutor's office that set in motion the polygraph. It was the prosecutor's office that made the statement to the court that 'Boy, if we're not satisfied after this, we'll dismiss it,' planting that seed in anyone's mind who would hear it. It was the prosecutor's office that chose an employee of their office to give it. It was the prosecutor's office that, when they testified that she was so upset the test was inconclusive, they gave it to her anyway, and it was the prosecutor's office that when it came back as a devastating revelation to their case they chose—after the fact again—to deny it. And it was the prosecutor's office that chose not to do a report that would reveal what it was."

The judge wasn't through. He was leaning over the bench in the direction of Ray, his face hard and his eyes hard agates. "It was the prosecutor's office that went forward to the court and counsel and did not indicate that it was inconclusive, did not indicate anything other than 'Boy, now we're ready to go,' and it was the prosecutor's office that chose not to give her another polygraph, despite her repeated request to do so, and it was that same prosecutor's office that did not deliver those results to the special prosecutor when all of the other papers were delivered to him. When you look at the totality of these facts, it is pretty rough." Haas leaned back and waited for Ray's response.

Ray said, "It *is* pretty tough to conclude that it was a wise decision, Your Honor, but I think prosecutorial misconduct cuts a bit deeper than that. And it must be remembered, of course, that Judge Gardner presumed from the statement that it was inconclusive."

"*Where* did that come from?" I demanded.

Ray abruptly changed the subject. Without answering, he gave the judge an ingratiating smile and said, "Well, Your Honor, I'd like to talk about the extrajudicial statements."

Ray said Stapleton's releases to the press were unwise but didn't amount to prosecutorial misconduct. Besides, he said, there was an apparent conflict in my representing both Sandy and Little Mike.

But Judge Haas would hear nothing of it. Stapleton knew little of our defenses to these two cases, Haas said. "Seems to me you'd want to know something before you started making those types of accusations."

When Ray insisted that there was an apparent basis for Stapleton's statements, the judge asked, "Is the morning newspaper the place to resolve it?"

"No, Your Honor," Ray admitted, the same tolerant smile.

"When a person is charged with murder?"

"It is not, and it was unwise and—"

Haas interrupted, "I remember Mr. Stapleton testified that he didn't think it was prejudicial. I said, 'You mean to tell me if a person is going to go to trial for murder, facing a potential thirty years in prison, and you issue a statement to the public of Lincoln County that if these two lawyers go forward representing her that she is represented *by unethical lawyers who will be disbarred*—that that is not prejudicial?'" Haas stopped for a moment. "I'm sorry, I'm interrupting you."

"That's quite all right," Ray said. I could see by the way he was handling Haas he was a veteran in the courtroom. He repeated that Stapleton's statements were unwise and smiled sadly at the judge. He said that he understood that both Michele and I had turned these matters over to the Oregon State Bar and that a preliminary opinion had been issued by George Riemer, of the bar, that no ethical violation had occurred.

Ray concluded by saying that Haas had done the right thing by removing the DA's office from the case and by changing the venue. Stapleton's face was impassive at hearing his own lawyer admit that. Haas, Ray insisted, had preserved the rights of Mrs. Jones. He felt that the prosecutors' removal had been an appropriate sanction, enough punishment. Once more he apologized to the judge for Stapleton's statements but continued to claim the statements did not constitute misconduct.

When Ray said he had no further comments to make, Dawson, with a worry of his own, spoke up. The tape issue was still hanging around undecided. Well, the judge wanted to know, what should he do with the tape?

Dawson quickly replied, an eagerness in his voice, "I guess it's our position you could rule on that without sending the tape out. I don't think there's any testimony of any tampering and—"

"I just think in fairness to the Attorney General's Office and to the defense, it would be better to test it and clear the air of that."

Dawson paled. Then he immediately objected to the tape's being sent to anyone we selected. He wanted it sent to a neutral party.

I reminded His Honor how I'd begged Dawson not to ruin our chances with Judge Gardner for a fair disposition in Little Mike's case. Gardner still hadn't ruled on what he was going to do with Little Mike. "What interests me from Mr. Ray's statement," I said, "is that 'Judge Gardner presumed the polygraph *inconclusive*.' Now where did he get that information except through the interview conducted by Mr. Dawson? There's nothing on the record from which Judge Gardner could have *presumed* that this was *inconclusive*. Nothing!" Not once had Toliver claimed the results were *inconclusive*. Toliver had declared the test *invalid*, because Monica Gerttula was upset, but there were conclusive results of deception on the polygraph's charts.

Judge Haas said he'd take all matters before him under advisement, thanked the lawyers, and hurried from the bench.

We watched him go. I looked at Sandy. She was pale and had aged.

"Well, that was a big nothin'," said Eddie. "We coulda stayed home."

"Yeah, but Haas was pretty pointed," Michele said, gathering up our files and books once more and stuffing them into boxes. "Quoting chapter and verse like that from the prosecutor's own ethics book—that's pretty serious stuff."

We walked out of that strange old courtroom, hopefully for the last time. We said our good-byes to Michele, who promised to handle Brown's appeal. We were glad to leave, but we were this tribe, and the leaving itself seemed sad.

And down where I always worry, I knew the trouble was just the beginning.

30

Trials are wars. Wars bring on retribution. That all of us, the prosecutors included, were good, decent persons was lost in the war. We shed our sensitivity for the enemy, and to that extent we forfeited our own humanity. As in all wars, the time for retribution had come. We'd shamed these prosecutors, and now, back in Lincoln County and in front of Judge Gardner, a judge more to their liking, they attacked.

On July 11, 1986, the Lincoln County DA's office filed their motion to disqualify both Steve Lovejoy and me from further defending Little Mike in the juvenile court. Their grounds, of course, the eternal argument that pointed the long, ethical finger at us—we'd placed ourselves in an unethical conflict of interest by representing both Little Mike and Sandy.

In return we filed a similar motion with Judge Gardner to disqualify the Lincoln County DA's office from further participation in Little Mike's case—the polygraph matter, of course. As we saw it, their agreement to dismiss the case if Monica Gerttula failed the polygraph was a contract. We thought their conduct in that matter, now established in the record many times, was enough to cause any sitting judge to follow Judge Haas's lead and remove the prosecutors.

Gardner ruled, instead, that he would await the disposition hearing on Little Mike—when he would decide what to do with the boy—to determine whether the prosecutors should be removed. At the same time he overruled the DA's motion to remove Steve Lovejoy and me as attorneys for Little Mike, saying, "The court assumes that the attorneys are aware of their ethical obligations. This is not a matter for the court to decide."

Did we dare leave Gardner on the case after the state's investigator Stafford had talked to Gardner alone and had secretly taped the man? We couldn't forget that the tape itself revealed that the whole of the conversation between Stafford and Gardner had not been preserved. What, if anything, had been said and then recorded over? After Marquis had seemingly agreed to dismiss Sandy's case if Monica Gerttula wasn't telling the truth, then charged forward in the case even more vigorously than before—how had that affected Gardner's judgment of Monica Gerttula's credibility?

But Gardner was claiming his memory was deficient on what exactly had been said by Marquis. We remembered that Gardner told Stafford on the tape he "*assumed* the results were *nonconclusive*." How could he assume that? Why hadn't he assumed she passed, given that Marquis had passionately plowed forward after she'd taken the poly? If we confronted the judge for having taken part in an *ex parte* conversation with Stafford, it would only infuriate Gardner more. We'd cornered ourselves. We'd been successful in getting the man kicked off Sandy's case by the Supreme Court of Oregon, a matter the judge would never forget. But if we left Gardner on the case, we feared for Little Mike. Could the judge separate his enmity toward us from a calm, caring decision for the boy? We asked him to step down from the case. Then, predictably, Gardner refused to appoint another judge to hear us and simply overruled our motion.

We thought our chances were better with the Oregon Supreme Court. We filed our "Petition for a Writ of Mandamus" asking that the high court remove Gardner. He'd become a witness, we claimed, as a result of the misconduct of the state when Stafford had interviewed the judge. But the gods on high—those sitting on the Supreme Court—were not smiling this time. On August 19, 1986, the court entered its order denying our petition.

That left us standing before Gardner, this judge we'd blatantly confronted, perhaps humiliated, a man we'd often angered and who held Little Mike's life in his hands solely as his possession. Every participant in the boy's case had been shot at by someone: We'd taken after the judge twice. We'd attacked the prosecutors, and they, us. What calm goodwill was left for an innocent child when all of us were engaged in this holy war against each other? We'd fought the war hard, perhaps too hard. By now both sides were inextricably entrenched.

"We're fucked," Steve groaned.

"We maybe fucked ourselves," Eddie said. None of us disagreed with him. But while our attention was turned to Little Mike, on August 1, 1986, Judge Haas entered his final order dismissing the charges against Sandy, and on August 26, Brown filed his notice appealing Haas's dismissal. There'd be no end to this miserable war. Never.

That fall I went off to Nepal on a trek with Imaging. The trek took six weeks and lifted me into a strange world of innocent, beautiful people, the Sherpas, who knew little of our grasping for wealth and power. The only power these people sought was through their prayers that their legs would hold out and their lungs would absorb enough air to live one more day. Finally we'd reached the base camp of Mt. Everest at over eighteen thousand feet. It was a stark, beautiful land of honesty and innocence. Nothing could be hidden where the only goal was to put one foot in front of another in a journey dedicated not to winning, not to killing with words, but simply to *being*.

When we returned, I got a call from Michele.

"Well, the jury hung." With her customary direct manner, Michele jerked me back to the real world again.

"What jury?"

"Peck's jury. Jesus, where've you been? The jury convicted Peck on four misdemeanors, found him not guilty on a couple charges, and hung on twenty-one."

"That doesn't help anybody, Peck or us," I said. "Is the state going to retry the case?"

"Don't know," she said. "Aren't you getting tired?"

Her question made me feel suddenly exhausted again. "I was born tired," I said. And we laughed. If Peck took a plea of some kind, his case would be over, and if the Court of Appeals reversed Haas, we'd be at it all over again.

Back in Gardner's court once more, we moved for a dismissal of Little Mike's case or, in the alternative, a new trial. Gardner set our motions for hearing for November 24 and 25, 1986. Marquis, of course, brought in Toliver, who testified as before, and once more, on cross-examination, I laid out the same set of facts we'd proven to Judge Haas. That Haas would hold one way on these facts while Gardner would hold the opposite underlined the truth about the law—that it is a pea pod floating in the ocean moved by whatever wave happens to grab it.

During the arguments, Marquis had been after Little Mike for having supposedly violated the terms of his release agreement when he'd gone with Sandy to visit a family friend in the hospital. He wanted the boy put away. The boy was not allowed to be in Lincoln County. I'd risen to the argument.

"Now what we're seeing here is a prosecutor saying this boy is doing something wrong when he goes with his mother to visit a friend in the hospital?" Moreover, Marquis wanted Little Mike to undergo psychological testing and discuss the facts of the shooting, which I thought a further harassment of the child.

I argued, "We're seeing a prosecutor who is saying that unless this boy tells the psychologist what happened, that maybe he'll have to be disposed of in some bad way." I backed up and took in the judge during a long silence. Finally I said, "To me this is such a mockery of the function of the juvenile court that it makes me physically ill."

Judge Gardner jumped up, his finger pointing at me. "You stood over there at counsel table and basically said this court is making you sick to your stomach." I had said no such thing. The judge's face was red, his voice animated and loud. I was surprised at its sound. At last he'd come alive. He started for the door and then turned back to me and said, "I'm exercising the one last prerogative I have left as a judge. I'm recessing this hearing." Then Gardner stormed out of the courtroom.

I said to the record, "Note the judge has left the courtroom." Then despite my many entreaties through his court reporter and clerk, he refused to return to the bench.

"Now what's he gonna do to Mikey?" Sandy asked. I could see fear take over her face.

We had to get out of there and think.

Outside, a great Oregon storm was blowing, the wind so powerful it was hard to get to the car. The whitecaps on Yaquina Bay were running at the shore. I thought of home. I was a Wyoming man. I didn't belong here. We live in the isolation of our experience. I wanted out of this insane place where judges blew, and storms brewed, and when it was over, nothing changed, the landscape the same, the child still trapped, the war still on, the fear still brewing in the basement of my heart.

By now I'd actually come to see Judge Gardner as a man who wanted to do right. He was proud but stubborn. I thought he wanted to be a good judge and that he devoted great energy in that direction. I thought he actually cared about Little Mike, but was leaning in the other direction—in the direction of guilt, not innocence. Yet his decency to the boy on several occasions had not gone unnoticed.

That night back in my hotel room I grabbed a yellow pad and began to write a supplement to the record to show Gardner that I'd not directed my comments to him: "I have been remiss in failing to acknowledge His Honor's sensitive handling of the child in such a manner that the boy has been able to progress so well. Indeed, His Honor could have sent the boy to MacLaren had he chosen to do so. I did not feel it appropriate to express my own very deep gratitude, or the boy's, since I believed His Honor's decisions concerning the child were made because he thought his decisions were the right thing to do and in the child's best interest, and I thought that any overt expression of gratitude would be improper. But we are very grateful.

"What made me physically ill," I wrote, "was that the prosecutor or the juvenile department should demand that this child give up his Fifth Amendment rights in order to save himself from the threat of MacLaren [the psychological testing], and I am further repulsed that his mother should face the same threats while her case is pending. These threats have hung over these people now for many months and have caused this child and his mother untold misery and anxiety. That the child has been able to function so admirably under this sort of stress speaks strongly of the child's great commitment to his covenants with His Honor. This is and has been a serious and egregious threat to the constitutional rights of these citizens that should not be tolerated. I felt compelled to call the same to the court's attention, and to express my own acute feelings concerning the same, but these feelings were not directed to the court."

Marquis immediately filed his response. He wrote, "Mr. Spence's conduct reached its depths when, after a long day of invective aimed primarily at counsel for the state, and in another effort to intimidate the court, Mr. Spence once again resorted to shouting and declared the court process was making him physically sick."

He flailed at my claim that the state was bringing "untold misery and anxiety" on Michael. "No mention is made by Mr. Spence of the dying agonies of Wilfred Gerttula or the grief suffered to this day by his widow, who continues to be victimized by counsel in a fashion that goes far beyond any interpretation of proper zealous representation."

Then Marquis launched into a rant about my "collaboration" with Judge Haas against him, how I had defamed, insulted, and intimidated counsel and the court. He brought up the conflict of interest matter once more, then charged me, in consort with Judge Haas, with having "laid the costs of this case at the feet of Mr. Marquis," a finding made by Judge Haas in his letter decision of June 24, 1986. There Judge Haas wrote: "The cost of the Special Prosecution team, defense team cost, and venue change cost has been substantial." Earlier critical comments in the local press about the costs of the case had rankled Haas. He wrote, "The unfortunate cost of this case, as in other Lincoln County cases removed to Multnomah County in the past year and a half, rests at the feet of the Lincoln County Prosecutor and Mr. Marquis." Marquis was livid. He ended his response by asking the court to "take appropriate action," which, easily interpreted, meant to find me in contempt of court.

The worm turns. Now *both* Little Mike and I were at the mercy of His Honor, Judge Robert Gardner.

31

During the fall and winter of 1986, while we were fighting over what would happen to Little Mike, a new war was being waged on a different front. In September of 1986 a race to the Oregon State Bar Association and the Judicial Fitness Commission had exploded. Judge Haas filed a complaint against Stapleton and Marquis. The complaint against Stapleton was for his "extrajudicial statements" concerning our claimed unethical conduct in taking on the defense of both Little Mike and Sandy, specifically, Stapleton's public assertion that we would be subject to disbarment were we to represent Sandy. The judge said that the statements were made "to influence public opinion against the defendant, and to frighten the defense from the case." He also thought Stapleton's statement to the press about the cost of the defense was improper for the same reasons. Stapleton never mentioned, of course, that our firm was working without a fee from either the state or Sandy, nor were either paying our expenses.

In his complaint, Haas included the Monica Gerttula polygraph fiasco, laid out a short summary of its history, and ended by saying, "The prosecutors went further and made false statements to the Judge and defense indicating that Mrs. Gerttula passed the polygraph."

In the meantime Marquis filed a complaint against

Haas with the Oregon Judicial Fitness Commission, the exact nature of which we were not apprised since complaints against judges are confidential in the State of Oregon. But one thing was certain: Marquis asserted he had filed his complaint with the Judicial Fitness Commission against Haas *first*, and that Haas's complaint to the Oregon State Bar against him was backdated and retaliatory.

Marquis emphasized over and over that at *no time* during the case did he disbelieve Mrs. Gerttula. "She is the widow of the man who Judge Gardner ruled was gunned down by Michael Jones Jr. She was present when those shots were fired, and she suffered beatings at the hands of Mrs. Jones." I have no doubt that Marquis believed her. We each had our own set of beliefs. I had never claimed Marquis did not *believe* Monica Gerttula. I never claimed he was intentionally, knowingly, evilly prosecuting innocent people. I never claimed he lied under oath or otherwise. We believe what we want to believe—indeed, what we must believe.

No one can define truth or justice. They are beliefs. We take a side, and if we are worth a damn, we fight with all we can muster for it. In the courtroom, lawyers play word games they would not otherwise play. They make desperate arguments. They flail at their opponents. It is not a sign of evil or unethical lawyers. It is a sign of lawyers who care about themselves and their clients, and who, at last, believe.

Marquis laid out his standard scenario of the case to the Oregon bar—the one he believed. He claimed that I had "persuaded" Amish to say that based on the gunshot-residue tests of Mrs. Gerttula, it was more likely than not that she had fired a gun that day, even though Amish had written his report with that conclusion long before I ever met him. Now Marquis claimed that "the amount of gunshot residue found both on Mrs. Gerttula, and an even greater amount found on Mrs. Jones, were consistent with both Mrs. Gerttula and Mrs. Jones being in the general vicinity of a rifle blast from a .30-30 rifle such as that held by Michael Jones, Jr."

I took it that Marquis's beliefs shut off his memory of the facts. The problem was that the gunshot residue on Sandy Jones contained only barium, which was consistent with a .22, and which she admittedly fired. The gunshot residue on Mrs. Gerttula contained high levels of *both* barium and antimony, which was consistent with a gunshot from a rifle or a large-caliber pistol. And we remembered that the Crime Lab had never been able to come close to duplicating the level of gunshot residue on Monica's face and hands, even when Bekkedahl, the criminalist, discharged the rifle so near the dummy that the rifle blast knocked it over.

Then Marquis went on to assert in his complaint to the bar, "I find it extremely distressing that Judge Haas has adopted wholesale all of Mr. Spence's contentions, most specifically that Mrs. Gerttula had changed her statements." Beliefs trump memory.

As for the polygraph, he argued that "the squigglings" contained no exculpatory material in themselves. "You will note from a careful examination of Mr. Toliver's testimony, a transcript of which he enclosed, that despite Mr. Spence's and Judge Haas' *misrepresentations* [my emphasis] only in a single answer could anyone construe a 'deceptive response.' The other responses were within the range considered 'inconclusive,' even given a valid test."

Then Marquis nicely turned things around: he said Stapleton did not specifically instruct Mr. Toliver *to prepare a report*. Judge Haas concluded Stapleton had told Toliver *not* to prepare a report—this based on Stapleton's own admission under my cross-examination. Marquis insisted he'd turned the entire polygraph file over to Brown and told him the results "were inconclusive," but he'd obviously failed to tell Brown what a minus-14 meant on such a question as "Did you shoot a firearm at the scene that day?"

In Marquis's response to Haas's complaint to the bar against him, Marquis forewarned the bar that he was preparing another complaint against Haas, this time based on Haas's membership in the bar *as an attorney*. He wrote, "I do not believe a judge abandons his ethical duties as a lawyer when he assumes the robes. Judge Haas has obligations not only as a judge but as a lawyer." Marquis promised he wouldn't backdate this complaint against Haas as he claimed Haas had backdated his against Marquis.

Then Marquis ended his response: "In conclusion, I wish to state I have worked as a prosecutor since I passed the Bar in 1981, and despite the relatively low pay and extreme aggravation generated in my profession, I take great pride in doing the right thing as a prosecutor. I have never knowingly prosecuted any person I *believed* [my emphasis] to be not guilty of an offense. I did not do so in this case and I find the high degree of Judge Haas' involvement and his advocacy for the defense unseemly and improper." In short, Marquis had pulled out the big guns, the personal guns, the guns intended to do in a judge. Besides, Marquis knew what smart generals know—a good offense is profoundly better than the best defense. He'd launched his attack, and soon he'd level his guns on us. The second front in the war had just been opened.

Back in Lincoln County: On January 20, 1987, Judge Gardner held his "disposition hearing," the judge's way of saying he was about to decide how to dispose of a juvenile named Michael Jones Jr. The judge had taken great pains to author a bulletproof decision denying our motions for a dismissal, or for a new trial. It was his turn to join the war and to strike out at us. But before he made his findings concerning me, he decided to even things up a little all around.

He started with Stapleton: "Mr. Stapleton is very aggressive and very opinionated. On several occasions in the pretrial hearings he was openly hostile to defense counsel—particularly when it involved discovery. At times he gave this Court the impression that he felt that defense counsel and the courts were troublesome interferences to him. An example of this is as follows: After the polygraph operator told Mr. Stapleton the results of the polygraph, and Mr. Stapleton and Mr. Marquis decided not to disclose them, Mr. Stapleton told the polygraph operator not to prepare a report. One of his reasons, which he testified to in the *State vs. Sandra Jones* hearing, was so there wouldn't be any written report that the defense could discover." Although the state resisted discovery, the judge said, "in fairness, whenever the court ordered something produced, it was produced." Such was not my memory of it. But memories, too, fade in war.

It was my turn now to receive Gardner's personal judgments of me: "Mr. Spence's national reputation, presence, and style appeared to intimidate the prosecution and make them somewhat defensive. Communication between the prosecution and the defense, at least that of which the court was aware, was not good. Mr. Spence indicated that, based on the lab's gunpowder residue tests, the Jones' defense would argue that Mrs. Gerttula had a handgun and shot her husband. This created an unsettled and tense atmosphere.

"Mr. Spence was also very confrontational. He has absolutely brilliant skills in phrasing questions, in recalling facts, and in thinking quickly. He has a great deal of energy and enthusiasm. However, his style, at least as observed by this Court, is extremely confrontational." I thought his last comment was fair.

But how can one be *nice* in war? How can one be nice when the unlimited forces of the state are hurled against a powerless woman and her child and you are all that stands between them? I should not confront the judge or counsel when the rules of this war were violated? I should bow and speak in a quiet voice, cloaking honest feelings while the prosecutor, the witnesses, and the judge "dispose" of this woman and her child? Charge me with being confrontational. Aggressive, yes. Charge me with wielding a shameless passion for justice. But do not charge me with being nice. Judge Gardner did not.

"Mr. Marquis," Judge Gardner wrote, "although to a much lesser degree [he had inserted the word "much" in handwriting as an obvious helpful afterthought], responded in kind. Therefore, it was not very long into the trial when there were accusations of misconduct, ethical violations, fraud, intentional misrepresentations, etc. There were any number of angry exchanges."

The judge said he "recalled requesting the State to try to set aside the animosity generated in the pretrial proceedings, and to try to fairly evaluate the strength of their case." But Gardner forgot then, and seemingly forever, that he was told, in effect, by the prosecution that they would, indeed, evaluate their case, give Mrs. Gerttula a lie detector test, and dismiss the case if she was shown not to be telling the truth—that's how we heard it. Then Judge Gardner had once more recited his order to the prosecutors: "If there is any deceptive result of material questions, then you should convey that fact to Mr. Spence."

Gardner offered up his own defenses for Marquis and Stapleton concerning the polygraph—four of them: The first was that Mrs. Gerttula's emotional state rendered her test invalid. (Gardner also found that Toliver genuinely *believed* she was emotionally unfit for the test because she had just learned that she was accused of shooting her husband and that therefore the test was rendered invalid.) Second, that because the results of the test were not admissible evidence, they would not come under the *Brady* rule, which, in general terms, requires the state to turn over to the defense any material or evidence that could be favorable to the defendant. Third, Marquis and Stapleton thought that if they disclosed deceptive answers, this information would somehow come to Judge Gardner's attention. Why, I wondered, didn't the prosecutors want the court to know the truth? But Gardner took care of that by simply saying that he assumed the results had been inconclusive. How had he arrived at that conclusion considering the record was utterly silent on the matter? And finally, the judge blamed the "confrontational attitude of the attorneys that discouraged any open communication between counsel." My confrontation had been in open court. Had he forgotten how we'd pleaded in vain with His Honor to order the prosecutors to give us the results of the lie detector test? Still the judge did admit that he had "vacillated somewhat" on his discovery ruling on that issue, but he saved himself once more by emphatically asserting that the polygraph results had nothing to do with his decision.

In the end Judge Gardner found "the District Attorney's decision not to reveal the results of the two questions was incorrect and improper. Even in gray areas"—*gray areas?*— "the prosecutor must be 'above board' and err in favor of disclosure. If Mr. Marquis was not sure what the Court wanted the prosecution to disclose, he should have gotten clarification."

As for Peck having taken the Fifth, Judge Gardner said, "It would be pure speculation to infer that Officer Peck must have done something intentionally wrong or dishonest with the evidence. Likewise it is pure speculation to infer that Officer Peck was in some sort of a drug-induced state that caused him to do a poor job of collecting the evidence." Then Gardner resorted to his own speculation. "Were all of those matters to have been brought out at trial, they would not have changed this Court's decision." He had concluded that Michael Jones was a boy who had recklessly killed another human being. No evidence and nothing I could do would change his mind.

The judge was now ready to dispose of Little Mike: when I heard his words my heart stopped. "So the terms of the disposition will be as follows: the court is going to order that Michael be committed to the custody of the Children's Services Division for placement at MacLaren School for Boys for a time period not to exceed his 21st birthday."

After the shock of it, it was hard for me to hear him add, "But I am going to suspend that commitment and place Michael on probation to the Juvenile Department under the following terms and conditions . . ." The judge's conditions included that Little Mike could not come to Lincoln County, his home, without permission; that he continue to live with his grandmother; that he not be in the vicinity of any weapons; that he continue school and counseling. "And I'm going to indicate that before the Court will terminate probation I will have to be assured *that the counseling program has touched on his involvement in this incident* [my emphasis]." There it was again, the state's attempt, by one means or another, to trample the boy's constitutional right to remain silent. The state had given the right to remain silent to its own, Detective Ronald Peck—but not to a fifteen-year-old child who, at last count, had equal rights as a citizen.

Little Mike was not to reside with his mother, the judge said. She could visit the boy at his grandmother's. Again the judge emphasized he would not allow the boy to go home where he longed to be, unless for some short visit that was first permitted by the Juvenile Department. And even then, Mrs. Gerttula would have to be given notice that the boy was in the county, as if the judge believed the woman would be in some kind of undisclosed danger.

I thought the judge *believed* he was doing right. Had he possessed an evil heart, he could have sent the boy off to MacLaren. Had he been a vindictive man, he could have found me in contempt of court. Had he been a blindly prejudiced man, he would have overlooked chastising Marquis and Stapleton for failures concerning the polygraph. He, too, was a man who *believed*.

Now he looked down on the young, open-faced Little Mike, whose eyes were wide as half-dollars.

"A lot of people have gotten behind you and supported you: your tutor is here and had very good things to say about you, the school has had very good things to say about you, your grandmother has obviously devoted a lot of time and love to you, and I think what you have to consider when you look at these terms and conditions, and some of them may seem onerous, I think you have to realize . . ." The judge stopped to catch up with his thoughts. "I guess what I'm trying to tell you is life's a series of alternatives; if this had happened when you were an adult, you would be looking at ten to twenty years in the penitentiary. You should think of that if you ever get to feeling sorry for yourself about not being able to go back and live at your home."

Then he turned to Mrs. Gerttula and members of her family, who had sat through the whole proceeding as if to remind the judge that their retribution was his responsibility. "I guess my final comment would be to the Gerttula family, who have attended all of the proceedings. I suppose the hardest thing for people not involved in the system is to say, 'Here's a boy who's killed my husband and here he's going to go live with his grandmother,' and all I can say is that that relates to the fact that we have a juvenile system. I think it relates to the fact of the particular circumstances under which he was raised and the particular circumstances of his involvement. More than that I cannot say."

Later we sat around the tables at Mo's Annex, eating bowls of steaming chowder. "Gerry," Eddie said after we'd sat there a long while, too drained to move, "we won Mike's case." The crab boats were motoring by, pots stacked on deck, the men unloading their catch at the fish plant next door. "Now he's going to be free when he's twenty-one and with no record. His juvenile court record will be sealed."

"That's right," I said.

"This judge may have been wiser than we thought all along." Eddie was like that. Sometimes he saw things through a clearer prism. "Gardner found the boy guilty so he could keep control of him for a while. I think the judge did believe he killed Gerttula in the defense of his mother. But if Little Mike did, well, he still killed a man. His mother is charged with murder. You can't send a kid home to a mother charged with murder, not the mother that Gardner sees, until that matter is cleared up. He thinks this kid is a good kid. If he really thought he was guilty of a reckless killing, he'd send him off to MacLaren so fast it'd make your head swim."

"That's right," Steve said. "Little Mike'll come out of this without a record and without having spent a day in jail. We may not have convinced the judge that Monica Gerttula fired the shot, but we sure convinced Gardner that Little Mike was an okay kid. Okay kids don't kill people without a reason."

"Yeah," Michele said. "And Gerry, Gardner didn't

much like the prosecutors, either. He just disliked you more. Gardner did have some doubts."

"If he had doubts, he should have acquitted Mikey," I said. I was still hurting.

Michele was silent for a moment. "Keeping this boy away from the family farm, in school, and working might be just what Little Mike needs."

"Gardner was acting like God up there," I said. But that was his role. I was the kind who always wanted unconditional surrender.

"Maybe God would have ruled the same way," Steve said.

We pushed back from the table and went outside onto the bay front. And all I saw were the silent stars. I listened, and all I could hear was the sad, long bellow of the whistle buoy guiding the boats into safe harbor.

32

No doubt Judge Haas's complaint against Stapleton and Marquis was of considerable embarrassment to them. On December 20, 1985, the *Newport News Times* carried a blaring headline: "Portland judge files complaint against DA, deputy." Full-column photographs of both Stapleton and Marquis smiled out from the page. Haas's charges were reviewed in the story, and to each Stapleton replied, "I believe this complaint by Judge Haas is simply a vindictive response to Mr. Marquis' judicial fitness complaint."

Marquis made his own explanation to the press: "At no time whatsoever during this case have I disbelieved the veracity of Mrs. Gerttula," again quoting Toliver's conclusion that the test was invalid based on the fact "that just before testing Gerttula had learned that Spence thought she had fired the gun that killed her husband." And Marquis now asserted a new reason for Stapleton's instructing Toliver not to prepare a report. Such, he said, "is not uncommon where there is no stipulation or legal purpose to be served by preparing such a report." Marquis told the press that the test charts were kept and were made available.

The newspaper was having a marvelous time of it. The *News Times* simultaneously carried the story of Marquis's complaint against Haas. That headline read, "Complaint filed against Haas, too." Although by Oregon law a complaint against a judge was to be held confidential, the story led off with the following: "Joshua Marquis has divulged via letter that he considered some of Judge Harl Haas' actions 'prejudicial to the administration of justice.'" Marquis used his response to Haas's complaint to now make public Marquis's complaints against Judge Haas. In his bar response Marquis complained, among other things, that Haas had removed Marquis from the Jones case to "prevent contamination," then had contaminated the case himself by allowing the Gerttula lie detector test to be discussed in open court; that Haas had tried to prevent Marquis from responding to Haas's charges by attempting to withhold certain transcripts in the Jones case; that Haas did not provide complete transcripts to the Oregon bar of Toliver's testimony, implying that the parts left out were crucial to Marquis's position; and that Haas had decided early in the Jones case how he would rule. Marquis concluded by saying that Haas's complaint against him was vindictive, and that Haas had attempted to backdate his letter to the Oregon State Bar "to conceal or falsify dates on which matters were received or sent."

Michele, Steve, and I weren't to be spared. On March 5, 1987, Stapleton and Marquis filed their complaint with the Oregon State Bar against us. They wrote that Michele and Steve were associated with me and were responsible not only for their own wrongful conduct but for mine as well.

By this time Brown had appealed Sandy's case to the Oregon Court of Appeals. Conventional wisdom in the legal community was that Haas's dismissal of the charges against Sandy would be reversed and Sandy's case would be sent back for trial. Beyond mere vindication, I thought Stapleton and Marquis had revealed another motive for their complaint against me when they wrote, "Furthermore, although Mr. Spence is an out-of-state attorney, a finding of a violation of our Disciplinary Rules would allow the Supreme Court to exercise its discretion in allowing or denying his further appearances in Oregon state courts." They'd had enough of me, and clearly, I thought, they were attempting to use the disciplinary process to do that which no judge had yet thought proper—to deprive Sandy her choice of counsel.

Stapleton and Marquis claimed I'd violated the rules when, *before* I took either of the cases, I told the local press, on November 21, 1985: "We are investigating the facts of the case, and if we find she and her son are innocent of the crime, we will ask the Oregon courts if we can defend her, along with her present attorney."

I was quoted as saying on November 25, 1985, that I was interested in the case because "it has all the ingredients of a woman's case. Sandy Jones's treatment is typical of the kind women get from law enforcement, not the careful treatment that men get. This powerless woman goes to the law for help and doesn't get it. Instead she gets persecuted."

I told the paper I was impressed with the local lawyers working on the case, but, with a certain braggadocio I'd grown to regret, I said, "This case needs me." Marquis and Stapleton claimed these utterances constituted a violation of the rule against making out-of-court statements of the lawyer's personal opinion of the guilt or innocence of his client and, further, that they were designed to influence public opinion.

They charged Steve and me with issuing "a false process" when we subpoenaed Mrs. Gerttula into the juvenile court for her deposition. No such process, they claimed, was permitted in the juvenile court since it is a criminal proceeding. *A criminal proceeding?* When before we had wanted a jury in the boy's case, Marquis had argued that since it *wasn't* a criminal case no jury should be allowed.

Their favorite charge, of course, was their perennial claim that I was guilty of a conflict of interest when I defended both Sandy and Little Mike. They went on for two pages about that one. But if the conflict of interest wasn't enough to get rid of me, they said they'd heard I was going to write a book about the case, that I had obtained a release from Sandy granting me such rights, "and, if true, this would further underscore the serious conflict which would prevent the exercise of independent judgment by Mr. Spence on behalf of his client." Of course, I'd had no such agreement with Sandy or Little Mike.

Then Marquis and Stapleton threw an independent charge at Michele. During Little Mike's trial, by checking the records at local gun stores and by looking at public courthouse records, Steve discovered that Raymond Gerttula had purchased ammunition and that he owned three large-caliber handguns that had come into Wilfred Gerttula's possession. Because Michele had represented Raymond Gerttula previously, Marquis and Stapleton alleged she had revealed confidential client information. Not only had Michele not disclosed it to us, she had completely forgotten about it.

"Oh, for Christ's sake," she sputtered on reading their complaint. "That's all public record. The DA has it, the court has it—hell, Ulys and Josh should have disclosed it to us as exculpatory evidence!"

Marquis and Stapleton wrote that their complaints against us had been prepared the year before, and that Marquis had contacted the bar's general counsel concerning them, but they'd waited until after Sandy Jones's case had been disposed of "to avoid allegations that the Bar complaint was filed to interfere with the preparation or pursuit of a vigorous defense." Publicly, we were once again charged as unethical lawyers, and if Sandy's case was reversed by the Court of Appeals and sent back for trial, the very poisoning of the jury pool that Judge Haas had tried so hard to prevent still loomed dangerously overhead.

On April 3, 1987, Michele, Steve, and I filed our joint response to the complaint, a forty-five-page document that answered each of the charges and included numerous exhibits including letters from two respected members of the bar pointing out that since we were imposing a family defense, there was no conflict of interest for me to represent both Sandy and Little Mike. To make certain we were on ethically solid grounds *before* we entered Sandy's case, we'd obtained legal opinions from both Jim Shellow and Charlie Burt. Shellow, a premier criminal defense lawyer and former president of the National Association of Criminal Defense Lawyers, wrote in a letter dated January 15, 1986, that under the circumstances of this case no conflict of interest existed. He observed, "Unfortunately, motions to recuse defense counsel for imagined conflicts of interest are becoming increasingly routine in high profile criminal cases . . . it follows a pattern which has been of concern to the criminal defense bar for the past several years."

And Charlie Burt, that sweet old fighter for little persons' justice, now passed on, a highly respected Oregon criminal defense lawyer, also writing *before* we entered Sandy's case, said, "Under these facts I can see no possible conflict of interest on your part. Indeed it seems to me that these two clients have a community of interest. . . . I would not hesitate to undertake both cases if I were in your position."

And so this damnable war had escalated even further. If, once we'd been worried about our clients' lives, we must now also be worried about our own professional lives, for our right to practice law was being officially questioned, and under agreements between Wyoming and Oregon, any misconduct on my part in Oregon would be a matter that could result in my discipline in Wyoming as well.

We hoped that Marquis's and Stapleton's complaints against us would be summarily dismissed based on our thorough factual responses. But the materials submitted to the bar on each side were vociferous and vitriolic. After our lengthy response, Stapleton and Marquis imposed further acrimonious arguments against our defenses, which required us to give even further explanations. We were defending ourselves, and the more we defended, the worse it seemed to get. Like struggling in quicksand. No statement, no matter how insignificant, was left unchallenged. Lengthy rebuttals and endless caustic editorializing filled the bar's files. In the meantime, the same bitter process was taking place with Haas's charges against Marquis and Stapleton.

Finally, seven months after the first complaint had been filed, the Oregon bar felt compelled to make a summary of the entire free-for-all. The charges and countercharges had become so voluminous and confusing no one could make sense of them. The bar's summary rambled on for forty single-spaced pages of its own. One thing was obvious to me: the entire matter was beginning to look more like an uncontrolled catfight than anything else. I thought that had been the DAs' strategy from the beginning and that we had fallen into it.

On July 6, 1987, the Judicial Fitness Commission wrote Judge Haas, "This letter is to inform you that the Commission has completed its review of the above referenced matter [Marquis's complaint against Haas]. In accordance with Oregon statutes, which require the proceedings be confidential, we can only report that the matter is now terminated." That decision did not please Marquis. Almost immediately he filed a new complaint against Haas, but, as he had threatened previously, this time with the Oregon bar, his contention still being that since Haas was not only a judge but a lawyer as well, the bar therefore had the authority to review Haas's conduct.

The judicial commission's review was confidential so that no attorney could interfere with the judiciary's independence by filing a complaint whenever some lawyer might get miffed over a judge's ruling. I thought Marquis was circumventing that process with the apparent strategy to subject Haas to the same public scrutiny that Stapleton and he had suffered. His language was far from temperate. He wrote, "I have found myself forced off a case in an unprecedented manner and then subjected to deliberately false and malicious lies by Judge Haas."

Haas answered by attaching his response to Marquis's earlier complaint before the Judicial Fitness Commission, asking the bar to dismiss the charges in view of the fact that Marquis's latest complaints had previously been dealt with by the commission and dismissed.

But Marquis wouldn't let it go. "If Judge Haas believes the Judicial Fitness Commission will clear him, I invite him to authorize the commission to release its findings." Then Marquis filed yet another paper with the bar in which he argued his major positions anew and ended his complaint by writing, "He [Haas] has grossly abused that office, made blatantly untruthful statements, and still refuses to even address my charges."

On November 9, 1987, Judge Haas, rising to Marquis's bait, wrote the Judicial Fitness Commission asking the commission to release its findings in his case, "because of Mr. Marquis' insinuations about the commission's actions in dismissing his complaint." The commission refused. Still Marquis's complaint against Haas before the Oregon bar lingered on unresolved. Haas, it seemed, was now caught in the same trap that ensnared us.

Our hope for a summary dismissal of the prosecutors' complaints against us was soon dashed. On September 15, 1987, the entire mishmash was sent over to the Mult-nomah County Local Professional Responsibility Commission to investigate, and E. Joseph Dean, a Portland lawyer, was named as the special investigator by the bar's general counsel. His mandate: to turn over every stone. This was bad news for us. I'd learned from long experience that people who are given the duty to investigate too often interpret it as one requiring them to make charges. I was angry and worried. For having undertaken the defense of a poor person without cost to the State of Oregon, I was now being investigated as an unethical lawyer, and because Michele and Steve had served as co-counsel, they were caught along with me. So was the judge for having bravely taken the action he thought was just and right.

"I'm sorry I got you guys into this," I said.

"Oh, bullshit," Michele said. "You didn't get me into anything. It was the other way around. I think they just want to fry your ass because you're a big-shot lawyer and they aren't. The only power they have is to show the big shot he ain't such a big shot after all."

"I don't know," Steve said. He sounded sick, he who never entertained a negative thought in his life. "I think that Marquis and Stapleton can't figure it out. So they pawn it off on some investigator to figure it out for 'em."

By July 1987, our briefs and the state's reply brief had been filed in Sandy's case on appeal, and the court had set oral arguments for September 4, 1987. Terry Leggert, assistant attorney general, appeared for the state. We'd been worried that the "big-shot lawyer factor" could work against us if I appeared before the appeals court. For several reasons, we thought that Michele might be just the lawyer to do the argument. She'd written the brief and knew the case inside and out. And most of all, she was capable and aggressive and certainly wouldn't wither under fire.

When the day came for oral arguments Marquis had decided to drive to Salem to hear them in person. Although Sandy's case had never been his case, Marquis had by then adopted the entire Jones matter as his personal issue, as had we.

The courtroom was not large as courtrooms go. It was mostly notable for its stained-glass seal of the State of Oregon on the ceiling. Facing the bench were tables for counsel with a podium in the middle. Arguments before the court were usually made without much of an audience, and there were no rows of wooden pews as in the typical trial courtroom. Instead there were chairs all along the back wall of the room. There Marquis took a seat. Michele said he got up and sauntered over to the table assigned to the state's appellate counsel, Terry Leggert, laughed, and made faces. She was touchy. Everybody was.

The court gave each side only fifteen minutes to argue what had taken more than a year to fill thousands of pages of transcripts. The judges were busy. Fifteen minutes was all the time they'd spare.

After the arguments we waited. And waited. Finally on December 30, 1987, the Court of Appeals gave an ugly, belated Christmas present to Sandy Jones. They said she'd be given the opportunity to stand before her peers for trial. With cold judicial dispatch, Judge Edward H. Warren disposed of every troublesome argument that Michele had made. In his opinion he wrote:

> The trial court found that "Peck's unavailability as a witness is due to the state's failure to grant immunity

from prosecution after the defendant requested that the state grant Ron Peck immunity. Although it is probable that, but for the state's refusal to grant immunity, Peck would have testified, the issue is not whether the state had some causal effect on Peck's assertion of the privilege, but whether the state acted with the purpose of depriving defendant of the benefit of Peck's testimony." *In the absence of any evidence that the state sought to influence the witness to assert the privilege, there is no state violation of the defendant's privilege under the state Confrontation Clause* [my emphasis].

Of course the state hadn't *influenced* Peck to take the Fifth. Then the court provided us with another marvelous insight: in effect the appeals court said that since Peck was not to be called as a witness, his unavailability would not violate Sandy's rights. The judicial dog had been set to chase its own tail. We had complained that Peck took the Fifth and therefore *we'd* been deprived of our right to confront him. Warren said, Yes, he won't testify, therefore you have not been deprived of anything!

As to our right to due process under the Fourteenth Amendment, which demands fair play, Warren said we'd proved nothing. Nothing at all. We'd been deprived of no evidence, especially since Brown had agreed we might put in Peck's testimony through the transcripts in Little Mike's case. This, of course, would deprive the jury the opportunity to test Peck's credibility, the way he would react on the witness stand to my cross-examination, the sound of his voice, his hesitation, his facial expression. I wondered how many murder cases Warren had ever defended.

As anyone might have predicted, the Court of

Appeals did not address the crux question: How is it that under the Fourteenth Amendment of the Constitution, which demands fair play, the state can literally buy the testimony it needs to convict the accused by making shameless deals with criminals, offering them lighter sentences, paroles, freedom, even new identities and a new secret life—the most scandalous kinds of bribery—while an ordinary citizen could not force the state to give simple immunity to Peck for his testimony?

Then the dreaded words followed at the end of the court's opinion: "Reversed and remanded for trial," which meant that Sandy Jones must once more face the music— perhaps the doomful requiem after a full-blown jury trial in a Multnomah County courtroom.

Michele didn't want to give Sandy the hard news over the phone. She drove out to the farm. The months had worn at the woman's health. Not much was left of her to absorb more punishment, to cope with the threat of prison for the rest of her life, which meant she would lose her family as well. To her that would be worse than death.

"I felt so sick for her," Michele said. "Nothing I could say would comfort her. How could I explain that irrational decision to Sandy or to anyone? There was no damn logic to it."

"I sure couldn't explain it," I confessed.

"God, the thoughts you torment yourself with, like maybe I didn't write a good enough brief, or I could have made a better argument."

"It's nobody's fault," I said. "Not even the judges'. They're just people looking at another damned criminal file. It's just business as usual, justice as usual from a court that sits too high to see the people below."

On March 1, 1988, Michele filed our Petition for Review in the Supreme Court of Oregon, Oregon's court of last resort. On May 24 of the same year, that court turned us away as well with one heartless word, in capital letters:

"DENIED."

33

When a lawyer faces the stark reality of a trial and sees the specter of prison bars across the face of his innocent client, his heart sometimes weakens. Was there some other solution to Sandy's case? I felt the gripping fear I always felt before I walk into a courtroom—maybe I couldn't convince a jury, maybe I'd stumble and fall in the trial, maybe Judge Haas, having been reversed, might not be as forgiving.

In June 1988, Michele wrote James Brown. Perhaps Sandy could plead to a misdemeanor, something like assault. No jail time. She'd already served seven months waiting to go to trial for a crime she didn't commit. And she and her family had suffered the agony of waiting for these nearly three years, their lives in roiling turmoil. Sandy said that when her old mother heard that she'd have to go back to court again, the old woman just lay in bed crying.

Michele called me. "Brown wants Sandy's ass in the pen. He wants blood."

I said, "The way I see it, if Sandy doesn't do time, he can't call it a win. He has to have something to show Lincoln County for all the money he's spent."

At Haas's urging, Michele and Brown finally met with the judge in September to try to settle the matter, but Brown's neck stayed stiff. Gerttula was dead. The people were entitled to justice, and he wouldn't accept a plea to anything but a felony, and with time in the penitentiary. He'd leave it to the judge to decide how much. But we'd often been forewarned about Haas's reputation—once the accused was found guilty, Haas was severe in his sentencing. We had no choice but to head for the courtroom. Then we came up with another strategy.

Marquis had forayed into politics and had run Ulys Stapleton's campaign for reelection. The recall petition against Stapleton hadn't gathered enough signatures to remove him, but it became the foundation for the ensuing campaign against him. That, along with the adverse publicity he'd suffered in Sandy's case, spelled his political doom as DA, and the voters turned Stapleton out of office. New county commissioners took office as well, one of whom was Norma McMillan, the woman who'd cared for Little Mike shortly after the shooting. She became the newly elected chairman of the board.

If we could get the case postponed until *after* the first of the year when the newly elected DA, Dan Glode, would take office, maybe he'd want to save the county money, be a hero of sorts, and dismiss the case—or at least accept Sandy's plea to some minor offense. Michele asked all three commissioners to sign affidavits that they had no objection to the case's being continued until after January 1, 1989.

It was November 7, 1988, and we were on a conference call with Judge Haas. Wayne Belmont, the county's attorney (not the DA), was on the line raging that Michele had gone directly to the commissioners without having talked to him. The new prosecutor, Glode, was also on the call. In his campaign Glode had made a major issue of the Jones case. He'd been critical of Stapleton's conduct and howled about the cost of the case to the county. But now he wanted no part of it. And Brown was complaining to the judge that he'd lose credibility with his witnesses if the case were again delayed.

I heard Judge Haas's voice get low and hard. The case was ripe for trial, he said. By then it had been three and a half years since Wilfred Gerttula had been shot. Haas's feet were set in concrete. No matter my arguments, he ordered that we proceed to trial on November 28, 1988.

When that morning came, I walked into the courtroom, the juices flowing, the adrenaline up, the mind-set of war having replaced the fear in the belly. I was ready and I wanted the fight. Michele was there along with my youngest son, Kent, just out of law school. Eddie had stayed at home fighting other battles for us. Then Judge Haas came in, gave us his usual impish smile, and called the court to order.

Yet one critical matter was unattended to. The attack by Marquis and Stapleton filed with the Oregon bar against both the judge and us lawyers was being investigated by the bar at the very moment we were headed into this trial. I filed another motion to dismiss. I wrote in the motion, "Sandy Jones must either sacrifice the attorneys of her choice and face the likelihood that she cannot obtain *pro bono* counsel with equivalent experience and competence, or she must proceed with her present attorneys, who are under fire, under investigation, and who will be in continuous jeopardy themselves during the trial of this case." This was a real conflict of interest, one created by Marquis and Stapleton, who, as I charged, "intentionally continued to assert themselves behind the scenes contrary to the order of this court to the end that their vindictive acts have deprived this defendant a fair opportunity to defend herself and may deprive her of the effective assistance of counsel"—another constitutional guarantee.

I argued to Judge Haas, "Here on the morning of the very

first day of trial comes the newspaper, and in big bold print is the story for the entire state to read that says we are bad lawyers." Once again I called Marquis to the stand to answer for his statements to the press. Derision was in his voice—he had First Amendment rights. He admitted he had "a driving interest in the case" and had, on a number of occasions, met with Carmel Finley, the Lincoln County stringer for the *Oregonian*. He admitted to conversations about the prosecution of the case with Wayne Belmont, county counsel, Dan Glode, the DA-elect, and a list of others. He'd spoken on dozens of occasions with an attorney named Ronnau, who had represented the Gerttulas against Sandy, and he'd discussed Michele's fees with the court administrator. He'd talked with someone in the Attorney General's Office about Little Mike's appeal and to Terry Leggert, the lawyer handling the state's appeal in Sandy's case. Leggert testified that Marquis had even written her a letter correcting factual inaccuracies in her brief. My memory was that this man had clearly been told by the judge to stay out of this case.

Marquis refused to admit that his bar complaint against us might affect our ability to effectively represent Sandy. "Do you make room for the possibility that that might affect a defendant's trust and faith in her lawyer?"

"Mr. Spence, the world's full of possibilities. Yes, I suppose it could. I don't know."

I asked him if he didn't concede that what jurors read in the press might affect a juror's state of mind. I said, "That's one of the reasons, isn't it, Counsel, that we're very careful about what we do to affect the rights of a defendant, especially in the public media?"

"Yes," he said, as if he were admitting nothing.

"And you knew that at all times when you were making statements to the press, isn't that true?"

"Yes."

Calling his attention to the fact that he had also charged Judge Haas with misconduct as a member of the bar and by that scheme his allegations were spread across the pages of the public media, I asked if he wasn't concerned that such adverse publicity could affect Sandy's right to a fair trial.

He gave his head a little stubborn toss and reluctantly conceded that it would have been wiser to wait until this case had finally been resolved to make his charges, but said that Haas had filed against him. Besides, he claimed, Sandy had committed murder. "If I did not believe in my heart that there was proof beyond a reasonable doubt establishing the guilt of a person, then it would be grossly wrong and unethical of me to bring a prosecution. I have not and would not do that, and did not do that in this case."

I put Wayne Belmont, county counsel, on the stand, who said that after the Court of Appeals sent Sandy's case back for trial, Marquis just walked into his office, sat down, and began telling him that the county was going to get stuck for a lot of costs—thousands. He admitted that Marquis spoke of the judge and me with "animosity." Marquis wanted the case to come back to Lincoln County so he could prosecute it. He said it was Marquis's position that Haas had removed Stapleton but not Marquis. I thought we must not have been in the same courtroom when the judge made his order ousting the Lincoln County prosecutors.

This case was totally out of control. Stapleton and Marquis were running wild, the press was poisoning the jury, we were swimming in a quagmire of charges brought against us by Marquis and Stapleton, and the judge himself had been smeared in the press. I wanted the high court to exercise its inherent supervisory control of the case. Haas needed help,

I thought. We needed help as well. I'd ask the judges of the high court to postpone the trial until the bar complaints had been disposed of.

I called Ulys Stapleton to the stand. He stomped in angry steps to the witness chair. In long hours of questioning he came close to admitting that Marquis's complaint against Haas may have been filed so that it would appear that Haas's complaint against them was retaliatory. "There were things along that vernacular" was how he put it.

"Let me ask you if there weren't conversations by Mr. Marquis to the effect that 'I'll get the old bastard [referring to Haas] for having dismissed the Sandy Jones case.'"

Stapleton: "I don't recall. He could have said those things. I don't recall specifically if he did. There have been conversations. There were some strong feelings about Judge Haas. There have been conversations of that nature before." And he admitted, under steady questioning, that a by-product of the bar complaint might be that Haas would have to take himself off the case. "It was in the back of our minds that that would be a consideration."

Stapleton admitted that the complaints filed against him by Haas had caused him anxiety and diverted his attention from his work. At last he conceded that we, too, could suffer a similar anxiety as a result of their complaints against us. I reminded him that not only was I acting without cost to the county, but I would now have to hire a lawyer to defend myself before the bar. He agreed there was a limit to the forces that Sandy could muster, and he knew by filing their complaints we would have to expend our effort and moneys to also defend ourselves. Not only that, he admitted that Sandy might be concerned whether our strategies in the case were in her best interests on the one hand or were adopted to protect her defense counsel on the other.

I asked Stapleton, "Did you know that Mr. Marquis wanted this case returned to Lincoln County so he could prosecute it?"

"I believe he'd like to prosecute it, especially if you're the defense attorney."

The next morning I called Marquis back to the stand. The evening before someone had violated the judge's standing order that prohibited any witness from discussing the testimony of another witness. The day before, on the stand, Mrs. McMillan had repeated some statements about Marquis that I have not revealed here or elsewhere since I thought them only hearsay. Contrary to the judge's order, some lawyer or witness who had heard her testimony in the courtroom told Marquis what she'd said, and Marquis had ordered a transcript of her testimony from the court reporter. I wanted to know which witness had told Marquis and had thereby violated the judge's order. Marquis repeatedly insisted he couldn't remember who told him.

"I don't believe you," I said. I asked the judge to order him to answer my question.

Judge Haas said if Marquis couldn't remember something that important from the night before, how could we believe his testimony concerning matters that had occurred months or years before? Haas said, "I'm *ordering* you to reveal the source of that statement."

"I don't recall. It was one of those people in the hallway."

Haas looked up at the ceiling as if pleading for divine guidance. He was doubtlessly considering contempt. But Christa'mighty, where would that lead us? It was as if the judge had, by the power of Marquis's arrogance, been somehow stripped of his own power. Before I released Marquis from the stand, he admitted that he and Stapleton had discussed "the likelihood that if a judge were under investigation or had complaints filed against him, he might not be able to sit on the case."

Once more I called Michele to the stand. She said the bar complaints had seriously affected her ability to prepare a defense for Sandy because she had to answer the complaints while Sandy's appeal was pending and she was solely responsible for the appeal. She said she'd spent more than a hundred hours in just refuting the continual "baseless allegations to the bar" that had been filed against us for nearly a year, none of which, of course, were billable hours even at the measly $45 per hour the state was paying her. She said so much had been made in the press about the cost of the case to Lincoln County that one attorney had actually stopped her and asked, "Which county are you going to bleed this time?"

"How did that make you feel?"

"Pretty awful." Then she expressed her understanding of the judge's order as it pertained to Marquis and Stapleton: "They are off the case. They have no further ability to participate in the case whatsoever, to contact anybody, to express opinions, to assist in appellate briefs, to make comments to the press, to do anything. They were removed from the case." She thought that the only way to stop the harassment was for Haas to again dismiss the case. Marquis would never stop. On the other hand, Sandy herself didn't want a continuance until the bar complaints were settled. Why should she have to wait months, maybe years more? This threat hanging over her head kept her in living hell. A normal human being can withstand only so much.

"Before I put you on the stand a few minutes ago, you had implored me not to put you on, hadn't you?" I asked Michele.

"Yes."

"You didn't want to testify for what reason?"

"Further testimony about the bar complaints."

"And about unethical lawyers?"

"Yes, sir."

"This room is full of lawyers listening to this testimony, is it not?"

"Yes, sir."

"How does it feel to look at your peers and have to deal with this, Ms. Longo?"

"It's pretty horrible, Mr. Spence."

"A representative from the press is sitting here?"

"Yes."

"You realize he has the power to publish everything that's been said in this courtroom?"

"Yes." She said she felt she might be hurting her client by testifying. Yet she had the obligation to do so.

"What can you do?"

"Nothing, there's no remedy except dismissal."

She said that Marquis's complaints against the judge were wild and baseless. Yet, she said, if the judge got off the case, that was exactly what the DA was attempting to accomplish.

I made my plea to the judge for dismissal. "So the tactics of Mr. Marquis and Mr. Stapleton have been well thought out. 'How do we get rid of the judge? How do we get rid of the attorneys? What do we do to poison the minds of prospective jurors?'"

I pointed out that Marquis insisted he had no memory of who, yesterday, had told him about the testimony of Mrs. McMillan. "How do you deal with such people? I tell you, Your Honor, I don't know what I would do if I were a judge. I feel like you're on the horns of a dilemma. I think that if you dismiss the case, you'll suffer further charges. If you dismiss the case, the prosecutors will charge you publicly with misconduct and will use your dismissal to prove the allegations that they've already brought, whatever they are."

I asked simple questions: "But what would Sandy say if the jury found her guilty? Would she ask, 'Why didn't I have a fair trial?' How do we protect ourselves? How does the judge protect himself? How do we stop them? I ask you not to drag either me or Ms. Longo under this cloud, with this burden." Then I also argued strongly for a continuance until after the bar complaints were settled. I needed a win—any win would help—a dismissal for sure, or at least a continuance.

A great sadness filled me. "I'm involved in this case, Your Honor, and I'll be involved in this case as long as Your Honor tells me to stay here. You have my assurance of that." I said I was no longer there voluntarily. I said I was there out of duty. I remembered when Michele said Sandy's only consolation after hearing she had to go back to court was that I'd still be her attorney.

I ended my argument to the judge by saying, "This woman is a citizen of the United States. She sits here presumed innocent. She has the right to the protection that any other citizen would have. And if we can't protect Sandra Jones, if the judicial system of Oregon cannot protect Sandra Jones from this sort of treatment, nobody in this state is any longer safe."

Brown made a brief closing, the thrust of which was that Sandy had received the "highest level of legal representation," and that the rest of our complaints were simply explainable in terms of the case's complexity. It was three and a half years since Gerttula had been killed and it was time for the case to be resolved.

Judge Haas said he wanted to mull it over and would have a decision for us in the morning. I didn't sleep the whole of the night.

34

The next morning Judge Haas looked down at us, cleared his throat as usual, took a swig of water, and said, "I've been a lawyer for twenty-seven years and eight of those as a district attorney in this county. I've seen a lot of lawsuits and I've seen a lot of attorneys. I've seen people do things in a courtroom that were not the right thing to do to get a verdict. But I've never seen anything like Joshua Marquis in my life," someone, he said, who was apparently attempting to poison the well of public opinion to influence the outcome of a case, especially after he'd been removed from it. He said he wasn't going to hold anyone in contempt because "that would result in this judge, who has felt the sting of Mr. Marquis's pen, being judge, jury, and sentencing judge, and I don't think that would be fair to Mr. Marquis."

Haas said he was shocked "that there's been an attempt by the former prosecutors to manipulate who the judge would be through the charge-filing technique." He said there was no question in his mind that there'd been an attempt to get him off this case. He referred to the "unflagging zeal of Mr. Marquis to just want to knock off the doors of the courthouse to get into court to try this case. And for the life of me, I can't understand those motivations. They're certainly not healthy."

He thought the worst thing he could do for Mrs. Jones

was to grant a continuance. He said he was tempted to dismiss the case. "That would be an unhappy crown of thorns to place on the DA's brow. But this is not their case. This case belongs to the State of Oregon."

The judge waited to see what we had to say. If we were going to trial, how, I asked, could the state put on the testimony of Monica Gerttula when the polygraphs measured her responses as deceptive? I read the Canons of Ethics to Brown: "It is unprofessional conduct for a prosecutor knowingly to offer false evidence." Once more I argued that Brown was on notice of Mrs. Gerttula's polygraph. I said, "Mr. Brown can *believe* anything he wishes, but he must act reasonably and within his responsibility. The former prosecutors did not believe that Mrs. Gerttula told the truth and chose a method to resolve that disbelief—the polygraph." I argued that since the method chosen showed that their disbelief was well founded, they were not permitted to simply say, "I believe." I said reasonable sanctions required that Monica Gerttula be disqualified as a witness.

But Brown argued, "If Monica Gerttula Steele [she was now remarried] were here seated in the courtroom, she would ask, 'When do I get my turn to tell the people what I saw, and when do I get my opportunity to respond to all those accusations that I'm a liar?' We submit, Your Honor, her turn is long overdue." In fairness, so did His Honor. Despite our attempts to exclude Monica Gerttula's testimony from the trial, Haas ruled that she'd have an opportunity to tell her story to a jury.

But that morning the searing question that continued to burn at His Honor was who had, in violation of his order, told Marquis the essence of Mrs. McMillan's testimony? Haas ordered in all the witnesses who'd been in the courtroom the day before and interrogated them in an attempt to find out who had told Marquis about Mrs. McMillan's testimony. But no one admitted they'd told Marquis anything. Then with a resignation bathed in frustration Haas said we'd pick a jury the following morning. I thought he was embracing an unrealistic hope. The next morning, we challenged the entire jury panel and here's why:

Those on the master jury list were selected only from voter registrations when they should have included names from automobile registrations and perhaps other sources. But that wasn't the only problem. I called Janice Hall to the witness stand in support of our motion to quash the panel. Ms. Hall had been the jury supervisor for the past seventeen years and had, during all of those years, dutifully followed the policy laid down for her by her superiors. She admitted that routinely she excused mothers with small children, old people who were capable of serving but who found it inconvenient to attend court, nurses, doctors, pharmacists, attorneys, ministers, priests, blind people (contrary to an Oregon statute), people with certain religious beliefs, all self-employed persons who wished to be excused, people earning their living by commission sales, people with planned vacations, all people not reimbursed by their employer for jury service, people with medical problems (serious or not), members of the military or National Guard, and she excused any other person who requested off whether or not the grounds were sufficient to constitute "extreme inconvenience or undue hardship," which was the statutory grounds by which a citizen could be excused for jury service. What I saw were politicians who let anyone off who wanted off.

Nor was any proof required of the grounds for excusing the juror. No criterion was laid down to establish "undue hardship." No records were kept showing why a juror was excused. Sixty-eight percent of those originally called were excused. In practice, the court administrator was selecting our jury, and only those who actually *wanted* to serve remained. I've always maintained that people who want to pass judgment on others ought not to be allowed to do so. Besides, any competent defense lawyer in a case such as ours would want mothers with children. The government and large corporations pay their workers for jury service. Did we want a jury of government employees and corporate minions judging Sandy, a woman who might, to them, appear to be a pariah of sorts? Did we want only people who were deeply invested in the very system we were up against? I was convinced that a jury that represented less than half of those called to service was not a fair, representative panel. His Honor listened to my arguments carefully. Finally he threw up his hands: "We're going to try this case." He denied our motion to quash the jury and wished us all a happy weekend.

It was raining again. We spent the weekend holed up in the River Place Hotel preparing another petition for a writ of mandamus. First thing Monday morning we were in chambers smiling at the judge again. Of course, he smiled back. Then he said he'd thought about our motion to quash the jury panel over the weekend and was having second thoughts. I asked for time to take the matter to the Oregon Supreme Court. But it was hard to keep the man focused. He was still concerned about Marquis. What if Marquis waited until we were about five days into trial and filed another series of public complaints against Haas that again challenged his ethics? That would further poison the jury panel and affect Sandy's right to a fair trial. I could see that Haas was thinking about stepping down from the case.

But if he quit the case, any attorney, by filing groundless charges, could get rid of the judge. "You cannot be disqualified by the intentional misconduct of Mr. Marquis," I argued. I pulled my chair up a foot closer to the judge's desk, looked him in the eyes, and said in a quiet voice, "If you get off this case, I'm going to get off this case, too." I believed Haas's foremost concern was that Sandy get a fair trial. What would happen to her fair trial if both he and I stepped down? Haas turned to Michele. He wanted to make sure Michele understood that his insisting that Sandy get a fair trial was one thing. If she was convicted, his sentencing would be another. "She may think that if she stands in front of me convicted of manslaughter that I would be that same judge." His eyes grew suddenly hard. "Remember, I told you."

Finally he said he was going to give us a couple of days to prepare our mandamus motion to the Supreme Court on the jury issue. But he said there was no way he'd postpone the trial while the bar disposed of its complaints against us. That could take as much as a couple of years. "We'll start picking a jury Wednesday afternoon at two o'clock."

We prepared a thirty-six-page motion to the Oregon Supreme Court and asked that court to stay the proceeding in Haas's court until the Supreme Court had passed on the merits of our motion. I outlined the entire history of the case, the polygraph issue, the gunshot-residue facts, the changing stories of Monica Gerttula, the engineer who testified that the boy could not possibly have shot Gerttula, the whole liturgy of misconduct by Stapleton and Marquis, the continued insertion of Marquis and Stapleton into the case after they'd been removed, and how Marquis had admitted he wanted the case returned to Lincoln County so that he could personally prosecute the case against Sandy Jones.

I wanted the Supreme Court to take supervisory control of the case, to order the trial continued until after the Oregon State Bar resolved its complaints against both Judge Haas and us, and I wanted the high court to take such action as might be necessary to hasten the bar's disposition of the pending complaints against us.

I set out the facts surrounding how the jury list had been selected and asked the court to order Judge Haas to quash the panel.

The next day we drove to the appellate court building in Salem and filed our motion. We got there around four in the afternoon and waited, hoping the court might yet respond that afternoon. It was dark when we finally left the building and it was pouring rain. The only response that we got was from the Supreme Court's lawyer, who told us that our petition had been denied. But he said, The judges thank you for the large-print type. Honest to God, that's what he said.

The next morning we trudged back to Haas's courtroom. I was exhausted. I looked at the prospective jurors filling the pews, a random group of citizens you might find filling a shopping mall in Portland, these good citizens who wanted to be jurors, who wanted to judge Sandy Jones. I wondered what they thought of her lawyers, who'd been charged with professional misconduct, these lawyers who'd cost Lincoln County and the State of Oregon thousands of dollars while they tried to get a murderer off through one of their slick lawyer loopholes. And this judge: there'd been complaints against him as well. Were these dreadful thoughts only in my troubled mind?

It was then that Brown offered to take a plea from Sandy to manslaughter in the second degree, a felony. How much time she'd actually have to spend in prison would depend on Haas. And Haas wouldn't hint at what he had in mind for her. But I thought under the circumstances of this case he wouldn't sentence her to more than a year or two. On the other hand, even if the jury compromised their verdict, she could end up convicted of manslaughter in the first degree, which carried a maximum penalty of twenty years. And if we won this case, Brown would likely be after her in yet another trial on the attempted-murder charge we'd been successful in severing from this case. I tried to explain it all to Sandy.

"I never did anything," she said. "I never shot anybody. I never asked Mike to shoot anybody. And he never shot anybody. I'm not guilty of anything and I'm not pleading guilty to anything I didn't do."

"A jury could find you guilty of a lot worse than manslaughter in the second degree," I said. "You'd probably be out in a year or two, and it'd all be over. But it's your life. You have to make the decision. We'll fight for you. We've come this far. I think we can win. But you know it's no guarantee."

"I know. I'll pray on it." Then she turned to me. "What do you think I should do?"

"I think you should pray on it," I said.

35

Judge Haas asked the standard questions of the jurors. Had they heard or read about the case? Most had. Did they have relatives or friends in law enforcement, or had they been in law enforcement? Some had. One man had been a security officer for Pacific Northwest Bell. He claimed to be totally unbiased. Another was a research analyst for the Oregon Criminal Justice Commission.

"Great," Michele whispered. "Just who we need!"

Of the first twelve jurors called, seven of them, or members of their families, had been victims of crime. One woman's uncle had been murdered on Christmas Eve, and one woman's sister-in-law had shot an intruder between the eyes in a hotel room. The judge asked about their hobbies. One juror collected frogs. One woman spent a lot of time as a volunteer on the National Executive Board of the Presbyterian Church. I looked at Michele. She knew what I was thinking. I was leery of potential zealots of any denomination. They're more likely to hang your client than forgive him.

When the judge turned the first panel of twelve jurors over to me for my *voir dire* examination, I introduced the jurors to the clerk, Jay Moody, to the court reporter, Dana Hodges, and to Michele. Then I walked over to Sandy, put my hand on her shoulder, and introduced her. I said simply, "She is charged with murder."

I looked at the panel for a moment. Then I said, "I noticed that when the judge told you Sandy was charged with murder, several of you looked at her, which is a natural thing to do. What does a murderer look like? Can you see it in their eyes, in their face? I just wondered if any of you believe, as you looked at Sandy, whether you could tell by looking whether she's innocent or guilty?" No response. The jury was shut down tight, afraid to speak out in this hostile place called a court of law. My job was to release the jurors of their natural hesitancy to speak out, to get past the masks we all wear every day. Finally Juror 7 said, "It's hard to be in that chair"—he pointed at Sandy—"and to know how to be—people judging you and all." He was a thirty-seven-year-old personnel coordinator with a college degree.

I told the jurors I, too, was anxious. Afraid, even. I had a big responsibility. This woman's life, her children's, were in my hands. But there'd come a time in the trial when she and her children would be in the hands of each of them. I said, "Let's go forward to that time. Do you think you might feel a little afraid, too?" Juror 1 said she'd have no anxiety about it at all. She was twenty-two. But when I said it was hard to talk about our fears, she admitted that, yeah, she'd had such feelings. When I asked the panel about it, most raised their hands to say, yes, they felt some anxiousness of their own. Then I asked an eighty-seven-year-old retired lawyer on the panel if he'd like to trade places with me today. "No," he said, "it might not be too much fun." He'd never tried a case.

What does the presumption of innocence mean? Juror 9 said, "I believe her to be innocent and they have to prove it to me that she's guilty." I thought that was as good as I could get. Then I talked to the retired master sergeant. He was used to taking orders. I said, "When the judge says we should presume someone innocent, we say, 'Yes, sir. I will.' But there's a difference between saying it and *feeling* it, isn't there?" "You betcha," he said. He was a serious man.

I talked about television cop shows, and how the cops are usually right and break down the doors and shoot people and we see blood all over. But if Mrs. Jones was innocent, well, the cops must have made a mistake. "We have become a cop-embracing society because we hate criminals so badly." When I asked if they could make room for the possibility that cops make mistakes, they all raised their hands that they could.

Juror 11 admitted he really wanted to sit on the jury. Something different to do, he said. The responsibility wouldn't bother him. Juror 2 hadn't tried to get off because she thought it would be a great learning experience. Well, yes, but I asked, "Have you ever been inside a penitentiary?" Then I asked her if she'd ever considered that she *alone* had the power to stop a verdict of guilty, because the verdict had to be unanimous. "Each of you has the power to decide her life, forever." I had my hand on Sandy's shoulder. "Considering that fact, is there anybody who wants to get the hell out of here?" A couple of jurors raised their hand. They were the ones I wanted. Before I was through I had each juror tell me if he or she believed Sandy was innocent, could he or she stand alone against the others? One woman had been a rose festival junior princess and said that her classmates had decided to hate her, and she felt alone. "It was like her sitting in that chair." She pointed at Sandy. On the other side of the question I had the jurors agree that if they stood with the majority, they'd respect the right of a person who was standing alone. That's what made the system work—a mutual respect for each other.

Another juror wanted to stay on the jury "to see that justice was done."

"What do you mean by *justice*?" I asked. She said it was the right and the wrong of it. "But from whose side?" I asked. The woman sat very proper and straight, her ankles nicely crossed, her hands folded over her lap. I said, "Sandy Jones is here to get justice. Will you give her justice?" She nodded, but I doubted we were working with the same definition of the word.

Juror 7 said she wanted to tell me what was going on with her. "Actually it's happening in two places. One, right here"—she pointed to her head—"and the other down here"—pointing to her stomach. She wanted to remain impartial, but she might not be able to. "There's also a lot of real nervousness about sitting up here and being judged myself, whether or not I will be found worthy of this thing or not." I wanted this juror. She knew herself and was honest about herself. I thanked her.

I told the jurors that as an attorney I had a right to choose the cases I took. If I didn't feel good about a case, I wasn't required to take it. Every lawyer can't take every case. Every person can't be a juror on every case, either, I said. "If I decided I couldn't take a case for some reason, it wouldn't be a comment on my worthiness. It would be a statement about my being a human being." I talked with the jurors about *their* right not to sit on this case if for some reason they didn't feel comfortable about it.

We'd been talking about prejudice. Suddenly I said, "I'd like you to be prejudiced on behalf of my client." The jurors looked surprised.

One said, "I'm sure you would."

"I think I'm entitled to have your prejudice," I replied. "Sandy is presumed innocent." The juror nodded in agreement.

Then Juror 12, the old master sergeant, unexpectedly blurted out, "Frankly, I got those feelings down here, too."

But he said Sandy Jones was innocent until "that gentleman over there"—pointing to Brown—"proves to me that she's not."

"Thank you." The sound of my voice exposed my honest feeling of gratitude.

"You're welcome," he said.

And how do people interpret facts? I said, "If I were your husband, and you were my wife—you smile—I know that's hard to imagine, but if you came home at one o'clock in the morning, I could say, 'Honey, I'll bet you had a flat coming home or you were talking with your friends and the time slipped by,' or—"

A juror interrupted me, "Or you could say, 'Where the hell have you been?'"

"Right." During this trial, I said, they'd hear testimony they could interpret either as innocent or otherwise. I asked how many had been accused of things they hadn't done. All but one juror's hand went up. It was Juror 1 again. Then I asked Juror 1, "Do you agree that there are people who always give the guilty interpretation to whatever fact they look at?" She nodded. I told the jurors they'd hear testimony that Sandy had made threats. They could conclude that she was an evil person or a frightened mother wanting to protect her children. It was up to them to decide.

Juror 2 said, "That doesn't give her the right to threaten someone. Where's it going to stop? We all have to live by the same rules." But when I asked her if she could conceive of a situation where she might do worse than merely threaten, that she might actually use a gun, she suddenly said she firmly believed in self-defense. Many jurors said they'd lay their lives down in an instant to save their child. Even so, Juror 2 wasn't sure that shooting someone would be right. No one was above the law, she said. I made a note. By the time the evening recess came along, the jurors and I were openly discussing our feelings and our view-points.

That evening in chambers Brown was complaining: I'd referred to the defendant by her first name, which is for-bidden in most courts. The judge warned me. Then Brown complained that I was giving the impression to jurors that I didn't take cases unless I believed the defendant was inno-cent.

"To come in here and whimper about things like that!" I said to Brown.

"Let's keep it on an up-tone," the judge warned us, as if he were speaking to feuding siblings. "You guys have a nice evening. Good night." It was 5:02 P.M., December 7, 1988.

Whether Sandy might take a plea to manslaughter was still deeply troubling her, and us. Jury selection was going well. The judge was giving me loads of leeway. Brown seemed willing to sit by and watch it happen. Sandy was pale, and obviously frightened. She said she'd been praying with her family on the plea offer. She was worried that the judge might be mad at her for not pleading guilty and that if she was convicted, he'd punish her further. She was afraid I was mad at her, too. I tried to reassure her. A full trial was her right. It was her life. She had the right to make her own decision. We couldn't make it for her. I could only say I thought things were, so far, going our way in jury selection.

The next morning, the first order of business was not jury selection. Mr. E. Walter Van Valkenburg, an attor-ney for the *Oregonian,* was before the court by the order of His Honor. He was the lawyer who'd solemnly promised the judge to keep in his possession the notes of the *Oregonian*'s reporter Judy Pinckney, and to bring the notes into court when ordered. He was the judge's custodian of the notes.

We remembered that, armed with the results of the autopsy that showed that Wilfred Gerttula had been shot with a large-caliber firearm, not a .22, Trooper Geistwhite had once more gone to interview Monica Gerttula, presumably to get her explanation for insisting that she saw Sandy shoot her husband point-blank with the .22. When Trooper Geistwhite arrived at Monica Gerttula's home, he'd met Judy Pinckney, who was just leaving. We believed Pinckney's notes would reveal that Mrs. Gerttula had stated to Pinckney that she saw Sandy Jones shoot her husband point-blank with the .22, and that we could therefore prove that her recollection disappeared only after Geistwhite told her the hole in her husband's chest was from a large-caliber weapon, which refuted Monica Gerttula's attempt to nail Sandy with the crime. Obviously, the Pinckney notes were crucial to our defense.

We gathered around the judge's desk in chambers. Van Valkenburg, seemingly above the whole matter, told us he couldn't produce the notes that had been entrusted to him by the judge. He claimed that his law partner Charles Hinkle had been under the impression the case was resolved and had sent the notes back to the *Oregonian*. The *Oregonian* had disposed of the notes and Ms. Pinckney moved to California. I asked that Van Valkenburg be sworn. I wanted to examine him under oath.

Sandy was upset: "Hey, if I destroyed evidence, I'd be in jail."

I had the record of Van Valkenburg's promise to the judge. I read the record to him. "Your Honor," he had assured the court, "I will maintain the notes and they will not leave my possession." In place of the notes we desperately needed, he now produced only a feeble apology.

"I understand your apology," I said, "but would you take Mrs. Jones's place in the penitentiary if she can't produce the evidence she needs for her defense?" He answered saying he'd broken the promise, but not intentionally. When I asked him if he'd read the notes, he admitted he had. Then I said, "I'd bet my bottom dollar you won't have any memory now what those notes said." Right. He had no memory of anything specific. He'd looked for Ms. Pinckney but she'd disappeared without leaving a forwarding address. Of course. It was all that simple.

I punished him with more questions. If he'd lost a $10,000 bill, he'd have a specific proposal on how to go about finding it, wouldn't he? But he couldn't give us any more assistance on how to find Ms. Pinckney. Fred Leeson, a reporter from the *Oregonian*, was sitting in the back of the courtroom. I challenged Leeson by asking Van Valkenburg, "Do you think he [Leeson] will publish *your* testimony?" I pointed at Leeson. Van Valkenburg had no idea. "Don't you think the public should know that the *Oregonian*'s own attorney, charged with the responsibility of retaining the notes upon which the defendant's life depends, has *lost* them and claims that they can't be found? Don't you think the public ought to know that in *blaring headlines* across the paper? If you were an honest editor, wouldn't you publish that?"

"I don't know how to answer that, Mr. Spence."

I called Van Valkenburg's partner Charles Hinkle to the stand. Hinkle had written a letter to Judd Randall, assistant managing editor, that said, "Enclosed are the notes that Judy Pinckney left with us several months ago. You can return them to her or dispose of them as you see fit." He claimed he'd never talked to Van Valkenburg about it. At the time of Hinkle's letter, the Court of Appeals had not yet made its decision on Judge Haas's dismissal of Sandy's case. And I noted this was the same firm that had sued Judge Haas to force the judge to lift his gag order on the attorneys in our case. The judge called a recess.

Michele said, "We need to talk." We walked down the marble-floored hall and leaned up against the wall. "Listen, the bar's investigator—Joe Dean, the one who's been appointed to see if we're unethical?"

"Yessss," I said slowly, expecting the worst.

"Well, he's with the same firm as Van Valkenburg and Hinkle." I looked at Michele. We both started to laugh. It was too much. Too damn much. We notified Judge Haas of the problem. He said he'd call the bar and make sure the bar got our files the hell out of that firm. Then the judge took under advisement the issue of contempt against the *Oregonian*'s lawyers. No judge would dare attack the only statewide newspaper in Oregon. Freedom of the press is a double-edged sword. As someone said, "We have freedom of the press only when we own one."

During that same recess we learned that Ms. Pinckney wasn't so hard to locate after all. The judge had asked the state's investigator Carroll to find her, and the judge said it had only taken Carroll ten or fifteen minutes. Now His Honor gathered us in his chambers to talk to Pinckney on a conference call. I knew already what she'd say. She wouldn't have her notes and her memory would be vague. And that's exactly what happened. But one thing she did remember. After the interview, Monica Gerttula had called Ms. Pinckney and asked her not to publish her interview. *Not to publish the interview she'd just given?* Why?

In the courtroom again, I put Judd Randall on the

stand. He admitted after laborious questioning that the *Oregonian* probably didn't own the Pinckney notes and that nevertheless he'd thrown them away.

"Don't you have a duty to be as honest about your own misdeeds, your own failures, your own negligence, your own willfulness, as you have about publishing others'?"

"Absolutely," he said.

"Don't you think the public has the right to know that you *suppressed* evidence?"

"If that were the case, yes."

"Well, haven't you?"

"It would be a part of a story on this hearing, yes." I beat on him for another hour on a variety of issues. At last it became clear to everyone: the paper's position was that the right of a reporter to her notes trumped the right of a person charged with murder to a fair trial.

A week later, on December 15, a story on the hearing appeared in the *Oregonian*. It was buried at the bottom of page 10 of section C and bore the same-size headline as a story on farm workers receiving money owed to them from a berry farm. The story recounted a Milquetoast summary of the hearing, quoted me as calling the *Oregonian* lawyers and editors "'First Amendment fanatics' who exhibited 'bad faith' by destroying notes that were under the protection of a court order." The story went on to say, "Spence contended, 'The *Oregonian* destroyed the rights of this defendant to defend herself.'" Then, to show balance, the paper quoted Doug Dawson as saying, "We still don't know what was in the note," another of Dawson's masterful statements of the obvious.

Three days later, as if to placate me, the paper ran a story in the same section, also at the extreme bottom of the page, with a picture of me with my cowboy hat. The story was about how trial lawyers had been squeezing into the spectators' gallery to watch me work. "To describe Spence as just a trial lawyer would be to describe Bruce Springsteen as just a New Jersey musician." If Sandy Jones was convicted and I sued them for their willful destruction of evidence, they could show how fair they'd been.

The next morning we met with Sandy in the courtroom before the trial began. Had she decided to accept Brown's offer for a plea? It would have been easy for me to urge her on to trial. But if we lost the case, none of us had to serve the sentence Haas would give her.

"It's like everybody wants me to give up," Sandy said.

I said, "No, we worry just like you do."

"Well, I been really praying. And the Lord spoke to my heart and told me to flip a coin. And I flipped the coin. Heads, I fight on. Tails, I plead guilty. Then Mikey flipped a coin and Shawn flipped one and Big Mike, and everyone got heads." She handed me a coin. "You flip it."

"I don't make decisions that way, Sandy."

"Flip it, Spence. Just flip it."

Finally I flipped it. *Heads.*

"Tell Brown that God's on our side and we're going to go ahead with this trial."

The basis of Sandy's decision was as good as any. No one could foretell what surprises the trial would hold in store for us. No one could read this jury for sure. I thought we could win. We had a fair judge. The jury pool didn't include the wide spectrum of people I'd wanted and was entitled to under the law. But the judge was letting me talk to them and I thought they were responding favorably to me in various ways. What haunts the trial lawyer is something he can't see, some dynamic in the courtroom he doesn't understand. We are only human beings trusting our instincts. If our instincts are wrong, our clients pay with their lives.

I walked up to Brown in the hallway and told Brown his offer was declined. Then I held on to his biceps, one with each hand, and at arm's length I looked him in the eye. With a small smile I said, "God is on our side." A fleeting look of astonishment passed over his face. Then he turned and walked away without saying anything.

Back in the courtroom we continued our selection of the jury. The jurors began to discuss among themselves how they would cope with fear. Juror 5 told about a mean older brother who had rolled him up in a rug and left him there, and how he'd nearly choked to death from the dust inside the rug. He told how a gang of kids couldn't catch his brother so they caught the juror and locked him inside a rest room and cut off all of his hair.

"Pretty helpless feeling to be bullied, isn't it?" I asked.

"Yeah."

When I asked Juror 7 what he'd do if he asked for police protection and didn't get it, he said, "I'd probably look to my own resources. If I was a helpless female, I'd probably invest in a gun." Juror 12 said his wife was "adept at firing weapons," and he'd expect her to use them if necessary. Juror 5 agreed. Juror 1 owned a gun. Juror 7 didn't. Juror 2 had a .25 caliber pistol. She used to carry it and had it in the house because she lived in "a crappy neighborhood."

They all had stories to tell. Juror 3 told how her husband had shot a starting gun (a gun used to start races) at her. Scared her to death. Juror 3 had been robbed six times in six years. She and her husband were even robbed on their honeymoon. Juror 5 had a dozen guns. He hunted. He'd killed elk.

"How do you tell the difference between an entry wound and an exit wound?" I asked.

"When it goes in, it's small. When it comes out, it's blown out."

Thinking of Gerttula's exit wound, I said to the sergeant, "You can put your fist through the exit wound, everybody who's hunted knows that, isn't that true, Sergeant?"

"You betcha!"

"Don't have to be an expert to know that."

"No."

Then Brown took over. He spoke softly to them, kindly, but he spoke in his usual distant, abstract way, using words that sounded as if he were reading from a law book. He talked about circumstantial evidence and finally got down to it with an example about a kid who got into the cookie jar. You find a chair in front of the shelf. There are crumbs on the counter.

Juror 9 interrupted, "Yes, but his brother could have done it."

"No," Brown said. "The older brother is down the street playing with some other kids. But the youngest son has cookie crumbs on his lips."

"Yeah," the juror said, "that would be circumstantial evidence." Brown questioned them about the length of time it had taken to get the case to trial, three and a half years. Juror 7 said it made him curious about what had happened. Juror 2 wanted to know if Sandy had been in prison those three and a half years. Brown said, "I can't tell you."

"You can't tell me?" the juror asked, astounded.

"No."

I interjected, "It's all right with me if he tells you."

Then Brown made a tactical error. "Well, thank you, Counsel, but we're going to work with the rules of Oregon in this case. And I guess maybe I'm getting used to the idea there's some things you're not going to know." That was not only a put-down, but also it left the jurors with the impression Sandy had unfairly been held in prison all those years and that Brown didn't want them to know.

Juror 2 said she didn't like that. Juror 8 wanted to know, was that a speedy trial? Brown didn't answer the juror and instead turned to the Peck matter, told the jurors an officer in the case had been convicted of three crimes involving, among other things, drugs, and could they believe such an officer? Apparently he was going to call Peck after all.

Juror 1 thought she might have trouble believing him. Other jurors joined in. Brown tried to defuse their skepticism: "If a team's got an ineligible player, do they forfeit the game?" Juror 12 thought so. That had been our argument all along.

Brown suddenly dropped that discussion and wanted to know if, because the defendant was a woman, the state would have to prove more than if the defendant were a man. "No," Juror 3 said. But another juror said he'd protect his woman. And he had a retarded son and he'd protect him, too.

Then something set Juror 2 off. She remembered the news stories about the dispute over the road: "Guy's probably a real jerk, but what if he is? Maybe it's because of my gender, but I think men can be more jerky than women." She told Brown she was changing her mind. "If you don't like the way I feel, I'll get down right now. I think she [Sandy] was probably wrong, but I probably would have done it. And I don't even know the story so you probably better let me go." Brown struggled with her but it didn't get better. Then Judge Haas saved Brown by calling for the noon recess.

*   *   *

After the recess Brown again began talking about this officer who'd been convicted of crimes and who was going to testify. Juror 9 finally gave Brown what he wanted. His crime probably had nothing to do with the case, the juror said. The officer maybe regretted what he did. The juror would listen and weigh the man's testimony.

Juror 2 piped up, "Can I say I disagree? Because if he was dishonest once, he's probably been dishonest his entire career."

Juror 9 and Juror 2 began to argue. The judge said, "Let's not direct our questions to each other but to the lawyer." Then Juror 2 said, "I don't think he'd take his oath in this box any more serious than the oath of his job." Brown tried to get her off the jury by asking if she could be fair and impartial to both sides. But she checkmated him. Yes, she said. She could be fair and impartial.

With no place else to go, Brown returned to the cookie jar. What if the older boy told the younger boy to get the cookies? Would the older boy be as responsible as the younger boy?

I objected because Brown well knew there would be no evidence that Mrs. Jones told anybody to do anything. The judge overruled me, but the jurors got the message. Brown forged on. Could they convict the defendant if she was responsible for another person doing the killing? Several said they could. But Juror 2 said she might not realize the impact she put on somebody else, and in that case she might not be responsible.

Brown, too, talked about fear, the jurors continuing to tell their personal stories. One juror was with her husband when he died. The master sergeant had made 119 jumps out of an airplane. Brown was again oblique in his language. He talked about people being "startled" and suggested they might not remember clearly. However, he didn't tie it into the facts of the case. When it came my turn again, I did.

I told the jurors outright what Brown was getting at: that Mrs. Gerttula, who saw this shooting, might have been so stressed that she testified to things that didn't happen. Then I asked, "On the other hand, do you make room for the possibility that this widow had some animosity against Mrs. Jones and that she may have attempted to convict my client with statements that weren't true?" "Yes," Juror 7 said, and the entire panel agreed to keep an open mind on the matter.

I told them I had to cross-examine the widow in detail. Could they see my cross-examination as an aid to the performance of their duties—to find the truth? They said they could.

I asked the sergeant, "If you had a fifteen-year-old boy, and his mother was in serious danger of her life, or he thought she was, you would expect that boy to do something, wouldn't you?"

"You bet your life," he said.

"And if he didn't, he'd disappoint you?"

"He'd hear from me."

"Would you think it unjust if the prosecution turned around and charged your wife with murder because of what her boy did?"

"I'd think there was some injustice, yes." No one disagreed with the sergeant.

I talked about how Sandy was different from other folks, her small farm, her interest in Indian spiritual matters, things of that nature. Juror 7 said she valued people who were different from her. She was my kind of juror.

Then I said that every lawyer has a problem in a criminal trial: Should I put my client on the stand? If I put her on the stand, folks might think she was lying to save herself. On the other hand, if she doesn't take the stand, people might think she must be guilty because otherwise she'd want to tell her story. I asked the jury if they could understand that dilemma. They nodded. "My client will do what I ask her to do. She trusts me. But what if I don't put her on the stand? Will you hold that against her?"

Juror 7 said, "But what if she has information I think I need? I might wish you'd put her on the stand."

I thanked the juror. I said that brought up an extraordinarily important matter. "The defendant isn't required to produce any information of any kind under the law. Did you know that?"

Some didn't know that. That led me into a discussion about the Fifth Amendment. "It was made for us, for American citizens, to be protected against the police."

The master sergeant said, "That's what the Constitution was written about."

"That's what we've been fighting for in those wars, isn't it," I echoed.

"You bet your life," he said.

Then I talked about Little Mike, that I might not put him on the stand either, reluctant as I was to put a boy up against a lawyer like Mr. Brown.

And what about me? Some had seen me on television before. One man said he didn't remember what I said. He only remembered the cowboy hat. I asked if it raised their curiosity a little bit why someone like me would be involved in this case. "Could you make room for the possibility that I might take the case simply because I wanted to?" Juror 3 said he did. I said, "That's because you're a lawyer." And everybody laughed. Then I turned to the judge and with a smile and a nod of approval toward the whole panel, I said, "I accept the jury for cause."

* * *

The next morning we began questioning more jurors to take the place of several who'd been excused for various reasons. I said to the new prospective jurors, "First off, I'm a proud daddy, and I'd like to introduce you to my little boy, Kent." Kent stood up. He's six-four. "He's a young lawyer who's just graduated from law school and came to watch his father in the case to see if he could learn something. So he'll be going in and out of the chambers with me and with Ms. Longo and that's why, and that's who he is."

The questioning went on all morning in a conversational manner, covering with the new jurors the subjects we'd discussed the day before. I thought the prospective jurors felt free to discuss the important issues they'd have to face in the trial. A good *voir dire* helps jurors understand their duty, the issues, the rules of court, and how the law works in a trial.

We talked about judging people. We judge everyone. They were judging me, I said, and I them. We judge out of our own experience. Then I asked them what they thought might disqualify them as a juror. Juror 18 thought she was too sympathetic, that it was a weakness. I replied I reveled in that weakness. But were we cops in our hearts because of all the crime? Juror 16 said, "I saw a comedy act the other night where the fellow asked, 'You call Domino's Pizza and the police department at the same time and guess who will arrive first?'" Everyone laughed.

We talked about how Perry Mason always solved the crime. I said, "I've been at this for more than thirty years and I've never gotten anybody to confess, ever." More laughter. I told them it was not the obligation of the accused to solve the crime. The burden of proof rested entirely with the state, and the proof had to be beyond a reasonable doubt. Then I explained that I might not call a single witness, and that even if the state called a whole raft of witnesses, the state could fail to prove its case beyond a reasonable doubt. You don't count witnesses on each side to decide whether the proof was made or failed.

During lunch, the Joneses were in the park across the street from the courthouse eating sandwiches they'd brought from home. Mike Jr. reported that a man had tried to sell him some marijuana. When Mike said he didn't want any, the man offered him crack. When Mike said he didn't want that either, the guy asked Mike if he wanted to trade something for it. Mike said no. We were in chambers and on the record. It just happened, I said, that Carroll, the state's investigator, was standing nearby watching. "Now that's all I can say. I don't know if it was just a coincidence that he was there in the park when this occurred or whether the state is attempting to set up one of our witnesses."

Brown was livid, as livid as I'd ever seen him. "The innuendo that the state would mess with your witnesses is deeply offensive." He assured the judge that Carroll had been with them during lunch. If one of the state's investigators was attempting to set Little Mike up, I thought revealing it at the first opportunity in the record was the wisest thing to do.

Then, back in the courtroom I talked with the jury about the indictment, which is only a charge made by grand jurors who had heard but one side of the story. We weren't permitted to be present. Did they believe that where there's smoke there's fire? "When you read something about a crime in the paper, don't you say, 'Why, that dirty so-and-so did this and that. It says so right here in the paper'?"

Juror 21 said, "When I read something like that, that's what I feel."

"Would you all agree that Mrs. Jones hasn't had the

chance to tell her story? Still, she doesn't have to say anything?"

Juror 21 said, "I didn't even know that last Monday."

I went on talking randomly from juror to juror, being sure that I talked to each separately. None of us likes to be excluded or ignored. We continued to talk about what the juror could think of that might disqualify the juror. By this means each juror could do some self-appraisal, a task we are not often called upon to do. It gave me an opportunity to see how each juror thought. People who know little of themselves can understand little of others, and a juror must understand the accused before the juror can pass judgment.

When I was finished, and it was again Brown's turn, he said I could continue. He would not require any additional time. Maybe he thought I was overextending my welcome with the jurors, or maybe he realized that any further questions by him would only risk my playing off of his questions to his detriment. I thought he'd made a mistake. I'd broken through the wall that often separates lawyers and jurors. I went on for another hour and grew to know some of the jurors better than some folks I've known a lifetime. That's what should happen in a good *voir dire*. A lawyer ought not to be required to put his client in the hands of strangers.

Had the jurors made decisions that affected the lives of others? Many had. What were they most proud of in their life? Some were proud of their family. Some weren't particularly proud of anything. I spoke of our lives as the work of a sculptor and asked, how many felt they had more sculpting to do? Most raised their hands. Brown sat soberly at his table without objections to my questions. I was revealing who the people were, and by making careful note of their answers, Brown would know best whom to strike when the time came for peremptory challenges. But mine would be an open relationship with the jurors who remained.

Then the time was upon us: Who would be stricken from the jury? Each side could strike six persons from the jury for no cause at all—these strikes are called peremptory challenges—so that lawyers can take off the jury any they feel might be prejudiced against them or their case, even though the lawyer might not be able to recognize an exact, actual prejudice. Often it has to do with nothing more than the chemistry existing between the lawyer and the juror. Juror 2 was stricken by Brown. He also struck others I would have wanted. I likely struck some that Brown would have wanted most to keep. He struck those who seemed more capable of empathy and revealed any sort of attraction to me. I struck those who seemed most ready to judge and who were most judgmental. And I preferred the intelligent juror.

In the meantime Haas said he had been considering contempt against the *Oregonian* lawyers, but he was going to turn the matter over to the District Attorney's Office for Multnomah County for further investigation. I thought it would die there. In fact, it did. The Multnomah County DA needed to be in the good graces of the paper as much as the judge did. Besides, His Honor was adamant about going forward with this case. He wasn't going to delay the trial to hold a contempt hearing.

In the days following, we examined another panel of twelve jurors to fill the vacancies of jurors excused by our peremptory challenges. Brown began in the same way with the same series of questions he'd used. His examination was brief. He said he didn't want to give the jurors the impression "that he was less anxious to know them," but he felt he had had sufficient time to talk to them and turned them over to me.

Again I played off Brown's questioning. A juror had said he wanted to know *for sure* concerning the guilt of the party charged. But Brown had said, "Sure, sure. You want to have as much information as you can get." Now I said, "The issue, as Mr. Brown well knows, is that you don't convict people with 'as much information as you can get.' You can convict them only on proof beyond a reasonable doubt." I'd listened carefully to Brown's abstract language. He'd asked if Peck's conviction would be "distracting" to the juror. I told the juror "distracting" would not be the issue. The issue was whether the witness could be *believed.*

I asked the new panel if they had one thing in the world they could change, what would it be? One wanted children to read more. Another wanted peace. Another, medical care for everybody. Another wanted no more homeless people. Another wanted justice for all.

Again I asked these newest prospective jurors if any had been victims of violence. Juror 24 said, "A Jap stuck a rifle in my belly and pulled the trigger. He failed to load it properly. Another fellow who was with me killed him before I could." I needed that juror. Finally I said, "I'm going to say one last thing to you that you're going to be delighted to hear. I have no further questions." The jurors laughed. I like happy jurors.

We exercised our remaining challenges. Brown left the old sergeant on. I thought I knew why—the man had spent a lifetime obeying commands. He would be more favorable to authority. I left him on because he would be my ballistic expert in the jury room. I hoped he'd convince his fellow jurors that Gerttula was not shot with a rifle. The exit hole was too small. In the morning we'd pick two alternate jurors and be ready to begin the trial.

In the meantime Judge Haas reported to us that he'd arranged to have his trial order served on Marquis and

Stapleton, who were potential witnesses, an order that required witnesses not to discuss their testimony outside the courtroom. The judge told us he'd been advised by the process server that Marquis would not come out of his office to receive the service. After that the judge arranged for the sheriff to personally serve him.

The next morning, December 14, 1988, we began arguing motions *in limine*—lawyers on each side wanting the judge to rule in advance of the trial that certain evidence would not be permitted or referred to during the case or that certain contentions by the parties could not be submitted or argued before the jury.

Since the judge had separated the attempted-murder charge against Sandy for a later trial, we wanted the pictures of the bullet hole through the windshield excluded and any testimony with respect to it also excluded. Michele argued long and hard. The judge overruled her. Pictures of the windshield and testimony about Sandy having shot at Gerttula with the .22 would come in to prove motive.

Then once more I moved His Honor to dismiss the case based on the *Oregonian*'s intentional destruction of the Pinckney notes. I argued knowing that His Honor would not grant my motion. But by our motions the issues were preserved for appeal. I argued that Van Valkenburg had been made the court's representative, its *custodial legis*, when Haas had permitted Van Valkenburg to keep the Pinckney notes rather than turn them over to Haas. The state's case rested with the testimony of Monica Gerttula. I said, "When the *Oregonian* destroyed the Pinckney notes, we lost our last chance to defend this case. The court should say, 'This has gone far enough. I'm going to dismiss this case. This woman doesn't have to take that risk anymore, particularly when the court's own *custodial legis* violated the court's trust.'" In short, it was the court's agent who had failed the court. It was the court's duty therefore to protect us from its *own failures*.

Dawson argued that the notes could only have been used to impeach Mrs. Gerttula's testimony. Proof that we were prejudiced by the loss of the notes was our burden. But the judge was troubled. He said, "If you have Mrs. Gerttula talking to Ms. Pinckney, and then the state police comes on the scene and interviews her, then the phone call by Mrs. Gerttula to Ms. Pinckney saying, 'Please, don't print what I told you'—can't we draw something from that? It would be exculpatory evidence, would it not?" But Dawson said Monica Gerttula's call to Ms. Pinckney was consistent with Mrs. Gerttula having been told by the police not to make any public statements. The judge said he saw that side of it, too, and overruled my motion.

We'd traveled the long, torturous journey to trial. We'd been unsuccessful in diverting the system away from its course. The system had remained firm, the judge tolerant, the prosecutors intransigent. For Sandy it had been a journey through hell. We are a frightened species, and the only palliative against our fear is hope. Hope is like the mast of a ship in the storm. We would grab hold of the mast and begin our trial in the morning.

The judge smiled at the jurors sitting in their hard-bottomed chairs and told them, "We want fourteen uncluttered minds." He told them they were not to talk about the case or let anybody else talk to them about it. They were not to read the newspaper. Then he said, "First you'll hear the state's case and then you'll hear the defense's case," and with a few more words he started to dismiss the jury, then I asked to approach the bench. At the bench I reminded the judge we had no duty to put on a case. He nodded. He turned to the jurors again. "As counsel reminded me, the defendant does not have any obligation to put on any evidence whatsoever. I appreciate counsel pointing out that slip of the tongue." He graciously thanked the jury and recessed until ten the following morning.

I liked our jury. The *voir dire* had cut through the barrier that most often separates jurors and lawyers. The judge had permitted us to get to know the jurors and them us, and by his forbearance had encouraged an atmosphere of congeniality and trust. Despite my fear to the contrary, we had a pretty fair cross-section of citizens. If I could make a solid opening statement to the jury in the morning, perhaps we had a chance to win this case.

36

___

James Brown stood before the jury in a light gray suit, his head balding, his brown hair cut short, his pale skin, a man of small stature, thin of bone and flesh, of quiet voice and narrow face, a memorable feature of which was a stubborn nose. He stood at the podium to make his opening statement. He seemed nice enough, distant, but nice, a little hard to follow, but nice, pleasant without emotion, without word pictures that might excite the senses, but nice. He was in every way a nice man.

He spent more time telling the jury about the geography the jurors would encounter as they were bused to the scene than the facts of the alleged murder itself. He went into exquisite detail about how they'd travel to Lincoln City and, after that, mile by mile to the scene of the alleged crime. He explained the course of the river to the ocean, the mileposts, the vacation homes, the gardens, the farming, the neighbors of the Joneses, and almost foot by foot up the road past the Joneses' house to the third gate—"an eastern-Oregon gate, the kind pulled across, wires with a couple stays in the center, and then stretched or forced in place to complete the fence to close off the road." After that he went into the legal chain of title to the Jones property. The Gerttulas had once owned the farm, sold it to others, and finally the Joneses had bought the place.

When he got to the story of the shooting, he sounded

as if he were reading a report on a corporate stock. The defendant and her son had confronted Dick and Nye, held them at gunpoint, and finally let them leave. He mentioned that Mrs. Gerttula had remarried, but at the time of the incident she and her then husband, Wilfred, were confronted at the same gate by the Joneses. He gave an account of the shots fired into the tires of the Gerttula pickup and the bed of the truck. Mrs. Gerttula and the defendant had wrestled over the camera, and Mrs. Gerttula's glasses had been knocked off. She had difficulty seeing without them. He described how the defendant had left Mrs. Gerttula at the gate, how Mrs. Gerttula had to run down the road after the pickup and was bitten by the Joneses' dog. She got help from a neighbor, who took her on to the Cleveland place, where she found the pickup, her husband inside—dead. Brown referred to Sandy as "the defendant," the prosecutor's way to depersonalize a human charged with a serious crime. It is always easier to convict nonpersons.

Brown admitted that Mrs. Gerttula had given two statements. She told the officer that the defendant had shot her husband. "It certainly looked that way," Brown said. "It was a time of unbelievable emotional stress. I'll tell you that her first impression was that the defendant fired the fatal shot and the statement was reviewed with her again by Sergeant Geistwhite, at which time she became uncertain about what she really saw. But we will tell you all about that because that is something that you need to know and you're going to need to consider."

When he got to Peck, he said, "Part of your decision is whether or not Detective Peck soured the case." As if in passing, he spoke of the gunshot-residue tests and admitted that Monica Gerttula had residue on her hands. "We will present testimony explaining what that means and doesn't mean. I want you to be aware of that, too," he said with a slight shrug of the shoulders.

His statement took no more than half an hour, and he concluded it by saying in the same level, quiet tones, "We expect to prove that Mr. Gerttula was, together with his wife, confronted by the defendant and her fifteen-year-old son; that they were both armed. We're going to contend and we expect to establish for you that they were waiting for the Gerttulas; that at that time shots were fired into the pickup, the tires, through the windshield, and that a single shot was fired that hit and almost immediately killed Will Gerttula. We expect to show you beyond a reasonable doubt that the defendant, Sandra Jones, is responsible for the death of Will Gerttula by intentionally committing acts herself that, under the laws of Oregon, render her as responsible for the murder of Will Gerttula as if she herself had pulled the trigger. Thank you for your attention." He picked up his notebook and hurried back to counsel table and sat down next to Dawson. The court took an early recess.

In chambers I renewed my motion to dismiss and demanded a bill of particulars. I said to Judge Haas, "Here we are, three and a half years later, this case having gone to the Supreme Court and back. Yet all we get in his opening is a legal conclusion. There's not a single act, and Mr. Brown knows it, that Sandy Jones has ever done which would cause a reasonable person to conclude that she knew that whatever she did would result in the death of Wilfred Gerttula." The judge said almost automatically, "Overruled."

Haas was set on busing the jurors to the scene. I objected. It had been three and a half years since the incident. The shooting had taken place in the full bloom of summer. There were leaves on the trees that created certain shadows that witnesses would testify to. Now it was December and the trees were barren. The property was in scandalous disrepair. I thought the jurors would conclude that the Joneses were not only poor, but lazy. The past years had separated the family and exhausted their resources. Anticipating the jury's view, we'd asked Mike Sr. to clean up the place as best he could. His Honor was bent on the outing. After my opening statement the jury was going to go to the scene, and that was that.

Kent, Michele, and I grabbed a sandwich for lunch in the courthouse coffee shop. "No surprises in Brown's opening," Michele said. She was elated. Every trial lawyer's nightmare is that after the other side puts all of the evidence together, it adds up to a scenario you'd never anticipated.

"That jury doesn't have the slightest idea what this case is about," I said.

"That's his style," she said. "He's the master of the understatement."

"I'll try not to be the master of the overstatement," I said.

After lunch when I rose to make my opening, I knew one thing: I had to tell the jury the *story* of the case. A trial is only a story. It has heroes and villains. It has drama, human emotion, and conflict, and how that conflict was resolved would be up to the jury. We hoped for a happy ending. This jury would never acquit Sandy unless they knew her, understood her, empathized with her, and at last grew to care about her. Moreover, the jury would never embrace her if they didn't embrace me, because after many days of trial, the trial lawyer gradually grows to take the place of the defendant. He speaks for the defendant, acts for her, and finally becomes the surrogate defendant himself. The jury must trust the lawyer. That means the lawyer has to be trustworthy.

I began by telling the jury that the opening statement was a time when the lawyers, if they have a case, should present it. I said I'd given Mr. Brown the opportunity to tell us the facts of his case, and that I had not caused any "distraction"—a word, I said, Mr. Brown was "comfortable with"—and that I had not objected once to anything that he'd said. Now, it was my turn, and I hoped he'd give me the same courtesy. "My opening will be considerably longer than his, because I have some facts to give you."

I pointed out that Brown had no trouble describing the "eastern-Oregon gate" in detail. He admitted Sandy Jones had shot no one. Yet in no way did he explain how she was responsible for Wilfred Gerttula's death. He'd said only that she had "'committed acts that she knew would cause Mr. Gerttula to be shot.' I think you'd like to know *what* those acts were, wouldn't you? What was it that she was supposed to have done? There has been a discussion about the cookie jar and crumbs, and a lot of hinting going on, but now, after three and a half years, he is unable to come forward and tell us straight-on, face-to-face, eye-to-eye, what Sandy Jones *did* that caused her son to shoot Mr. Gerttula, that she *knew* would cause him to shoot Mr. Gerttula, and that she *intended* him to shoot Mr. Gerttula." I turned to stare at Brown. "We were entitled to know that, to defend ourselves."

I said the case was not about eastern-Oregon gates and oceans and rivers. This case was about people. About two families. I told them the story of Big Mike and Sandy, how they'd saved their money and bought this little swamp-bottom farm. They were poor and proud and didn't take welfare. I told them how Mike Jones had been injured and how Sandy Jones was working as a security guard at a trailer park. I covered Sandy's concern for Medicine Rock, and the right of the Indians to worship their ancestors in a sacred place. She had a troop of young Boy Scouts and among other things taught them gun safety. I talked of her caring for the environment and how she had confronted the good old boys about the illegal landfill that would change the course of the river.

Gerttula had connections to the good old boys. One of the people involved in the case would be Fred Ronnau, a lawyer. Ronnau had been county counsel and represented Lincoln County in civil matters. As county counsel he advised the Planning Commission. It was Ronnau, in representing the Planning Commission, who had found that the Gerttula subdivision was illegal. It had no sewer or water and was not provided with a public road.

Gerttula had other interesting connections to the good old boys. He'd been a schoolmate of the local circuit judge, who had the same authority as Judge Haas. It was that judge who would end up trying many of the cases between the Gerttulas and the Joneses. The road commissioner's son-in-law was the game warden. I said that for twenty or thirty nights this game warden spied on the Joneses with infrared light watching to see if he could catch Mike Jones Sr. illegally taking salmon out of the river. Gerttula was a friend of the sheriff's, and Monica Gerttula was connected to one of the most wealthy and influential people in the county, Mrs. Reed. As for Monica Gerttula, I said, "I think you will find that she is a tough woman, that she knows how to fight, and how to cry. She grew up in hunting camps. She disclaims knowledge of guns. I think you will find that disclaimer untrue."

I told how Fred Ronnau, the attorney for the Planning Commission, had admitted there was no actual road to the Gerttula property. The road existed only on a map.

The river had changed course and the road on the map had been washed away. As platted, it had never been constructed. I was drawing on the board. The changing course of the river had threatened the house when the Gerttulas owned the Jones property, and the house itself had been moved. Then to steel them for the unsightly view they'd have of the Jones property when they were taken there by the judge, I said, "When you go to the scene, you'll see a property that is no longer the beautiful place with the gardens, the house, and the flowers, the place all neat and beautiful and happy. That was the way it was in July, three and a half years ago. Many things have happened to that dreadful place since then, that little paradise that was once theirs."

The Planning Commission had issued a cease-and-desist order on Gerttula and said, "You will not sell any more of these lots. No road." In the meantime people had been buying lots from Gerttula and were complaining. The trail that the Gerttulas claimed was a county road was slipping away in mudslides, and it went through sacred Indian burial grounds. The Indians had come to Mrs. Jones and begged her to intercede.

The Joneses and the Gerttulas had once been friends. I showed the jurors pictures of the families together, Gerttula sitting next to little Shawn, his arm around the child. Together they'd fought against the county's illegal landfill. But problems arose over the road, and the Gerttulas hired the same Fred Ronnau who had previously represented the Planning Commission, now in private practice. "He was a very crafty and very talented lawyer," I told the jury. "Where once as the Planning Commission's attorney he claimed this was an illegal road, he now took on the case of the Gerttulas to force a road through the Jones property. The Joneses didn't have money to hire lawyers through a protracted court battle. Gerttula's approach to the case was to break the Joneses, to frighten them, to harass them, to exhaust them, and to use the power he had with the connections he had."

Sandy had gone to the Planning Commission along with others who were protesting. "'This is wrong, the way you're doing this. You run roughshod over little people and you sit there and you serve the good old boys of the county. Now why don't you stop it? We're all citizens. We all have these rights.'" Sandy had been representing herself. Then the harassment began.

I told the jurors how the Joneses had found their fences cut and their livestock getting out. Then the Gerttulas filed complaints against them for livestock running at large, which carried a possible jail sentence and up to $1,000 in fines, fines that Sandy Jones and her husband could no more pay than they could build Rockefeller Center. Two days later they were charged by the Gerttulas with maintaining an illegal septic tank. The Gerttulas lived miles away—what concern was it of theirs? The reason the Joneses hadn't thought the tank was illegal was because it had been built by the Gerttulas themselves when they owned the property.

Sandy filed her papers in court. I said, "I wish you could see her briefs. She can't type. The lines are all straight, setting out her arguments and her reasons why she thought this was wrong. She took a copy of her brief to Ronnau, and within a half hour afterward another complaint was filed for livestock running at large. For this charge the Joneses had to face a jury and hire a lawyer."

At the trial Gerttula came into court with a picture of several of the Jones cattle and testified that the cattle had been at large in December. "But all the trees had leaves on them and the grass was green. The jury threw the case out.

That made no difference to the Gerttulas. What Gerttula had in mind was that through this process of continued harassment the Joneses would cave." I saw the sergeant just shake his head.

The following May, Gerttula filed a complaint against Mike Sr. for obstructing a county road, this road on the Jones property that Gerttula's own son had built, not the county. In June, Gerttula's old classmate, the judge, issued a temporary restraining order that, in effect, said that you are stopped from obstructing this road during this lawsuit or I'll throw you in jail.

In August, Mike Sr. complained to the sheriff that Gerttula had tried to run him down on this road. Nothing was done. "It was during that month that the Jones children had been home alone when Gerttula drove up. They hid, as they'd been told. Then they heard the cistern lid slam shut. As soon as the vehicle left they rushed out to the cistern and opened it up, and there floating in the cistern was a dead raccoon." Several of the jurors winced. Again Sandy called the sheriff. A deputy came out and interrogated the kids, then thirteen and ten. They probably didn't know the difference between the sound of the pickup door slamming and the sound of the cistern lid. They sounded different, the kids insisted, but they couldn't say exactly how. Who could? The deputy left and nothing was done.

That same month someone filed a complaint against Mike Jones for building on the Jones property without a permit. A permit wasn't required. They were only repairing their barn. Mrs. Jones went to the Planning Commission and took a neighbor friend along. The friend demanded to know who'd filed this complaint, and after a lot of arguing and demanding they finally found out that, yes, it had been Wilfred Gerttula. The Jones property was jointly owned by Sandy and Mike. But only Mike had been charged with the offense. If Mrs. Jones had also been charged, she could have represented herself. But since she hadn't been charged, she was not permitted to represent her husband. She wasn't a lawyer. She even went to the Planning Commission and asked that her name be put on the complaint, but they refused. Mike Sr., an uneducated man, was not capable of defending himself. So again they had to scrape the last of their money together to hire an attorney. Three hours before the trial was to begin, the county attorney came in and dismissed the complaint. But by this time they'd already spent their money on the lawyer.

In the meantime Gerttula would come to the Jones property, take pictures, talk to the Joneses, and try to tape-record them to gather evidence for use in the legal proceedings Fred Ronnau was bringing against them, a proceeding to make that private trail into a public road. In September, the first contempt action was brought against Mike Jones Sr., Ronnau claiming that Mike had violated the court's temporary restraining order by cutting down a tree that fell across the trail. Still they had no lawyer. The judge found Big Mike guilty and gave him fifteen days in jail, suspended until the case was concluded.

I told the jury how the children were shot at during the following February. The kids were close to the house, out in their own pasture. Mike Jones Sr., hearing the shots, flattened himself to the ground. A neighbor also heard the bullet splat. Mike Sr. looked up and saw a Jeep Wagoneer of the kind and color owned by the Gerttulas.

In April the trial on the road was held. Sandy Jones struggled to defend herself and her family. "And people laughed at them," I said. "Lawyers laughed at her and the judge laughed at her. Gerttula thought it was funny seeing this woman trying to defend herself." In June the judge ruled that that trail was a county road. But how, I asked the jury, could the judge find this was a county road when the county hadn't been made a party to the suit? The county had said, "We don't want the road." Even to that day, the road had never been opened.

Then one day in June, Mike was plodding down the road. The Gerttulas drove up and Mrs. Gerttula yelled out, "Will, he's not going to get off the road." And Mr. Gerttula answered—and this was all in the public record—"Neither are we." And he hit Mike and knocked him down. I told the jury that Mike was big but fragile. He went into paralysis easily from a serious back injury. "Mike is lying there on the ground. Mr. Gerttula thinks this is very funny. He is laughing and took a picture of Mike lying there."

Mike was taken to the hospital and examined in the emergency room. You know the kind of care that people with limited resources get at a hospital, I said. The people at the hospital claimed they could see nothing and shrugged their shoulders. Mrs. Jones went to the sheriff again and asked for protection. The sheriff did nothing. But the Joneses had seen it happen, and the children had seen it. I said, "It would be a normal response for a child to be totally terrorized of Gerttula, this man who'd put a coon in the cistern and had run his father down."

In the same month the children were up above the Jones property on their two little ponies riding on the alleged county road near the Gerttula subdivision when Gerttula shot at them. The children ran home, breathless, petrified with fear. Sandy called the sheriff again. A deputy came out to investigate. He talked to Gerttula. Do you have a gun? Yes, he did—a .22. The sheriff smelled the gun and realized it had recently been fired. He asked permission to swab Gerttula's hands for gunshot residue. Gerttula refused. He couldn't be required to submit to the test unless he was under arrest. Gerttula claimed he'd been down at the barn shooting rats, but when asked, he also refused to take a lie detector test. When the deputy interviewed Mrs. Gerttula, he asked her, "Does your husband ever take the gun to the barn?" She said, "No, he doesn't take the gun to the barn." The deputy wrote up the report and turned it over to the district attorney, Ulys Stapleton, to evaluate for prosecution. Nothing was done. Mrs. Jones was becoming desperate. She couldn't get any protection from the law. Little Shawn was having nightmares and Sandy sent the little girl to her mother in Portland to take her away from "this war scene," as I called it.

In the meantime, Gerttula sued the Joneses for $30,000, more than the farm was worth, and later Ronnau upped the ante to $250,000 because the Joneses had blocked the road. Sandy didn't know what to do. They'd been sued for a quarter of a million dollars. They couldn't hire a lawyer. The kids were terrorized. The family had been broken up. They'd been hauled into court repeatedly on trumped-up charges, none of which had been made to stick.

"Now follow her logic," I said to the jury. "You might not have done this, but she says to herself, 'I can't get justice here, and the people in charge of justice are the judge and the prosecutor and Mr. Ronnau.' So she sued the judge and the prosecutor, Mr. Stapleton, which will prove to be the worst thing that ever happened in her life. And she sued Mr. Ronnau. She represented herself." With respect to Mr. Ronnau, she claimed his influence was used to "intimidate and harass this defendant in numerous and frivolous lawsuits and complaints." She served all of them and summoned them into court.

I told the jurors that Mrs. Jones didn't know that under the law the judge and the prosecutors couldn't be sued for failing to perform their jobs. I said that probably some of the jurors didn't realize that any more than Sandy did. She asked for an order restraining Gerttula from terrorizing her family. The judge she sued got off their case. But in the courthouse she was now seen as a troublemaker, a nut, and the new judge threw out all of her cases without a trial.

In May, before the shooting, Mrs. Jones had asked the new judge for a restraining order. She was asking the system to please listen to her. She needed help. In effect she was saying, If you won't help me, "I'm going to end up where I have to face Gerttula myself and take the law into my own hands." She was, in effect, saying that everywhere. Please help me. She went in to see the new judge. He told her to go down and talk to the Victim's Rights Office maintained by Mr. Stapleton. The woman in that office said, "Why don't you hire your own lawyer?"

At the recess Brown warned me in the record that if I mentioned the Monica Gerttula polygraph, he'd move for a mistrial, and the judge said, "Yeah, I ruled on that. That's excluded." Then the judge wanted to know if I wasn't about through. My opening had taken all afternoon and I hadn't spoken yet of our defenses. I told the judge it would be way past five o'clock and that I was getting tired. His Honor said he was going to hold my feet to the fire—to force me to finish that night. It was 4:10 P.M.

Brown said to me, half mocking, "Are you going to keep me from my little boy's Christmas program, Mr. Spence?" Christmas programs are important. I thought of Little Mike and how he'd been deprived of his family. I thought of my own kids and how I'd missed events important in their lives. Michele had a husband and two small boys at home. How she was managing this I had no idea. And then I thought about Sandy, and what she'd miss if we failed.

"How'm I doing?" I asked Kent after I'd walked back

to counsel table. I relied on those close to me to tell me what was going on in the courtroom, how the jurors seemed to be reacting, was I reaching them, were they hearing me? Even after all those years in the courtroom I was still anxious.

"They're hanging on every word," Kent said. I missed Imaging. She was my eyes and ears in a courtroom. Lawyers get caught up in themselves and sometimes can't see. Imaging could judge me better than anyone else I knew.

"What's Sandy think, so far?" I asked Michele.

"Well, honestly, Gerry, she thinks you've got her motive for killing Gerttula laid out pretty well. You might want to talk to her."

"I know. I've been doing Brown's work. I think he's been pretty damn happy with what I've done so far. But this jury has to understand Sandy. Those facts are going to cut in both directions. If they think Gerttula had it coming, they'll find a way to acquit her. If I can make them care enough about her, they'll never let Brown haul her off to the pen."

After the recess I told the jury the story I'd related so many times in court, of how Little Mike, frightened, on that day in July of 1985, had called Sandy at work. Gerttula had left the gate open again, the ponies were out, and Little Mike had heard shooting. Sandy wanted to know what the shooting was about. She told Little Mike to stay in the house. She ran up the hill. Sandy had no sooner got to the upper gate when Little Mike was there with the .30-30. "I thought I told you to go back to the house." But he was fifteen. And this was his mother. He was crying. Then before she could settle the matter with Little Mike, along came Dick and Nye in their old car. I told the jury that Dick and Nye were "a pretty seedy-looking bunch." Dick was a gruff, old guy, and I said I didn't know if the jury could tell by his testimony whether he was drunk or sober. "You'll discover that Mr. Nye has been convicted of crimes. They won't admit that Gerttula was shooting, but they will admit that they heard shooting up there."

Then along came the Gerttula pickup. I was drawing at the board. I drew in the so-called road, the gate, the river. The story never changed, the story I could prove from the testimony of the witnesses, Monica Gerttula's story, and how Wilfred Gerttula had said to her just before Sandy stopped them at the gate, "Now we're going to have some fun." Gerttula gunned his pickup at Sandy. "Varoom! Varoom! She was absolutely terrorized." The pickup was not moving forward but kicking up dirt from behind as Gerttula braked and clutched it and threatened to run her over. Sandy shot at the tires. The big man got out of the car. He was strong. He knew Sandy wouldn't shoot him. He dropped his tape recorder and grabbed her gun with both hands, throwing her around and around. "She was hanging on to the rifle for dear life.

"What do you suppose Mrs. Gerttula is doing all this time?" I asked. I took the jury through the facts as seen through Sandy's eyes, Gerttula's staggering back to the truck, the fight over the keys when Monica Gerttula was so hysterical she couldn't drive the pickup, and how Sandy drove the truck down with two flat tires, a dying man inside. She finally stopped at the Clevelands', where she ran in. "Call an ambulance," she said.

I told the jury that in this case I had to defend not only Sandy Jones but Little Mike as well, "because if the boy is guilty of nothing, then obviously his mother can't be guilty of aiding and abetting him." I looked at the jurors, one by one. "Is that clear?" They nodded. Detail by detail I accounted for all of the bullets in the .30-30, the gun in Little Mike's possession. I explained to the jury what gunshot residue was, how this residue of barium and antimony was found on Mrs. Gerttula's hands and face and how the state's own expert would testify that it was more likely than not that she had fired a gun that day. "When the state wants that evidence to put somebody away, that evidence is unimpeachable. It's absolute. It's the standard. But it was against their own principal witness. So what did the state do?" I told how they'd tried to duplicate the residue on dummies. I asked Michele to sit down in front of the jury.

"Here's the dummy's head." I pointed at Michele's head. "You're no dummy," I said to her, and smiled. The jury smiled. Michele smiled. The judge smiled.

I went through the entire procedure of the state's testing. No antimony in a .22 cartridge. But plenty of it on Monica Gerttula's face. Same with the .30-30, which contained antimony in the residue—but no antimony on the dummy's face. None.

It was five-thirty. I was exhausted. I told the judge in the jury's presence that I was getting feedback from the jurors. They were awfully tired and I was tired. If we could start at eight in the morning, I promised to be done by ten.

Revived in the morning, I was at it again, telling the jurors about Monica Gerttula's inconsistent statements, and about the Pinckney interview, how Geistwhite had come, and after that, how Mrs. Gerttula could no longer remember. I covered the whole *Oregonian* affair, their attempt to quash the subpoena for the Pinckney notes, and how, later, the *Oregonian* destroyed the Pinckney notes.

I asked, "Where is the gun that, according to our position, was in the hands of Monica Gerttula?" She said she picked up the recorder and dumped it behind the seat. I told the jury where the recorder was found—down over the side of the road just short of the river. But the gun was never found. "They've known for years that the position we've taken is that *there was that gun*." I turned and looked at Brown. He was smiling. "He smiles," I said, pointing my finger at him. "To this day there has not been anybody from the state to go look in that river."

Then I went into the Peck issue, and how he was convicted by the jury on some of the counts involving drugs. I talked about Peck's failure to do elemental, first-grade measurements at the scene; about Vargo, who had never in his life performed an autopsy on a person shot with a gun. And looking straight at the old sergeant, I discussed the exit wound in Gerttula's body, a small wound inconsistent with the exit wound one would expect from a rifle bullet.

At last, ready to conclude my opening statement, I said, "Ladies and gentlemen, the evidence is going to show that Mike Jones Jr. didn't shoot anybody. Secondly it is going to show that he doesn't have a malicious bone in his little body. The only thing he wanted to do was protect his mother. Mrs. Jones had no malice. She could have shot Mr. Gerttula and Mrs. Gerttula a dozen times had she wanted to. The malice in this case, ladies and gentlemen, isn't on this side of the table. I think you will find that the malice rests with the Lincoln County prosecutor.

"At the conclusion of this trial I'm going to ask you to do what nobody else has done for Mrs. Jones. I am going to ask you to protect her, *to protect her* as a citizen under the Constitution. I'm going to ask you at the conclusion of this case not to leave her any longer at the mercy of the state.

"That, ladies and gentlemen, is the great calling and the great function of an American jury, and that's what we're here to do today, to achieve justice. Thank you very much." I walked back to the defense table and sat down. It was 9:30 A.M.

After that the jurors were hustled into a waiting bus and we proceeded to Lincoln County, a good one-and-a-half-hour drive from Portland. The jurors were driven through the Jones farm, which, to my surprise, Mike Sr. had cleaned up pretty well, the old junkers covered with plastic, the No Trespassing signs down. They walked up the hill and through the several gates to the scene of the shooting. They milled about, looking, the men with their hands in their pockets, not sure what they should do or look at, the women in twos and threes, already having made friends, the old sergeant seeming to know what had happened. He looked here and there and nodded as if he were making mental notes.

Suddenly Carmel Finley, the stringer for the *Oregonian*, jumped out from behind some trees where the shooting had occurred. She began snapping photos. No attorney and no member of the court or officer of the court knew she'd be there. She'd been lying in wait, hiding in the bushes.

At the first opportunity after we left the scene, I stopped our caravan with the judge and the lawyers at Gesik's Auto Sales in Lincoln City. The court reporter was with us. I dictated in the record how Finley was the author of the "scathing and inaccurate article" that had been published on the date of this trial, how she'd secreted herself behind trees and bushes at the scene of the shooting. I said it was my contention "that the *Oregonian* has intentionally and arrogantly, without interruption, interjected itself into this case from the beginning. It has done so for its own purposes, which have always come ahead of the right of the defendant to a fair trial."

I went on, "Now the last straw has occurred. These jurors have a right to come to the scene without being photographed, without being afraid their picture will appear in the paper." I said the court had been careful to make certain the jurors were protected even from the video camera that was in the courtroom during the opening statements so that they'd not feel any intimidation or pressures as a result of their being photographed. The scene of the shooting was a "quasi courtroom," I said. "We simply can't get a fair trial." Once more I moved the judge for a mistrial. His Honor said he'd take the motion under advisement. "You guys can argue it in the morning."

37

I'd been up since 5 A.M. and was primed and ready for my cross-examination of Monica Gerttula. Brown told us he'd call her as his first witness. We had hundreds of pages of her past testimony to review. Every statement she'd ever made in regard to what we called "the accident" had been retrieved and her inconsistencies carefully noted.

Enormous amounts of information had been generated in this case. Michele had painstakingly managed all of it. Outside of court she could often be found sitting on the floor sifting through files, pulling out gems for me to use the next day. Wryly, she once said she'd really wanted to be a librarian, but had screwed up and gone to law school instead.

Stapleton, not having yet been replaced by the newly elected DA and knowing that Michele was in the middle of this trial, again subpoenaed her to testify before the grand jury in another case. Haas said he'd quash the subpoena, but our team didn't need that kind of a worrisome interruption on the day the state was calling its star witness.

The harassment didn't stop. In chambers Brown requested that Sandy, in the presence of the jury, be required to stand up alongside Monica Gerttula to demonstrate the difference in their sizes. Sandy was at least six inches taller than Mrs. Gerttula. I objected. The jurors could see the dif-

ference in the sizes of the women. I said it would be a blatant demonstration intended to prejudice. The judge shook
his head. "This has been a trial that if something could go
wrong, it has gone wrong. I'm not going to risk anything
occurring out there in the presence of the jury that could
cause a mistrial." I thought he could envision one of the
women losing it and taking a swing at the other.

Then I invited Brown to show some compassion. All
witnesses had been excluded by order of the court. But
wouldn't Brown permit Mike Sr. to stay during the trial?
"No," Brown said. "If he's going to be a witness, he must
abide by the court rule." I pled with His Honor. Little
Mike and Shawn were excluded because they'd been listed
as Brown's witnesses. Couldn't the court permit Sandy to
have one member of her family with her—just one—during this ordeal by fire? The judge was firm: "Mr. Jones Sr.
will be treated like any other witness." Lonely, deadly
place, a courtroom.

Monica Gerttula took the stand. She'd been transformed
from a dowdy widow to a smartly dressed woman. She
wore an attractive suit; her hair was styled and her makeup
neatly applied. The smiling, black-rimmed glasses were
gone. Brown started with a few preliminary questions about
how Mrs. Gerttula had been born in Austria and had come
to this country as a refugee. When he got into the road dispute, she stated that the road had been maintained by the
county for over thirty years, that the road grader had gone
up a little beyond the house, "but during their maintenance program *Sandy Jones run the grader off with a pistol.*"
Calmly, I stood, and asked the judge to instruct the jury to
disregard the answer, and he did. Sandy was upset. She'd
grabbed Michele's arm.

"Don't worry, Sandy," Michele whispered. "There's
gonna be hell to pay for that cheap shot."

Then we retired to chambers for my newest motion for a mistrial. It was a slick move, I thought, if Brown primed his witness to volunteer something like that—something she'd never seen. Was Brown trying to force Sandy to give up her Fifth Amendment rights? The only way Sandy could refute what the woman had just said would be to take the stand. I asked the judge to bring Monica Gerttula back to chambers and admonish her, which he did in his soft, friendly way. He told her she could only answer the question put to her. None others. Did she understand? Yes. She acted like an abused child, her head down, speaking apologetically into folded hands on her lap. Back in the courtroom the judge again admonished the jury. "You are instructed, *strongly instructed,* to disregard the statement made."

Brown guided Mrs. Gerttula through the early morning of the day of the shooting—from the toast she had for breakfast to her memory that her husband, at their subdivision, had taken off his shirt to clear around some survey stakes. She said she put a new roll of film in the camera and she and her husband were headed home. When they got to the gate, they saw Mrs. Jones standing on their side of the fence. Her husband said, "You better take a picture of this." She said, "I opened up my side of the door, I stepped out, I aimed the camera, and I snapped, and she shot the ground right alongside of me."

Brown handed her the photograph that showed Sandy shooting the rifle in a downward direction, the smoke coming out of the barrel. Mrs. Gerttula said she hollered to Sandy, "Are you crazy?" She said the boy was hiding in the shadow of a stump behind and to the right of her. She turned to take a picture of the boy, but she was so rattled, she didn't forward the film in the camera. She said she felt a blow at the back of her head. "She hit me on the side of the head with her rifle. It knocked my glasses to the ground. I was warding the blows off with my right arm, and with my left hand I was groping in the dirt to try to find my glasses, so I was stooped over. And she continued to hit me."

Both tires, the right rear and the left front, were hissing. She had her glasses by then and heard Little Mike say, "You shot at me, you shot at me." She said, "I was facing into the cab, across-ways where the driver's door was open, and Will leaned on the door and I noticed a little speck of blood on his face.

"I remember shouting, 'Will! Will!' And I ran around the back of the pickup facing Mike. He didn't stop me. No opposition there. And when I got around to the driver's side of the open pickup door, Will had collapsed into the pickup. I heard him say, before he collapsed and prior to my running around on the side, 'Oh, my God! Oh, my God!'"

The woman wept as she told her story to the jurors. "He laid across the pickup seat. I picked up the tape recorder by the driver's side." She explained how she jumped into the pickup and tried to get her husband's foot untangled from under the clutch. She started to turn on the key and she said she heard Sandy holler to Little Mike, " 'Go get the key. Get the key out.'

"On her [Sandy's] instruction, the boy leaned the gun into the open door of the pickup on the right-hand side, reached over with both of his hands, and with both of his hands pried my fingers singularly away from the key that I was trying to turn, and he got the key."

Mrs. Gerttula said, "I couldn't start the pickup. She was yelling at me, 'Give me the camera. You're not going anywhere for help until I have the camera. Give me the camera.' I screamed and screamed. She said, 'Shut up, don't scream. Give me the camera. We're not going to call for an ambulance until you give me the camera. How's your money going to help you now? How much is that camera worth to you now? Give me the camera.'"

The woman was sobbing. I looked at the jurors. There were tears in some of their eyes. Then Mrs. Gerttula said, "She had her hand through the open window and grabbed me by the hair and had me part out of the window. I knew I'd thrown the camera behind the pickup seat." She said she was grappling to give Sandy the camera so she could take her husband to the hospital. Then she said Sandy shouted, "'You got a gun back there? You got a gun back there?' I didn't have a gun back there. I just wanted to give her the camera."

Monica Gerttula asked for a Kleenex. The clerk handed up a ready box to her. Then she said Sandy yanked the door open and pulled her out by the hair, took over the pickup, and Mrs. Gerttula got in on the passenger side and "sat by Will's head." She said she grabbed at the steering wheel and honked the horn for help.

When they got to the next gate, Sandy ordered her to open it, and when she did, Sandy stepped on the gas and drove down the road leaving the woman behind. Mrs. Gerttula said, "I was screaming and screaming." She ran down the hill and at the Jones place tried to get one of their old junkers started, but she couldn't find any keys. Then the dog bit her. When she got down to the Ferris house, she asked for help. She said Ferris was an old man, and slow, and she was screaming for him to hurry all the way to the Cleveland residence, where she saw the Gerttula pickup parked. The woman was openly weeping again and the judge called a recess.

After the recess Mrs. Gerttula testified that she went to the pickup where her husband lay and held his head in her arms and kept talking to him, assuring him that the ambulance was on the way and that everything was going to be all right. "Some fellow came to the door and said that Will was dead. I said, 'No, don't be stupid. Go get the ambulance.'" Then Trooper Geistwhite led her from the pickup and told her it was too late. She sat down on the lawn. She was nauseated. "I started telling the story of what I just told you today. He made notes. He was very nice and kind."

After she was seen at the emergency room, she was taken to the police station, where she gave Trooper Geistwhite a recorded statement. The next day Geistwhite came to her house and took pictures and recorded yet another statement from her. She admitted that Geistwhite "mentioned that it could have been a larger caliber than what I'd been saying, that it was Sandy's gun." And later she'd gone to the sheriff's office and the sheriff told her it was a larger-caliber gun than a .22.

Brown had her testify as to her height—five feet and half an inch—and her weight at the time—152 pounds. She was left-handed. She admitted that the officer swabbed her hands for gunshot residue. She denied having any weapons in the pickup. She denied firing a gun that day.

"Did you try to shoot the defendant?" Brown asked.

"No."

"Did you shoot your husband?"

"I did not." She was firm, her chin set. Some of the jurors looked at Sandy to see her expression.

That ended Brown's examination. He'd been his usual laconic, matter-of-fact self, even through the weeping. The jury had been open to her. I could feel her pain, her horror. I thought the jurors had as well.

In chambers the next morning, Brown told the judge he had some new exculpatory evidence. One of their witnesses, a Don Shaffer, was told by Gerttula on the Sunday before he died that he, Gerttula, had done "something stupid." Gerttula admitted he'd seen the Jones kids on their ponies across the river and he'd yelled at them and shot into the trees, but not at the children. We were being told this three and a half years after all of this took place, and on the morning I was to cross-examine the state's star witness? The facts were contained in a new report by the state's investigator Carroll, who'd recently interviewed Shaffer.

Back in the courtroom I confronted Mrs. Gerttula. I spoke to her in a kind but firm voice. It soon became apparent that she wept when Brown questioned her but fought stubbornly against giving a straight answer to the most obvious questions that I asked her. She couldn't remember if Mrs. Jones was a religious person. I asked if at the party for the little girl, Shawn, and before refreshments were served, the family had said a prayer. She didn't remember the party. She wouldn't admit that Sandy had prayed with her, nor would she admit that Sandy had befriended many of her neighbors. She did recall that once Sandy had given Wilfred a tailgate for his pickup because the old one kept falling out and her husband had been hurt by the old one.

Reluctantly, she finally admitted there'd been problems created when her husband sold lots prior to the time the Gerttula subdivision had been approved by the Planning Commission. She acknowledged the cease-and-desist order issued by the commission against her husband, but only when I read it to her aloud in front of the jury. But she claimed that the commission's order had been issued before they were married in 1972. I handed her the order, which was dated six years *after* they were married.

She wrestled with me over every fact. She didn't remember. She didn't know. She answered questions I didn't ask. I could see that some of the jurors were becoming impatient with her.

I had her tell about their complaint against the Joneses for livestock running at large, and how the Joneses had to hire a lawyer for the jury trial that followed. She admitted her husband had claimed that his photo of the Jones cattle had been taken in the winter, but she remembered that there was "some difficulty with the photograph, the shadows weren't in the right position to the time element that Will testified to." She agreed there wouldn't be leaves on the trees in December. I left the jury to draw their own conclusions whether her husband had offered false evidence in an attempt to get a conviction against the Joneses.

She'd heard of the complaint about the raccoon but that was "ridiculous," she said. Reluctantly she admitted her husband had dug the hole for the septic tank the Joneses used, and she also admitted that her husband had later filed a complaint against the Joneses for that same septic tank although they lived more than ten miles from the Jones property. It was she, she said, who'd taken pictures of the Joneses repairing their barn, and it was her husband who'd then filed a complaint against them for building without a permit.

I asked, "Did it bother you a lot that they were building out there? Did it interfere with your life or diminish your property or cause you any problem?" She said they had to get a permit so she thought the Joneses ought to as well. Finally I said, "You've said that three times, but you haven't answered my question. If you don't want to answer the question, just tell me and we'll go on."

"Okay, let's go on."

I looked at the jury. Some looked solemn, and one juror was shaking her head. The old sergeant had thrown himself back in his chair and was looking down at the witness over his nose.

Then the crux question on the issue of Gerttula's harassment: "And Mr. Ronnau gave you advice to the effect that you should file complaints against the Joneses for anything that you thought they were doing illegal, isn't that true?"

"Yes," she said, but she denied the strategy was to bring the Joneses to their knees because of their poverty.

Suddenly I asked about her present husband. "What does Mr. Steele do?"

"I think my marital status doesn't mean a thing here now."

"No, please. What does he do?"

"He works at Georgia Pacific. So what?" she snarled. "What's it your business?"

I questioned her about the time her former husband had run over Mike Jones Sr. She admitted she told her husband, "He's not stopping," referring to Mike as he walked down the road, and that her husband said, "Neither are we." She heard the ring of the bucket Mike was carrying and said she knew they'd run into him. Her husband got out and with his ever-ready camera took a picture of Mike lying on the ground.

She agreed that the judge who had sat on the Gerttulas' lawsuit against the Joneses was a classmate of her late husband's. I read to her from Sandy's handwritten request for a restraining order that she'd filed to protect herself and her family from Gerttula. It set out many of the details of the Gerttulas' harassment. The hearing on Sandy's request for a restraining order had been set for July 29, 1985, six days following the death of Will Gerttula. Again she swore her husband carried no firearms in the pickup except during hunting season.

I offered into evidence the deputy's report on Sandy's complaint that Gerttula had shot at Little Mike and Shawn. We argued in chambers for an hour over its admissibility. The report would show Little Mike's frame of mind—that the Joneses were motivated in whatever they did by fear of what Gerttula might do to them, not by malice toward him. The judge was tired. We were tired. The jury seemed tired. Mrs. Gerttula must have been exhausted having wrestled with me for hours. The judge took the issue under advisement and recessed until 9 A.M. the following morning.

The next morning, after another hour's argument, the judge allowed the officer's report to go to the jury. He deleted any reference to Gerttula's refusal to take a polygraph. I read the report aloud to the jury. The deputy reported that Gerttula had admitted he'd yelled at the kids and that he heard shooting at the time, but he denied he was responsible for the gunfire. The report stated that Gerttula refused to have his hands swabbed for gunshot residue and quoted Gerttula as having claimed he shot a rat. Then the report quoted Mrs. Gerttula as saying that her husband did not normally take his rifle to the barn. She had not heard any shots fired that day.

Then without objection from Brown, I read aloud Carroll's report of what he'd learned from Don Shaffer: "'Gerttula stated [to Shaffer] that he'd been driving on the Siletz Highway when he looked across the river and saw the Jones kids riding their horses and saw their cattle on his property. He yelled at them and shot into the trees.'" According to Shaffer, Gerttula was adamant that he'd not shot at the children. Gerttula told him that he knew he shouldn't have done it, "'but he was frustrated by their free use of his property.'"

Back to Monica Gerttula. Concerning the handguns we were interested in, she said she'd been told that her husband had once had in his possession a handgun that belonged to his brother, but she insisted that during her marriage to Wilfred Gerttula, he'd never owned a handgun. What about the Luger his son, Brian, had pawned? She said that her husband had never got the gun back.

I pressed her. Hadn't she previously denied under oath that she or her husband had *ever possessed* a handgun during their marriage?

"You want to play with words," she hissed. "All right. That's true."

"Now if you had a handgun in the front seat of the car, would you say that either you or your husband had *possession* of the handgun?"

"Yes."

"If the handgun was in the glove compartment but you didn't have your hand on it and the glove compartment was closed, would you say you had *possession* of it?"

"If it had been there, yes." But once more she denied there had been a handgun in the pickup.

I tried to get her to admit that she'd gotten out of the pickup and stood there loading the camera outside the pickup. She denied it. But the officers had found the foil of the film wrapping on the ground. I asked her how it got there. She didn't know.

"And at the time you were supposedly taking Mrs. Jones's picture, didn't she tell you to drop the gun?"

"No, there was no gun."

"I call your attention on page 186 of your testimony before Judge Gardner on December fourth: 'Now at the time you were taking her picture, did she holler something to you?' Read what you answered." I pointed to the place in the transcript of her testimony.

"'Drop the gun. Drop the gun,'" Mrs. Gerttula read in a faint voice. She said that had been a mistake and that she had later corrected herself.

About the stump where Little Mike was supposedly standing, Mrs. Gerttula claimed the boy had been hiding behind it. Didn't she know that the jury had been to the scene and that there was no stump there? At first she said it had been removed. Then, I pointed out that the officers had taken a video of the scene at the time of the accident and there was no stump. Finally I had her get down from the witness stand and, on a schematic drawing, show us where the stump was. She drew it in. I had her estimate the distance from the stump to the nearest track of the roadway. Ten feet, she said.

My cross-examination went on for hours. The woman's attempt to avoid the questions, her contradictory testimony, and at last her openly hostile demeanor seemed, from the jurors' overt responses, to grant me permission to press her further. Step by step I wrote down on a flip chart what she claimed had happened in the order of their occurrence, from one through thirteen. Again and again she amended the order of the events. By this time she no longer claimed she had seen her husband through the open pickup doors as he hollered, "Oh, my God. Oh, my God," and fell into the seat of the pickup. And she admitted that, as she ran past Little Mike, he could have shot her if he'd wanted to. "Not once, but he could have shot you and Mr. Gerttula many times, couldn't he, had he wanted to?"

"He did."

"You don't claim you ever saw Mike shoot your husband."

"No. I was told that later." By the sheriff.

Then I asked her plainly, "Didn't you learn in Austria the law is that if you shoot somebody *accidentally* you may still be guilty of a crime?"

"That's anywhere, not just Austria."

"It's anywhere, that's what you think?"

"Of course."

"That's your belief of the law as you sit here today, isn't it?"

"Yes."

"You knew, didn't you, Mrs. Gerttula, that if you ever admitted that you accidentally shot your husband, that you would be charged with the crime? Didn't you know that?"

"Yes."

We recessed early that day because the judge said he was coming down with the flu.

Was I being too harsh on the woman? No matter how successful the cross-examination had been, it could all dissolve into a puddle at my feet if at some point the jury felt that I was being unfair to a poor, abused, perhaps confused widow who thought she'd seen her husband murdered in cold blood, and that my cross-examination was merely the tool of a crafty attorney plying his weapon unfairly.

I asked Kent and Michele about it that evening.

"I don't think so," Michele said. "I've been watching the jury."

"So have I," I said. "But a lawyer has to be careful," I told Kent. "The fact that you may be all hyped up about your client's cause doesn't mean that the jurors feel the same way you do."

"Well, I don't know, Dad," Kent said, "but I think you're being patient. You haven't raised your voice. I think you're okay." Then he laughed. "I've seen you a lot worse."

"I don't think the woman came off sympathetically," Michele said. "She's been evasive and confrontational. I think so far it's okay with the jury. I'll let you know if I think you're on the edge."

* * *

The next morning my cross-examination of Mrs. Gerttula began concerning the "acceleration marks" left by the Gerttula pickup at the scene. "Isn't it true that your husband was goosing the pickup at Sandy, who was caught between the pickup and the gate?"

"No, it's not true."

My question and her denial created a mental picture of it. Hadn't her husband used the pickup as a weapon before? Had she forgotten that she'd admitted that her husband ran into Mike Jones Sr. with his pickup? She also denied that it was when her husband was goosing the pickup at Sandy that she'd taken the smoking-gun picture of Sandy trying to shoot out the front tire of the pickup to defend herself.

Again she denied that a firearm was in the pickup. I read the first recorded statement she'd given to Geistwhite on the day of the accident. Geistwhite had asked, "Did you have any guns in the car?" And her answer: "Ah, no, I was fumbling around looking—not that I know of. I'd never seen a gun back there." She also claimed she didn't see what had gone on at the front of the pickup—never saw her husband there. Now she admitted what was obvious from the blood on the hood of the pickup—that that was where he'd been shot.

Suddenly I said, "You were there, too, weren't you?"

"No, sir!"

"The reason you've steadfastly stated all these years that you went around the *back* of the pickup and that you never saw your husband at the front end of the pickup was because that's where your husband was shot, and you shot him, isn't that true?"

"No, I didn't shoot Will. I had no gun."

She admitted she saw the tape recorder on the ground. She told Geistwhite that she had picked up the tape recorder with her right hand and that she had had the camera in her right hand and that she had thrown both behind the seat.

"Your husband had just been shot and this was the first thing you did? Actually you threw the recorder over the bank, didn't you?"

"No, sir. Not at all."

"Your husband didn't throw it there."

"Not very well."

I asked if the reason she threw the recorder over the bank was because she was afraid it contained, among other things, Sandy's statement to her to drop the gun. She said that she wasn't afraid of that at all. Once more she denied it was she who had thrown the tape recorder over the bank.

"That's where you also threw the gun?"

"No, sir. There was no gun."

Next I went over each of the *ten separate times* that she'd told Trooper Geistwhite that she'd seen Sandy Jones shoot her husband point-blank in the chest with the .22. She steadfastly denied she was attempting to make Trooper Geistwhite believe Sandy had killed her husband. But the next day when Geistwhite again questioned her about the shots, she said she couldn't remember. "Mentally I was blocked."

What about Pinckney's visit just before Geistwhite arrived? Mrs. Gerttula denied having given an interview to any reporter who came to her home, and she denied calling any reporter to ask that the reporter not publish the interview. I reached for the transcript of Pinckney's testimony. Brown objected. At the bench he contended that the Pinckney transcript we'd taken over the phone in chambers couldn't go into evidence because her testimony wasn't sworn. Geistwhite's notes also showed that Pinckney had been there. But now Brown claimed that Geistwhite, despite his notes to the contrary, had changed his mind. Geistwhite would claim that the Pinckney interview had been by telephone.

Then Michele saved the day. She pointed out that the Pinckney interview was under oath after all. In the melee we'd forgotten that the judge had sworn her. Both Brown and I had interrogated her. The transcript had already been used in the case to impeach Van Valkenburg—days previously. With that showing, the judge overruled Brown's objection and said he'd permit us to read the whole interview to the jury.

During that same recess I advised His Honor that Dr. Michael Hecker, the man who had tested the Rose Mary Woods–Nixon tapes, had just made his report on his findings concerning the tape recording of Judge Gardner. Stafford claimed he hadn't turned on the recorder until Gardner was part way into the interview. We wanted to verify that representation. I said, "Dr. Hecker is going to testify that that tape *was* meddled with. And it was not a matter of the tape just being turned on in the middle of Judge Gardner's testimony. It was a matter that the tape was intentionally, in his opinion, obliterated at that point. We are prepared to bring the witness here and our motion for a mistrial will follow." I was angry. "If we obliterated a tape interview with a judge about a material matter in this case, I think we'd be in jail yet." I looked accusingly at Dawson. Dawson said nothing.

Back in the courtroom I read aloud the entire transcript of the Pinckney interview to the jury. Pinckney stated she'd not only interviewed Mrs. Gerttula but that an officer had arrived at the time she was leaving and that Mrs. Gerttula had called her and asked her not to print the information she'd given her.

Once more I turned to Mrs. Gerttula on the stand. She admitted she'd never seen Little Mike shoot her husband. She said she'd never seen Little Mike up at the front end of the pickup. Nor did she ever hear Sandy Jones say anything to Little Mike prior to her husband's death. She still insisted that when Little Mike shot out the tire, "he was in the stump vicinity."

She claimed the welt on her head—you could clearly see it in the photographs—was from Sandy hitting her with her rifle. She said Sandy came around and grabbed her by the hair. "She yanked the door open and pulled me out."

"In the process of pulling you out, you fought back, didn't you?"

"I tried." But she said it was ludicrous to suggest that she had got the bump on her head when Sandy was jerking her by the hair to get her out of the pickup. At the hospital she told the nurse she'd been hit over the head with a shotgun.

I said, *"Shotgun?"*

"I meant a long-barrel gun." Despite the fact that she'd shot many species of birds with a shotgun, she tried to say she wasn't familiar with a shotgun.

Then I asked her if she could account for as much as thirty minutes from the moment she said she'd been left at the second gate until she arrived at the Cleveland residence with Mr. Ferris. Ferris had seen the pickup speeding down the road and would testify that it was as much as twenty to thirty minutes later before Mrs. Gerttula appeared at his door. It would take but a minute or two for her to run down the hill from the second gate, and minutes after that she would have been at the Ferris home.

"Actually, Mrs. Gerttula, you stayed up at the scene of the accident and it was then that you found the recorder and threw it over the bank?"

Brown objected. The court overruled him. She was

angry. She pointed her finger at me. "I was in a pickup. She ordered me out. I opened up the second gate and she drove off. I have always said that. I maintain that. Don't change my story!" She was shouting at me.

Brown, who'd been hunkered down during most of my cross-examination as if to object would only make it worse, had no questions of his witness on redirect, an intelligent decision. I thought there was no one more eager to see a witness get down from the stand than Brown himself. It was four-fifteen in the afternoon. Judge Haas wanted the hell out of there, too. So did we. But more than we, I thought that Monica Gerttula was relieved that the torture of her cross-examination in a packed courtroom and before a jury was finally over. I watched her go. It hadn't exactly been a fair fight, this frightened woman against a seasoned lawyer. Yet, she'd stood up to me, and although she hadn't done her case much good, still I had to admire her pluck under fire. But tougher witnesses were on Brown's agenda. Tomorrow would be a different day.

38

Christmas, a season of love and forgiveness, of family togetherness and joy, was a time of fear and pain for the Jones family. Shawn cried at night. The enemy was out there, the enemy that no one could identify—the state, the police, the sheriff, the prosecutors, the good old boys—an indefinable, amorphous, omnipotent, vicious mob. Sandy was numb with fear. And we were afraid to leave her. Yet we had to leave her.

We'd all gone home for a fast holiday, our own families not on our minds as much as a woman and her kids in that foggy, swamp-bottom farm, the husband in the house crippled and not able to offer much except his quiet, bewildered presence. It was hard to be joyous when we knew that at the moment we were hugging our own kids, our families safe, that another family we'd grown to care about was in peril. I thought that Brown, too, was likely not thinking of his family but was preparing his witnesses and honing his case with the object of putting Sandy Jones behind bars.

On the morning of December 27, 1988, we were relieved to see Sandy back in the courtroom in her blue polyester slacks suit. "Hi, Spence, Happy New Year," she said. She smiled and took her seat at counsel table as if this were the place she'd chosen to spend the rest of her life. She wore a red velvet ribbon in her long, dark blond hair.

I opened my trial notebook. We'd begun our fifth week of trial and we'd only completed the state's principal witness, Monica Gerttula. Brown got right to his case. He called Robert Longley to the stand. On the day of the shooting Longley had accompanied the body of Wilfred Gerttula from the Clevelands' to the hospital, where the body had been x-rayed, and from there to the funeral home where the autopsy was performed. Brown's questions didn't take ten minutes. I was to spend the rest of the day with him. My strategy—to prove our case on cross-examination so that we wouldn't have to call witnesses of our own who would then be cross-examined and their credibility impugned by Brown.

Longley had been the officer who'd investigated Sandy's complaint about the raccoon in the cistern. I read his report to the jury. His report included a photo of Little Mike, a cute, skinny little boy with curly red hair standing there in his bib overalls with Shawn, who was holding up the dead animal by the tail. Longley agreed there was no way the animal could have crawled into the cistern by itself. When Longley concluded that Little Mike couldn't explain the difference in the sound of the cistern lid slamming shut from the sound of Gerttula's pickup door, I dropped a coffeepot lid on the table. Then I dropped my glasses on the same table. "Can you hear the difference with your ear?" I asked. Yes. He could hear the difference.

"Could you explain the difference in words?" No, he said.

"That doesn't mean that I didn't drop the lid from the coffeepot, does it?"

"That's right."

He hadn't slammed the cistern lid and then slammed a car door to see if the kids knew the difference. He never talked to Gerttula—said now he wished he had. Did he think he might have done things differently had it been the mayor's wife instead of Sandy Jones? "Yes," he said. I was surprised at his frankness. I saw that the jury was, too.

Longley remembered the time when Gerttula had brought charges against the Joneses for livestock running at large. Oscar Granger, head of the Planning Commission, was at the trial. Fred Ronnau, Gerttula's attorney, along with two county commissioners, was also there. Why, I asked Longley, had all of these "bigwigs" come to hear this trivial case of livestock running at large? He had no answer. I thought perhaps the jury speculated along with me: the good old boys were after this woman.

Although Longley had been back to the scene of the shooting, he'd never searched the river for a gun. Nor had Brown or Dawson requested him to do so. I looked over at the jury as if to ask, why? Yet he admitted he'd learned in the "Gardner proceedings," as he called the juvenile court hearing brought against Little Mike, that a claim had been made about a missing gun.

I turned then to the autopsy. Longley had seen the corpse opened, seen the lung taken from the corpse, and seen Dr. Cushman begin to take the bullet fragment from it. Dr. Vargo, Marquis's expert, wasn't there at that time. The autopsy had been performed in the basement of the funeral home. When I asked Longley if there weren't a lot of people standing around, Brown objected. At the bench I told the judge, "The autopsy was a circus. The prosecutor was there, a number of his deputies, his secretaries, and others who had no official business or capacity were there. It reflected upon the professionalism and credibility of the work done." When the judge allowed the testimony, Longley said that he, Dr. Cushman, Officer Groat, two deputy district attorneys, the district attorney, and one secretary were all present and possibly a couple of other secretaries he couldn't remember.

"It was an event that was being observed by curiosity seekers who had no official capacity there and who, in fact, were permitted to be there by the district attorney, isn't that true?" The judge sustained Brown's objection, but the macabre scene had been set for the jury.

Longley said Peck admitted to him that he'd taken drugs from the evidence locker. "Officer Peck had put many people in the penitentiary for narcotics, hadn't he?"

"Yes."

"And you discovered he'd been using that evidence, those narcotics himself?"

"Yes." Like anybody else, jurors have a hard time with hypocrisy.

I asked him if he knew that Peck had taken the Fifth and refused to testify when called at an earlier time in this case. Brown failed to object. Longley said he knew that.

Back in the hotel that night, we ate fresh Dungeness crab Michele had brought from her husband's boat in Newport. Michele pampered us: she handpicked the crabs and made huge mounds of sweet meat to dip in hot butter and eat with sourdough bread.

"Look, oysters are great," she said, laughing, "but what you need is brain food. Keep eating."

The next morning, December 28, 1988, Brown began to bring on a string of witnesses we dreaded, witnesses intended to paint Sandy Jones as a vicious, aggressive, pistol-packing, rifle-toting bitch who was on the verge of killing anyone who crossed her path. His first witness, Jack Dick, was a hard-looker who came to court dressed as if he'd come back from a month in logging camp with a week's growth of whiskers like a burned lawn. He eased up to the stand as if it were the electric chair. He spoke with singsong sorts of sounds. He said he'd come across "the lady," pointing to Sandy at our counsel table, at the gate and that she was hysterical. He said, "She told me to get back in the car or she'd kill me. I said, 'Okay, lady, don't shoot me. I'm an innocent party.'" With those words Brown turned the witness over to me.

I cross-examined Dick like a patient father talks to a misbehaving child. Yes, Mrs. Gerttula had left one of the gates open when earlier in the morning he and Nye had followed the Gerttulas up to their subdivision. He got mixed up on which gates were which. He said Mrs. Jones told him her boy had heard some shots, and, yes, as a father it would distress him if someone had shot at his children. After I led him through some of Sandy's experiences with Gerttula, he said he now understood her better. He added, "This woman really wasn't there to do harm but to protect her children." Then he was even quick to volunteer, "If I'd been in her shoes, I'd be scared and mad."

"Bingo," Michele whispered to me. "Their menacing charge is done. Over!"

But Brown was going to keep throwing witnesses at us until he hit us with something I couldn't fend off. As if Dick had said nothing hurtful to his case, he called Dale Nye to the stand. The man looked as if he'd been driven up to the courthouse from a local shelter for the homeless.

Nye claimed Monica Gerttula had closed *all three gates*. The most Nye would say to Brown about Sandy's supposed threats to kill was that Mrs. Jones had her gun pointed at them. The kid was there, too, he said, and was armed.

When I cross-examined the man, he thought there were *four* gates, not three, and that the Gerttula pickup was red instead of blue. I read him his testimony before Judge

Gardner in which he said that *Wilfred Gerttula*, not Mrs. Gerttula, had opened and shut the gates.

"Now, Mr. Nye, as a matter of fact, the gates were opened by Mrs. Gerttula and left wide open, and you drove right on through and *nobody* closed the gates, isn't that true?"

"That's true. I remember them being—stayed open and left open. I believe they were closed, but I might be wrong. I can't remember."

I pressed him. "And the reason you can't remember is because the Gerttulas threw the gates open, you drove right on through and left all three of the gates open, and you knew that livestock get out of those open gates."

Brown didn't object to my objectionable multiple question. "That's right," Nye admitted.

He said while he was up there, he heard one shot. I read to him from his previous Gardner testimony when he said he'd heard *two shots*. Then I went through Sandy's whole story once more, starting with Gerttula's shooting at the kids. "From her standpoint, under those circumstances, you understood what she was doing?"

"Yeah," Nye said, "I had a lot of sympathy for her at the time."

"You didn't ask the sheriff or anybody else to file a complaint against Mrs. Jones, did you?"

"None. No, I didn't."

"And as a matter of fact, Mr. Nye, you would agree that she's been through enough, wouldn't you?"

"I would agree to that, yes, indeed."

Then the judge released the witness and he hurried out of the courtroom with steps on the edge of a trot.

Brown called to the stand Sandy's neighbor down the road, the eighty-four-year-old Dutchman, Cyrenus Ferris, a pleasant old man with a slight accent. He sat down stiffly, as if he'd been hoeing the garden all morning, smiled at Brown, and told how Mrs. Gerttula had come up screaming, "They shot my Willy in the tummy." In the *tummy*?

Mrs. Gerttula had asked Ferris to call the police and take her to the hospital. Because he was Dutch, he said his habit was to take off his shoes before he entered his home. Mrs. Gerttula had rushed to him with his shoes in her hands beseeching him to hurry. He had put his shoes on and then taken her as far as the Clevelands', where they came onto the Gerttula pickup. At the Cleveland residence Mr. Cleveland came out of the house and told Ferris that he, Cleveland, was a mortician and knew a dead body when he saw one, and Gerttula was dead. After that, Ferris left Mrs. Gerttula there and drove back home and finished his coffee.

I gently cross-examined the old Dutchman, who told the jury he'd seen the dust left by some vehicle that had come driving fast by his house when he'd just sat down to eat, and he was still eating when Mrs. Gerttula came screaming. She'd arrived twenty to thirty minutes after the vehicle had driven past his house, the one that had left the dust trail he'd seen earlier. That helped establish the probable time that Monica Gerttula was alone on the Jones property following the time Sandy had left her standing at the gate.

Then Brown called the fire chief, Jay Williams, a lean, lanky, sandy-haired man who identified some photos of the deceased. He said when he got to the Clevelands' at 12:57 P.M., he saw Mrs. Gerttula leaning into the passenger side of the pickup. A trial lawyer looks for a witness he can pass without cross-examination so jurors don't conclude he questions every witness whether he has something important to interrogate them about or not. "I have no questions," I said.

Brown immediately called Daryl Laube, a local fireman. Laube had taken the distraught and disheveled Mrs. Gerttula to the hospital about an hour later. She told him she'd been hit in the *back of the head* with the *butt* of a gun, not on the forehead with the barrel of the gun as she'd earlier told the jury. I asked if he'd examined the back of her head. He had. He saw no injury. She needed no emergency care.

I asked Michele to take a chair in front of the jury. "Supposing," I asked Laube, "the occupant is grabbed by the hair and is jerked out the window of the pickup. The woman is struggling, fighting, holding on to the steering wheel and her head is being pulled. The bump could be as the head is turned in this fashion?" I demonstrated with Michele, pulling her hair and turning her head. Laube agreed. And that ended it for the day.

The next morning Brown called Charles W. Bergman, a police officer in the sheriff's department who said he'd arrived at the Cleveland residence at 1:09 P.M., and that when he saw Sandy, she seemed to be in shock, she'd been crying and was in pain. She was holding her arms across her abdomen and bending over. She said she had a hernia. He testified that Deputy Peck arrived, that Mrs. Jones got in Peck's car, and that he followed them to the first gate, where he was posted to keep security.

On cross-examination he said Sandy asked him if Gerttula was dead. "I told her I wasn't sure. I didn't need to tell her."

"So this woman who was not only in serious pain was also worried about Mr. Gerttula's life, isn't that true?"

"It appeared that way, yes."

Bergman said Peck had been alone at the scene with Sandy for twenty-seven minutes. The distance from the second gate, where Mrs. Gerttula said she'd been left by

Sandy, to the Ferris residence was approximately eleven hundred feet. Bergman said if Mrs. Gerttula could run as fast as he could walk, she could probably cover the eleven hundred feet in three to four minutes.

As if he were working from a checklist, Brown put Sheriff Larry Spencer on the stand. Spencer identified the firearms that were taken from the Cleveland residence and said he had given them to Deputy Peck. He acknowledged he'd taken Peck off duty once the investigation of Peck about the missing evidence had been launched. Brown had the sheriff on the stand for less than five minutes. I had him on the stand the rest of the day.

"Now there came a time when you discovered that Officer Peck was a *crook,* isn't that true?"

The word *crook* set the sheriff back. "I don't know what you mean by *crook,*" he said. I asked if he didn't sometimes refer to ordinary people who used narcotics as *crooks*? "I suppose so, yes, I do."

"So, I thought when the tables were turned, it would be fair if we referred to a sheriff with the same language. Fair is fair, isn't it?"

"I guess so."

I smiled at him. He wasn't smiling. I led him along. Was he a fair man? Yes. Did he treat people all the same? Yes. When the time came when he once found Peck drunk in his car, did he charge him with drunk driving? No.

"How many cases against dopers had to be either reinvestigated, dismissed, or compromised because of what Officer Peck did?" I asked.

He finally estimated between thirteen and fifteen.

Under some deal the special prosecutor had made with Peck, he was given probation. "And he gets probation!" I said in amazement. "And you think everybody is treated with evenhandedness in your community?" Yes, they were.

He admitted that if officers fail to gather evidence properly, innocent people could go to prison. Then I asked, "Do you think officers should use triangulation in a homicide investigation?"

"If it was important, yes." He admitted that the location of the pickup truck and the acceleration marks should have been triangulated. He said he might not expect a rookie cop to know how to do this, but he'd expected that Peck would know how.

Although Monica Gerttula testified she had talked to the sheriff out in the county garage where the state had stored the Gerttulas' pickup, the sheriff denied having ever talked to the woman. And about our missing gun—he'd never ordered divers to go look for the gun. "If you found the gun, it would blow the state's case, wouldn't it?" He fought me on nearly every question.

"After you found out that Peck was a man who stole evidence that had been entrusted to him, didn't you feel you should also reinvestigate the Jones case?"

"No." He tried to pass the buck to Stapleton.

"Did you know that Mrs. Jones had sued Mr. Stapleton?"

"No, I didn't."

"Do you know whether Peck was under the influence of drugs when he investigated this case?"

"No, I do not."

"Don't you care?"

"Of course I care now."

"Well, now that you care, what are you going to do to resolve that?"

"Nothing. We are resolving it here."

"Are we? The jury can't investigate the matter. The only investigative arm is you, Sheriff."

As he often did, Brown objected that my question was argumentative, and often the judge sustained his objections. The question itself made my argument.

"Sheriff, you can't represent to this court that Detective Peck didn't alter evidence from the Gerttula homicide scene, can you?"

"No, I cannot." The blond woman juror in the front row was scowling at him.

"And you can't represent to this court that Officer Peck reported or logged in *all* of the evidence that he collected at the scene, can you?"

"No, I cannot."

There's always a time when a good cross-examination should end, when one more question could ruin it. "I have no further questions," I said.

The judge was eager that we stand in recess for the holiday and recessed early. "Happy New Year," he said in a too cheerful voice, and we walked out of the courtroom, grateful for the few days we had to prepare ourselves for the remaining witnesses in the case. One thing I knew: Brown was holding back the key witnesses, those he believed would finally convict Sandy Jones.

39

During the break for the holidays I celebrated my sixtieth birthday. Imaging put together a gala surprise party for me with friends coming in from across the land. I was staggered and found myself pleasantly distracted from what otherwise stood as the painful, frightening passage into the winter of my life. Perhaps we were celebrating that I should yet have the opportunity to fill out the last chapters with something meaningful. There was this trial. It seemed to take on a life of its own, and for reasons that weren't yet clear to me, I felt it touched important issues that extended beyond the facts of the case and the people involved. After the party Kent and I flew back to Portland.

The following morning I began my cross of Detective Groat. What had happened to the guns belonging to Raymond Gerttula, Wilfred's brother? Long after Wilfred Gerttula was dead, Groat, at the direction of Stapleton, had picked up the weapons from Mrs. Meisenger, Wilfred Gerttula's sister. But he'd retrieved *only two:* a .357 Magnum and a .380 Italian weapon, the name of which I couldn't pronounce. Juror 4, fluent in Italian, pronounced it for us. "Thank you," I said, and smiled at her. "You see, there's an inherent wisdom in jurors." The jurors were still smiling back.

Groat was unable to account for the third weapon listed

on the court order, a .38 Special revolver, nor could he explain why these guns had been placed in the hands of Mrs. Meisenger, a woman who by her own admission was terrified of guns. Prior to any of the facts in this case, the court had ordered Wilfred Gerttula to sell the weapons. Soon I had Groat admitting that the guns could have been delivered to Mrs. Meisenger *after* Gerttula had been shot, leaving open the real possibility that one of Gerttula's guns could have been used in the shooting. Yes, Groat agreed, he could only take her word for when she had received the weapons. And where was that .38 Special? I looked at the jury and raised my eyebrows at the question. What about Mrs. Castle, Gerttula's first wife, who had told Groat that Gerttula treasured the German Luger—a relic of World War I, given to him by an uncle. Gerttula's son, Brian, then a convict still at large, had hocked the Luger, and Gerttula had redeemed it for $35. Mrs. Castle told Groat that Gerttula had two handguns. *Two handguns?* I was still reading aloud from Groat's report to refresh his memory: "Mrs. Castle said that she knows Will was married to Monica *at the time,* and she was sure that Will would still have the Luger, that she was positive in her own mind that he would."

I looked at the old sergeant on the jury. Then I asked Groat if he was a hunter. Yes, he said, and proudly laid out an inventory of his kills: nine deer, two elk, and a porcupine. No, he didn't know that a rule of the woods was that you're not to kill porcupines. They're to be protected so that persons lost and without food could kill one with a club. He said he shot a .30-06 and a .30-30, either of which would leave an exit wound larger than the entry wound, and depending on the bone it hit, it could leave a hole as large as your fist. The old sergeant nodded his head in agreement.

After I turned the witness back to Brown, his redirect

examination didn't get off to a good start. "Do you know of any reason why Mrs. Castle wouldn't be available as a witness in this case?" I walked swiftly to the bench, gestured for Brown to come forward, and moved for a mistrial.

"The question by counsel, as he full well knows, is an impermissible comment on the obligation of the defendant to call witnesses," I said. Brown was caught. He tried to argue that through the hearsay representations of Arlene Castle I was attempting "to generate an issue about a missing gun that does not exist."

His Honor leaned over the bench and whispered to Brown, "What about your question being a comment on the defendant's obligation to call witnesses?"

Brown said he'd been surprised.

His Honor: "How could you be surprised? This was all evidence that was in the hands of the state."

"It was a surprise in the sense that we had not prepared for this in our case," Brown whispered back.

His Honor: "*You* could have called her."

Yes, but Brown complained that Mrs. Castle was hostile to both Wilfred and Monica Gerttula. The judge denied our motion for a mistrial, but I'd put yet another wrap around Brown. I wanted him tied up tight and afraid to take risks. The judge's ruling was a warning, like a referee's in a boxing match when he warns a boxer about his low blows. When would the next low blow disqualify Brown and give the match over to us? Haas turned to the jury and instructed them that we had no obligation to produce any witnesses or any evidence and that the sole responsibility for the production of evidence to prove the charges in this case was on the prosecution.

Brown wasn't ready to give an inch. Matter-of-factly he

called a witness we'd been dreading, a man named Rocky Marrs. Marrs ambled to the stand with a long, rocking gait. He had a scruffy beard, dangling, dirty hair, and a skinny frame on which hung grungy, loose-fitting clothes. Under Brown's careful questioning Marrs said that three weeks before Gerttula was shot, Sandy Jones came up to him while he was clearing brush at Gerttula's end of the road, pointed a pistol at him, and said, "Next time he comes down here, I'll just blow him away."

"To whom was she referring?" Brown asked ever so innocently.

"Will Gerttula."

Brown showed him Sandy's Charter Arms .38. "Tell us whether or not that looks like the pistol that you saw in the hands of Sandy Jones on the occasion that you described." Brown was holding the weapon in front of Marrs's face. He wasn't sure, he said, but one thing he was sure of. The pistol he saw was loaded. "I could see the lead cartridges in the cylinder."

This guy, an ex-con, seemed always available to the police as a witness. I think more innocent people are in prison today because of snitches who lie on the stand and who seek some kind of favor from the state for their lies than from any other cause. Before the trial I'd talked to Marrs over the phone and had taken careful notes. Now on the stand I got him to admit that he'd helped the police in several other cases, one against a man charged with the arson of a trailer house, and on another occasion he'd turned someone in for poaching deer. I handled him carefully, friendly-like. I asked him about threats against his life by third parties—he claimed six—and as I went over them, one by one, the picture began to emerge of a man who kept the company of questionable people or of one who possessed a vivid imagination.

"So sometimes you tell the police the truth and sometimes you don't, that's fair, isn't it?" I asked.

"Yeah," he mumbled.

"And you've been convicted of a felony?"

"Yeah, burglary, when I was younger."

"And since then you've learned that if you cooperate with the police in situations when they need help that they treat you pretty well?"

"At times they will."

"Isn't that true?" I insisted.

"Yeah."

He admitted that he told Brown's investigator Carroll that the pistol Sandy wielded had a four-inch barrel. "And you told him that it was chrome, didn't you?" I had Carroll's report in hand.

"I couldn't—well, yeah, but I really couldn't tell in the sunlight."

"Well, if you couldn't tell in the sunlight, you would have told him that you couldn't tell in the sunlight. But you told him that it was chrome."

"Chrome or nickel-plated."

"That means something that was shining. Here's something that's chromelike." I picked up the coffeepot lid again. "We both know they make guns in three styles: in chrome, stainless steel, and blued, isn't that true?"

"Yeah."

"You thought that when Mr. Carroll, the state's investigator, talked to you that he was being fair to you?"

"Yeah."

"And when he asked you what the gun looked like, you said it looked like a .38 or a .357 with a *four-inch* barrel and it was *chrome,* isn't that true?" He saw me thumbing through Carroll's report.

"Yes."

"And when Mr. Brown came up and showed you the gun just now, you said you couldn't tell for sure, right?"

"Right."

"But the gun Mr. Brown showed you had a *two-inch barrel* and it was *blued*, right?"

"Right."

"And you know that a gun that has a two-inch barrel and is blued does not look like a gun with a four-inch barrel that's chrome?"

"No."

"And when Mr. Brown asked you if it looked like this"—I picked up Sandy's .38 Charter Arms pistol—"you should have told him no, it didn't look like this, shouldn't you?"

"Correct."

"And it didn't look like this, did it?" I was still holding up Sandy's pistol, which had been holstered at her hip when the shooting took place.

"No."

Marrs testified that Sandy had ridden up to him on a Honda motorcycle. I asked its color. Maroon or purple, he said. I asked him if he hadn't told me previously it was brown. He said he could have. Then he said it was "brown or maroon or red or something."

"So if you told me it was brown, why do you tell the ladies and gentlemen of the jury that it was maroon or red, please?"

"Because you got me upset, is why."

"What am I doing to upset you?"

"Your questions."

"And that's why you don't tell the truth?"

"Yes."

"Were you nervous and upset when Mr. Brown was asking the questions?"

"A little."

"Were you nervous and upset when the police officer was asking you the questions?"

"A little."

"Were you a little nervous and upset with me, or a lot?"

"Just a little."

"That makes it pretty much even, doesn't it? So shouldn't your testimony be the same?"

"Yeah."

"You shouldn't be telling it one way to one person and another way to another, should you?"

"No."

Then I reminded him of his answers to Brown's earlier questions when he'd said that the confrontation with Sandy had taken place two weeks before Gerttula's death. Within minutes he'd also said the incident had taken place early in the spring or late in the fall. And once he'd said the confrontation had been three weeks before the death of Gerttula. Obviously, all the dates couldn't be true, he admitted, and soon I had him acknowledging that he'd told Gary Stafford that the confrontation had occurred not in 1985, but 1984. Surely Brown had known how squirrelly this witness was. Yet Brown was prepared to convict Sandy Jones on his testimony? At the recess I asked that the man's testimony be stricken. The time of the alleged confrontation, 1984, was too remote. But Judge Haas allowed the testimony to stand. It was an issue for the jury, he said.

After the recess I took one more swing at Marrs. "The reason you were even able to identify Mrs. Jones was because you saw her picture in the paper, isn't that true?"

"No," he said.

I said to the court reporter, "Would you read the last question back to the witness to make sure he heard it correctly?" I picked up a report from my table as if I were ready to show him another prior inconsistent statement. He wanted out of there.

"Yes, I seen her picture," Marrs hurriedly admitted. I looked over at the jury. They were staring with open distaste for the man.

When I sat down, Sandy whispered to me, "Somebody ought to punch Marrs out. Why would they call somebody like him?" I couldn't answer her question. But it had something to do with the mental composition of prosecutors—their willingness to believe any witness who had something incriminating to say about the accused, a mind-set that interpreted whatever the accused said and whatever anyone said against the accused in the worst possible way. Accusers are that way. It's their nature.

Brown wasn't backing down. He called Donald Buford, a truck driver, a clean-cut Mr. Average Good Citizen. I knew what was coming. So did Sandy and Michele. I could hear them stirring uneasily in their chairs. Buford in a calm, believable voice told the jury about an occasion when he, too, had had a conversation with Sandy Jones. Mike Sr. had been there and was walking with a cane. Sandy told him that Gerttula had run over Mike with a pickup. Then Buford came out with it: "Sandra told me that she'd have to kill Gerttula if she didn't win in court. I told her, 'Sandra, it's not worth going to jail over,' and she said, 'I don't have any choice, if we lose, I have to kill him.'"

Then with a little shake of his head as if he were shocked by Buford's testimony, Brown turned the witness over to me for cross-examination. I could almost hear the penitentiary doors creaking open and slamming closed on Sandy Jones. I didn't dare attack the man. The jury liked him. I had to turn him into our witness. You feel your way through things like this. Again I started out in a friendly way, getting him to tell the jury that he'd gone to the sheriff after he'd read of Gerttula's death in the performance of his duty as a good citizen. I smiled my approval.

"So it must have shocked you to find out that this nice woman turned out to be a murderess."

"Well, I don't know that she is a murderess," Buford said. "I think she probably is, but it's not for me to decide."

"Of course not," I said, still cordial. "The jury will decide that, but we're just wanting to know your state of mind, and I appreciate it very much that you're helping us understand that."

Wasn't he a person naturally inclined to understand people? Yes, he agreed. And Mrs. Jones discussed her problem with him because she liked him? He said he hoped so. She saw him as a sensitive person as most folks did? Again he hoped so. Referring to the fact that Gerttula had run over Mike Sr., I asked, "Did you ever know anybody who was intentionally run over with a car? Ever see that done before?" No, he hadn't.

"Do you think that would be frightening?"

"I'm sure it would." Then he agreed that if this had happened to his brother or his wife, he would have gone to the police and demanded protection.

"That's our right, isn't it?"

"That's correct."

"And suppose that you went to the police and they gave you no protection at all? Would you take steps to protect your wife yourself?" Yes, he said he would.

Then I asked, instead of presuming Mrs. Jones guilty, as he had, what if he had adopted a state of mind, as the jurors were required to do, that Mrs. Jones was innocent until proven guilty? Could he adopt that point of view for a moment? Yes, he could. After that I went through the list of grievances he'd known nothing of, including Gerttula's shooting at the kids, the raccoon in the well, and the rest of it. I ended the series of questions by telling him that the authorities had given Sandy no protection.

"Wouldn't you need those facts to interpret correctly what Mrs. Jones said to you?"

"Perhaps."

Sometimes a wee voice in the subconscious, without stating the reason, tells me to ask a certain question. Suddenly I asked, "Did you ever threaten to injure somebody severely?"

There was a bulging, pregnant silence. Finally he said in a raspy voice, "Yes, I have." I gently pressed him for the details. "I had an argument with a man in a feedstore. I threatened to stab him with a pitchfork." I could hear a gasp in the jury box.

"To run him through with a pitchfork?" I said, my voice bathed in incredulity.

"Yes. I wouldn't have done it. I said it in anger."

"Does that mean you are an evil man?"

"I hope not."

"What would happen if we found the man dead the next day?"

"I would be a prime suspect."

"What if the person next to you at the feedstore came in and testified to a jury as you are testifying to a jury against Mrs. Jones, that they heard you say you were going to run him through with a pitchfork? How do you think you could make them believe that you didn't kill the man?"

"I honestly don't know."

"Stop and think a minute, Mr. Buford. You've just said to the ladies and gentlemen of the jury that Mrs. Jones made a threatening statement against Mr. Gerttula. How can she now defend herself?"

Brown objected that it called for the witness's speculation. The judge sustained him. I needed to say nothing more. I thanked the witness and sat down. Once more we'd been snatched free of the snapping jaws of the state. But before I could catch another breath, Brown called Delores Baxter.

The woman, a bank teller at the Security Pacific Bank, said she knew Mrs. Jones, nodding toward Sandy. "She's the woman sitting between Michele and Mr. Spence, the woman in the blue dress."

Ms. Baxter said she'd talked to Sandy when Sandy came to the bank and that Sandy was very distressed over certain events that had taken place. Mrs. Baxter didn't enumerate. She did say Sandy had sued a judge and had lost that case. "She seemed very frustrated. And as she was leaving the bank, she got up to the front door, turned around, and came back and raised her jacket and said, 'If I can't stop them, this will.' There was a holster on her waist." She couldn't tell Brown what was in the holster. All she saw was the leather. It frightened her.

I did what lawyers ought not to do: I was taken in by my own distaste for the witness. To me she seemed the sanctimonious sort and displayed a haughty air. I launched a frontal attack where a more gentle cross might have been better. "If you were frightened, you didn't go to the sheriff and tell him that you were frightened, did you?" No, she hadn't. I asked her for the date. She didn't know.

"Could it have been the year 1984?"

Brown saw where I was going and objected. The court overruled. I asked the question again.

"I don't think I should answer if I can't answer correctly."

"I just asked you if it *could have been* 1984?"

"It could have been."

"Could it have been 1983?"

"Again, it could have been."

"You really don't know, do you?"

"I really do not know the time frame, the dates."

"I have no further questions," I said. Brown had no redirect examination. It was the end of the day and Haas called a recess until the following morning.

Walking out of the courtroom, I said to Sandy, "We're still in this game."

She looked pale. "I got a terrible headache. I get 'em all the time."

"What you're listening to is enough to give anybody a headache," I said.

"I'm afraid to look at the jury. I'm afraid if I do, I'll look guilty. Do I look guilty?"

"You're doing fine. You look as innocent as a lamb." I laughed.

"Thanks, Spence." Then she thought for a moment. "Sometimes it doesn't seem like it's me who's on trial. Sometimes I pretend it isn't. I get by that way."

Brown had insisted he was going to call Ronald Peck as his first witness in the morning. I doubted it. Yet we had to be ready. Michele gathered up all the Peck materials, organizing the ammunition. She recalled an incident I didn't think I'd be able to use, but it gave me another clue to the man: "This happened before Peck's own drug investigation came down. I had this client who'd been busted for growing pot. No prior convictions, employed full-time, middle-management type. I talked to the deputy district attorney handling the case, trying to get a diversion for a first-time offender—you know, if he successfully completed treatment, didn't get popped for anything else, in three years the case would be dismissed with no conviction on his record. The deputy DA says, 'Well, the cops get pissed when we dump these cases out like that, so you better talk to the cop for me, get his okay, and I'll think about it.' So, there I am doing a lazy DA's job, and I go find the cop, who happens to be Peck. Caught up with him one day in the coffee shop and asked him to okay a diversion for my client. 'No way,' he said. 'The guy's got to end up with at least a felony—I want it on his record. No deal.' Then Peck's troubles came to light and the DA dismissed my client's case outright along with a bunch of other cases, thanks to Peck's own misconduct. Karma kickback, I called it."

The following morning Brown did call Peck. That surprised me. I'd probably forced him to it. What would the jury think if Brown didn't put the man on? Maybe Brown knew what I knew—that it might be better to call him and face my cross-examination than to hear me say over and over on final argument that the state took the Fifth, to hear me shout across the courtroom pointing my finger at Brown, "And tell me this, Mr. Brown: *Where is Officer Peck?*"

I could feel my heart pounding up around my Adam's apple. I'd made a big issue of Peck. He'd become the hub of the state's case. If he came off as a humble sinner seeking atonement, if the jury forgave him, if they resented my attacking a man who was trying to right the wrongs of his life, if I couldn't win the cross-examination, it could all backfire. I watched Peck walk to the witness stand with a strange sort of slump. Peck had gained weight since we'd seen him last. He seemed subdued, even humble. Suddenly I felt sorry for him, the embarrassment of having to face a jury as an officer who had put many a criminal behind bars who, himself, was now on probation.

Brown did as I would have done. He had Peck admit his conviction. The way Peck spoke of it, it was as if he'd come nobly forth and confessed his crimes. He took responsibility for what he had actually done, but he insisted he wasn't under the influence of drugs when he was investigating the Jones case, and, no, he wasn't a drug addict or an alcoholic.

He told the same story we'd heard so many times before, a story that began when he'd arrived at the Clevelands' and continued on through his investigation at the scene of the shooting. He seemed honest enough, straightforward and believable. I thought Brown made a solid decision in calling Peck.

Now the onus was on me. I'd laid too much of my case on Peck's misconduct. My job was to convert this man from a wounded officer who was seeking redemption for his misdeeds into an unreliable, amoral conveyor of half-truths. If I failed, our case could be severely damaged. I had Peck's criminal trial transcript. I confronted him patient question at a time. Hadn't he actually come forward to admit his crime only *after* a fellow officer, preparing for another trial, had gotten into the evidence locker and found cocaine missing? Yes. Didn't that fellow officer have a photo of the cocaine that had been confiscated, a cup or a cup-and-a-half-ful? Yes. After that, Peck had come back to the evidence locker with a bag of a white powdery substance and his fellow officer had weighed it and it didn't weigh up right. Yes, that was true.

And there had been pills missing? Yes. The bottle of pills that Peck had returned was only half-full and they weren't the same pills. He admitted that. Considering that he brought back the wrong pills and had also produced some cocaine from an unidentified source, hadn't he tried to *manufacture* evidence? He denied that he had "manufactured evidence" but admitted he stole seventy-five tablets of Valium.

"As an officer, you were charged in this case with the sworn duty to preserve the evidence, weren't you?"

"Yes."

"So when you steal evidence, sir, when you steal pills, you're not only stealing like a common thief, but you're also violating your responsibility as an officer, isn't that true?"

He looked down at his hands. "That's true, I violated a very sacred trust." The Peck jury had convicted him of three misdemeanors: second-degree theft, possession of a controlled substance, and official misconduct. That jury had also found Peck not guilty on eight counts and was unable to decide on the twenty-one remaining charges. Facing a retrial, Peck had pleaded guilty to a charge or two, was sentenced and placed on probation.

I wanted to show that during the time Peck was being investigated he was also investigating Sandy's case, and that the man was mentally unstable.

"It's true, isn't it, Officer, that in May or June of 1985, that you threatened your girlfriend with physical violence?"

"If I did, I don't remember it. It's possible."

"Should the jury take into consideration your consumption of drugs or alcohol as an excuse for your lack of memory?"

"No."

"And you continue to deny an excessive use of alcohol, don't you?"

"Yes."

"And you deny that you were habituated to drugs during that period, don't you?"

"Yes."

"And so neither of these account for the fact that you don't remember having threatened your girlfriend with physical violence, isn't that true?"

"Yes."

"But you make room for the possibility that you did threaten her, is that correct?"

"Yes."

"Do you think that those threats to your girlfriend might be considered as evidence of emotional instability?"

"No."

Now to tie this into our case I asked, "You took into your possession certain items in the Jones case?" Yes, he had. "You were entrusted with their care just as you were entrusted with the care of the drugs in the other cases?" Yes. He admitted he was probably involved in about forty other cases at the time. "That means that there were forty human beings charged with crimes, the evidence of which you were entrusted with, isn't that true?" Yes, he said.

Perhaps he didn't always tell the truth: "On the one hand, you say you took nothing for your own use, except Valium. Then you pled guilty to a set of facts in which you admit to have taken Dilaudid, isn't that true?" That's true, he said.

At first Peck said he was at the scene of the shooting alone with Sandy for a total of five minutes. But under cross he didn't deny that he could have been there for as long as twenty-seven minutes. Other than taking some photos that he couldn't account for, what had he done outside the car at the scene? He admitted that Sandy seemed incoherent at the time but he refused to agree that she seemed "dazed." I called his attention to his testimony before Judge Gardner when he'd said, "She appeared to be more or less in a daze." Then I asked, "Why do you argue with me when I ask you that simple question now?" Brown objected. The judge sustained him. The jury looked on.

He agreed that he took gunshot-residue swabs from Sandy and turned them over to the state lab in the ordinary course of business. But he wouldn't admit that he should have taken swabs from Wilfred Gerttula's hands. He'd previously testified in Gardner's court that it was proper procedure to swab the deceased's hands for gunshot residue. I could see the jurors were becoming impatient with the man as he became more and more contentious, fighting me now on every question. I was glad for it.

He testified that he'd emptied the .30-30 rifle when he'd taken it into custody. Yet he'd sent it off to the state lab with a *live shell in the chamber*! Had he been sober? Had he been under the influence of drugs to make such a blatant, dangerous error? No. No, not at all.

He said he did triangulations to locate the position of the cartridge cases at the scene. But what good would those measurements be if we didn't know where Gerttula was? Did he measure where the front of the vehicle had been? No. Did he take measurements of the acceleration marks? No. Had he taken measurements where the blood on the ground was located? No. Had he made measurements from the front of the pickup to the gate? No. Had he made a measurement from the ground to where the bullet in the alder tree was found? No. And on and on for more than two hours. Still Peck insisted he was alert on that day.

I called his attention to a large, vicious-looking machete that was in the truck. He remembered that. "Where is the machete?" I asked.

"I don't know." *He didn't know?*

"Was there blood on the machete?"

"There may have been."

"I am not suggesting by my question that the machete had a damn thing to do with the case. But I am asking you if you don't think a competent officer, who was alert and bright, would have preserved a machete that was found in the truck of a person who was shot, where there's a charge of murder?" He thought the machete wasn't relevant.

"What about the recorder? Was there blood on it?" I handed him the tape recorder, where a brown, bloodlike stain was obvious. I displayed it to the jury.

"There's a discoloration, yes," Peck admitted.

"Did you request that those stains be examined?"

I gave him his report. The report was silent on the issue.

"Are all of these defects in the evidence—evidence that would have been gathered and preserved by any competent officer—explainable by your emotional state of mind at the time?" Brown objected. The judge overruled.

"My emotional state of mind had nothing to do with that."

Then I reviewed the failed evidence, item by item, and ended my cross-examination by asking him, "Mr. Peck, would you say that the investigation that was conducted into the death of Mr. Gerttula was one that this jury could justly and fairly rely upon?"

"Yes, I do." I looked over at the jurors. I didn't think they believed him.

"Thank you," I said. Haas recessed court for the day. We'd survived what I thought must surely be the heart of the state's case. But James Brown had other plans.

40

Brown did what good trial attorneys do. He called the witnesses we would have called. He had Dawson take on John Amish, the lab technician. Dawson tried to muddy up Amish's testimony about the gunshot residue on Monica Gerttula's hands and face. His question reminded me of a blind man drawing a picture of the donkey before he tried to pin on its tail. "What the hell is he talking about?" Michele whispered.

"He's Mickey Mousing the evidence," I whispered back. "He doesn't want the jury to know what he's talking about." After more than an hour of high gibberish, Dawson concluded his examination as if he'd made a great and deciding point to the jury, looked like a cock about to crow, bowed slightly, and said to me, "You may examine."

I asked Michele to sit in a chair in front of the jury. I put some Saran Wrap around her face and body, took out a can of Johnson's baby powder, opened it, and smacked the bottom of the can in her direction. The powder, like gunshot residue, stuck to the Saran Wrap. Amish admitted this was the mechanics of the test that had been attempted by the criminalist Bekkedahl in the state lab. Only one problem— when Bekkedahl had fired Little Mike's .30-30, he got no antimony residue on the dummy and low quantities of barium, while the levels of both antimony and barium found on Monica Gerttula's face and hands had been high.

"Now after all of the talking you've done with Mr. Dawson, do you wish to change any of the testimony you gave to the ladies and gentlemen of the jury under my cross-examination?"

"No, I do not."

"And the bottom line is that you're still a truthful witness, isn't that true?"

"That's correct."

"And you still believe that it's more probable than not that Monica Gerttula fired a gun on the date in question, irrespective of all the things that we've now heard, isn't that true?"

"That's true," John Amish said.

But Brown wasn't ready to concede the issue. He had Lieutenant N. Michael Hurley waiting in the wings. If Brown's tactic had been to muddle up Amish's findings, he brought on Hurley to undermine the younger man's testimony. Again Dawson did the questioning in a hard, damaging voice. Hurley claimed that Amish didn't have the experience he had and was obviously not up-to-date on the most recent data in the literature. He stated that the cutoff levels for positive gunshot residue had been *lowered*, and according to his tests and the current literature, gunshot residue from the bullet's primer travels *farther* than unburned gunpowder, this despite that unburned gunpowder is heavier than the mist-like gunshot residue. Hurley looked over at the jury as he gave Dawson his answers, and after another hour of what appeared to be mostly monumental nonsense, Dawson again bowed slightly in the direction of his witness, as if to say he'd shown the whole of Amish's testimony as unreliable.

"Jesus, Gerry," Michele said. "This guy is shooting at the moon."

"He's trying to confuse the jury. Let's see if we can de-confuse them." I started by giving Hurley a fair chance. "You're not suggesting by your testimony that the conclusions of Mr. Amish are improper or inaccurate, are you?" If he had answered my question no, I'd have thanked him and sat down. Instead the man was going to take me on. He said, "At *that time*—"

I cut him off. "No! *Today!*"

He gave me a contemptuous stare. His answer was gilded with authority. "Today I would not come to the same conclusion as Mr. Amish." There it was. If I let that answer stand, and if the jury was confused, maybe Monica Gerttula could get off the hook for the residue on her hands and face.

But if Amish was using a higher cutoff level for antimony and barium than the one Hurley would use, it meant that Monica Gerttula had *more*, not less, gunshot residue on her hand than was required to establish she'd shot a gun on that day. Hurley wasn't bound by logic. Amish, Hurley said, was wrong when Hurley's own testimony said Amish was right. The jury looked confused. I'd have to take the man on, question at a time.

Could he tell me of a single test he'd made? Of course. What gun was used? A .30-30. What make? Well, he couldn't say. The cartridges he used? Various. That's no answer. What specific cartridges? He didn't remember. How far did the gunshot residue travel? He couldn't remember. Could he produce a record of the test? He had none. Could he give me the specifics of any test he had run? He tried to evade the question. "The specifics would be we've done testing with both handguns—"

I interrupted him, "Give me a test, sir. Don't Mickey Mouse it. Give me a test. You know what I mean!"

Dawson jumped up hollering, "I object to the Mickey Mouse, Your Honor," to which a cascade of laughter came rolling out from the gallery of spectators. The judge looked down from the bench. "He's talking about *any* test that you've personally performed," the judge said. Finally Hurley admitted he'd done one test in the summer of 1988. What kind of a revolver? He couldn't say. What kind of ammunition? He couldn't say. What were the results for antimony? He didn't know. It was impeachment of the most fundamental sort that suggested the witness was guessing, perhaps worse than guessing.

Did he think Amish was an honest technician? Yes. He had to say that. Did he think he was competent? He said he was competent to run the instrument that did the testing. "Well, is he a competent man now, today?"

"Competent to do what?" he asked.

I stopped and looked at him. The jury waited. "Are you afraid to answer the question?"

Hurley raised his chin an inch and his lips formed a small sneer. "I don't believe he knows as much about gunshot residue as I do." With that I had him turn to the jury and tell them he knew more than Lieutenant Telyea, as well, another lab technician. "You know more than both of them combined?" I asked. I looked over at the sergeant on the jury and raised an eyebrow.

"Yes, maybe more than them combined."

"If these men don't know what they're talking about, it would be a terrible crime to turn them loose in the courts of justice in this country, wouldn't you think?" He didn't answer the question. "Well," I pressed, "do you think both of these men would be qualified to testify to a jury on these matters?"

"I believe they were and I believe they are."

Then I put the lid on the issue: "So it isn't a matter that they're not competent, it's just that you think you know more than they do?"

"Yes, sir."

"Did you ever tell Amish that his results were incorrect?"

"His results I don't know to be not correct," he said, stumbling over his double negative.

I wanted to know about his claimed search of the recent literature that had advanced his learning beyond that of both Amish and Telyea. Where were these articles? I could see him trying to weigh his answer. Finally he said he had several in the car. The evening recess at hand, I requested His Honor to instruct Hurley to bring the articles into chambers. Then Michele and I stayed with him and speed-read through his books, and with yellow stickies we had him mark every place he thought established that gunshot residue would travel farther than unburned powder from the cartridge.

When, two hours later, we finally left the courthouse, Michele said, "He's busted. What did he think—that we wouldn't read 'em all? He must think we work for the state."

In the morning Hurley had to admit that the books he'd brought to court were compilations of articles published years ago, most written in the sixties and seventies with references as early as 1940. "So the most recent reference would be about ten years old, is that correct?" I asked.

"That's when the author of that chapter is referring to."

"Tell the jury the truth, did you do any literature search specifically for this case?" He played with his words without answering. I asked the question again. Finally he said, "No, not specifically for this case."

I turned to his books with the yellow stickies marking the places and began to read what he'd marked in the judge's chambers the evening before. It soon became apparent that none of the references stated that gunshot residue traveled farther than unburned powder. Each time I read one of his selections, I let silence fill the room and stared at the witness. He stared blankly back. Finally I said, "Is there a single area in any of that literature that says that gunshot residues travel farther than gunpowder residues?"

"I don't understand your question." The jury understood. Patiently I asked the question again. His answer, finally: "In those specific words, no."

"I thought you were telling the ladies and gentlemen of the jury under your oath about a *new* discovery that Mr. Amish and Mr. Telyea didn't know anything about. Isn't that what you told the jury?"

He started to evade again. "This information—"

I interrupted, "Didn't you tell the jury that?"

"I don't believe I did tell the jury that." The jury had its own memory and again I let silence fill the courtroom.

One of the articles was about how a scientific witness should establish his credibility with the jury by "frequent eye contact with the jury, or by a slight gyration of the witness chair which will give you eye-to-eye contact with the most important person or persons in the courtroom [the jury]." After having read those sentences I asked Hurley, "Don't you think that the best way to be credible is to be painstakingly accurate and painstakingly honest?" He had to admit it.

"Do you still maintain that you know more about this than Mr. Amish?"

"Yes, sir, I do."

I reminded him of my call to his home several weeks before at seven-thirty in the morning. "I asked you then if you would argue with any of Mr. Amish's results, and didn't you tell me that you would not?"

"Not with his *results*. You didn't ask me about his *conclusions*," as if the two words meant different things. Addressing my final question to the jury instead of the witness, I said, "All right. When we're talking to scientists, we better be very careful to use the correct words, hadn't we?" Some of the jurors smiled, and there was audible laughter from the gallery. After that I had no further questions for N. Michael Hurley.

Still Brown had more witnesses. He called Trooper Richard Geistwhite to the stand. Since the shooting, he'd been put on security detail for the governor and was driving the governor around as his chauffeur. In less than an hour Brown took the cop through the testimony we'd heard several times, but before he turned him over to me, he had Geistwhite identify a photograph of the dead Gerttula lying across the pickup seat. "Is that how he appeared at the time you pulled Monica Gerttula out of the pickup away from her husband?"

"Yes, it is," Geistwhite said. I felt the horror of Monica Gerttula's experience. The jury looked shocked and sickened. For a final shot, in his answer to Brown's next question, Geistwhite pulled an old cop trick. He referred to the shooting as "the time of the murder." I interrupted, asking His Honor to instruct the witness not to refer to the incident as a murder, nor to refer to the place of the incident as "the crime scene." Brown quickly played the other side of it: "Can we agree not to use the word *accident*, Your Honor?" Words are powerful. They can save and destroy. The judge said, "Yes, let's just call it the scene."

Geistwhite admitted that Monica Gerttula repeatedly stated at police headquarters that Sandy had shot Wilfred Gerttula "point-blank in the chest with the .22." She even mentioned the sound of the .22, a "spat-spat," and she'd told Geistwhite her husband had never been in front of the pickup, which, by now, everyone knew was wrong because of the massive amount of blood on the hood and grille. Then

I posed the crux question to Geistwhite: "Did Monica Gerttula ever even suggest that Little Mike did anything at the scene except shoot the rear tire?"

"No."

"Did she make any claim that Sandy Jones did anything to cause her son, Mike, to shoot Mr. Gerttula?" He tried to avoid the answer. I asked the question again.

"Not that I recall," he finally admitted.

To underline his answer I said, "That's an important issue in this case, isn't it?"

"Yes."

I heard Sandy mutter, "Thank you."

One thing I knew from long experience—prosecutors sometimes prime their witnesses to suddenly blurt out forbidden, prejudicial statements when they're cross-examined, statements that would result in a mistrial if they'd given the same answer to a direct question posed by the prosecutor. Without warning, Geistwhite unloaded one on me. I'd asked if it didn't surprise him that Monica Gerttula would be out there taking pictures of somebody with a gun if she was really afraid of Sandy?

"Well, they'd encountered the Joneses when the Joneses were armed in the past."

I heard Sandy gasp. I objected immediately. "That's improper and it's not true," I said quietly so as not to emphasize his answer. Judge Haas stepped in. Did Geistwhite have any firsthand knowledge of the matter? And when the man answered no, Haas instructed the jury to disregard his statement. I asked the judge to hear me in chambers. The jury watched us leave the courtroom, Geistwhite trailing behind us like a schoolboy on his way to the principal's office.

In chambers I asked Geistwhite further questions. Personally he knew nothing of the Joneses having confronted the Gerttulas with arms in the past. He couldn't name any officer who had. The judge called it "bootstrap hearsay," and I argued for a mistrial, but having gone this far, Haas wasn't going to mistry this case. He'd give an additional instruction to the jury. "Ladies and gentlemen, the court is instructing you that there is no evidence that the Joneses ever had a prior encounter with the Gerttulas when the Joneses were armed, and you're to disregard totally the officer's statement in that respect."

What about Monica Gerttula's sudden loss of memory after the autopsy? Geistwhite admitted that the day following the autopsy he had gone to the Gerttula house and told the woman that her husband had been shot with a larger caliber gun than a .22, and that her husband had been at the front of the pickup.

"And after you told her that new set of facts, it was then that you turned on the tape recorder."

"Yes."

"Don't you think it would have been fair for this jury to have heard that conversation *before* you turned on the recorder?"

"Yes. I wish I'd have taped that particular part of it." I doubted that. I thought it might well have been Geistwhite's unrecorded conversation with the woman that caused her to suddenly block out all of her previous memory to the contrary.

"So her last statement was diametrically opposed to the statement she gave you on the day of the shooting when she told you what kind of shots they were and who shot what gun—this was all blocked out now?"

"Yes." But Geistwhite denied seeing Ms. Pinckney, who was leaving the Gerttula residence as Geistwhite had entered it. "I had a phone conversation with Ms. Pinckney," he now insisted, "and I told her that any statements had to come from the DA under his press-release policy."

"You knew Ms. Pinckney talked to Mrs. Gerttula before you were able to tell Mrs. Gerttula about the size of the bullet in her husband's chest and the blood at the front of the pickup, isn't that true?"

"Yes."

"And the reason you didn't want Mrs. Gerttula to make any statements to the press is because what Mrs. Gerttula told Ms. Pinckney would have been contrary to what you were able to get her to tell you—about blocking out her memory of the shots, isn't that true?"

"No. These statements would be very prejudicial to a fair trial."

"You never have much problem publishing the facts against the accused party," I said. The judge didn't like that comment and on his own sustained an objection to it. I let Geistwhite go.

Brown brought Mary Ross to the stand, whose testimony had become the hook upon which Brown had hung his case—that Sandy spoke of killing Gerttula to Ross and that this conversation had taken place in the presence of Little Mike, who was thereby prompted to kill Gerttula himself. We heard it all again as we'd heard it before—that Sandy said maybe she'd have to kill Gerttula and that she'd spend less time in jail than all the time she'd suffered from his continued harassment.

Had Ross's diminished memory been replenished from other sources? Early on she'd given Officer Longley a statement, but in it she'd made no reference to Little Mike even being present, much less that he'd been listening to the conversation. Nor did she tell Longley anything about comparing jail time to the problems she was encountering with Gerttula.

"So, Miss Ross," I said, "are you adding things to your statement over three years later? As time goes on, does your memory get better about these things?" No, she said, it all had come to her memory shortly after the interview.

"Sandy told you Gerttula put her husband in the hospital, didn't she?" Ross didn't remember the details. "Is that because you weren't much interested in what she was saying to you?" She said no. In her entire life had she ever known another woman whose husband had been run down intentionally with a truck? No. That would be quite a memorable occasion, wouldn't it? Yes. Had she, in the entirety of her life, talked to a mother whose little children had been shot at by the same man? No. That was quite a memorable occasion, too, wasn't it? Yes. If Mrs. Jones was hysterical, that would be something that you would understand? Yes. The police would do nothing, the prosecutor would do nothing, so she had told Sandy to see an attorney? Ross admitted she'd never talked to Stapleton about the case. She'd talked to no one about it.

"You would have been desperate in her shoes, wouldn't you?"

"Yes."

"And to threaten to defend yourself or to defend your children is no crime, is it?" Brown objected but the judge allowed the question.

"No."

At the last I asked her, "Would you as a sensitive, caring, understanding victim's rights representative have fully understood her fear in her position?"

"Yes."

Brown acted as if I hadn't touched the woman in my cross. What was I missing? What did he see that I didn't see? I asked Michele, "What's going on?"

"I don't think she hurt us," she said. I asked Kent.

"Maybe he wasn't listening," Kent said. I worried. A lawyer can never know for sure what's really happening in the courtroom, not as it all comes sifting through to the jurors. Perhaps it was Brown who had missed it. My cross completed, Brown chose to leave her testimony stand as I had left it.

"Call Ben Kowitz," Brown said. Kowitz was a short, stout, older man who took the stand and sat nervously waiting for Brown's first question while the lawyer shuffled through his papers. Sandy told me Kowitz was a tinker—had made a handgun out of scraps, a kiln from a campfire, and a pottery wheel that was water-driven. She said, "Once I was really sick after I got out of jail. Ben sent over some homemade lamb stew. It was so good and I held it down and started to get better. He's a little man with a big heart."

According to Kowitz, he'd been driving up the road and had stopped at the Clevelands', where he discovered Gerttula lying dead in the truck. Sandy came out of the house and asked Kowitz to go get Little Mike. Kowitz was on his way back to the Joneses' to fetch the boy when he met old man Ferris on his way down to the Clevelands' with Monica in his car. Kowitz found Little Mike at the Jones place and brought him back to the Clevelands', where Sandy was waiting for the police to arrive. When I had no questions for the man, Brown immediately called Tom Cleveland.

Cleveland was one who could make the jurors laugh in the midst of this macabre drama. They liked him. "I raised ten kids, twenty-three grandkids, I'm sixty-four. In good health. Anything else?" The jurors laughed. He said when Sandy drove up, he was in the backyard. "My wife was laying in the sun and I was working. That's the way we do it. She lays in the sun, I work." More laughter.

Sandy asked Tom to help her get Gerttula to the hospital. He was already dead, and it was forty-five minutes before any police arrived. "When they did arrive, there was a bunch of 'em. They were running every which way. It was really kind of a mess. There were twenty, twenty-five policemen running around, some in Levi's and everybody asking questions."

Cleveland took Sandy's pistol and the .30-30 from the pickup and laid them on the bed in the bedroom. He said Mrs. Gerttula was out there crying and raising hell, and he didn't want a shooting war of some kind to erupt. That's why he took the guns. He told about how he'd been waiting to tell the cops when this tall, dark-haired cop said, "What the hell are you doing there?" And Tom Cleveland said, " 'I live here, partner. I'm on my own property.' And the cop said, 'Get the hell off, we're talking business.'" So Tom said he thought, "Well, that's fine. I was going to tell them about the guns." The next day he called Sheriff Spencer and the sheriff came and got the weapons. Cleveland said he never asked Sandy what happened and she never told him. Said it was none of his damned business.

When I cross-examined Cleveland, he said he thought about Little Mike, who was all alone, a man shot, his mother in the hands of the police, and his father off somewhere. Cleveland went down to see the boy, who'd been hiding. He tried to get Little Mike to come home with him, but he said, "No, I better stay, because they kicked my dog. He was tied up and they hurt my dog." Then the boy threw his arms around the man and started crying. Later Cleveland told the jury how one of the officers, the same big one with the dark hair, had said, "Well, we'll get that little bastard. He hasn't told us everything yet."

Then my last question: "You're telling me, Mr. Cleveland, that they left that body out there in the road in that pickup from noon until eight o'clock that night with the temperature as high as a hundred degrees?"

"Yes, sir. Just about that much time."

After a recess, Brown had Gerttula's sister, Mrs. Terry Meisenger, testify how Raymond Gerttula's guns had come into her possession and how the officer had retrieved them from her—two of them. But they weren't taken from her until January 6, 1986. That was all Brown wanted from the witness, but on cross, Mrs. Meisenger readily admitted that Monica knew all about these guns. Monica had been there when Mrs. Meisenger picked up the guns from Wilfred Gerttula. And that was all I needed from her as well.

Once again it was Dawson's turn. Brown called Terry Bekkedahl to the stand, and Dawson, in his gruff, authoritative manner, lumbered through his direct examination. He droned on hour after hour about factual details that didn't resolve any of the matters at issue—who shot Gerttula and why? Bekkedahl testified how he had found the Kodak film wrapper on the ground at the scene, the one I'd questioned Monica Gerttula about earlier.

Dawson labored through Bekkedahl's experiments to reconstruct the gunshot residue found on Monica Gerttula's hands and face. Again his testimony seemed confusing. But finally, under my cross-examination, he admitted he'd not been able to come close to duplicating those residues, even when the .30-30 was fired within a few inches of the dummy's head and fired so close that the blast knocked the dummy over. Bekkedahl admitted his previous testimony—that the reason he had failed to test Gerttula's clothing for gunshot residue was that if there'd been no gunpowder on his clothing, which there wasn't, he knew that the gunshot residue had not been able to reach the deceased because gunpowder traveled farther—

which was exactly opposite of Hurley's testimony. The jurors seemed to understand that. I left the witness, and Brown promptly called Dr. Cushman, the pathologist who'd performed the autopsy.

Again Dawson questioned the witness for what seemed to be an eternity. Cushman's testimony was burdened with the virtually meaningless vocabulary of his profession, words like "the bronchi," "the pleural space," "the medial border," "subpleural bruising," "mild multifocal arteriosclerosis," and on and on. No one knew what the hell the man was talking about, and soon I doubted that many cared. He talked about "the axilla." Finally Dawson said, "You mean the armpit?" and after that it got worse, such as "the distal phalange of his left fifth finger." But one thing the jury learned. Gerttula had bled to death from the wound in the right lung, the doctor surmising he hadn't lived for more than ten minutes.

I asked Cushman if anyone had told him that the man had lain in the hot pickup for over eight hours. No, he didn't know that. Then came Cushman's autopsy two days later, after the body had been embalmed. Not the best of conditions, he admitted, for one to give his opinions on anything, and moreover, he also admitted he wasn't a forensic pathologist. He did say the bullet took a downward course. Either someone shot the man from above, like in a tree, or he'd been stooped forward at the time he was hit, in a position as if he were wrestling with Mrs. Jones for her .22. Not only that, bruises on the man's side could have been inflicted with the sharp edges found on the sight or the butt of Sandy's .22, a bruise consistent with Gerttula's and Sandy's fighting for her rifle. He admitted that he found no particles of copper from a copper-jacketed slug, the usual rifle bullet, and by the end of my cross-examination he said he couldn't tell us whether this wound was from a rifle or a pistol. He wasn't qualified to say.

Relentlessly Brown was calling every witness, whether they could present telling testimony or not, as if a witness might somehow slip through my cross-examination and unexpectedly deliver the fatal blow to Sandy Jones. Dawson called Dr. John M. Vargo to the stand. He was a dark sort, three-quarters bald, a black fringe around his shiny head, a luxuriant black mustache. Dawson went to great lengths to establish that Vargo, the district medical examiner, was an expert on gunshot wounds. Although he'd never done an autopsy in his life, he claimed he had witnessed over a hundred autopsies where gunshots were the cause of death. He had directed Dr. Cushman to do the autopsy. Vargo said he had ordered X rays of the body and claimed he was present for the autopsy after the chest cavity had been opened.

Vargo, too, talked to the jury with the intimidating words of the expert, like the "cavitation" he observed, caused, he said, by a high-velocity projectile that blew out the bone and tissue as much as six inches around the course of the bullet. He spoke of the small fragments of metal making a "snowstorm" effect, which meant a high-speed projectile consistent with a rifle, not a pistol, had passed through the body. Dawson smiled his pleasure at his witness's testimony and turned Vargo over to me.

My examination began by getting the man to admit he was merely giving his opinion, that he didn't know what gun killed Mr. Gerttula, nor its caliber, nor the kind of bullet. Then I began to test the knowledge upon which he based his opinion. He didn't know if a .30-30 was faster or slower than a .30-06 or a .30-40, the hunting rifle used by both my father and by me as a boy. Finally he admitted he didn't know the velocity of any cartridge, nor did he know where the velocity of the gun was measured—that is, at a few feet out or at the muzzle.

He was not a pathologist, much less a forensic pathologist, who could testify as to the cause of death in a criminal case. He wasn't a criminalist, and he admitted he didn't know much about ballistics. He had never hunted. He didn't own a hunting rifle. Once he saw a deer that had been shot, but he hadn't observed the exit hole. I pressed him for more details on his expertise. He thought he'd seen about ten autopsies where a rifle had been the death weapon. Did he think that seeing ten autopsies made him an expert on whether this was a rifle or a pistol wound? He could remember only three bodies that had been shot through the chest. One male, one female, and a child. He didn't know the kinds of rifles they'd been shot with. As my interrogation went on and on, the witness became more vague, with a memory that began to fail him. He'd never seen the "snowstorm" effect before. He admitted that so far as he knew, in the entirety of his career he'd never seen a body shot with a .30-30. Moreover, whatever expertise he had in the field of ballistics was based solely on what an officer named Hansen had told him. Finally I asked him, did he know a single forensic pathologist in the entire world who was an osteopath? "No" was his grudging answer.

He admitted that a pistol bullet could do massive damage, break ribs, tear up the lungs. Then I began to test his knowledge of the anatomy from a standard anatomical drawing. He got sadly mixed up on how many arteries, how many "segmental bronchi," how many thises and thats there were in the human body. He began to hedge and to turn red, often claiming he didn't understand simple questions. He admitted he'd read only one article on the "snowstorm" effect, which was supposedly the trail of tiny particles of lead left behind a high-speed rifle slug.

"If a qualified forensic pathologist had read two articles, I guess he'd be twice as qualified as you, wouldn't he?"

"Am I supposed to answer that?"

"No," I said in a kindly way, "you don't need to."

Vargo, himself, had approved of the embalming before the autopsy. He assumed that a jacketed bullet when it traveled through the body and struck bone would expand. But he had no explanation why the exit hole was smaller than the entrance hole. At last he admitted he didn't know for sure if Gerttula's wound was from a rifle or a pistol. It was the end of the day. We gathered up our files and headed out into the rain.

The following morning Dawson called to the stand Dr. Reay, the chief medical examiner from Seattle, Washington. About six feet three, this man gave the appearance of a retired athlete who'd taken on the vestments of the irreproachable scholar. He was a forensic pathologist with those profoundly impressive credentials, and when he walked into the courtroom, he was also a professional witness, one who'd been on the stand hundreds of times against the best lawyers around. In the courtroom there is no way to measure the knowledge, the truthfulness, the final conclusion, of any expert witness except by cross-examination, and most often that merely reveals the skill of the cross-examiner pitted against the skill of the witness. Still, on occasion, the truth will out, and in the end one has to rely on the innate wisdom of the jury. The expert might fool one set of ears, but could he fool twelve?

Reay said that every year he'd seen at least forty bullet wounds to the chest, mostly from handguns. He used words at the outer edge of the layman's vocabulary but he spoke in understandable English. He thought it was difficult to determine if the weapon was a pistol or a rifle based only on the exit wound. He said the exit wound was usually a bit larger. A bit larger? I looked again at the sergeant.

Reay described the "snowstorm effect" he saw on the X ray, which he claimed was indicative of a high-velocity firearm. That no copper jacket was found within the body meant nothing. He said that Dr. Cushman, who did the autopsy, might have missed it, or it simply went out the exit wound with the bullet. After reviewing the damage to the tissues and bone, he concluded this was a wound inflicted by a high-velocity bullet consistent with a rifle.

Reay had done damage. He could hurt us even further in my cross-examination. Too often the strategy of the expert is to lie in wait for the opportunity to deliver the killing blow. Reay watched me approach. He'd been in such a place countless times. He looked as if he were eager for the contest. I could feel a new surge of adrenaline. In physical battle I would have charged. In the courtroom I walked calmly to the lectern and called Reay's attention to Dr. Brady, our expert. "He is a man of great stature in your profession?" I asked.

"Yes, sir."

"Respected by his colleagues?"

"No question about that."

"You are aware that Dr. Brady is going to give an opinion based on reasonable medical certainty that is exactly opposite of yours?"

"I've been told that. But that happens."

"That happens? That staggers me. How can men of science, both qualified, both honest, come to different results, and both claim their results are based on reasonable medical certainty?" Reay said it had something to do with different backgrounds. I thought it as likely that it had to do with which side hired which expert.

I said, "What this means is that although you are both men of stature, men respected in the profession, professors, people who are board-certified, people who are lecturers, people who are looked up to as leaders and authorities, that nevertheless you can come to opposite conclusions. Now that means that somebody is damn sure wrong. Either you are wrong, or Dr. Brady is wrong, that's obvious, isn't it?"

"Yes, I think we have opposing opinions, yes."

"Well, Dr. Reay, in fairness to both truth and honesty and Dr. Brady, could you leave room for the possibility that you are wrong?"

"Absolutely. I could be wrong, sure."

"I've been in this business for over thirty years, and I don't think more than twice in my life have I ever heard a witness say that to me, and I thank you for that."

He admitted that embalming could exaggerate the swelling of certain tissues and make wounds appear more pronounced. Cushman's report, which he had reviewed in arriving at his opinion, was inadequate. That the body had lain out in the hot sun in the pickup eight hours before it was taken to the mortuary could, he admitted, cause decomposition, which would in turn cause gas inside the body and affect the way the wounds appeared.

I called his attention to Dr. Cushman's belief that the bullet had been wobbling when it entered the body; that is, the entry wound was slightly oblong. I walked over to Jay, the clerk, and asked him if he had an apple or an orange in his lunch bucket. He pulled out an orange, handed it to me with a big grin. I took the orange, thanked him in the name of justice, and poked a hole in it with my ballpoint pen at an angle instead of straight in. It left an oblong entry wound.

"Do you want your orange back, Jay?" I asked.

We all laughed, the jurors, too, a little relief during the intensity of the interrogation.

Reay admitted that, hypothetically, he could have seen Monica Gerttula accidentally shoot her husband with a pistol, performed the autopsy, and been surprised at the findings, findings that would have suggested a high-velocity projectile instead of a pistol. And he knew of no studies in which the "snowstorm effect" of high-velocity bullets and low-velocity bullets had been compared in experimental animals.

Dr. Reay said he'd been born in Rock Springs, Wyoming. "Being a Wyoming boy, aren't you a hunter?"

"Just birds, at one time."

"You never shot a deer?"

"No, sir."

"Have you ever walked into a cold-storage plant in Rock Springs and looked at the hundreds of deer and elk carcasses hanging there?"

"No, no, I haven't."

I called his attention to the large exit holes made by the hunters' expanding bullets. I thought that after the cross-examination of the witness it had become clear to the jury—for the bullet to go through Gerttula's body and do the damage we saw to the ribs and yet not expand so that the exit hole was even smaller than the entry hole—well, something was wrong someplace. My cross-examination over, Reay ambled from the witness box with a friendly nod to me. Then I heard the words. I couldn't believe I'd ever hear them come from the lips of James M. Brown.

"The state rests."

I turned to Michele. "Did I hear correctly?"

She smiled. "I doubt it. Make him say it again," she whispered.

Yes, the state had rested, and Brown had never called

Little Mike or his father. Both had been kept from the courtroom because Brown had listed them as witnesses and the prosecution therefore had the right to exclude them from the proceedings. I wondered if Brown had known all along that he'd never call the boy or his father against Sandy. What could they have possibly said to convict her? And what would a jury think of a prosecutor calling a son against a mother or a husband against a wife? Sandy could have exercised her privilege that protected her against a husband testifying against his wife, and even if there had been a divorce in their background that had not been nullified by another marriage ceremony, still, what would a jury think of prosecutors who took advantage of such a technicality to force a husband to speak against his woman? I thought Brown knew all of this from the beginning, that he had never intended to call either, and that he had exercised his power to keep them out of the courtroom, where they might have been of some comfort to Sandy. Still, I give an honorable man the benefit of honorable intentions, whatever they might have been.

41

Of course, as was our right and our duty, at the conclusion of the state's case we asked Judge Haas to acquit Sandy Jones. Our motion was based on the failure of the state to make out a *prima facie* case against her. This judge, this Harl H. Haas, was the same man who had, on his own, once dismissed this case on evidence no better than the evidence Brown had just presented over these past weeks. Now Haas had the opportunity to do it again. We talked about it at breakfast in the hotel dining room.

"He's not going to dismiss this case," Michele said, pouring a bowl of cereal. "Not a chance in hell. He's been burned by the Court of Appeals once already."

"If he dismisses the case, it'll be double jeopardy this time. Court of Appeals can't touch him," I said. "He can thumb his nose at them."

"He's not the kind to do it," Michele said. "He's got a jury. Maybe thinks they'll acquit and then everybody'll be off the hook. If he doesn't agree with the jury after we put on our defense, he can always grant a new trial."

As soon as I walked back into the courtroom, I moved His Honor for an acquittal. Judge Haas said, as was his way, "Let me tell you where I am on this." He smiled. "As you know, the state, at this point, gets its evidence viewed in the most favorable light to them. They have evidence that Wilfred Gerttula was at the scene, that Sandy Jones was there, that Mrs. Gerttula was there. They have evidence that Sandra Jones had a .22 and that Michael Jones Jr. had a .30-caliber, high-velocity weapon at the scene that was fired. The evidence accounts for all of the bullets. And they have produced evidence from two doctors that the gunshot wound that Mr. Gerttula received was from a rifle. You have only one person at the scene with that kind of a weapon. The more difficult question is, did the boy intentionally take the life of Wilfred Gerttula? And more difficult yet, did Sandy Jones aid and abet him? That's the one I'm struggling with." He turned to me to hear my argument.

"This is a case that cries out for responsibility. The buck stops with you, Your Honor." I smiled at the judge. "Even if you assume that Little Mike shot Gerttula, it has to be shown that he did so with malice."

The judge stopped me. "That only gets you down to a manslaughter charge."

"Well, how do you become guilty of aiding and abetting manslaughter?" I asked. "I don't think there's such an animal in the law. And what did Mrs. Jones do to aid and abet? Her every action, even at the victim's aid office, was couched in self-defense. The state has the duty to prove it *wasn't* self-defense."

I was on a roll again, chipping away at the foundation of the state's case. You never know which argument will finally bring the whole house down. "Even Mrs. Gerttula said that Sandy Jones made no command to the boy. She said the boy remained in the shadows, made no hostile move toward Mrs. Gerttula, and never attempted to interfere with her free movement at the scene. She said she saw the boy do nothing, ever, and that the only time that she ever saw the boy, he had the gun in a relaxed position. That's the testimony of the only eyewitness. There's no evidence that Sandy Jones aided and abetted Little Mike to commit a crime, if, indeed, he committed one. So, the state's case fails."

When I stopped to take a breath, Judge Haas quickly turned to Brown before I could carry on. "Jim, what's your position?"

"We disagree one hundred and eighty degrees." Brown had gotten up and was pacing the floor in front of the judge's desk. "The issue is the defendant's mental state. At this juncture we're entitled to have the evidence viewed in the most favorable light to us. There were threats expressed by the defendant, expressions of anger and hatred. The threat made to Mary Ross was made in the presence of the boy. The defendant was the custodian of the child. They were together a half hour before the fatal shooting. They were both armed, acting in concert, lying in wait for the Gerttulas. My recollection is that Nye said the defendant pointed a rifle at Dick and that the boy covered him with a rifle. They fixed the gate below by tying it with a rope. There was only one way out."

Brown stopped his pacing directly in front of the judge. "We think the jury could find that the defendant shot directly at the victim with her .22 while the victim was seated in his pickup. Her conduct is the best expression of intent. All of that conduct is evidence from which the jury could deduce, properly, that the defendant's mental state was what she had previously said: 'Yes, I am going to kill him!' A child armed in her presence has to be deemed acting with her knowledge and approval. They set up a cross fire. The jury can find that this defendant intended the death of the victim."

Judge Haas turned to me. "Do you want to respond?"

"Well, Your Honor, there isn't a case in the history of the world that holds that even if the defendant was standing at the scene screaming, 'I hate you, I hate you, I'm going to kill you,' and she shot her gun into the car, that that constitutes aiding and abetting the boy, if the boy was the one who shot him. The law does not provide that if I act out a murderous intent against a victim and am unsuccessful, that that constitutes aiding and abetting someone who has no intent to kill and was successful."

I started to argue further, but His Honor stepped in. "All right. I have a couple of cases I want to review. It won't take long. I'll give you a ruling shortly."

After that we walked out into the courtroom once more and waited. There was always the chance the judge would hold for us. We waited. But why should he take the case from the jury, which was his right under the law, when the jury had dutifully sat for weeks listening to the evidence? Why would one man substitute his judgment for twelve? We waited. At last His Honor walked in and the court came quickly, silently to order. Still we waited. He cleared his throat, smiled at both sides, and began.

"If you give every favorable inference to the state's evidence, well, I think it is a relatively close call. The court is going to deny the motion. Be ready to proceed with your defense in the morning, Mr. Spence." We gathered up our files and walked silently out of the courtroom.

Fear began to grip me once more. It's one thing to shoot down the case of your opponent. It's another to put on your own defense and lay it all out there for the prosecutors to get their hands into, to sort through it, to finger it and rip it apart until it can no longer be recognized as anything human, anything decent. I had mauled their witnesses and torn apart their case. Sometimes I shook them like a terrier does a rat in its mouth. Sometimes I played with their witnesses like a cat with its catch. Now I had to decide whether I would give the prosecution the same chance at our witnesses. I could always rest our case and put no evidence on at all. I had done that many times in a career, and successfully.

Worse, I had to make that damnable decision, the one every defense attorney faces. I'd made that decision in the back of my mind, but only tentatively. Now was the time. I had to decide, would I put Sandy Jones on the stand?

If I didn't call her, there'd be those who'd think she must be guilty or she'd take the stand and defend herself. Innocent people want to proclaim their innocence to any who will hear. This jury had been waiting these many weeks to hear Sandy Jones's story, this woman whom they'd only seen shake her head, only seen look sadly down, or jump at some testimony that surprised her. They'd watched her and attempted to gauge her innocence from the way she conducted herself in the courtroom. But now they wanted to hear her, to judge her. It was their job, and to them it would seem their right.

On the other hand, if I put Sandy on the stand, some might see her as trying to talk her way out of a horrible crime she'd committed. Was she trying to fool them? Was she lying to save her guilty hide? If she took the stand, the jury would test her as they had tested the state's witnesses. But worse, Brown would cross-examine her, pummel her with leading questions, and as is often the case, the innocent would appear as if she were trying to hide her guilt.

Fear, ah, the damnable fear that comes marching in and screams in your ears and laughs and mocks and causes the bravest to take pause. It was my fear, and Sandy had lived with hers all these years. In ways she was like me: when I am afraid, I am more likely to attack than run. The lion, afraid, charges. And we kill the lion. On the other hand, when we're afraid, we sometimes hide. But we do not trust those who hide, who evade, who run. They must be guilty. Fear is the witness's enemy in the courtroom. Still, fear can serve the trial lawyer well. When I am afraid, I know that I care. When I feel my fear, I know that I face danger and I gather my forces. Fear confirms that I am alive and readied to fight. It heightens my senses and brings to the battlefront the best of me. But I had dealt with my own fear for many years and knew its power and its dangers. A witness has little experience in dealing with fear in the courtroom. And often, too often, fear defeats the witness, especially the innocent. I had always known that the sociopath, void of normal human emotion, does best on the witness stand, and Sandy Jones was no sociopath.

But Sandy had the absolute right to make the final decision. It was her life. If she insisted, she could sit up there and tell the jury the whole sordid story as she remembered it. And she wanted to take the stand. On the other hand, if I talked her out of it and she was convicted, she would always believe that had she testified the jury would have believed her. It's easy for a lawyer to bow to the client's wishes, to put the client on the stand, and when the jury convicts, to blame the client. It's a lot harder to make the decision for your client, to keep the client off the stand in the proper case, and if the jury convicts, then to wonder forever if it was your decision that put your client in the penitentiary.

That night our little tribe of warriors met at our hotel to finalize our defense. Michele was there. Eddie had flown in. Imaging and Kent were there. Would Sandy testify?

"You gotta be kidding, Gerry," Michele said. "I can't believe you're even considering it. A little pressure and she'll split open like a melon hitting the pavement."

Kent chimed in, "Yeah, but those jurors are gonna want to hear her say, 'I didn't do it.' What kind of case do we have if she doesn't at least say what happened at the shooting? Sandy was there. She could answer a lot of those questions."

"No," Imaging said. "Those jurors know what happened up there. Gerry's told them, and I think they know that's what Sandy's told you. They believe you, Gerry. That's what matters."

Eddie nodded. "Leave it be, Gerry." He paused. "If she'll let ya."

I thought Sandy was too near the surface to take the stand. She was who she was, and there was no preparation I could put her through to ready her for a successful cross-examination by the prosecutors. She'd been badly hurt by the years of persecution she and her family had suffered. The endless torment of trials and appeals, and the threat to Little Mike, had caused deep scars. She didn't have an accurate feel for who she was or how she appeared to others. She could lose it all if she veered off on any one of her many themes that ranged from the crooked cops who were always watching her, to the holy Indian land on Medicine Rock; from how the Gerttulas were certified devils, to how she'd prayed and that God was on our side. She was hurt, and her anger often covered her hurt. Brown could easily cause her to explode as I had Monica Gerttula, and if she blew, it could all be over, then and there on the witness stand.

That night I met early with Sandy. "There's been too many lies told about me, Spence," she said. "I want to testify."

"I know, Sandy. But you saw what I did to Monica Gerttula on cross-examination. Brown can do that to you."

"Yeah, but I'm not gonna lie."

"It isn't what you say. It's how you say it, Sandy. You're pretty hotheaded sometimes. If Brown gets you mad, you know what the jury will see?"

"What?"

"They'll see you losing your temper up there, raising hell with Gerttula, getting Little Mike all excited—and you know the rest."

"Well, I didn't kill anybody and Little Mike didn't either."

"I think the jury understands that now. But what happens when Brown starts after you? He'll get you to tell all of the things Gerttula did to you, and how it hurt you and made you mad as hell. If you deny that you were mad, the jury won't believe you. If you admit it, they could figure you wanted Gerttula killed. You can't win this one, Sandy."

"I trust that jury."

"Do you trust yourself?" When she didn't answer right away, I said softly, "Do you trust me? We've come a long way together."

"Yeah, Spence, I trust you."

"If I put you on the stand, I pit you against Brown. Brown is a professional. He knows what to do to make you look guilty. You're an amateur. The contest isn't fair. Brown will win and we'll lose what we've gained. We're ahead. Let's stay ahead."

"What will the jury think if I don't tell 'em what happened?"

"I already told them your story. You can't tell it any better. When I was selecting the jury, I prepared them for the possibility that you might not take the stand. By the time the final arguments are over, they'll forget it anyway."

"Okay, Spence. I came this far with you. I'm not changing horses now."

That night, late, I was awakened by the telephone at my bedside in the hotel room. It was Michele. She was excited, her voice hollering at my sleeping ear.

"Jesus Christ, Gerry! Sandy was right. God *is* on our side!"

"What are you talking about?" I mumbled.

"My husband called me from Newport. Said he took a call for me from a guy named Robert Wheeler. He's a cop in the Newport Police Department. Bob said I should call this guy right away. I did. And guess what?"

"What?"

"God *is* on our side!" She was laughing.

"Come on. What's this all about? We got work to do in the morning." I needed my sleep.

"You aren't kidding we've got work to do! We have a new witness!"

42

After years of waiting, Sandy finally had a chance to defend herself. A new, palpable energy filled the court-room. The jurors were ready, visibly leaning forward, wanting to see what hand we'd play.

I announced, "Call Robert Wheeler," and a clean-cut young man walked forward. Looked like your typical grown-up Boy Scout. He settled down in the chair, looked nervously over in Brown's direction, and waited for my first question. "Mr. Wheeler, we met for the first time in the hallway this morning?"

"Yes."

He was the cop who'd called Michele. Been a cop for three years. We'd protected him with a subpoena so his fel-low cops couldn't claim he'd voluntarily jumped over to the wrong side. He worked in Newport.

Wilfred Gerttula was his second cousin and a close friend. He knew Monica, his wife. In fact, he was presently living next door to Monica Gerttula. He'd first become acquainted with the Gerttulas in the summer of 1972, a month before Wilfred and Monica were married, and had his first summertime job with the Gerttulas at the age of twelve. Put up hay, pulled the weeds, and as he got older, fixed fences, mowed, and ran a Caterpillar tractor—general ranch work. He was employed by Gerttula in each of the following summers up to and including the summer of

1985, when Gerttula was shot. "Haying was over at the time of his death," he added. "But I'd been working with him right up to that point."

I showed him a picture of the blue pickup belonging to the Gerttulas. "Do you recognize that vehicle?"

"Yes, I do."

"Did you ever drive it?"

"Yes."

"Now before I ask you this question, let me ask you if you've discussed your testimony with the state?" He had. Probably the day before. "So before you took the stand, as a police officer you felt it your duty to tell the state what you're about to tell the ladies and gentlemen of the jury?" Yes, he said. I looked over at Brown. He looked uncomfortable. "So what you're about to tell the ladies and gentlemen of the jury is no surprise to Mr. Brown or Mr. Dawson, that's true, isn't it?"

"Yes."

Monica Gerttula, of course, had repeatedly testified there'd never been a handgun in the pickup. I got right to it with the witness. "I want to put you in that blue pickup between 1978 and 1985. Had you driven it a number of times?" He said he'd driven it around the farm many times when they were haying.

"Now between the years 1978 and 1985, did you have occasion to look in the glove box?"

"Yes, I did, to get something—cattle-hauling slips, things like that. There was quite a bit of stuff in there."

"When you looked into the glove box, what did you see?"

"A lot of papers and things."

"And?" I waited.

"A firearm."

"What kind of a firearm?"

"Small automatic-type pistol."

"How many times do you think you saw that small automatic pistol there between the years 1978 and 1985?"

"Approximately four to five times. The gun was smaller than the forty-five that I carry."

I showed him Raymond Gerttula's automatic pistol, Exhibit 79. "Would Exhibit Seventy-nine be a size smaller than a forty-five automatic?"

"Smaller than the one I carry, yes." I had him leave the stand and go out of the courtroom and unload his gun. When he came back, I had him show the jury the two pistols side by side.

"Now, Officer, nobody knows whether Exhibit Seventy-nine or a gun like it was the one you saw in the pickup. If I understand your testimony, you're saying that Exhibit Seventy-nine, like the gun in the pickup glove box, was a size smaller than your forty-five, is that correct?"

"That's correct."

"Thank you, Officer, for your service."

Brown got up slowly and walked to the lectern to cross-examine. His excessive nonchalance bordered on weariness. Had the witness seen any shells or clips in the glove box? No. Had he ever seen Gerttula fire the gun? No. The witness said an automatic pistol, when fired, kicked the empty casing randomly out the top of the pistol. That was the extent of Brown's cross-examination.

I forced the attack further. "You never took the gun in the glove box in your hands?"

"No."

"You never examined it?"

"No."

"Let's be frank with the ladies and gentlemen of the jury. As a young man, you already knew that that handgun constituted a concealed weapon, didn't you?"

"Yes."

"And you didn't want to get too familiar with that situation involving your cousin Will, isn't that true?"

"I would say that is correct."

"Do you have an opinion based on your thirteen years with the Gerttulas whether Monica Gerttula knew that that handgun was in that pickup?"

Brown jumped up. "Excuse me, Your Honor."

I looked over at Brown. "Does that mean you're upset about that?"

"Your Honor, if the court please," Brown said exasperated, "that's not proper."

Judge Haas said, "I don't think there's sufficient foundation. I'll sustain the objection."

I didn't let it go. I started again. "Mrs. Gerttula, for thirteen years, had the same access to the glove box as you did, didn't she?"

"Yes."

"Objection," Brown said. "Calls for speculation."

"Oh, I'll overrule that," the judge said.

"The glove box was never locked, was it?"

"No."

"Thank you for coming, Officer," I said.

As I watched the man walk out of the courtroom, I thought of the first time, three and a half years before, when Eddie and I had heard those two young lawyers, Michele and Steve, complain that the Joneses were innocent people and that there was a missing gun. I thought of our efforts during all of those years to find the gun, our pleas to the sheriff and the DA to search the river for it. As I saw the man walk out the door, in my mind's eye I could see that automatic lying rusted and covered with moss at the bottom of the Siletz River. Now it all made sense to me—the gunshot residue on Monica Gerttula's face and hands and her failing her lie detector test. Whether my view of it was accurate or not, I could see it all clearly in my mind—Sandy and Little Mike there, armed, stopping the truck, and Sandy confronting Wilfred Gerttula—What the hell were they doing shooting up there? Why had they left the gates open? Why had he shot at her kids? Why? Then Monica had gotten out of the pickup with her camera.

Gerttula wasn't going to answer this woman, this Sandy Jones, not this crazy woman who was stopping the development of his subdivision. "Get the hell out of the way," he probably said, and when she stood her ground, her .22 in hand, he had gunned the truck at her—left those acceleration marks in the dirt. And when he'd charged her again with the pickup, her back to the closed barbed-wire gate, she fired at the front tire to stop his assault. When that didn't stop him, on his next charge with the truck she fired into the windshield.

Gerttula felt the lead from the .22 spray into his face. That was enough! I could see him jumping out of the pickup. See him running over to the woman at the front of the pickup where she stood with her rifle ready. He'd take that damned gun from her. He started to wrestle her for it. She was a strong woman and was not about to give it up. Not Sandy Jones. Then Little Mike hollered, "Leave my mother alone. Leave my mother alone." The kid had already shot out the rear tire when Gerttula had charged his mother with the pickup. Now he fired twice more to scare the man off, one bullet into the pickup bed, another into the alder tree above the pickup bed.

Then in my mind's eye I saw Monica Gerttula take the automatic pistol from the glove box. She was in a war. Guns were being fired all around her. She ran up to the front of the pickup where her husband and Sandy were wrestling for the gun and aimed the automatic at Sandy. She wasn't much of a hand with a pistol, but that woman was fighting along with her husband and bullets were flying around. Wilfred Gerttula was bent over struggling for the rifle. When Monica fired, perhaps to scare Sandy, perhaps to shoot in the defense of her husband, the bullet hit the man while he was still wrestling with Sandy. His blood began to drip down on Sandy's moccasins. Sandy said she thought she'd been shot. Suddenly, Gerttula let loose of the .22 rifle and turned and grabbed the front of the pickup, where he leaned on the hood for a moment, the blood running freely onto the pickup hood and grille. After that he staggered to the pickup door and, barely able to crawl in, collapsed, where he died a short time later.

Sandy realized that Gerttula had been shot. She asked Monica, "Do you have a gun?" The woman was screaming hysterically, trying to push her husband over so she could drive the pickup. Sandy knew she had to get the man to the hospital, that Monica was too hysterical to drive, but she wouldn't get out of the pickup. Sandy told Monica to get out, but she wasn't answering. She just sat there letting out scream after scream. Sandy told Little Mike to get the keys. Then Sandy took hold of her hair and began pulling her out, the woman fighting to stay in. Sandy pulled and pulled at the woman, sometimes knocking her head against the door opening to the pickup, until the woman finally fell to the ground. Little Mike put his rifle in the pickup and opened the gate and Sandy drove off leaving Monica Gerttula there at the scene.

Gerttula's recorder was on the ground. In my mind's eye I saw the rest of it. Mrs. Gerttula sat there for a while collecting her senses. She was exhausted and in shock. She saw the recorder, and fearing it had recorded her and her husband's actions, she threw it over the edge of the precipice. But it never got to the river. Perhaps she picked up the gun where she'd dropped it and threw it as hard as she could in the same direction. Maybe she picked up the shell casing and tossed that, too. Then she came down the mountain. When she got to the Joneses', she tried several times to get one of their vehicles going. Bitten by the dog, she was weak with fatigue, shock, and hysteria and stumbled on down the road until she got to Ferris's. After that we knew the rest.

Whether Monica Gerttula had killed her husband accidentally we would never know. My opinion is only my opinion. Others have had opinions to the contrary. I wonder, what if Stapleton and Marquis had decided to charge *her* with murder instead of Sandy Jones? Plenty of innocent people were in prison on circumstantial evidence less compelling than the evidence that could have been garnered against Monica Gerttula. Had the prosecutors searched for witnesses who could testify to quarrels between Monica and Wilfred, perhaps they could have found people who would willingly take the stand against her. And there was the insurance and the quick remarriage (which I believe had nothing whatever to do with the death of her husband). Whatever the facts, I believed then and I believe now that Monica Gerttula was innocent of any crime. If she shot her husband, it was an accident.

This was a case where no one, not Monica Gerttula, not Sandy Jones, and not Little Mike, was guilty of any crime. It is no crime in America, not yet, to defend one's self or one's loved ones. That right extended not only to Little Mike but to Monica Gerttula as well.

I turned to the judge. I had one more witness before we rested. "Call Dr. William Brady," I said. A tall, slender man in his late fifties walked in businesslike steps to the witness stand. Brady had gray, wavy hair, clear blue eyes set in a handsome, thin face, and a ready smile. He was a forensic pathologist, the former director of the Oregon State Medical Examiner's Office, with the day-in, day-out responsibility of determining the cause of death of the bodies presented to him. He supervised thirty or forty pathologists in the state who also did autopsies. He'd been the head man at the state examiner's office for fifteen years.

After medical school he'd done a residency at Harvard for two years and took postgraduate training in the Medical Examiner's Office in Manhattan—fifteen years of medical training in all. He'd passed all of the requisite boards and was certified by all of the relevant specialties. He was a full professor on the clinical faculty at the University of Oregon Medical School. This was a true expert. The jurors looked at him with obvious respect.

He'd seen many deaths from rifles and his share of deaths from pistol shots. He'd looked at the same material that Dr. Reay had reviewed and was ready to give his conclusion. But before he gave his opinion, I asked him if he'd previously given the same opinion to DA Ulys Stapleton. He said he'd met with Stapleton in a motel in Lincoln City on the morning before he was to give his opinion the first time he'd testified—in Little Mike's case.

"So, your testimony here today is no surprise to them?"

"My testimony is pretty repetitious." Brown and Dawson knew of his testimony before they'd found Dr. Reay.

Dr. Brady said the "snowstorm effect" came from an earlier Texas article, but there had been no studies on that phenomenon before or since. "It certainly doesn't have an awful lot of scientific basis," he said. "You see these particles in both high-speed gunshot wounds and slow-speed gunshot wounds as well."

He spoke of the three impacts made by the slug that had killed Gerttula: one as the slug entered the body, one as it struck the front ribs, and a third as it hit the ribs on the back. At each impact particles of the bullet sheared off. It was not a "snowstorm" effect but a "clustering" of particles on each impact. He said, "This is characteristic of a low-velocity bullet, Mr. Spence, losing portions of its surface as it goes through the body. It is certainly not, in my opinion, characteristic of the type of spread that would be produced by a high-velocity weapon."

He spoke of a high-velocity, semijacketed rifle bullet. "It's like a spinning eggbeater and would have ripped a hole in the tissue of the back and done exactly what you would expect an eggbeater to do, namely open it up, destroy, tear, rip tissue, and create a gaping wound of exit. And this simply is not present here." Once more I looked up at the old sergeant on the jury. He nodded his head in approval.

And if it were a high-speed rifle shell, as claimed by the state, what about the copper jacket? "The jacket," Dr. Brady observed, "is not inside the body. If there was a jacket on the slug when it went in the body, only one of two things happened: either it stayed in or it exited. It's obvious it didn't stay in, because it wasn't seen on the X rays. So it went out."

"How would it get out without creating a large wound?" I asked.

"It can get out only in two ways: if it stayed attached to the slug, we have the spinning eggbeater ripping things out—the big hole. If it separated from the slug, then it will exit creating its own, separate hole. There would be two exit wounds."

"So do you have an opinion as to whether or not this was a rifle slug that went through Mr. Gerttula?"

"I do."

"And what is your opinion?"

"I don't believe that a rifle slug went through this gentleman's body."

"And is that opinion based on reasonable medical certainty?"

"It is, sir."

"Do you think there is a likelihood that you are wrong?"

"No, Mr. Spence, in this particular situation I believe I am right."

"Thank you, sir." I turned to Dawson. "You may examine."

Dawson asked for a recess. He had something up his sleeve. When court took up again, he brandished a book by Dr. Brady, one written for prosecuting attorneys and physicians doing death investigations. In the book Brady had given the formula for kinetic energy. He'd left off the reference to gravitational force. Brady said he'd taken the formula from the *Army Ordnance Manual*.

"Basic high-school math, isn't it?" Dawson asked.

"High-school physics," Brady said. "It left me a long time ago."

"That applies to the things that keep us all here on earth, doesn't it?"

"That's right."

"And, it's actually thirty-two-point-two, isn't it, Doctor?"

"Mr. Dawson, you've looked it up more recently than I have. I'm certainly not going to argue with you."

"Well, actually, I spent some time last night calculating."

"Good for you," Brady said cheerfully. A sprinkling of snickers came from the audience.

"Why did you leave that out of your book?" Dawson demanded.

"The mathematics become exceedingly complex. My intention was to explain the basic principles and I hope I've done that." Then Dawson went through each of the three editions of Brady's book and continued to beat at the man for not having corrected this error in any of the editions. After half an hour I thought the jurors were weary of it. Some were looking down at their laps. Others gazed at the ceiling.

"What's this all got to do with me?" Sandy asked impatiently.

"Beats me," answered Michele. "I skipped physics in school."

I let Dawson drone on. Finally Dawson wanted to know if the doctor knew what a one-in-twelve twist meant. Brady said he didn't know. Dawson told him it meant a complete spin of the bullet once every twelve inches. With that information and a bullet traveling at the rate of two thousand feet per second, Dawson's point was that the bullet would have gone through the body without making a complete spin. Where, then, was the eggbeater effect? But the spin, of course, whatever it was for whatever type of bullet that had killed Wilfred Gerttula, would have been altered as it struck bone and tissue.

Dawson was after him about another formula in his book concerning the rotation of the bullet. It was, Brady said, still another formula he'd taken from *Army Ordnance*, and because it was so difficult, he'd left it out of the subsequent editions. After that Dawson turned the doctor over to me for further questions. Even though he'd been wearisome, I worried that Dawson had done damage.

I began by saying, "Except attempting to embarrass you for making unnecessarily complicated formulas simple, do any of the formulas that we've been educated on by Mr. Dawson have anything to do with the conclusion that you reached?"

"No. They are esoteric. The day-in, day-out application of the material can be made pretty simple and hopefully explained in commonsense terms, which I've tried to do."

"Do you know any pathologist who uses these formulas?"

"No, I don't offhand."

"Do you think in fairness if you were to judge yourself impartially that the fact that you left off the *G* on a formula renders you either incompetent or a liar?"

"I think not. I hope that it does not impart that opinion to the folks we're talking with." He looked over at the jury and gave them a quick smile. He was good. I went on reading from the book that Brady had authored. It told how high-velocity projectiles generally leave large, gaping wounds at exit. I went through the book page after page finding language that supported Brady's opinions, sometimes nearly verbatim—about the expanding jacket on hunting projectiles, and how the organs hit with a .30-30 bullet are disintegrated, shredded. In Mr. Gerttula's body they were not. I must have read from more than a dozen pages.

Then I ended with this question: "Based on your review, your own observation, and your knowledge from your work, is there any question in your mind as to what kind of bullet caused this injury?"

"No, there isn't, Mr. Spence."

"Just so I can hear it once more, what kind of a bullet caused this injury?"

"This injury resulted from a low-velocity missile characteristic of that which would be discharged from a handgun."

Dawson had no further questions. I saw the doctor nod politely to the jury and walk proudly up the aisle through the audience to the courtroom door.

I turned to the judge. *"The defense rests,"* I said.

After scores of witnesses, hundreds of hours of testimony, thousands of pages of transcript, and years of struggle and waiting, we had finally laid Sandy's case in the hands of the jury. I could hear the jurors' thankful mumbling.

Then all the lawyers walked into chambers. Eddie was with us. I made another motion for a judgment of acquittal, mostly for the record in case of a conviction and our need to appeal, a motion the judge summarily overruled. The decision would be the jury's.

In the judge's chambers followed hours of endless haggling over exhibits that had been offered into evidence and that the judge had taken under advisement. Then our arguments raged endlessly over the instructions that the judge would give the jury, the lawyers bickering over every proposed word. Could Little Mike be guilty of only negligence and Sandy be guilty of aiding and abetting a negligent killing? We argued there was no such thing as aiding and abetting an unintentional killing. *Intent* was the key— Little Mike's intent. Brown argued that it was a matter of Sandy's intent. I argued vehemently, vociferously, against the judge instructing the jury on "lesser includeds," crimes contained within the charge of murder such as a lesser degree of murder, manslaughter, reckless endangerment, and even negligent homicide. If the jury were unable to agree, they could compromise on one of the lesser crimes. We wanted to win it, all or nothing.

It was past five in the evening and we were all worn-out and testy. Finally the judge threw up his hands, his withering patience exhausted. "I'll give each side fifteen minutes to argue this in the morning. Then I'll make my decision."

Still we argued on. "I have no problem if Mr. Brown argues that Sandy's statement to Mary Ross may be evidence of her intent, but if he gets up and argues that this was the encouragement that she gave her son to kill Gerttula, we're in real deep shit." The word slipped out. The judge was too tired to care.

The arguments filled the room, the jangling cacophony of months of passion unloosed. Even Brown's voice raised an octave, his voice suddenly piercing. It was past six o'clock and the judge, weary, threatened he was going to cut us back to five minutes in the morning. We couldn't stop the arguments, the melee over every word, each side afraid the jury might focus on that one word in the instructions and then all could be lost—on a single word. It happens many times.

At six-thirty the judge finally saved us. Wearied, our patience ragged, the judge said good-night to all, put on his coat, and walked out the chambers door.

In the morning final arguments would begin, and the fate of Sandra Kaye Jones would, at last, be left to the jury. I felt shredded and worn, too worn to face the fear that every lawyer must face, a fear that now descended over me like a smothering shroud.

Would I have the power to answer the prosecutor? Could I convince the jury that Sandy Jones was innocent? What if the jury saw me as too smart, too clever, too noisy, too pushy, too arrogant, to be believed. Had I made a mistake in convincing Sandy not to tell her story? What if, in the morning, I failed? My God, what if after all of this I failed?

43

We sat in the judge's chambers, Sandy Jones sandwiched between Michele and me, the judge, absent his robe, seated behind his desk, his pinkish, good-humored face emerging from an old cigar of a suit. Brown and Dawson, as usual, were off to the right—the far right, I thought. Sandy wore the same baby blue slacks suit, her hair falling in tired curls past her shoulders, her eyes weary. For many weeks she'd sat silently through the endless arguments of the attorneys. Never once had she uttered aloud a single word, as if her tongue were my tongue, her brain, her feelings, mine. Now she wanted to say something to the judge.

The State of Oregon represented the enemy to her. The State of Oregon was prosecuting the action. The prosecutors were the State of Oregon. The State of Oregon wanted to put her in prison. I said, "Your Honor, my client has asked that I ask you to tell the ladies and gentlemen of the jury that she, too, is a part of the State of Oregon."

"I don't know what to say," she said in a low, crumbling voice. "I am a part of the State of Oregon." Her logic was irrefutable. She *was* a landowner, a citizen, and if the State of Oregon was prosecuting her, well, then, was she not prosecuting herself? Her mind worked like that.

Judge Haas looked up at her, thought about what she had said, and shook his head like a father dealing with a precocious child. What could he say? He chose to say nothing. Instead he gave us the good news. After all our haggling the afternoon and evening before, he said, "I'm satisfied that there is really no evidence that Sandra Jones intended to aid and abet a negligent or reckless act. She either intended to aid and abet an intentional killing, or nothing at all." He read the instruction he'd decided upon: in order to find Sandy guilty of murder, the state had to prove beyond a reasonable doubt that Little Mike intentionally caused the death of Gerttula, and that neither he nor Sandy was acting in the lawful defense of either themselves or one another. We rejoiced in silence.

The judge read through the rest of the instructions he'd give the jury, provided each side with a copy of his instructions, and then said, "Gentlemen, it's time to go in there and face the jury."

It was January 20, 1989. I looked over at Eddie and Michele. They were as solemn as monks. We sat down at counsel table. Eddie put his arm around me and gave me a squeeze. He'd been with me at this moment so many times, for so many cases, for so many years. Michele said, "This is it. Here we go." I looked for Imaging, then Kent, and found them sitting in the front row along with my handsome secretary, Rosemary McIntosh, who'd come in to help and who, like every good legal secretary, is mother, brains, and rudder to her boss.

"God's on our side," Sandy said.

"We can use all the help we can get," I said. Then the jury marched in, sat like a choir readying for the sermon. Some folded their hands on their laps and some their arms across their chests. They also looked tired.

Then we heard Judge Haas speaking to the jury from the heights of the bench. "Ladies and gentlemen, before I instruct you this morning, I know this is the longest jury trial all of you have sat through, and I want you to know it's the longest one I've sat through. Probably for counsel, too." He began to read his instructions to the jury about how the jurors should judge the credibility of the witnesses, that if they thought a witness lied, they were entitled to distrust the remainder of the witness's statement. He told the jurors that the defendant had an absolute constitutional right not to testify, and a decision not to testify could not be considered an indication of guilt. He defined direct and circumstantial evidence and said that the filing of the charge was not evidence of guilt. He defined reasonable doubt, which existed "when after a careful and impartial consideration of all of the evidence, you do not feel convinced to a moral certainty that the defendant is guilty."

He instructed on the law of self-defense and gave the aiding and abetting instruction he'd earlier read to us in chambers. He defined the elements of the crime of murder and told the jury that the state had to prove all of the elements of the crime beyond a reasonable doubt. Then he turned to Brown. "Mr. Brown," he said, nodding to the lectern.

Mr. James M. Brown, special prosecutor, walked in his usual, small, efficient steps to the lectern. The state has the right to both open and close, the defense's argument stuck in between like a prisoner guarded on both sides by the police. Brown was as colorless as ever, as pale as ever, as thin of body and emotion as ever. He smiled at the jury without pleasure and began.

He spoke of the inauguration of President George Bush, the parades and speeches and of the sunshine that had invaded the courtroom the day before, suggesting that spring would be coming, new grass and fresh breezes. He said it was hard to talk about the death of a man. "We don't like to talk about death." He mentioned the "distressing pictures," and the need to make one last big effort to resolve the case. Then he thanked the jury and said, "One of the hardest things is to sit quietly and just listen without the opportunity to interrupt or ask questions or make any observations." He looked at each of the jurors before he began again.

"Next Monday is January twenty-third, 1989, which will be three years and six months since Will Gerttula died. Yours is the job to determine whether Mr. Dawson and I have proved to you beyond a reasonable doubt that the crime of murder was committed by Mike Jones Jr., and that the defendant, Sandra Jones, committed acts that resulted in the intentional infliction of violent death on Will Gerttula." Having arrived at the point where his argument might begin, Brown suddenly drew back again. He spoke of nearly everything but the facts—that his statements were not law, his memory of the facts not supreme. He spoke of the right to competent counsel and finally he said that Will Gerttula was entitled to justice under the law in Oregon.

But once more he balked from argument as if he were afraid to enter such a forbidden area. He spoke of the "literal warts on the case," defects he would lay out for their consideration. It was like a puzzle, he said, with twenty-seven witnesses called by the state and eighty-one exhibits. Again, instead of entering into the argument he began dragging the jury back through the chain of title to the Jones property, outlining the various conveyances that the records revealed, the lawsuits over the road, the surveyor's testimony, and on and on. The jurors' eyes were beginning to glaze over. Finally he mentioned how Mrs. Gerttula—he referred to her properly as Mrs. Steele—had given gifts to the Jones kids and how when the Joneses were having trouble with their electric power, the Gerttulas had given them flashlights, and when the Joneses didn't have enough money for gas, Mrs. Gerttula had put a $20 bill inside a flashlight so when the Joneses couldn't figure out why it didn't work, they would open up the flashlight and see the money. "I think that was a sensitive thing to do, a recognition of another person's pride," Brown said. I thought it was Brown's good effort to try to rehabilitate Monica Gerttula in the eyes of the jury. And, without doubt, she was a woman with goodness.

Brown spoke of how Will Gerttula had been "frustrated in his legal right to develop his property. Why Sandy Jones felt she had a right to keep the man out of his own property may never be known. If you are the last property owner on the road, you then have free range of pasture without having to worry about fencing stock in. You own not only your own lots but Gerttula's other lots as well. Not a bad deal. Maybe she had a feeling of power, that regardless of what Will Gerttula owned or developed that she could inhibit that."

He dwelt on the fact that the Joneses had been enjoined from blocking the road. "Certainly," he said, his voice still as drowsy as a sleepy teacher's, "the defendant would not be the first person frustrated by the decision of a court. But in our society, courts make decisions. There are mechanisms for reviewing them, mechanisms for appealing them, but courts make decisions that are binding on us and have to be honored." I thought of mechanics with greasy hands under old clunkers, of railroad mechanics with huge iron wrenches. Mechanics.

At last, beginning to warm slightly to his argument, Brown started with the witness Donald Buford. "The defendant said to Mr. Buford in the feedstore that she was going to go to court and if she were unsuccessful, she guessed she'd have to kill that individual. Mr. Buford was concerned, because she sounded serious. She'd just have to kill that man."

Then it was Rocky Marrs. "He was up there working with a chain saw and he became aware that the defendant had come up behind him and was pointing a pistol at him, and her words were, in fact, the next time Will Gerttula comes up here 'she'd blow him away.' I suggest that what occurred had a very significant impact on his memory. Scared the heck out of him. He remembers even seeing the ends of bullets in the revolver.

"Now in early July 1985, it appears there was some kind of setback in the defendant's efforts to get reconsideration on the judge's road decision. And so she ended up talking with Mary Ross, a lady who worked for the Lincoln County district attorney. Mary Ross went out and talked with her. All kinds of inferences may be urged on those circumstances. But you saw Mary Ross, not a person to put somebody down, not a person to put somebody off, but the defendant was agitated and Mary Ross thought it better to talk with her outside the office." Brown looked down at his notes. "They sat down in the hallway, where the defendant recounted her grievances. Now Mary Ross testified that the defendant said she'd been harassed by Will Gerttula and recounted these grievances in the presence of her son, the boy Mike Jones Jr. And in this hallway of the Lincoln County courthouse, a public place, when it appeared that Mary Ross wasn't going to do what the defendant wanted, the defendant said, 'I'll have to kill him myself'—or words to the effect—that she knew the law: 'I'll spend less time in jail than I'll have to spend putting up with him.' That was early in July."

Brown glanced at his notes again. "Then along came Dick and Nye, who encountered the defendant." Brown nearly always referred to Sandy as the defendant. "My recollection of the testimony is that the defendant pointed a rifle at the head of Jack Dick and that the boy covered

Dale Nye with a rifle and scared the heck out of these guys. She confirmed, if she didn't already know, that it was Will Gerttula who was up the road. Sandra Jones and the boy were acting together. I submit to you that their memories of having rifles pointed at their heads is very vivid, very clear.

"Dick and Nye went down the road and encountered the next gate, which someone had tied in such a manner that they had to use a cigarette lighter to burn off the rope. Maybe it was tied that hard, and maybe those guys were so frightened by their recent experience that it was hard to make their fingers work to untie the rope. But they wanted out of there and they burned that rope and they got out of there." When Brown started into the testimony of Monica Gerttula, the court ordered a short recess. The jury filed out and Michele and I compared notes.

"The guy's building a picture of an evil bitch who had her kid maliciously kill Gerttula, instead of a woman scared to death that Gerttula was going to kill her kids," Michele said.

"That's his theory of the case," I said. Lawyers with words, like artists with paint, can take the same words, the same paint, and end up with different pictures. A lawyer can paint one of innocence or one of guilt. And if a defense attorney fails to answer a strong argument, one that captures the eyes of the jurors' minds, at that moment his case can be lost. If, on the other hand, he lets the prosecutor drag him into the prosecutor's case instead of arguing his own, he can also lose. I sat back, closed my eyes, and tried to relax. I had to trust my mind's ear to sort out what I needed to rebut and what I needed to ignore.

When the jury filed back in, Brown began his argument anew by saying in a quiet voice that "Mrs. Gerttula Steele has submitted herself to questions here for four days." He took his time with her testimony, how they didn't pack a lunch and how they'd been with Dick and Nye. When he finally got to the time, I opened my eyes to watch. Some of the jurors sat up in their seats. "Dick and Nye saw the defendant with a rifle, and Monica Gerttula became aware that the boy was back to her right, also with a rifle. Now Will Gerttula may have said, 'Oh, there's Sandy. You better get a picture of this.'" Brown handed a juror in the front row an enlargement of the infamous photo of Sandy aiming her .22 rifle in a downward line of fire, the smoke coming out the end of the barrel.

Pointing to the photo, he said, "The gate's closed. The defendant and her son were there and they were waiting. She wasn't on the other side of the gate. She was on Gerttula's side of the gate, and she was waiting." The jurors were crowded forward viewing the photograph.

"Now if you're going to shoot a rifle, you need your feet comfortably spread in a balanced position. She even has both sleeves rolled up. This is not a person who has, just instants before, somehow scrambled under a barbed-wire fence. She's there, she's squared around. She's ready. She has a rifle to her shoulder. She's aiming, and the photo was taken literally milliseconds after the trigger was pulled."

He pointed to a small portion of the pickup in the corner of the photo. "See, it's not blurred, that's clear. *It's not in motion.* That's not a pickup that's lunging, it's simply there and it's *stopped!* The photo shows the expression on her face. That's an expression of anger, animosity, even hatred. This is not a person who is standing in the middle of a road frightened. She's blocking that pickup from leaving." The jurors peered at the photo and passed it along.

"Monica Gerttula told you that as she was taking that picture, she turned to take one of the boy, and that the defendant struck her with such force it knocked her to her knees. Knocked her glasses off. She said she needed those glasses to see." He spoke of her injuries, one on her forehead and one over the right temple. "She was hit, repeatedly. Can you imagine what kind of blow it took, what kind of anger, what kind of force to raise that kind of bump on your head? How do you feel when you're hit like that? What do you see? What do you hear? What"—he paused—"do you remember?" I thought he was into it pretty well, and his voice took on new life. The jurors were listening.

"Shots were being fired past her, and she's being struck repeatedly and driven to her knees without her glasses. At that point she can't tell you exactly what happened. She remembers the words 'Give me that camera! Give me that camera!' The camera is broken. The next thing that Monica Gerttula is clearly aware of is that she saw her husband, probably through the open doors of the pickup, with blood on his face. Then she was aware that he was clutching his chest.

"Now Mrs. Gerttula Steele can't tell us exactly what happened after those moments that she received these blows, and she's getting her glasses and trying to recapture her senses. Most probably those events took a very short period of time." With a photo of the truck in his hands Brown pointed to the bullet hole on the left side of the windshield. "Sometime immediately before or immediately after the blows to Monica Gerttula came the shot into the cab of the pickup that caused the facial wounds to Will Gerttula. Monica Gerttula was aware her husband had blood on his face and heard him say something like 'Oh, my God' and clutch his chest, and so it seems that Will Gerttula was toward or near the front of the pickup when he was hit by the shot that killed him. Monica Gerttula didn't see him there. Whether she was still trying to find her glasses, whether she was still on the ground having been struck by the rifle butt or barrel, we're not going to know exactly. Monica Gerttula recalls running around the pickup, seeing the boy with a rifle, who was saying something to the effect, 'You shot at me, you shot at me.'" As I heard her story as painted by Brown, I thought his picture was beginning to make sense. I could feel the blows landing. I had to answer. I wanted to jump up and shout that this was all wrong. What if the jury thought he was right?

"The claim, the argument, or whatever—there's no evidence of it—but nevertheless it has been said repeatedly that Monica Gerttula must have shot her husband. I want to talk about that for a moment." He looked as if he had been insulted by the suggestion. He pursed his lips and squinted his eyes against the words he was about to deliver. He pointed to Sandy, saying she was five feet eight inches while Monica Gerttula was but five feet and a half inch tall. "That makes you reflect for a moment, on the disparity," he said, "on the unequal combat that we've described. Monica Gerttula was simply overwhelmed."

Then Brown pointed out that to the highest center section of the front of the pickup was four feet two inches. "Where is a person's arm when they hold it straight out?" he asked. "Is it twelve inches below the top of one's head? She was clearly on her side of the pickup at all times." He argued that if she had shot her husband, in order to shoot over the pickup she'd have been shooting up. If he were struggling with somebody, he would have been below the level of the pickup. "It couldn't happen. It didn't happen. Will Gerttula was shot by the boy from behind as Will Gerttula most likely got out of the pickup, shot by the boy in fear and anger after Gerttula had been directly shot at by the defendant. What Monica Gerttula most probably saw was the defendant swinging her rifle toward Will

Gerttula. She didn't tell you exactly because she was hit with such force.

"Will Gerttula made it back to the pickup, crawled in, and collapsed. Monica Gerttula's whole focus was to get him to the hospital. You got to think about the reaction then of the defendant. Here's a man shot in the chest and she's thinking of the camera, telling the boy to take the keys away from Monica Gerttula, and Monica Gerttula is overwhelmed again by two people *who are acting together.*" He underlined the words with a new, stronger voice.

"And the keys are forcibly pulled out of her hand. But she won't give up. She goes around to the driver's side and gets in and she was screaming and screaming, trying to attract attention, hoping there was someone on the river to hear her. She's trying to get Will to the hospital. At the second gate, probably the gate that had been tied shut that Dick and Nye burned their way through, the defendant says, 'We're not going anywhere until you get out and open the gate.' Monica got out, opened the gate, and the defendant drove away and left her." Then Brown told how Monica Gerttula had run to the Jones place, tried to get a car started, was bitten by the dog, how she ran to the Ferris home and came up to the house hysterically begging for Mr. Ferris to take her to the hospital. He described how slow Mr. Ferris was, how the old man took his time unlocking the car and having her put on her seat belt.

Brown argued that just as Sandy had arrived at the Clevelands', Ben Kowitz was driving up the road and stopped to talk to the defendant. He looked in the pickup and saw that Will Gerttula was probably dead. Sandy Jones asked him to go get Mike Jr. "And so Kowitz is on his way back up to the Joneses to get Little Mike when he meets Mr. Ferris on his way down. Not only that, but Jay Williams of the Depoe Bay Fire Department says twelve forty-five P.M., and that it took him twelve minutes to get to the Clevelands'. Monica Gerttula was there by the time he arrived. Mr. Ferris was nowhere to be seen. He'd come and gone. There is no way that Monica Gerttula stayed at the scene." Brown paused to let his version of the facts register with the jury.

Brown's face became an angry landscape. "There was no phantom gun. There were no empty casings from an automatic pistol found on the ground. There was no tape recorder thrown by Monica Gerttula over the edge—which, interestingly enough, she told the police about. You're asked to believe that she thought this recorder was incriminating, that she threw it away and then told the police about it." That was a point I hadn't thought of.

Brown claimed that Sandy didn't stop at the Ferris place, where she had often used the phone, to call for help. "Instead she went to her friend Tom Cleveland, who hid out the boy. He got the guns and didn't tell the police, hid those, too, and kept that evidence from the police! Cleveland also said he saw the rifle in the pickup. Monica Gerttula never saw that rifle being placed in the front of the pickup. How and when that got there is not clear from the evidence in this courtroom."

Brown paused again, cleared his throat, and once more scanned his notes on the lectern. He claimed that Monica Gerttula was initially wrong in what she thought she saw. "When the police talked with her at the Clevelands', she's vomiting, she has released urine, her pants are wet. And later that afternoon she is interviewed. And at that point this is a lady that I suggest to you can't begin to calculate the adrenaline, the fear, the grief, the frustration, she's experienced, these emotions and physical things that have been inflicted on her. Then she gives a statement to Sergeant Geistwhite. Think about what she has experienced," Brown said in a voice that edged toward a shout. "No breakfast. No lunch. She'd been beaten, shot at, she's been with her husband when he died, in the hospital and had thrown up. At four o'clock when her statement was taken, she had nothing in her stomach, and now we are going to take a statement from her!"

Again, anger took over the man's face. "But three and a half years later she gets to sit here for four days while a row of lawyers pounce on every single discrepancy and accuse her of being a liar. Imagine! Imagine the nightmare! The nightmare of a person who's a victim of a crime and suddenly *she's* the accused! And Monica Gerttula is charged with lying because every single word, every single impression, isn't precisely accurate. That's not right! That's not true! I told you the truth. It would be a surprise if there were no discrepancies in the details of what she saw. She came here and she told you the truth. She looked at you and she held her head up and she came back for four days in a row and she told you the truth. And you ought to believe her!" Brown waited as if he expected the jurors to shout their accord. I thought Brown and Dawson believed her, that Marquis and Stapleton had believed her, that Judge Gardner had believed her. Wouldn't the jury believe her?

Finally he turned to the gunshot residue. "That young criminalist, Mr. Amish, who filled out the box that said, 'Your residue level is this level,' claims that means you probably held a gun. Well, they don't do that anymore, but we're stuck with the fact that he filled out the form." Brown mentioned Hurley, saying there were many things they didn't know about gunshot residue yet. Then without elaborating he said, "You might think of it like painting a fence with red paint and you come in with red paint on your hands. Someone says, 'Aha, you must have painted the fence.' It may also mean that you put your hands on the fence, or you shook hands with somebody who did paint the fence, or that you moved the paint bucket." I thought it one of Brown's best metaphors.

"I have two boys," Brown said quietly. "One is eight and the other is almost ten, and I asked the older boy's permission to use this story. If I tell my boys that I don't want the water turned on in the backyard, and they both come in wet, that doesn't tell me who turned the hose on. It tells me they're both wet. I guess under my experience I would send them both to their rooms. They've learned. The crime lab has learned that the residue accumulates, that there are a number of variables. We know that gunshot residue means that Monica Gerttula was in a gunshot environment. And for that matter, so was Will Gerttula, because one of them killed him."

He said that the acceleration marks occurred at the gate in one of two ways. Gerttula may have been in the habit of slipping the clutch while he was waiting for Monica to get out. When the shot came through the windshield, that would be the time he'd have let his foot off the clutch and killed the motor. He said the more likely cause of the acceleration marks was when the defendant drove the truck away after the right rear tire was fired into and was flat. The defendant, he said, was unfamiliar with a vehicle with a standard transmission—another scenario that had never occurred to me. He argued that Gerttula's foot was down on the pedal. The defendant was excited and in the effort to get that truck started and out of there, the acceleration marks were left behind.

Then Brown went into the autopsy. "Dr. Reay, the chief medical examiner from Seattle, saw the classic pattern of the lead snowstorm associated exclusively with high-velocity gunshot wounds. There was one high-velocity weapon at the scene, and that was held by Mike Jones Jr."

And what about the intent to kill? Brown's lips suddenly stretched thin. "It was not only the defendant's intent, he said, but also Mike Jones Jr.'s intent when he pulled the trigger that fired the bullet that killed Will Gerttula. Now there isn't any little machine that you put your hand on that says this is your intent, that permits you to look inside people's heads. We have to look at two things: What do people say, and what do people do? We look at all the circumstances.

"In this case the defendant repeatedly told people of her dislike and antagonism toward Will Gerttula. She made little threats, 'I guess I'll have to kill him.' She made the threat in front of that boy two or three weeks before this occurred. She communicated to the boy in the presence of a witness, in a public place, her feeling, her antagonism. She and the boy acted together. He acted as an *extension of her* in confronting Nye and Dick. They were working together, literally, as partners. Not equal partners. We're talking about an adult and a fifteen-year-old boy. The adult is the custodian of that boy and she's placed loaded weapons in that boy's possession. And she, together with that boy, are pointing those weapons at people, pointing them at adults, and, as she said before, 'I guess I'll have to kill Will Gerttula.'"

Brown stopped to look the jury over. Satisfied, he said, "They knew that Will Gerttula was coming down that road and they waited there. With that foliage that was a situation for ambush. They were in a position of cross fire. The camera was a threat because it was going to be evidence.

"It wasn't a spontaneous exchange of shots, it was one that was thought about, talked about, planned during the twenty or thirty minutes while they waited behind that closed gate. It is almost as big a tragedy that the boy was induced to commit that act, that the boy was *an extension of the defendant.* That was a tragedy of itself!"

Then Brown closed his notebook and stood silently before the jury for a moment. In a voice barely above a whisper, a painful sweetness in the sound of his words, he said, "Ladies and gentlemen, Will Gerttula was killed by a .30-30 rifle. Under the circumstances, we submit to you that the shot was fired at him by Mike Jones Jr., who intended that he be hit, and that the necessary intention of hitting somebody with a .30-30 bullet is that they die, that that was known and expected and advised and counseled under the totality of the circumstances. Sandra Jones intended that Will Gerttula die, intended that he be shot and killed. Based on the evidence in this case, we ask that you find the defendant guilty of the crime of murder."

James M. Brown walked back to his table. "Thank you," he said, and sat down. His face regained its expressionless mask. I saw no sweat on his brow. He was a cool one, I thought. He gave a nod to Dawson, who in turn patted him on the back. Then the judge ordered the noon recess. Sandy Jones's life now rested with me. I had one shot at the jury. Just one. The last one I'd ever have in the case, the last one Sandy Jones would have in her life.

44

No lunch, the belly tight, the adrenaline surging like seas in a hurricane. I hurried to gather up the arguments I'd worked on for weeks, and those I must now make to counter Brown's, some of which I thought were compelling. I wondered how a juror might feel after hearing both sides of the same set of facts. I knew if the case hadn't been won by the time of the final argument that rarely could a lawyer win it at that late stage. Yet the case could easily be lost in the final argument. Brown's argument, as was his style, presented a penumbra of the cool, the considered, the calculated, the imperturbable.

The case had presented two women and two lawyers who argued opposite stories from the same facts. The jury had to decide which woman to believe—the one who had been on the stand for four days and who had testified under oath concerning nearly every detail in the case, or the one who had chosen not to take the stand at all, who had remained stone mute. And the jury had to decide which lawyer to believe—the one who usually spoke quietly, with little emotion, and who often understated his case as if it were mere business, or the one who sometimes filled the courtroom with the sound of thunder.

It was the worst time for a lawyer to give a closing. The jury was already tired and nature's anesthesia had likely set in, the noonday meal, which casts all the world, except

America, into siesta. But as the jurors marched in, they seemed ready enough. They took their seats and looked over at me. I thought they were probably anticipating some magnificent close, and I didn't think I could deliver it. After all of those years of waiting to make this argument, after the scores of times I'd delivered it in the middle of the night or as I'd driven down some lonely highway, now that the time was upon me, my mind was suddenly blank. I was still that country lawyer from Wyoming. I had always been. People never change. Only people's perceptions of people change.

The judge took the bench. I could feel the fear rising in my belly. I saw nothing in my mind but white, empty light. The state wanted Sandy Jones—this woman who had dared rise up and challenge the good old boys. The state yearned for her even more after this so-called big-shot lawyer had come breezing into town. I wanted to expose the underbelly of the system, to display to all how justice is rendered to the poor and the powerless from behind the myths and lies that say justice belongs to everyone. I wanted to show how sometimes it can be purchased with the power of money. But what ordinary American could afford the legal team we'd thrown at the state for nearly three and a half years?

Yes, the state; yes, its loyal servants; yes, Stapleton and Marquis; yes, the police and the sheriff's officers; yes, Judge Gardner and now Brown and Dawson—all of whom stood for the entrenched power of Lincoln County—all of them wanted her. They had the duty to make their communities safe from murderers. I believed they believed that and were as dedicated as we on the other side of the case. But I also thought that Sandy Jones stood as a symbol of the rebellion of the poor that all power secretly, subliminally fears. If I failed her now, they would drag her away.

The courtroom was packed, the people crowded into the aisles and standing six deep against the walls.

"Mr. Spence," Judge Haas said, his permission for me to begin my argument.

As I walked to the lectern, I said one solemn prayer to myself. May I tell it straight and from the heart.

"May the court please." I smiled and bowed my head to Judge Haas. He was a judge entitled to my great respect. "My friends"—I was speaking to the jurors. "Jay"—I turned to the judge's clerk. "Dana"—I was addressing the reporter. "Counsel!"—I looked to the other side of the courtroom and nodded to Brown and Dawson. "Michele"—I smiled at my wonderful associate. "Kent"—I acknowledged my good son. Then I turned my back to the court and stretched out my arms in the direction of my client—*"And Sandy."* Then, before I began to speak, I walked over to the jury and took each of them in with my eyes, one at a time.

Finally I said, "I wish after these many years in the courtroom I were a wiser lawyer. I've spent a lifetime in courtrooms trying to become wise, trying to become some kind of a funnel through which justice might flow. It isn't easy to know what to do." I began to feel alive, the juices rising, the power returning. My arms felt strong. I spoke the truth. It always gives me strength when I see a jury in front of me. "If it weren't for a jury like you, I would have given up long ago, because but for the jury there isn't much justice left in this system.

"I get strength from another source. I get strength from the huge courage that it must take for someone like Sandy Jones to have gone through what she has endured, to have sat by silently all of these weeks, all of these years. What kind of faith must she have? Can you imagine how it is to be so powerless; to have someone else speak for you, to have other people decide your fate, to place yourself in the hands of twelve human beings whom you have never seen before and to sit quietly with that almost childlike faith? It must make you feel very proud to be on this jury. Your duty must feel very solemn and heavy, and you must be a little frightened, as am I.

"I wish I could hear what you want me to say to you. How it must be for you to sit there without being able to say anything to me, to exclaim, or even to get up and leave! You have been the most attentive jury I have seen in my career. I've never looked up but what you were watching and listening and considering. And your twelve minds are better and wiser than any single human mind anywhere. There is something that binds you together, a willingness to search for the truth. I wish I had the ability to express to you my gratitude and my great respect for that."

Again I took in each of the jurors. "I guess I have to begin by saying to you that I think you already know the just answer in this case. I believe you already know that Sandy Jones can't be found guilty in this case, that she's innocent. And if that's so, why don't I sit down? Is it that I don't trust you?" I looked at each of them again. "The reason is because I am a human and see this case through my eyes, through my experience. What if I've forgotten something? What if there is a question in your mind that I should deal with? I am afraid to sit down.

"There will come a time when I will never be able to speak for Sandy Jones again, when Mr. Brown will get up and have the last words in this case because the state has the last word. And so your advice might be for me to quit speaking. But I must speak to you and I will try to speak truthfully and fairly and out of my heart. I think lawyers have that obligation.

"I live in a little village in Wyoming called Jackson Hole. It's a place of vast and beautiful mountains and a rugged wilderness that go on for miles and miles. You could walk for days in places in that country and never see a human being. It's the place where I grew up. It is a place that has had a great deal to do with forming who I am and what I think and what I believe. I believe that a lawyer is like a guide in those mountains. You have a choice here. There are two guides, either of whom you can follow. There is the guide of the state, the prosecutors. And there are the guides at the defense table. These guides will lead you to different places. And, of course, there is your own beautiful common sense and your joint intelligence that will ultimately direct you to a just result. But I hope that I can show you a way that is fair and just and according to the law that His Honor has given you.

"One of the things that struck me as rather strange is that we didn't hear the prosecutor, who is here to enforce the law, ever speak to you of the law. We never heard Mr. Brown speak to you once of the instructions that His Honor gave about what the law is, this prosecutor, this man of the law. One wonders why?" I waited for the jurors to consider that question.

"The first law that His Honor gives you is that it's the burden of the state to prove its case beyond a reasonable doubt. Sandy Jones hasn't had the obligation to prove a thing. I haven't had the obligation to prove a thing on her behalf. I haven't had the obligation to question a witness. I haven't had the obligation to call a witness. I haven't had the obligation on her behalf to say a word. It was *their* obligation and it remains their obligation to prove this case to you beyond a reasonable doubt. I didn't hear Mr. Brown once say he had proved anything to you beyond a reasonable doubt.

"Do you remember when we began our first discussion here together—when you were being selected as jurors, when we were talking about how it was to be charged with something that you hadn't done, how it was to defend yourself from false charges, and that no matter what you did, there was somebody to make something ugly of what you did, somebody who would give a wrong connotation to what you did, a wrong interpretation?" I waited. Several jurors nodded. "I asked you then if that had ever happened to any of you, and you all remembered that sometime in your lives you had been accused wrongfully, and you remembered how it was when you tried to explain, because the more you explained, the worse it got. And I said that's why, in America, the law presumes us innocent. That is the law. And Mr. Brown never spoke of it. Everybody has afforded Sandy Jones the presumption of innocence in this case, everybody except Mr. Brown." I looked over at his table again. He was busy writing in his notebook.

"And you're going to notice how, at every opportunity, Mr. Brown gave an ugly, convicting, hateful, guilty connotation to the innocent acts of Sandy Jones, even to her desperate acts. I heard him say Sandy Jones must be feeling power. Do you remember that? She must be feeling *power*! I don't remember any evidence about her feeling power. I remember evidence of her being terrorized. I remember evidence of her being frightened for her children. I remember evidence of her being sick and hurt. But I don't remember any evidence of her feeling power." Once more I waited for the jurors' memories to catch up with my words.

Then I said, "Years ago when I was a young prosecutor, I thought that my obligation as a prosecutor was to prosecute the guilty and to protect the innocent. My obligation to protect the innocent was as powerful and as demanding, as ethically planted in the gut and soul of the system, as was the duty to prosecute those who had committed crimes."

I turned toward Brown and gestured. "Here is a man who says he's going to be fair but who has never given this woman, to this moment, a particle of fairness. It's as if there has been a terrible disease in this case. Why do they want Sandy Jones so badly? What is it about this poor woman that has infected the entire judicial system all the way from Lincoln County to this special prosecutor that requires them to strip away her presumption of innocence, to strip away even basic fairness, and to undertake every cover-up, every impropriety in order to convict her?" My voice was on the rise. "Why? What is it about her, about this simple woman who's trying, who isn't on the welfare rolls, who isn't out begging, who has never committed a crime in her life, whose greatest sin was that she didn't have enough money to get good legal advice and who one day decided to represent herself and to sue the prosecuting attorney, and to sue the judge, and to confront—*to confront*, my friends—the good-old-boy system of Lincoln County? It was a sin, I'm afraid, for which she will never be forgiven." My mind was not choosing words. The words were coming as freely as if the faucet had been opened.

"I didn't hear Mr. Brown talk about how the Gerttulas had decided to harass this family. Mrs. Gerttula admitted that this lawyer, Ronnau, said, 'We will harass her until she caves in.' Do you remember that testimony? Do you remember that she said that Ronnau told them to bring those actions, the suits for the cattle being out, for the septic tank that didn't meet code—the septic tank that Mr. Gerttula helped install—the suit for repairing a barn without a permit where none was required, suits that over and over and over again required the expenditure of money that they knew she didn't have until they would bring her to her knees, suits in court in which her own husband was barred from making an ordinary use of their road, suits in which she was sued, and her family sued for as much as a quarter of a million dollars, suits that were without end, without justification? Why haven't we heard a fair prosecutor explain what that kind of harassment does to an ordinary woman? An ordinary, decent, courageous woman?"

I walked from the jury over to Sandy and turned facing her. I waited. Finally I said, "Sandy, I'm proud to represent you."

I saw the tears in her eyes.

Then I walked back to the jury. "I don't know how you would feel if somebody shot at your children. What would you do? What would you do if you went to the police and they investigated and the police report showed there was evidence to support the prosecution of Mr. Gerttula, better evidence than has ever been introduced against Sandy Jones in this case, and the investigative file was filed away under 'Miscellaneous'? What would you do?

"What would you do if the children were out in the meadow with their own father, and the father had to hit the ground because of shots that were fired in his direction and the children ran frightened to the house?

"What would you do when finally you had to send your own little girl off to her grandmother's in Portland, to break up the family, to send this child away because you couldn't get protection from that man? And I suppose that as the parents complained about this, worried about this, as their children were terrorized by this . . ." I stopped.

"Please hear me. As these parents *complained*—that is what Mr. Brown calls aiding and abetting the murder of Wilfred Gerttula. The complaints, the fear, the frustration, and Sandy saying, 'If somebody doesn't help me, I may have to shoot him myself'—that's what Mr. Brown calls aiding and abetting without referring to the definition of aiding and abetting as given to us by Judge Haas—when a mother speaks in front of a child! *That* is aiding and abetting?

"What would we do if our husband or wife had been run down and when we go to the state trooper, he says, 'There's nothing I can do about it. Why don't you go back from where you came? Why don't you go back to Alaska?'

"Finally, as you remember, she'd gone to Judge Littlehales and begged him for a restraining order, and the judge sent her to the victim's rights people. Now I don't know, ladies and gentlemen, but if one of you came to my office, I hope I would see you as an important enough person to warrant enough respect to invite you in, not to ask you to sit down and talk in a public hallway. I would hope you would have the confidence to tell me the truth, not to worry, to open up your heart and say what was on your mind, to tell me your fears. After all, mine is a lawyer's office. There is a relationship of attorney and client, a privilege that is almost holy in the profession. How would it be if we couldn't speak to our lawyers or their employees, if we couldn't speak to our priests or our preachers, if we couldn't speak to our wives and our children without these people using what we've confided in them to prove that we are murderers?

"This woman"—I turned to Sandy—"was sent there by the judge to get help. She told the victim's rights person what her problems were. She said, 'I am afraid. I beg for help and I want a restraining order, and if somebody doesn't help me, and he continues to do these things, to shoot at my children and put them in danger, I may have to shoot him myself.' What did they expect her to say? What kind of help did this woman give Sandy Jones? How would you like to be helped by that kind of a person? How would you feel when she said, 'Go hire a lawyer,' and she didn't even go in and talk to Ulys Stapleton, the prosecuting attorney?

"Mr. Brown put Ms. Ross on the stand to testify that Sandy Jones is a murderess, that this is evidence of her intent to kill, and that you should use this evidence, during this beautiful coming spring that Mr. Brown talked about, to put Sandy Jones in prison—because Sandy Jones is a murderess! If this is the presumption of innocence in America, my friends, none of us wants it. If this is called fairness in America, don't be fair with me.

"Then they bring in this nice man, Mr. Buford, who sat up there on the witness stand, this sincere man who believed the state's story that Sandy Jones had killed Wilfred Gerttula. I remember looking at him and I said, 'Do you think she's guilty?' 'Yes, I think she's guilty,' and as a good citizen he told what he had to tell.

"I asked him, 'Didn't you threaten somebody one time, threatened to run a pitchfork through somebody?' Remember that testimony?" A couple of jurors nodded. "He said, 'Yes,' surprised, like, how did I know? And I said, 'You didn't really intend to kill anybody, did you?' and his answer was 'No, I didn't. I didn't mean it. I was just mad. I didn't mean it.'

"Sandy Jones meant it, but he didn't? Sandy Jones is guilty, but he isn't? Then I asked him the crux question. 'How could you make a jury believe you?' How do I make a jury believe me?" I was speaking softly. "I'm telling you it scares me to death. I don't know if you believe me." I waited a long time. "I look into your eyes and I can't tell whether you believe me." I waited longer and looked at each juror. "Do you believe me?" I waited. When I saw no answer on their faces, I fought on. Words were the weapon. Only words, which dissolve into the atmosphere, the distant echoes of which will leave only a shadow of themselves on the memory of the mind.

"Do you know how many people are in the penitentiary who are not guilty, but who are hated? History is filled with people who have been convicted not because they are guilty of anything, but because they were hated. That's the great technique: if you can make somebody hated and tell half-truths about them and rip out the presumption of innocence from them, and ignore the law that has been laid out by His Honor, if you can make people hate, well, then you can convict them without evidence."

I turned to the judge and looked up and smiled broadly at the good man. "With all due respect, Your Honor." I turned again to the jury. "Do you remember when Judge Haas said to you, 'If you talk to each other, I'll shoot you'? Do you remember that?" The jurors began laughing.

"Every one of you heard it and every one of you could testify to it. In print it is devastating evidence. What if day after tomorrow they find one of you dead? The conclusion could be that you talked, and that this judge is the guilty one." I pointed up at the judge again with a small laugh. And the jurors laughed again.

I reminded them of the judge's instructions about believing a felon, "that if you find that a witness has been convicted of a crime, you may only consider this conviction for its bearing, if any, on the *believability* of a witness's testimony.

"Why didn't we hear about that from Mr. Brown concerning his witness Rocky Marrs, who ended up not even remembering what year he was supposedly confronted by Sandy Jones, this man who told the officers her gun was shiny and who described the length of the barrel of a gun that wasn't in any way like Sandy's pistol? This was the man who described her motorcycle as brown, maroon, and later red. Mr. Brown didn't have to call Rocky Marrs. He didn't have to call Mr. Buford. He didn't have to call the lady from the victim's rights office. Why did he call these people? I suggest to you that he called them in order to make you believe that Sandy Jones is a vicious person.

"And they called Ms. Ross for another reason. I want you to stop and think about this with me for just a moment. Do you remember anybody saying that Sandy Jones told Little Mike to kill anyone, or encouraged him to do that in any fashion? That proof is necessary for the state's case." I waited for the jurors to contemplate the question.

"Now they bring in Ms. Ross. Their whole case depended upon what Sandy Jones was supposed to have said in front of Little Mike a month before this shooting. On cross-examination I asked Ms. Ross if she left room for the possibility that Little Mike wasn't present. Her answer: 'I *think* he was there.' *I think!* That's their case for aiding and abetting—*assuming,* ladies and gentlemen, that Mike Jones Jr. heard what Sandy said. That's the state's evidence for holding Sandy Jones in this case as a murderess.

"Now what do you think about that kind of justice in America? How would you like to have a prosecutor living next door to you, watching you, a member of the good-old-boys organization in your community, deciding whether you were going to go to the penitentiary or not based on that kind of evidence?

"If that's the law of this land, my dear friends, we can't live here anymore. It isn't safe for us to live here anymore. And that's why I'm here, if you want to know the truth. Is that proof beyond a reasonable doubt? If it is, tell me so. If that's the proof, send her off to prison. If that's the proof that it takes to substantiate this case, send her away!" I walked away from the jury toward the door of the courtroom. Halfway to the door I suddenly turned back.

"The Dick and Nye testimony. Can you see old Dick there?" I was smiling and there was laughter from some of the jurors. "If I was making a movie, I couldn't cast a better character than Mr. Dick. But, you know, I have to say something about both Mr. Dick and Mr. Nye. When it finally came down to it, they were honest, weren't they, even though they had been handled pretty roughly at the hands of the prosecutors?" I saw the jurors begin to laugh. I didn't know why. "There's a private joke going on here, and I don't know what it is."

Juror 10 said, "If I can't cry, I'll laugh." And the others were laughing, too.

I said, "Am I all right with you?" The jurors nodded and I went on, realizing they were laughing at the memory of Dick and Nye, who had, at last, been more comical than incriminating. "The testimony of Dick and Nye was important because they, too, had heard the shots that Little Mike had called his mother about. Do you remember Mr. Dick said, 'Yeah, I understood her. I think she'd gone through enough. I don't blame her.' Do you remember that? But Mr. Brown brought them here to tell you that she is a bad woman, that she is a person who intended to kill Mr. Gerttula."

I picked up the enlarged, poster-sized photo of Sandy with the smoking gun in her hands. "Now this picture was shown to you." I turned to Michele and said, "Ms. Longo, would you help me for a moment, please?" She held on one side of the photo and I held on to the other and we walked up close to the jury.

"Now the first thing we conclude is that because she had her sleeves rolled up she is ready to go to work, which is to kill Wilfred Gerttula? No, she is not going to kill Wilfred Gerttula, she is going to aid and abet her son in his killing according to some vicious plan! We can tell that because her sleeves are rolled up?

"The next thing we are to take from this photograph is

that she's standing comfortably with her feet in proper balance and that indicates she's spent some time in getting ready to do this?

"Then we are to look at the face. Michele, would you come up close with the picture and let them see her face? We are to conclude by looking at her face that this isn't a woman who is afraid. We are to tell that this is a woman who has hatred on her face, not fear. A vicious killer!

"The next thing we are to take from this photograph is that the camera was magical. The camera was fast enough to freeze the smoke from the exploding rifle but not fast enough to freeze the truck as it was charging Sandy Jones. This is what we were asked to believe, as if this courtroom in Multnomah County, Oregon, is populated with fools."

Then I pointed at the place on the photo where the front of the pickup could be seen. "With a step or two in any direction, Monica Gerttula would have been in range of Sandy Jones and Wilfred Gerttula as they wrestled for Sandy's rifle. Even if she shoots from where she took the picture, it's all over, isn't it?"

I demonstrated the point with Jay Moody, the court clerk, who, at my request, stooped a little to become five feet eight inches. And I invited a small woman in the audience to come forward. The woman was about five feet tall, the height of Monica Gerttula. I took a long wooden pointer and put it in a downward course at Jay's chest to represent the course of the bullet through Gerttula. Then I had Jay stoop over. The course of the bullet from the small woman standing with her arm extended, as if shooting a handgun, suddenly became parallel to the ground as Jay bent forward—the exact course of the bullet through Gerttula.

I asked the jurors, "If Little Mike shot Mr. Gerttula, where was the boy?" Monica Gerttula claimed that she was at all times near the open door of the pickup. In order for Little Mike to shoot Gerttula, he'd have had to be somewhere *in front* of Mrs. Gerttula. "Surely she would have seen him. Instead, she said he was always back in the shadow of the nonexistent stump. She said, 'Even when I walked around the rear of the pickup, he was standing there with his gun relaxed. He never said anything to me. He never tried to stop me. Mrs. Jones never said anything to him.' But what did Mr. Brown say? He said Sandy and Little Mike must have had this thing figured out. Is that proof beyond a reasonable doubt, or is that his assumption? It's his *presumption of guilt,* isn't it?"

I showed how all the shell casings from the .30-30 had been accounted for and how none could have hit Mr. Gerttula. To refute those facts, I said, Brown had to assume two things: one, that the Joneses had stored the gun with a shell in the chamber, dangerous to say the least, and two, that the sheriff's department, with its meticulous search, was unable to find the casing to this phantom eighth cartridge. That failure alone was reasonable doubt.

And what about the felonious intent the judge said the state must establish? "If Little Mike *intended* to kill somebody, he could have shot Mr. Gerttula anytime he wanted. And Sandy Jones had a pistol on her hip that she never unholstered, and everyone, including Mr. Brown, admits that. That gun was never fired. If she wanted to kill Gerttula, all she had to do was drop the rifle and pull her pistol out and shoot him. She didn't have to stand there and wrestle with him until she was beaten up and sick. Is that proof of an evil intent beyond a reasonable doubt?" I saw Brown shaking his head and smiling. The jury saw it, too.

I said, "Mr. Brown smiles. It hurts me when he smiles."

Then I turned and pointed at him. "This man right here, this nice man, pleasant face, nice smile, pleasant demeanor, who talks much quieter to you than I do, said,

'Sandy Jones put the gun in Little Mike's hands.' Where did that information come from? Is there any evidence that this boy is different from our children? Had my son abandoned his mother under such circumstances as these, I wouldn't have been very proud of my son. I'd hope that my son would protect his mother. And I'd hope there'd be officials in my county who, if my son had stayed there, wouldn't later come before a jury without any evidence, and in a soft and gentle voice tell a jury that my wife put the gun in my son's hands, and that they lay in ambush for the decedent. I would hope that I would never hear that."

I turned back to the picture of the smoking gun. "It is an extraordinary picture, as Mr. Brown says. It's the only case that I've ever heard of where there was a real picture of a real smoking gun. *The case of the smoking gun.* If it weren't for the picture, they would have claimed that Sandy had the .30-30 in her hands, wouldn't they? It's the picture that *doesn't* convict. *It's the picture that acquits Sandy Jones,* because she can prove that the .22 was in her hands, not the .30-30. Unwittingly, Monica Gerttula has saved Sandy Jones. It's the only decent thing that Mrs. Gerttula ever did for us in this case.

"You see the smoke coming out there? Mr. Brown tells us that this is gunshot residues going downrange, suggesting that that is how Monica got residues on her hands. But do you remember that .22s don't have any antimony? Who does Mr. Brown think we are?" I saw a juror becoming restless.

"Please, Judge, I'd like to have a recess for the jury."

During the recess Eddie came up to me and said I was doing just fine, to keep it up. Michele and Sandy spoke quietly. Kent kept his distance, knowing my mind was on the argument. I checked my notes that contained the points I still wanted to make. Then I walked over to Sandy.

"How are you doing?" I asked.

"Good. You're doing good. I'm praying for you."

When the jury came in, they sat down quietly and looked over at me. I was already on my feet, and when the judge nodded in my direction, I walked quickly to the jury box and began as if there'd been no recess at all. "If, in this case, I say this shooting was in self-defense, the state has to prove that it was *not* self-defense, and they must prove that beyond a reasonable doubt. In America the state must prove everything." I read from His Honor's instructions concerning self-defense that the jury "may consider any evidence of Wilfred Gerttula's propensity, if any, to engage in violent and assaultive conduct." I said, "The law is just common sense. Nothing mysterious about it. If you know that your neighbor is violent, you deal with that neighbor with quite a different set of thoughts than you would if your neighbor was a quiet, gentle, passive person. If you know that your neighbor has shot at your children or run over your husband or tried to poison your water supply, you certainly are quicker to act in your self-defense with that kind of a person than you would with somebody else." I turned to Brown. "I don't know why we haven't heard from counsel about that." This time Brown didn't smile.

I looked at the photo of Mrs. Gerttula with the swollen and bruised forehead. I held up the photo. "I don't doubt that she was struck on the head. I don't see how you can pull somebody out of the car who's holding on to the steering wheel and screaming and screaming *and screaming*, how you can grab them by the hair and pull them out so you can get the wounded husband to the hospital and not bump the woman's head in the process. I don't think that's quite possible.

"I have no doubt that Mrs. Gerttula was confused. This was a terrible tragedy. If I had shot my wife accidentally, I would likely be confused. I would likely be shattered. But something else would happen if I tried to cover it. And that's the problem in this case.

"Suppose that instead of telling about the tragedy as it happened, we try to cover up what happened. We know we have a picture of her with the gun, and so we're going to blame her. That's where this all fell apart. In this whole process Monica Gerttula went to an extreme to try to pin a murder on Sandy Jones that she knew that Sandy Jones didn't commit. Not once but ten separate times—I read them to you—she stated to Trooper Geistwhite that Sandy Jones shot her husband with a .22. And it wasn't just that she shot him. It was that she shot him point-blank. And it wasn't that she shot him point-blank, it was that 'I saw her pull the trigger.' And it wasn't that 'I saw her pull the trigger,' she demonstrated *how* she saw her pull the trigger. And she couldn't make it stick, so she suddenly couldn't remember. She had even gone to the extreme of explaining which shot was the fatal shot.

"She didn't remember that her husband had been at the front of the pickup when he was shot and that there was blood all over the front of the pickup. The story just falls apart, everywhere. The time that it fell apart the worst was the day she denied that she even talked to Ms. Pinckney."

I turned to Brown once more. "Mr. Brown said he was going to present the whole case to you, warts and all. Has it been the state that's come forward with the warts in this case? It was the defense who brought the testimony of Ms. Pinckney to you, who said that she talked to Mrs. Gerttula in her house, described the house, took five or six pages of notes, and then was told by Mrs. Gerttula not to publish them.

"And it was Geistwhite who said, 'I called up Ms. Pinckney and told her not to publish Mrs. Gerttula's statement because it was *contrary* to our policy.' What was contrary is that Mrs. Gerttula had given her statement to Ms. Pinckney just before Geistwhite came to the house and told Mrs. Gerttula, 'There's something wrong with your testimony. This man wasn't shot with a .22 like you said, and there's blood on the front of the pickup. So he didn't get shot over by the door like you said. He got shot up front. Now come on, what happened here? Let's get this straight.' And Geistwhite got her straightened out all right before he turned the recorder on. Had Ms. Pinckney's notes been available, notes that were taken just a few minutes before, what would we have in this case? We would have the ultimate proof of how that story got changed."

I turned to the packed gallery and searched the people. "I'm looking for the *Oregonian* reporter. Where is he? He's somewhere, listening, listening to my final argument. The *Oregonian* was charged by His Honor to maintain those notes so you could hear what they said. They were entrusted to the lawyer for the *Oregonian,* as an officer, a custodian of His Honor. And the notes were destroyed. I will guarantee you one thing, and you, the audience, within the sound of my voice, can go out on the street and broadcast it as loudly as you can broadcast it. The *Oregonian* destroyed notes that were essential to the defense of my client. That will never hit the headlines of that paper." A rolling burble of laughter came from the audience. Judge Haas let it roll.

"I'm just wondering if you think that Mrs. Gerttula lied to you. I don't like to use that word. I rarely use it. I don't like its sound. Do you remember when she said, 'My husband didn't own a handgun while I was married to him'? And I asked her if she were playing with words, *own* as opposed to *possess.* Then we got Mrs. Meisenger here, who talks about the three handguns that they had. Now these handguns obviously didn't shoot anyone in this case, but I am thinking of the court's instruction. Mrs. Gerttula knew they had those guns. Mrs. Meisenger said Monica Gerttula was there when she delivered the guns. She talked about another Italian gun that was in their possession. She talked about a family Luger that was in their possession.

"And I go stumbling through this case looking for the gun. Why do I have to look for the gun? It's not my obligation to look for guns. But I keep looking. And then we find the witness. Lo and behold, he lives next door to Monica Gerttula. Lo and behold, he had been there since that truck, that '78 truck, was new. He's driven it many times. He's seen the gun in the glove compartment many times. Monica Gerttula had many times over the access to that truck as that young man had, a police officer, who didn't want to be here, who was subpoenaed here, and required under the law to come and tell the truth as he knew it. And before he came, he walked over to Mr. Brown and Mr. Dawson and told them personally about the gun. He told them about it before they rested their case. And who presented that wart? There were warts all over this case. There were warts in very strange places in this case.

"Do you remember Mr. Brown's discussion about the hole in the windshield? If you were against a fence and being attacked by a truck—is the truck a deadly weapon?" Turning to Michele I asked, "Where's the deadly weapon instruction, Michele? You'll understand why I'm so grateful to Michele. She's been my brains. I'm but the mouth." I heard the jurors laugh with the audience. I read the instruction aloud that said that an instrumentality that is readily capable of causing death or serious personal injury is a dangerous weapon. "I suggest to you that a pickup is more dangerous than a .22. It was probably the most dangerous weapon out there.

"Mr. Brown said that Sandy Jones wanted the camera.

Yet if she wanted the camera, she had every chance to get it. It was there in the back of the pickup all the time. She never made any attempt to get the camera. She was making an attempt to protect her children, and herself. Once she realized Gerttula was shot, she wanted to get him to the hospital. When she got to the Clevelands', she ran into the house pleading to Mr. Cleveland to help her get the man to the hospital.

"Let me talk about another wart." I held up Sandy's moccasins, which Brown had brought into court and had introduced into evidence but had never mentioned to the jury. "Why wouldn't the state come forward with the simplest piece of evidence in this case that establishes what really was going on here—her moccasins? The blood that spattered down on her moccasin tops is almost irrefutable evidence of what happened. Gerttula was bent over and the blood dripped on them, and it is obvious that the blood fell on her moccasins as they struggled."

I put the moccasins back on the evidence table. "I want to talk to you about the gunshot residues. That has been the greatest travesty of justice I have seen in thirty-seven years in trial. I want to give you a certified guarantee: I guarantee to every one of you that if you were at the scene of a homicide and had gunshot residues on your hands, on both hands, on both the front and the back, and on the sides of your face consistent with your having shot a handgun, and you were the only one at the scene with that evidence on your hands, that that evidence would be respected by competent, honest law enforcement officers.

"They would respect it for a variety of reasons, one of which would be that that kind of physical evidence does not lie. A second reason is this: if you can't respect that evidence, then you've got to go up and open the doors of the penitentiaries and let the people out that are there because of it. But these residues were on Monica Gerttula's hands, and that destroyed their case against Sandy Jones. The efforts they went to, to destroy that evidence is almost unbelievable.

"I think of this young man, Amish. They had threatened him and intimidated him, suggesting they were going to do all kinds of bad things to him. Stapleton had written to his boss. The man had been called on the carpet for telling it like it was. He was only supposed to tell it like it was if it helped the state's case? But under cross-examination he still had to say there was a greater probability that she fired a gun than not."

Then I backed away from the jury and smiled. "Now please, folks, I can't do what Perry Mason does. I can't get Monica Gerttula to come trotting up here and say, 'I did it.' But we did find the gun for you. We did find the gunshot residues for you. We did establish for you that it was a pistol because in the final analysis you have to decide whether you believe Vargo and Dr. Reay, or whether you believe Dr. Brady. I think it might be a little easier to believe Dr. Brady because his testimony makes common sense. If this were a jacketed rifle bullet, the jacket was magical. It either somehow disappeared inside the body or it exited from the body without leaving an extra hole or by leaving a hole smaller than the entrance wound after it hit a rib. That's pretty magical to me. I was very proud to be able to present Dr. Brady to you.

"Anyway, about the Perry Mason thing that I discovered by listening to Mr. Brown. He was telling us how Dick and Nye were so upset that when they couldn't open the gate they burned the gate open—the second gate. Nye took a cigarette lighter out and burned the rope to get the gate open. Now the next thing we're told—watch this, Perry Mason, it amazes me—Sandy and Monica Gerttula are coming down to this same second gate and they stop for Monica Gerttula to *open the gate!* I don't know how it got closed again after Dick and Nye burned the rope in two. And it's there that Sandy Jones supposedly leaves Monica Gerttula."

I shook my head in disbelief. "Do we believe Mr. Ferris? He was a nice old man who wouldn't lie to anyone, and he was clear about what he remembered. He had just sat down to dinner when he saw the pickup go by. He eats slowly, took twenty to thirty minutes, and he was just finishing up when Mrs. Gerttula came to the door. When was all of this stuff thrown away if she wasn't up there? When did the recorder get thrown over the side of the road? What happened to the gun? It doesn't take twenty minutes to go from the second gate to the Ferrises'. It takes three minutes or four if she's running.

"But Mr. Brown wanted to know, 'Why did she tell police that the recorder was in the pickup if she had thrown it away?' Well, why did she tell the police that she saw Sandy Jones shoot her husband point-blank ten separate times? Why did she go through all of those stories? She just simply fell apart there. That's why. And I think Mr. Brown knows that's why.

"Here's another interesting little tidbit that shows the thinking of Mr. Brown. Mr. Cleveland is a felon! According to Mr. Brown, he hid the boy. I suppose Mr. Cleveland will be charged. Mr. Brown wouldn't even give Mr. Cleveland the decency of saying that this was an old man who let the boy go home without being faced with that misery at the Clevelands'. So you want to see how the brain works? Let me show you how the brain works, with all due respect. Here is an example that came out of Mr. Brown's head. It was a story about his children. I respect this man as a citizen and as a father. But he gave you an example about his two boys who came into the house with water on them after they'd been told not to turn on the hose. And he said, 'Which one turned on the hose? You can't tell because they both have water on their hands.' Then the clue as to how his mind works: 'I should send them both to their rooms,' he said. *Both* to their rooms? We don't give the benefit of the doubt to *anybody*, not even at home.

"Here is another quote from Mr. Brown. 'This boy'— referring to Little Mike—'was induced to commit that act, that tragedy. He was *induced* to do it.' Do you remember any evidence that Little Mike was induced by anybody? Stop and think about it a minute. How would you like to live in a country where somebody can make a murderer out of a little boy in order to hang his mother?" I let the jurors think that over.

Then I turned around to Michele. "Could you find me the instruction, please, that says that Mr. Brown has to prove Mike killed Mr. Gerttula intentionally before the jury can hold Mrs. Jones as an aider and abettor? Obviously you can't aid and abet a nonexistent crime."

I read the judge's instruction: " 'Before Sandra Jones can be guilty of murder by aiding and abetting Mike Jones Jr., you must find, first, that the state has proved beyond a reasonable doubt that Mike Jones Jr. unlawfully and *intentionally* caused the death of Wilfred Gerttula. As a part of its responsibility the state must prove beyond a reasonable doubt that Mike Jones Jr. was not acting in the lawful defense of Sandra Jones, or himself.' "

Over and over, many months before, I'd made these clear arguments on the law to Judge Haas. Surely Brown knew this would eventually be his burden of proof. Yet this case had marched on as if the law didn't exist. Perhaps I could now convince a reasonable jury to halt the travesty. I said, "The state has to prove two things before they can even start to talk about Mrs. Jones being guilty of a crime. They must first prove that her boy, Mike Jones Jr., is guilty of murder, and they have to prove that beyond a reasonable doubt. Even if they prove that he shot Mr. Gerttula, they have to show that it wasn't done in the defense of his mother. If it was done in the defense of his mother, she is not guilty of a crime, nor is he.

"Suppose this is the fact—which isn't the fact—but suppose the worst possible thing I can think of. Suppose Sandy is standing out there wrestling for this gun and she's screaming, 'Mike, Mike, shoot him.' Now is she guilty of murder if he shoots? Would she be guilty of the crime of murder, or would Little Mike? He would have shot in the defense of another, which the court tells you excuses the shooting."

I stopped speaking and looked down at the toes of my boots for a moment. Finally I said, "Where is this case? Where is the proof except a dastardly allegation that I resent and that I trust you do too, that, quote, 'She induced him to kill Mr. Gerttula, and they lay there in ambush.'

"Well, ladies and gentlemen of the jury, I think it's time for me to stop. When I sit down, there won't be anything else I can ever say to you again. Mr. Brown has the last words. You will see me squirm over here and you will know that I want to get up and answer him, because you know I can. But you will have to answer for me. You will have to argue the case of Sandra Jones for me because once I sit down I can't.

"Now, folks, there are two ways for you to conclude this case when you are deliberating, and it's not for me to tell you how to engage in your deliberations. But you can take the long road, or you can take the short one. I think most of you already know what the result should be in this case. As soon as you elect a foreman or forewoman, you can take a poll immediately, and if ten of you believe there's a reasonable doubt, the case is over in three minutes. I have a hunch you might want to do that because we have chewed these facts over and over like an old cow with nine stomachs.

"I have a reason for wanting you to do this quickly. Soon I will put Sandy Jones in your hands, and I, too, am there with her—in your hands. The time waiting for a jury's verdict is the most miserable time in a lawyer's life. But this woman will wait and wait. She has been waiting all of this time. And it's time for this travesty to end. It is time for this torturing to end. It is time, ladies and gentlemen, for you to send Sandra Jones home to her family. It's time for this to be over. This has been a long case for this woman. This has been an agonizing affair and I wish she didn't have to hurt any longer than necessary for you to do justice.

"There's something else. This may not be the end of it. These people"—I pointed to Brown and Dawson—"have the power to charge her with other crimes—menacing—like the Dick and Nye situation, or they can charge her with attempted murder claiming she shot through the windshield at Mr. Gerttula. These charges are not included in this case. I wish you would write something across the bottom of your verdict as a message to the people in Lincoln County and to this prosecutor. I wish you would just write across here"—I held up the verdict and pointed at a blank space at the bottom—" 'Please leave her alone. Let her go home. Leave her alone.' I wish you would write that.

"Now, ladies and gentlemen, I have to say something on behalf of myself and Michele. I am about to leave you. I've been a long time with you in a kind of strange relationship. I know each of you in a way that I would never know you if I lived next door to you. We've never spoken to each other. But we have shared things together. We've shared laughter, and we've shared tears. We've shared tragedy and we've shared patience. We're going to share justice. That is quite a rich relationship. It's quite a fulfilling relationship.

"I have each of your faces indelibly in my mind. I'll never forget you, any one of your faces, ever, as long as I live. And yet, when I walk out this door, I will never have embraced you or thanked you or even said anything to you except 'Good morning.' That's quite a strange relationship. Yet it is a very dear one to me and I'm proud that we have had it together. So I am going to say good-bye to you. I don't like to say good-bye. I'll say, 'I'll see you tomorrow, some-place. I'll see you tomorrow.'" I walked back to the table where Sandy and Michele sat. I walked behind Sandy and put a hand on each of her shoulders.

"And so, ladies and gentlemen of the jury, I give into your hands my client, Sandy Jones."

As soon as I sat down, James M. Brown hurried to the lectern like a fireman to the fire. He didn't begin by addressing the jury. He didn't smile. His lips looked dry and his eyes were hard. He started right off:

"If it please the court, I only have a few things to say. I need to emphasize that you must find that Will Gerttula was the aggressor before you may consider any evidence of a propensity for violent behavior." He was speaking of the right of self-defense in the face of past aggressive action on the part of Gerttula. "It's not the other way around as was, I think, the impression given." Then he wanted the jury to understand that "deadly physical force is the use of an implement, a gun, capable of readily causing death." He was talking over my head. "It is a matter of the apprehension of genuine risk, substantial risk, and you'll need to rely on your recollection of the instructions, and they will be avail-able to you."

Once more there was no emotion in his voice; his voice was like a rock falling on pavement. "There has to be something more than someone losing a wrestling match before an individual is licensed or excused to kill some-body. And the evidence that's been referred to is that the boy had grievances, the boy had a grudge against Will Gerttula. The boy believed that Will Gerttula shot at him.

"The defendant knew that the boy had those feelings, these fears, this grudge, and the defendant had a grudge against Will Gerttula, and she made no secret of it. The boy knew that. The grudge went over a period of time, lawsuits, claims of harassment, claims of hitting her husband with a car, claims of shooting, claims of scaring the children, claims about the water system. So we start out talking about intent with clear, established feelings, animosity, antagonism, literally grudges against Will Gerttula."

I'd been waiting for this argument from the first time I'd heard the story from Michele and Steve Lovejoy. All of the harassment Sandy had endured at the hands of Gerttula did, indeed, establish an arguable motive for killing the man. But one thing Brown forgot: it also established a fact in paren-theses—that Gerttula may have deserved what he got. Jurors have an instinctive sense of justice. That's why we rely on them. While Brown saw Gerttula's malicious acts toward the Joneses as a motive for his murder, the jurors, I thought, could say he had it coming without ever saying it. And the same facts, on the other side of it, established the fear the Joneses had and their right to defend themselves.

"Will Gerttula was armed with a tape recorder and Monica Gerttula was armed with a camera," Brown con-tinued. "On the other side was a .30-30 rifle and a .22 rifle. If you're afraid because there was shooting up the road, why arm yourself and go off your property to seek out a con-frontation? Why block the only way out? Why tie gates? Why reset wire gates? Why obstruct the way out for the people you fear? Loaded weapons. Opportunity to wait as much as twenty minutes to half an hour, knowing that

Will Gerttula is going to be coming down that road. Why say, as the boy said after Will Gerttula was shot, 'You shot at me, you shot at me'?

"These were partners. Equal partners. They were there for the same purpose—to confront Will Gerttula. They shot together. They shot into the truck. Two people engaged in an ambush, two partners engaged in an ambush in pursuit of a common intent. The dominant one was the defendant, Sandra Jones."

He shut his notebook quietly. "We ask you to find her guilty of the crime charged. Thank you." James M. Brown walked to his table and sat down without saying a word to the scowling Dawson.

Then Judge Haas told the jurors not to discuss the case, and not to look anything up in any references. "We'll meet here tomorrow morning at nine o'clock sharp. At that time I'll give you the final instructions and we'll submit the case to you. You folks have a nice evening."

"Jesus God," I said to Michele. "I thought he'd give the case to the jury tonight and it'd all be over in an hour or two." I turned to Sandy. "This torture is going to be stretched out one more night. We've made it this far. We can make it the rest of the way." I smiled at her. She looked weak, the life gone from her eyes, her face hanging long, her muscles weary of holding on to her small smile.

"I'll be here in the morning, Spence." Then she pulled up a smile, from where I did not know. "And I'll be on time."

That night I couldn't sleep. I thought I would never sleep again.

45

At nine o'clock sharp Judge Haas called the court into session. Sandy was there, just a bare minute before. Our team of lawyers sat at our table, waiting. Fear gripped my chest. I could not force it out. I suffered from it every time I waited for a jury's verdict. It's the loss of control. It's putting the life of your client and your own life as a lawyer into the hands of someone else. It's a test of who you are. Have you been competent? Will you lose the case because of who you are? Would your client have done better with another lawyer?

I tried to concentrate on what the judge was saying. I heard him giving his last instructions to the jurors: "Each and every juror must agree on the charge in order to return a guilty verdict. Ten or more jurors must agree to return a verdict of not guilty"—an anomaly in Oregon law. He read the jury form to them, told them after they'd reached a verdict to sign it and signal the bailiff. Then he swore the bailiff, and although the jurors had requested that the two alternates be permitted to remain with them even though they'd not take part in the deliberations, the judge told them he could not permit that. He thanked the alternates for their service and discharged them.

Brown and Dawson took exception to the instructions the judge had given. They read their exceptions into the record. It made no difference. If the jury acquitted Sandy, any error on the part of His Honor in the instructions would not be grounds to set the jury's verdict aside. The constitutional prohibition against double jeopardy would save Sandy from another trial on the same charge. But Brown and Dawson might want to appeal just to make new law for the State of Oregon. They were the tough, the intransigent ones. We had no quarrel with the judge's instructions.

At 10:30 A.M. the bailiff brought us a note from the jurors. The judge read it aloud. "We, the jury, would like to now add an addendum to our verdict. We'd like to know that this matter will finally be put to a close and that our verdict does mean something. Please reply."

I looked over at Eddie and then at Michele. We thought we knew what that meant. The jurors were going to acquit Sandy Jones! And they wanted to know if they could add the language at the bottom of their verdict that I'd asked for. I felt an immediate discharge of the heaviness in my chest. I wanted to get up and shout, *Yes, yes. Write it there. Write it in plain and happy English. Leave this woman alone!*

Dawson spoke before I could muster the words. "There's no provision under our statutes for anything but a general verdict," he growled.

"Could I say something?" I asked.

"You betcha," the judge said.

"I told Jim Brown this a few minutes ago and I'd like to say it again. I have a huge respect for this whole process. My respect includes not only the prosecution that has stayed at this task, and this patient court, but for the jurors as well. The thing that is beautiful about these jurors is that, in a small way, they feel like they've made some contribution. I don't know whether they're naive or not. In this system, I don't know if they really have any power anymore.

But I have great respect for them, and for their hearts and for their souls and for their desire to join with us in making the system work. There isn't any provision against them writing anything they want to write on a separate piece of paper. There isn't anything that prevents them from communicating with us in any way they wish. This is still America. These people still have the right and the freedom to say what they wish, individually or as a group. They aren't just statutory tools. They're human beings. We have fought this battle, Jim and Doug, Michele and Eddie and I, over these years. Seems to me it's time for the battle to be over. Seems to me it is time to let these people do what they want to do. Whether it will do any good, I don't know, and whether it has any efficacy, well, we know it may not. But they have a right to speak their piece."

Judge Haas said, "You may be right. But you may not be right. Gerry, it appears you have a verdict over there." He nodded toward the jury room. "No one wants to go through this again."

"I can't see how it could possibly affect the validity of their verdict." I turned to Sandy. "Do you want the jury to write something?"

She said, "Well, I'd like the state to leave me alone."

Dawson said the jury could be coming in the other way, against us. And he didn't want any error in the record.

The judge thought a moment. "After the verdict, the jurors can say whatever the hell they wanted to say. We've invested too much in this case for me to run any risk now."

"What are you going to say to them?" I asked.

"I'm going to tell them to designate their verdict on the verdict form that I gave them. And after they come in, I will explain to them about it."

"All right," I said. "Let's do it."

Dawson asked, "Will you also tell them that the attorneys and parties are prohibited from discussing the case with them? I don't want a bunch of jurors running up to me."

"I'll tell them," the judge said.

At 10:44 A.M. the jury called for the bailiff and advised that they'd reached a verdict. "It's gonna be good, Gerry," Eddie said with a big grin. "It's gonna be real good!"

"You bet!" Michele said, hugging Sandy.

I was still afraid. In my head I thought we had weathered the storm and that we were sailing into the sun. Still I felt anxious. What if we'd misjudged the jury? What if they wanted to write, "We find her guilty. Go ahead and prosecute her for the rest of those crimes"? What if I had misjudged them completely? Yet I knew we must be all right. We must be.

The jury marched in. "Watch," I whispered to Michele. "If they look over at us, we're okay. If they don't, we're in deep." The woman in the front row looked at me and then at Sandy and smiled. I looked up at the sergeant. He was as stoic as a stump.

"Please be seated, everyone," the judge said. "Who's the foreperson?"

A juror raised her hand.

"Have you reached a verdict?"

"Yes, we have." She handed the verdict to Jay, who handed the verdict up to the judge. Slowly he unfolded the paper and carefully inspected it. I watched his face for a sign. He gave none. Then he handed it back to Jay.

"Mr. Clerk, would you please read the verdict."

Jay began to read. "Matter of the State of Oregon versus Sandra Kaye Jones. We the jury, duly impaneled to try the above-captioned case, do find our verdict as follows: to the charge of murder—*not guilty!*" Signed, *Foreperson.*

A tumult exploded in the courtroom. The audience

that filled the entire room and the hallway were on their feet cheering, whistling, whooping, and shouting, and Sandy was being hugged by all of us, and we were hugging each other. I thought for a moment I couldn't breathe. It felt as if I had never really known what happiness was. This was happiness—when justice was done and the blessed system was made to work. And we had made it work.

The judge was pounding his gavel. "I'll clear the courtroom," he shouted. But no one paid any attention to him. Finally when the pandemonium quieted, the judge said, "We are going to poll the jury."

He started with Juror 1. "Is this your verdict?"

Juror 1 said, "Yes," as did each and every one on down the line. Then the judge announced, "The verdict is unanimous." And again the cheering began.

At last the judge said to the jurors, "In response to your question: we only have the ability here to receive a general verdict. To have allowed you to say something at that point would be as if I allowed you now to stand up and express your opinions about the case. I think that would raise some question of impropriety if the court allowed you to do that.

"However, as soon as I discharge you, this court has no further hold on you and you're certainly, as citizens of this state, free to do whatever you want to do. I want to thank you. It has been a long and difficult trial, and it has put a lot of stress and strain on everybody, including you folks. You probably won't have another opportunity in your lifetime to participate in a case like this. So on behalf of the State of Oregon, and on behalf of the defense, I express their appreciation to you for the great effort that you've made. With that, this court is adjourned." Judge Haas hit his gavel with a resounding whap and descended the bench. His head seemed higher, his eyes atwinkle, and the same good smile lit his face as when I'd first seen him those years before in Lincoln County. Then we put our arms around each other, Sandy in the middle, and as in my fondest dream, we marched out of the courtroom, all of us free.

"God bless America," Eddie said.

"God bless that jury," Michele said.

"God bless you," Sandy said to me.

We were walking down the street, our arms still over each other's shoulders. The people stared at us. We just waved to them in happiness. Suddenly Eddie stopped, and when he did, we all stopped.

"Well, Gerry," he said, giving me his big Irish grin, "looks like we need to find us another good murder case. A trial lawyer isn't a trial lawyer without one, ya know."

AFTERWORD

Brown and Dawson continued to persecute Sandy Jones. On March 9, 1989, we returned to Multnomah County for the trial of the *State of Oregon v. Sandra Kaye Jones* on the charges that had previously been severed from the murder case by Judge Haas: attempted murder of Wilfred Gerttula, assault in the second degree against Monica Gerttula, and menacing against Jack Dick. Both sides waived the jury and stipulated to the facts that had been presented to the jury in the previous trial, neither side calling any witnesses. Sandy still faced up to thirty-one years in jail and fines of over $100,000. Brown argued that the evidence showed that Sandy had hit Monica Gerttula in the head with the rifle butt, a dangerous weapon. He also argued that Sandy had attempted to kill Wilfred Gerttula when she shot at the windshield of the pickup.

Judge Haas found Sandy Jones not guilty of all charges and ordered her bailsperson released. Mrs. Emburg, Sandy's mother, would finally get her home back.

The *Oregonian*, still a poor loser, struck back at us claiming that justice had been "murky," that Spence, "the superstar lawyer with a penchant for cowboy boots, Stetsons, and limousines," who specializes in "tumult and shouting," and who "returned again to issue one last, long ornery blast at everyone, even those peripherally involved in the case," had won through "his own majestic devices—not all of which fell within the usual court rules." The writer quoted Brown as saying he found my tactics "reprehensible, and I'm disappointed with him." The *Oregonian* ended its observations with the following: "Although truth is helpful in the highly charged adversarial system, the purpose of a trial is not a search for the truth. The foremost purpose of a trial, either civil or criminal, is to beat the other side. On that score Spence has few peers." Where they came up with my penchant for limousines when I drive pickup trucks, I can't imagine. They said nothing, of course, about their destruction of crucial evidence in the trial, nor did they mention that there had probably been a pistol in the Gerttula pickup after all.

On March 28, 1989, two months after Sandy's vindication by the jury, the Oregon Court of Appeals reversed Judge Gardner's conviction of Little Mike. It was more than a reversal. It was a *full acquittal.* Jenny Cooke, who had prepared and argued legal motions in Little Mike's case, wrote the brief urging the appellate court to reverse the conviction on the ground, among others, that the boy was simply innocent. Steve Lovejoy made the oral argument. The Oregon Court of Appeals stated clearly and eloquently, "We review *de novo* [which meant that the court sat as a jury] and conclude that the state failed to prove beyond a reasonable doubt that the child killed or aided and abetted the killing of the victim." Finally, Little Mike could go home.

The *Lincoln City News Guard* reported, "Nationally prominent attorney, Gerry Spence from Wyoming, who defended Sandra Jones, contended that the Joneses were victims of prosecution by the Lincoln County District Attorney's office and other elements of the local 'good-old-boy network.'" Josh Marquis was quoted as saying, "It is absolutely not true that Sandra Jones was the victim in this case." He said a Lincoln County jury would have seen through Spence's argument. As for Little Mike's acquittal by the Oregon Court of Appeals, Marquis's neck was still bowed. He made the same complaints, that "hundreds of thousands of tax dollars were spent on this case, and most of it went to the defense attorneys," in spite of knowing that we worked without any compensation from the State of Oregon whatsoever and paid our own expenses. Instead Marquis said, "I hate to see influence, power, and money control our justice system. And that's what happened in this case." Further, he failed to mention that James M. Brown, himself, headed the indigent committee that had approved these expenses and that Judge Gardner and Judge Haas had each independently reviewed and approved Steve's and Michele's fees and expenses in both cases.

Marquis threatened an appeal of Little Mike's acquittal. "It is not a question of whether we will appeal but whether we can appeal," Marquis said to the press. "If an appeal is possible, we will go forward with it." But the Court of Appeals had the authority to review juvenile cases as if the appeals court judges were the original sitting judges. Having acquitted Little Mike, double jeopardy finally protected the boy. Thank God for the Constitution.

Judge Gardner was equally distressed by the Court of Appeals exoneration of Little Mike. He abandoned judicial protocol and on April 19, 1989, wrote a personal letter to the appeals court judges. He said he had devoted four weeks to the trial, it was difficult, and he had given both sides "every opportunity to present relevant evidence. With all due respect, on the facts as I heard them in person, there was absolutely no reasonable doubt." In the final paragraph of his letter he wrote:

I am concerned about the practical aspects of your decision. First, a man who was doing what he had a right to do (drive on a public highway) was killed. Second, the juvenile who caused his death has been given the message that what he did was acceptable. Third, much of the progress that the Lincoln County Juvenile Department has been able to make with this young man over the past several years has been damaged. He is now free to return home to live with his mother in the same home, next to the same road where the same right-of-way dispute apparently still continues.

On May 5, 1989, Chief Justice George M. Joseph responded to Gardner's letter, pointing out that Gardner's letter came during the time when a petition for review to the Supreme Court could have been filed. "You apparently had not taken the trouble to familiarize yourself with the applicable rules of appellate procedure. Had you done so, I am sure you would not have written the letter when you did."

The chief justice concluded his response by writing, "Under Canon 3B (3), I am required to criticize you directly for your ethical breach. I trust that you will exercise better judgment in the future. I find it particularly unfortunate that you have created a situation requiring this action, because I consider you one of the best of a very good body of circuit court judges. I do not intend to take the matter any further than this letter."

But Gardner's "public highway" through the Joneses' property turned out not to be a public highway after all. Nearly ten years after Sandy and Little Mike were acquitted, George Steere, a property owner in the Gerttula subdivision, brought another suit against Sandy, a suit to declare that miserable trail a public road. As usual, Sandy represented herself. Judge Paul Lipscomb, another visiting judge, heard the case in the Circuit Court of Lincoln County and held that the right-of-way was not continuous, but had a ten- to twenty-foot gap in it, and that the road had never been accepted by the county as a public road. Moreover, the road as plotted no longer existed in places due to the landslides that Sandy had predicted all along. There had been no "public road," just as she had contended all those years in her fight against the good old boys.

All charges made before the Oregon Bar against all the lawyers and the judge in this case were finally dismissed.

On January 13, 1996, Mike Jones Sr. died of a heart attack he suffered while attempting to rescue a child and his mother who were trapped in a car that had been driven into the icy waters of the Siletz River.

Mike Jones Jr. and Sandy live on the farm, as does Shawn with her two daughters. They eke out a living as best they can, which at times is barely enough. But they are rich in their freedom and each other.

ACKNOWLEDGMENTS

This book would still be moldering in the dark recesses of my memory but for the painstaking and devoted assistance of Michele Longo Eder, who spent weeks, no, months helping me piece together those almost four years of often painful toil on behalf of Sandy Jones and Little Mike. Her memory was superb, her editing precise, her loyalty unyielding. If this book has any value to the legal profession and to the nation at large, it is because Michele believes that it does and devoted herself to the task of seeing that it finally came into being.

I also remember with great respect Steve Lovejoy for his faithful dedication to the case of a small boy who was wrongfully charged with a murder he did not commit.

I remember the Oregon Court of Appeals—a rare court, indeed—that actually read the transcript of Little Mike's trial in the juvenile court with understanding and had the courage to overrule a respected trial judge and acquit an innocent boy. Courts of appeals are better known for their affection for logic and their attention to precedent than to a vivid search for justice. This Oregon court's personal attention to the facts of Mike Jr.'s case was exemplary, for which an entire family is grateful.

I thank my faithful, talented, and wise partner, Eddie Moriarity, for his support. He has been beside me in most of the cases for which I have become known. His insights and efforts have been as much responsible for any successes I may have enjoyed as the work itself.

I remember the guidance and caring that was provided me by my darling, Imaging, who has always been there for me and who was powerfully there for me in this case. She read and reread every word of the manuscript and left the imprint of her good judgment on its pages.

I remember as well my good friend David Krieger, whose encouragement and insights were invaluable to me.

I remember my agent and dear friend, Peter Lampack, who, like the best of lawyers, is more concerned with the welfare of his clients than with his own and whose advice and representation teach lawyers themselves how to care.

I remember my editor and longtime friend, Lisa Drew, who has always argued and fought for a better judicial system and whose dedication to this book is incomparable. To her goes the credit for its publication, based, in part, on her belief that this book will have meaning to many who care about the delivery of justice in America. I have often said that Lisa should have been a lawyer herself. She would have been among the best.

At last I remember Sandy Jones and Big and Little Mike, who, each in their own way, fought bravely and honestly against a system that was bent to do them in.

GERRY SPENCE
Jackson Hole, Wyoming

INDEX